The Cove:

Historical Essay on the
Origin of the Abrahamic Faith
by Means of Deification,
with a foreword by
Professor Alex Zieba, Ph.D.

by BERNARD LAMBORELLE

BERNARD LAMBORELLE

ISBN-13: 978-1975832995
ISBN-10: 197583299X

To all men and women

willing to challenge their beliefs.

BERNARD LAMBORELLE

CONTENTS

Foreword

Once I'd heard that a journalist and a young Philosophy professor had their careers threatened for writing about this book, I knew it must be compelling, not just provocative: No-one reacts like that to crack-pottery. But history is replete with this reaction to truth. Reading it changed my view of the Bible and reconciled nagging questions that were part of my own spiritual journey. Perhaps this is what it was like to be a friend of Galileo's, enjoying a glass of wine after dinner as the last rays of daylight fade, when he passes you this odd-looking tube that had been lying on the table and says, nodding towards a sky you thought you knew, "Look what I found. You just have to peer through this to see the universe as it really is." There is at first the honour to glimpse a new paradigm just as the door opens, but then, as wonder and child-like thrill begin to settle into the myriad significance of what you are seeing, fear, anticipation, even some cognitive dissonance follow.

The vision at the end of Galileo's lens challenged accepted wisdom in a way perceived to undermine the Bible as a whole, and so threatened to undermine the entire Holy edifice it supported. It set the world in motion, after all. In time, the rest of us, even the Vatican, accepted that Galileo was, of course, correct--how could we have been so stupid?--and we (we Christians) adapted our moral sources to our new scientific paradigm, blamed medieval scholasticism for the error, and moved on with a new approach to the natural universe. We later described those periods of adjustment with words like "Renaissance" and "Enlightenment". Most of us moved on anyway, and the Jews and Muslims did not perceive a threat from natural philosophy, which came to be called "science", to start with. Unfettered from scholasticism and empowered by scientific method, we monotheists moved collectively towards a scientific and technological mastery that would otherwise have been impossible to even conceive.

Lamborelle's telescope is a formula, "the 6/10 multiplier", for correcting transcriptions of Babylonian base-60 to our decimal system, a moment of mechanical genius accompanied with persistence to reveal Abraham's history, and his Covenant with the Lord, as part of a coherent whole, tied firmly into the history of Egypt and the Middle East we already accept.

Formally, *The Covenant* is no more than the analysis of a few passages of Genesis, those at a critical early juncture establishing a Covenant between Abraham and the Lord. That moment will be the basis of moral, religious, judicial, and even scientific thinking, for a large portion of humanity, for thousands of years to come. Prophets will identify themselves, and their prophesy, as a piece of that action. Nations will be carved out in a conscious effort to interpret and satisfy its terms, and Empires will claim to be its fulfillment. Millions will pray and confess to the Lord of the Covenant, procreate and kill in His name, circumcise, marry, baptize, and bury, all in submission to His will. Because He said so and He is God. Ironically, a literal reading of the Bible verifying that this is a moment in history might be welcome by the faithful, if only it did not also demonstrate that Abraham was the leader of a large tribe, not sheep; that the Sodomites were not wicked in any sense we would acknowledge today (most of us would do the same in their shoes--you'll see); that the Covenant which we have taken as Holy was instead a pact drawn with a greater King, and was carried around later as the deed to the land promised in that pact. It's not welcome because the Lord then becomes, well, not *just* another man, but not a God either, like the other Kings, Baals, and Pharaohs around him. A Bible that is literally true may be void of magic and miracles, with no particular relationship to Divinity that we did not ourselves read into it.

A paradigm shift occurs when a new discovery, produced by a new way approaching a subject, has repercussions throughout many disciplines. Fulfilling the promise of a new paradigm, completing it, means applying the new way of thinking to the old data in these disciplines to learn what new and surprising truths emerge. Universities have for quite some time given courses on the influence of monotheism to Western culture, so these courses offer a list of disciplines affected by considering the Lord as a man, and the Covenant as history, a contract between nations. This shift runs as deep as monotheism itself.

A coherent historical reading of these early passages of Genesis, as Lamborelle has provided, invites approaching the rest of the Bible with a similar view to historicity. Instead of inquiry being guided by a theosophical hermeneutic presuming and insisting upon a consistent relationship with the same Lord, who is also the Holy Spirit responsible for creation, we read Biblical text as the documentation of historical events: the lineage, dynasty, and diaspora of a particular people. Shall the rest of the Bible similarly prove to have a real, very human history? This approach links the disciplines of history and Bible study in an unfamiliar and provocative way, laying out a pattern for new discoveries, beyond its confirmation of Abraham's life. The time-adjusted mapping of Biblical events to historical events enabled by Lamborelle's formula should make predictions about where anthropologists and archaeologists might explore to confirm or disconfirm new revelations provoked by other Bible stories, and enable them to approach existing historical artefacts afresh, reconciling contradictions and resolving controversies. Politics and Philosophy shall have to give up the textbook proposition that the first talk of a social contract comes during Socrates' dramatic self-examination by "the Laws" of Athens and recognize the Covenant as an actual social contract, an actual model from which our notions of justice and morality, and our actual constitutions today, had been drawn centuries earlier. Individual rights, citizenship, notions of reward or retribution, are demonstrably based on this human-made model.

These disciplines are within the broad scope and reach of Lamborelle's study. And then there are the possibilities. Abandoning medieval scholasticism as an empirical tool in favour of scientific method made possible discoveries about our material universe on an unprecedented scale, and technologies that, mostly, improve our lives. Can it be that a similar paradigm shift in our approach to monotheism, to social structure and law, leads us to discoveries about ourselves, our history, our human nature...which manifest as peace and justice in the world on a similarly unprecedented scale? Maybe. Historically, any respect, justice or sympathy we showed for our fellow creatures, we said was because He said so, his morality. The idea that justice might be adequate by itself didn't occur to us. Kant later said that without God, all is permissible, and that scares us. But it's not true just because Kant said it, or because we at first conceived of morality as submission to a superior will. Just as a child learns gratitude by being made to say "thank you", maybe we don't need to be told or threatened anymore to understand consequences. The road to success has always begun with the courage to look towards something at first terrifying that becomes ordinary, and eventually, obvious.

So we shall recover, as we have before, a little wiser and hopefully less violent and arrogant for the journey. Religion evolves again, but does not disappear. The identification of the Lord as a man depended partly on separating this historical figure from a Holy Spirit, and this Spirit shall remain an object of speculation, emulation and faith. At the same time, churches, minions, congregations, monasteries, have long been the repositories of societies' conscience, and so the source of its moral compass. We may not wipe them away in a stroke without undermining the social functions, which they serve. While part of this community cultivates conservative hegemony, another part has been adapting already, in the form of liberal, even atheist clergy, who have already separated and distinguished their moral and social function (ministering to a congregation) from its supposed metaphysical foundations. I predict we shall learn that the atheist-clergy are a larger group than we presently acknowledge. They are in this sense the forefront of applied social and moral thinking.

A. ZIEBA

Truth never penetrates an unwilling mind.

J. L. Borges

Preface

This book is the result of an investigation that began more than a decade ago and that has led me to a remarkable journey. It explores how taking an earthly perspective on the Abrahamic Covenant can dramatically affect our understanding of the biblical history, and how such a viewpoint might hold the key to unlocking our collective future. By adopting the perspective of a secular covenant with a powerful Lord instead of a religious experience with the divine, this book makes a solid case for a euhemeristic origin of this foundational episode of monotheism. It argues that by adopting such a viewpoint, it becomes not only possible to challenge existing conclusions, but also to offer a whole new understanding of the history of Israel that helps us better understand its evolution.

A prominent persona

It all started back in the fall of 2003 when I stumbled across the following passage of the Bible where God, accompanied by two angels, appears in human disguise to Abraham:

> *Ge 18:1 And the Lord appeared unto him in the plains of Mamre: and he sat in the tent door in the heat of the day;*
>
> *Ge 18:2 And he lift up his eyes and looked, and, lo, three men stood by him: and when he saw them, he ran to meet them from the tent door, and bowed himself toward the ground,*
>
> *Ge 18:3 And said, My Lord, if now I have found favour in thy sight, pass not away, I pray thee, from thy servant:*

Ge 18:4 Let a little water, I pray you, be fetched, and wash your feet, and rest yourselves under the tree:

Ge 18:5 And I will fetch a morsel of bread, and comfort ye your hearts; after that ye shall pass on: for therefore are ye come to your servant. And they said, So do, as thou hast said.

Ge 18:6 And Abraham hastened into the tent unto Sarah, and said, Make ready quickly three measures of fine meal, knead it, and make cakes upon the hearth.

Ge 18:7 And Abraham ran unto the herd, and fetcht a calf tender and good, and gave it unto a young man; and he hasted to dress it.

Ge 18:8 And he took butter, and milk, and the calf which he had dressed, and set it before them; and he stood by them under the tree, and they did eat.

The level of anthropomorphism and realism associated with this description of Abraham greeting God and eating with Him caught my attention. I sensed there was something oddly casual about this scene that didn't feel right. By focusing on a display of abundance and reverence rather than on the extraordinary nature of the encounter, this description appeared to better fit the visit of a high ranking official than that of a divine entity. This simple observation made me wonder: Could it be that the original author's intent was to narrate the visit of a prominent persona instead of a god? In this case, the elevation of Abraham's Lord to the status of divinity could be understood as the result of a later deification…

Is this notion nonsense, fabrication, or the result of serendipity? Because Pharaohs were regarded as living gods in ancient Egypt, I found myself questioning the logic of this three-thousand-year-old biblical story. After all, anthropomorphism and metaphors are commonplace in the Bible, and this particular example wouldn't be an exception. I had always been taught – and believed – that the Bible was never to be taken literally or as a body of historical literature. I also understood it to be riddled with anachronism, contradictions and incoherencies, and that many of its stories had been inherited from oral traditions that had been subjected to countless revisions. Even if my intuitions were right, would it be possible to verify? And what would it change anyway? These texts had been edited, over and over again. And just like a crime scene that has been tampered with by too many fingers, any original evidence would surely have been deeply altered and faded away a long, long time ago. Or at least, one would logically think so.

For the past twelve years, I felt as if Ariadne's ball of thread helped me maneuver out of the Minotaur's labyrinth. The many pieces of the puzzle easily fell into place, allowing me to articulate a radically different hypothesis on the origin of the Abrahamic faith that, in my view, is far more compelling, plausible and complete than the current catchall hypothesis that calls upon "oral traditions," which is really just another way to say "we can't deny this story must come from somewhere, but we're hard pressed to explain its origin."

On the methodology

All along, I sought to explore the topic in a multitude of ways, looking for contradictions and inconsistencies. I wrote this book with the goal of making it accessible, despite occasionally referring to scholarly notions. I adopted a scientific method, which consisted in performing extensive background research; constructing a hypothesis; testing the hypothesis against evidence; analyzing the available data and then developing a conclusion. Reader-response criticism provided the initial impulse and direction of this research effort. Textual criticism, aimed at identifying variants in the different textual sources came much later, as well as more formal narrative analysis.

Calling upon a mix of *intradiegetic* and *extradiegetic* evidence has allowed me to further solidify the case. Intradiegetic evidence is self-supporting evidence that can be found within the storyworld itself. It is essential to exhibit the logic, coherence and plausibility of the proposed biblical text interpretation. Extradiegetic evidence is external to the storyworld. It is found elsewhere in the Bible as well as in available data from historical chronologies, archaeology, etymology and even dendrochronology. Both types of evidence are essential to confirm that this interpretation fits the historical context of the Middle Bronze Age and allows one to understand the origin of the Covenant that is reported in the Bible. In order to be as thorough as possible, I did my best to approach the subject according to a historically accurate timeline, and avoid the trap of "twisting" reality or focusing solely on the facts that support my hypothesis.

Known limitations of this work

As the field of biblical research covers millennia and spans across multiple disciplines, it is very likely that this work still has a number of imperfections. Any bold claims, such as the ones made here, should be independently scrutinized and criticized. As Carl Sagan would say, *"extraordinary claims require extraordinary evidence."*[1] However, one also needs to start somewhere, and this book is an opportunity for me to share what I've discovered and learned, and to make a case for what I believe might be holding the elements of an important new theory that offers a far more coherent and plausible solution to a thorny problem.

It would nevertheless be hasty to take this work at face value, at least until it has been subjected to a healthy dose of criticism. One should keep in mind that, although substantial, the entire case currently rests on circumstantial evidence as well as a set of hypotheses that are elaborated on the basic premise that Abraham was a historical figure and that the lord with whom he made a covenant was a mortal. Yet, virtually all scholars are now in agreement with Finkelstein who rejects the possibility that Abraham ever walked this earth and considers him to be nothing more than a mythical figure. [2] There are no hard facts allowing us to affirm that the Patriarchs, *Baal Berith*, *Yahweh*, *Hammurabi* and the *Hyksos* kings were interconnected. This suggestion rests on a converging beam of evidence that is supported by textual, chronological and dendrochronological data. In this regards, and although Hammurabi is known to have made covenants with

---

[1] Sagan, Carl (December 14, 1980). "Encyclopaedia Galactica." Cosmos: A Personal Voyage. Episode 12, at 01:24 minutes into the show at www.youtube.com/watch?v=bimHmQmhh-l (retrieved 09/22/2015)
[2] Finkelstein, Israel and Neil Asher Silberman. 2001. *The Bible Unearthed: Archaeology's New Vision of Ancient Israel and the Origin of its Sacred Texts*. New York: Free Press. p. 33

neighboring states, no historical records indicate that he ever made one with the Levant or travelled to this region. In fact, some would even argue that his influence ever extended this far, despite the fact that one of his seals was recently unearthed in Lower Egypt[3]. The dating of the Hyksos kings and of the Santorini volcanic eruption also remain subject of debate[4]. And while I engaged in a fair amount of critical, textual and narrative analysis of the Hebraic text, much remains to be done for sake of thoroughness. Finally, and despite having spent two years studying biblical Hebrew, my knowledge of Semitic languages remains quite limited.

I nevertheless remain convinced that textual evidence alone is sufficient to support the basic hypothesis of an earthly covenant. The first objective of this book is therefore to reopen a field of research that has been largely abandoned due to lack of evidence by making a case for a historical Abraham and a mortal lord, and to demonstrate that the Jewish tradition, not only goes much farther back in time than what is currently accepted in the academic world, but finds its origins in the cult of the ancestors rather than in purported religious experiences with the divine.

Reception of this work

Although the historico sociological context of Canaan is conducive to such an investigation, there is so much at stake and such an aura of reverence around the Bible that simply raising these questions brings suspicion and skepticism. I learned this the hard way after publishing *Quiproquo sur Dieu* in 2009.[5] The feedback from readers was very gratifying, but the book suffered the faith of so many other publications and didn't break off the noise barrier. The reaction and discussion I had hoped for never materialized.

---

[3] Refer to work from archaeologist Manfred Bietak, director of the Austrian excavations at Tell El-Dab'a in the Nile Delta.

[4] Manning, Sturt W., Felix HöFlmayer, Nadine Moeller, Michael Dee, Christopher Bronk Ramsey, Dominik Fleitmann, Thomas Higham, Walter Kutschera and Eva Maria Wild. 2014. "Dating the Thera (Santorini) Eruption : Archaeological and Scientific Evidence Supporting a High Chronology." *Antiquity.* 88(342): 1164-79.

[5] Lamborelle, Bernard. 2009. *Quiproquo sur Dieu: 3,500 ans pour élucider la véritable identité du seigneur d'Abraham.* Montréal: Éditas.

It took me a while to grasp and then accept the harsh reality that those who should have cared weren't ready, and that those who were ready didn't care. Indeed, those who believe Abraham made a Covenant with the divine aren't interested in seeing their beliefs challenged, and those who view this story as a myth don't have much interest in learning more about it. In all cases, venturing off the beaten path to explore the idea of an earthly covenant requires letting go of intimate beliefs, fundamental religious concepts and academic presuppositions to embrace a whole new perspective that has never been thoroughly explored. In the case of the Bible, the challenge is augmented by the fact that countless frivolous claims have been made in the past that cast doubt and suspicion on any new bold claims. However, once the leap is made to accept this new perspective, there is simply no coming back as the facts speak for themselves.

As we seek to make sense of the world, we compare, analyze and interpret data through a lens – or filter – that is the result of our evolution, culture, beliefs, experiences and academic career. When discussing this research project, I am far more attentive to those who have strong emotional ties to the Bible, as they tend to adopt a far more defensive stance than those who don't – regardless of their academic background. Some are simply unable to entertain the idea of a mortal Lord. It is not bad faith per say, but rather a complete inability to deal with such a concept. They cannot dissociate the figure of Abraham's Lord with that of the divine God they cherish and view as the creator of the Universe. By dissociating these two entities, it is their ontological references – such as the understanding of the Universe and the place they occupy in it – that collapse as they are so intimately tied to their biblical views.

Given all of the above, I have come to accept the idea that this work is unlikely to receive much support from scholars in the field of biblical study – at least for the time being. Not that this research is not valuable, but because its premises, hypothesis and conclusion falls outside the realms of their normal expectations. The biblical scholars I have solicited for peer review politely declined to consider this work; invoking a busy schedule. I can't purport to know, but this work could also be rubbing them the wrong way as many of them have built their reputation by defending hypothesis that runs counter to the one presented here. There is also little upside for them in supporting a research that could be perceived as devaluing their knowledge and profession.

In order to apprehend the perspective offered here, I would therefore encourage everyone, and especially those who already have a set perspective on the topic, to read this book in its entirety at least once as if it was a work of *fiction*, before engaging in a critical analysis. This will hopefully help them better appreciate how the entire body of evidence yields strong support for the basic hypothesis.

Putting it all together

When taken on its own, this work is nothing more than an argumentation in favor of a revised scientific interpretation of the biblical history that might only raise interest among a very small niche of biblical researchers. Used as part of a collective reflection, however, it can turn into a powerful enabler to help those adhering to a fundamentalist interpretation of the bible question their convictions and increase the level of confidence they need to loosen up or let go of their religious dogma. A sincere and honest introspection awaits them. Such a reflection can prove valuable to weigh whether staying in the current paradigm (comfort zone) is truly serving oneself and the humanity – or not.

After having endured thousands of years of exclusion, hatred, and conflicts stirred up by a religious interpretation of this Covenant, isn't it urgent that we put a decisive end to this embarrassing nonsense? Looking back over the course of history, one can easily appreciate how science and rational thinking has contributed to pacifying the world by offering more objective, verifiable and consensual answers to questions that had until then remained subjective, and thus source of argumentation, conflicts, and hostilities. All along, scientific theories and hypothesis have acted as emulsifiers and have allowed people with varying backgrounds, cultures and levels of consciousness to smooth out their differences around the interpretation of objective facts and evidence.

It will take an enormous amount of energy and courage to face our historical shadows in order to overcome the status quo, break over the noise barrier, and challenge widely accepted academic views. New ideas must overcome inertia and accumulate momentum for themselves. The more people embrace it, the more difficult it will become for others to dismiss. And while those already at ease with a metaphorical interpretation as well as those critical of the scriptures will likely find this work of little value to their own spiritual journey, they nevertheless have a critical role to play in helping this work gain visibility by raising its awareness and by sharing it with others. Everyone can contribute to creating the safe space conducive to launching the difficult and much needed debate, instead of becoming the passive accomplice of a dangerous status quo. As Margaret Mead so elegantly expressed "Never doubt that a small group of thoughtful, committed citizens can change the world; indeed, it's the only thing that ever has."[6]

B.L.

---

[6] Lutkehaus, Nancy. 2008. *Margaret Mead : the making of an American icon.* Princeton: Princeton University Press. p. 261

Truth is by nature self-evident. As soon as you remove the cobwebs of ignorance that surround it, it shines clear.

Mahatma Gandhi

Introduction

The book of Genesis is nothing short of a *mémoire* of the people of Israel and their relationship with the divine. It describes the creation of the world, from the Garden of Eden to Noah's ark and from the Tower of Babel to the Patriarchs. The story of the Patriarchs is often presented as describing the fascinating lives of Abraham and his descendants, humble shepherds living in the Holy Land some 3,500 years ago, and of the special relationship they establish and maintain with a new god, *Yahweh*. In this story, *Yahweh* reveals himself to Abraham and makes a covenant with him, in exchange for his exclusive, absolute and unshakable faith. Abraham's unwavering obedience and willingness to sacrifice his beloved son to this new god is a cornerstone story of monotheism that has transcended time and captivated faith followers for generations.

The story of Abraham (i.e. Genesis 12-25) can be summarized as follow:

At God's request, Abram (who later becomes Abraham) leaves Ur in Chaldea with his wife Sarai (who later becomes Sarah) and his nephew Lot to travel to Canaan, the Promised Land (Ge 12). A drought forces them to spend some time in Egypt. Upon returning to Canaan, and as the pasture fails to feed the two herds, Abram offers Lot to separate. The latter chooses the fertile plains of Jordan and pitches his tent toward Sodom (Ge 13:12). Shortly after, four foreign kings loot the city and take away men and booty (Ge 14:5). When he learns that Lot has been captured, Abraham goes after them, defeats the kings, rescues the people and recovers the spoils. (Ge 14:16).

God then makes a covenant with Abraham: He blesses him and promises him many descendants (Ge 15:5). Unable to have children with his wife, Abraham fathers his first son, Ishmael (Ge 16:2), with his servant woman, Hagar. But, Ishmael quickly becomes a source of contention between the couple, and God intervenes with Sarah, in spite of her advanced age, so that she can give birth to Isaac (Ge 21:1). Meanwhile, God threatens to destroy the city of Sodom (Ge 19:25) because of the ongoing unrest. Abraham shows exemplary wisdom in seeking to save the righteous few who might still be in the city (Ge 18:23), but God ultimately destroys the city, for its people are sinners and wicked, and are threatening His messengers (Ge 19:5). Later, Abraham makes a covenant with King Abimelech to settle a dispute about a well (Ge 21:23). The story reaches its climax when God tests Abraham's faith by commanding him for the ultimate sacrifice—his son. Obediently, the Patriarch is prepared to kill Isaac when God, convinced of his faith, spares the child.

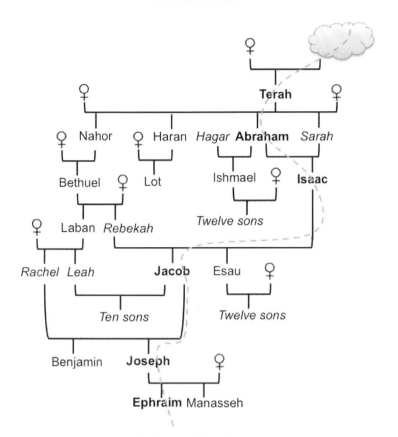

1: Abraham's family tree

The "Abrahamic Covenant" incarnates God's reward and mercy in exchange for an exclusive, absolute and unshakable faith. Jews, Christians and Muslims alike acknowledge this event as the cornerstone of the world's three great monotheistic religions, giving the Patriarchs the benevolent title of "the founding fathers."

And, while the three religions have evolved differently over time, the evolution of their respective beliefs find their roots in Abraham, Isaac, Ishmael, Jacob and Joseph, and especially in the covenant that God made with them:

> *Ge 15:18 In the same day Yahweh made a covenant with Abram, saying, Unto thy seed have I given this land, from the river of Egypt unto the great river, the river Euphrates:*

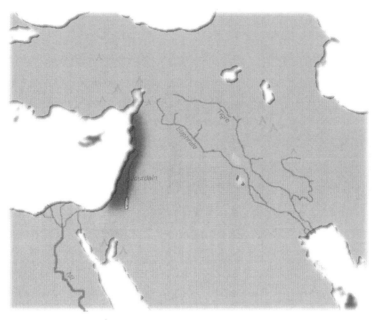

2: The Promised Land

After Genesis, the book of Exodus describes how Abraham's descendants, by now slaves in Egypt, reclaim their freedom when Moses, with God's help, leads them to the Promised Land and sets out the divine commandments, a pledge of their commitment and faith. These scriptures form the basis of all other subsequent books, not to mention an entire thought system that would become more diverse, complex and distinct over time.

The Jews claim to descend from Isaac. And, since God made a covenant with Abraham and his son, Isaac, they feel invested with a special charge:

> *Ge 17:21 But my covenant will I establish with Isaac, which Sarah shall bear unto thee at this set time in the next year.*

The Christians have always aligned with the Jews, since Jesus is a descendant of King Solomon, son of David, himself of the bloodline of Isaac. And, while they assign the Patriarchs a more secondary role, they cannot deny their importance and contribution. [7]

> *Matt 1:1 These are the families through which Jesus Christ came. He came through David and Abraham. 2 Abraham was the father of Isaac. Isaac was the father of Jacob. Jacob was the father of Judah and his brothers.*

For their part, many Muslims claim to descend from Ishmael, Abraham's firstborn son with his Egyptian slave. They also believe in the same God:

> *Sourate [2.136] Say: We believe in Allah and (in) that which had been revealed to us, and (in) that which was revealed to Ibrahim and Ismail and Ishaq and Yaqoub and the tribes, and (in) that which was given to Musa and Isa, and (in) that which was given to the prophets from their Lord, we do not make any distinction between any of them, and to Him do we submit.*

Muslims have always opposed the descendants of Isaac. The origin of this conflict might date back to the time of the Patriarchs, when Sarah cast out her servant, Hagar.

> *Ge 21:10 Wherefore she said unto Abraham, Cast out this bondwoman and her son: for the son of this bondwoman shall not be heir with my son, even with Isaac.*

Jews, Christians and Muslims all claim to be the legitimate heirs of Abraham, and, to this day, the blind faith in this Covenant continues to feed the most violent of conflicts and the deepest of passions. But what do we really know of the historical Abraham? Did he even ever exist? And why would a new god choose to establish a covenantal form of relationship with this fellow?

The writing of the Bible

A brief review of the origins of the Bible and the circumstances in which it was written will come in handy for understanding the broad strokes of the Abrahamic story's evolution, which are so intimately tied to its religious and political interpretations.

---

[7] Kaiser, Walter C. 2001. *The Old Testament Documents: Are They Reliable & Relevant?* Downers Grove: InterVarsity Press.

"Pentateuch" is the specific name given to the first five books of the Bible: Genesis, Exodus, Leviticus, Numbers and Deuteronomy. This name derives from the Greek (Πεντά) *penta* ("five") and (τεύχος) *teukhos* ("volume"). To the Jewish people, this set of books is called the Torah (תורה), which means "to guide" or "to teach." The stories found in the Pentateuch are common to all monotheisms and form the basis of the Old Testament as well as the Qu'ran. And although the Jewish tradition claims that the Pentateuch is based on historical facts dating back to the Bronze Age, scholars disagree. Monotheism[8] is a concept that simply did not exist during the Bronze Age, and no evidence of a people practicing a new religion or having a different culture was ever found in Canaan. Quite the contrary, it seems the digs have only served to exemplify the many contradictions that exist between the biblical story and the historical data. There is, indeed, clear evidence of widespread paganism throughout the land, and this is partially why the scientific community would like to brush aside the entire Abrahamic narrative as having no historical ground whatsoever.

This is also why most biblical scholars would now mock anyone affirming that the story of Abraham originated from a Middle Bronze Age (c. 2200-1550 BCE) historical event as purported by the Jewish tradition. Scholars are now convinced that it evolved, instead, from a much later myth or a legend that was transmitted orally over generations. They hold it that such a story would have been laid down in writing shortly after the Babylonian Exile, probably during the 6th or 7th century BCE. It was indeed under King Josiah, that the priest Hilkijah found, during some renovations, the "Book of the Law" that was hidden in the temple of Jerusalem (2 Kings 22:8). Although no one knows what this book actually contained, scholars believed it to be derived from legendary Deuteronomistic work. They also believe that this event sparked the reform that would eventually lead to the writing of the Bible as it happened right before the destruction of the First

---

[8] Throughout this book, the term monotheism refers exclusively to the three Abrahamic faiths: Judaism, Christianity and Islam.

Temple of Jerusalem by Nebuchadnezzar in the 6th century BCE, and the Jews' exile to Babylon. By seeking to give their story sacred meaning in order to forge a unifying identity, the Jews would have compiled their sacred texts into essentially the format we know them today.

The consensus over such an interpretation is so overwhelming among academicians that there has been virtually no more research conducted on the historicity of Abraham for the last few decades. Much of the same is accepted for the rest of the Pentateuch, which includes the story of Moses and the Exodus. The case is considered closed.

Modern significance of the Covenant

During the Babylonian Exile, many Jews believed that their misery stemmed from a weakening of their faith and a failure to follow the prescribed rules.[9] They were convinced that a return to the fundamental values of their faith would win them their freedom and their homeland. Fundamentalist believers of all faith denominations continue to adhere to this ultimate view and this is why many of them are seeking to impose their beliefs and practices on the rest of the world.

At the end of the Second World War, the Zionist movement managed to convince the international community to create the State of Israel on the "promised land," partially by invoking the legitimacy of the Covenant. As the Jewish diaspora from around the world returned to their so-called homeland, the Arab Palestinian population who was occupying this territory was forcefully expelled. Ever since the formation of the State of Israel, the neighboring Arab states have been at war with it.

---

[9] Gottheil, Richard , Victor Ryssel, Marcus Jastrow and Caspar Levias. "Captivity." Jewish Encyclopedia. http://www.jewishencyclopedia.com/articles/4012-captivity (retrieved September 10, 2015).

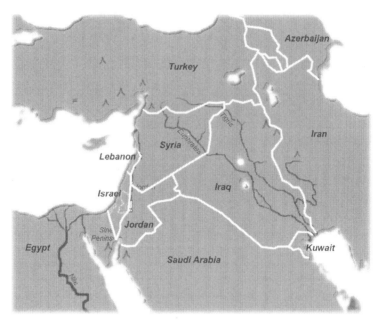

3: Modern Near East

Religious and political claims calling upon the Abrahamic Covenant continue to make headlines:

- *On August 30, 1967, General Moshe Dayan declared: "If one possesses the Bible, if one considers oneself to be the people of the Bible, one should also possess the biblical lands."[10]*

- *On February 25, 1994, Dr. Baruch Goldstein massacred 29 Muslims praying at the Tomb of the Patriarchs.[11]*

- *On November 4, 1995, Yigal Amir assassinated Yitzhak Rabin, Nobel Peace Prize laureate, for having signed the Oslo accords and agreeing to transfer a portion of the "Promised Land" to the Arabs.[12]*

- *On May 15, 2008, President George W. Bush declared before the Knesset: "Sixty years ago in Tel Aviv, David Ben-Gurion*

---

[10] *Jerusalem Post*, August 30, 1967

[11] *Time Magazine*, Vol. 143, no. 10, p. 48

[12] *Time Magazine*, Vol. 146, no. 20.
http://topics.nytimes.com/top/reference/timestopics/people/a/yigal_amir/index.html

> *proclaimed Israel's independence, founded on the 'natural right of the Jewish people to be masters of their own fate.' What followed was more than the establishment of a new country. It was the redemption of an ancient promise given to Abraham, Moses, and David – a homeland for the chosen people in Eretz Yisrael."*[13]

- *On July 5, 2014, at the pulpit of Mosul's Great Mosque, Abu Bakr al-Baghdadi, the leader of the self-proclaimed Islamic state asserted his position as caliph, or spiritual leader, of the Muslim faithful, calling himself "Khalifa Ibrahim," or caliph Abraham, a reference to the prophet Abraham, a key figure of the Quran.*[14]

Given so many political leaders, and their actions, are still influenced by the Covenant made with Abraham, there is no denying its importance to this day. Convinced that a divine creator casted these words in stone, fundamentalists continue to adhere to a literal reading of the Bible. They are unfortunately stuck in a paradigm of eternal conflict because they can't accept other's interpretations.

An intellectual comfort zone

The dating of the Bible to the 7th or 6th century is a conclusion that was reached by biblical scholars over a long period of time through resignation and absence of evidence, rather than because it has been proven to be this way. Certainly, archaeologists have confirmed there was no monotheism in Canaan during the Bronze Age. This fact is not being disputed. But what if we had been looking for the wrong suspect? What if the "key" to unlocking our historical truth had escaped us because of our religious biases?

Isn't it odd that ever since philosopher Herbert Spencer questioned the divine nature of Abraham's Lord over a century ago, it appears that nobody has seriously investigated the possibility that He could have been a mortal instead? Did focusing exclusively on the

---

[13] White House, *Presidential Speeches*, May 15, 2008. http://georgewbush-whitehouse.archives.gov/infocus/bushrecord/documents/Selected_Speeches_George_W_Bush.pdf

[14] New York Times, *Militant Leader in Rare Appearance in Iraq*, July 5, 2014. http://www.nytimes.com/2014/07/06/world/asia/iraq-abu-bakr-al-baghdadi-sermon-video.html?_r=0

"divine" nature of Abraham's Lord lead us to close off the investigation to alternative theories? While some research has raised important questions, there are no modern writings on this topic, despite the fact that it is well known that the cult of the ancestors – a practice consisting of preserving the memory of the dead through iconography, celebrations or other means – was widespread in Ancient Israel throughout the Bronze Age. Is this failure to investigate due to complacency, lack of curiosity, or simply a fear of straying beyond our comfort zone? The only reasonable explanation I was able to come up with is that, for anyone schooled in theology or interested in the Bible, the premise of a divine God is a *sine qua non* condition to any study on the topic. Unfortunately, when operating under this premise, anyone trying to correlate the early claims of Jewish tradition with archaeology is doomed to failure, as the evidence can't possibly match the allegations.

This is why we stand where we are today, and the reason scholars investigating the birth of monotheism are focusing all their research efforts on the late Babylonian Exile era, a period that is inconsistent with regard to Jewish tradition. J. M. Chladenius (1710-1759) was first to advance the theory that views of the same object can lead to dissimilar perceptions and stories without compromising the idea of unity of truth[15]. And it is my hope that the diverging views of the Abrahamic story held by fundamentalist followers and critical thinkers can be scientifically explained and eventually resolved.

Challenging the status quo

As our collective memories are populated with victors' tales, we naturally picture key historical figures as either hero or villain depending on which side of the battlefield they stood. We take it for granted that Abraham was a hero and that Bera, king of Sodom, was a villain. This assumption not only biases academic studies on the subject, but also affects our core religious values. As the symbol of God's infinite reward for *moral behavior* over *evil*

---

[15] Escudier, Alexandre. *De Chladenius à Droysen. Théorie et méthodologie de l'histoire de langue allemande (1750-1860)Annales. Histoire, Sciences Sociales 2003/4 - 58e année.* Paris: Editions de l'EHESS. p. 761

doing, one can easily see how this religious interpretation of the Covenant has even framed our sexual mores. Indeed, homosexuality remains deeply associated with sin, misconduct and sexual depravation, essentially because the story of Abraham tells us that the Sodomites were *wicked* and *sinners* before the Lord. In fact, the anathema over Sodom runs so deep in our cultural veins, that it gave birth to the word "sodomy." Could there be more to this homophobic attitude than tradition would like us to believe?

History continuously reminds us of how important it is to always put things into their contextual perspective. The biblical text is surprisingly ambiguous and allows us to ask the following questions: What if Abraham never made a covenant with a divine entity, but with a powerful overlord instead? And what if Bera, far from being a wicked man, simply stood in the way of those by whom we now remember him? Could his refusal to submit to a foreign power, rather than a lustful lifestyle, be the real cause of his demise? These questions might seem far-fetched, but surprisingly, and as this research will demonstrate, they aren't. They do show, however, how well conditioned we are and how little we dare question our beliefs and traditions.

It was not unusual during the Bronze Age for Kings or Pharaohs to be deified as living gods. Using a holistic, literal and secular interpretation of the biblical text, this study first demonstrates how the Abrahamic narrative (Ge 12-25) is far more coherent and efficient when considered from the standpoint of a mortal lord and the establishment of an earthly covenant aimed at pacifying the Valley of Siddim. It shows that Ge 14, far from being a late addition to the text with little value – as purported by most modern scholars, actually proves to be essential for understanding the revolt that was ongoing in the valley and justifies the covenant between Abraham and a Mesopotamian overlord. Using historical and archeological evidence, it then shows how, through the Bronze Age nomadic practices of necromancy and the cult of the ancestors, the descendants of Abraham would have celebrated the memory of their benevolent Lord, and how, through the "gift of the land" they would have adopted a sedentary lifestyle that would have led to the emergence of *Baal Berith* ("Lord of the

Covenant"), the enigmatic pagan deity of Shechem, a stronghold where Abraham and his descendant lived.

Once the paradigm of a mortal Lord is adopted, one can start re-establishing a handful of critical connections between known historical facts and the biblical text. The early Israelites would have gradually lost sight of these connections because they had become increasingly at odds with the developing model of a divine Lord. The greater the drift, the harder it would have been to maintain the connections; and so they had to be dropped for the sake of coherence, to the point of being negated and obliterated, as rejecting the past is often necessary to move forward when adopting new models. It would be this natural and religious evolution that gradually paved the way from the ancient cult of the ancestors to monolatrism and eventually to the monotheistic Abrahamic faith, as we know it today. Fortunately, evidence of the past existence of these connections can still be found, and one does not need to dig very deep to find them.

By studying the evolutionary stages of devotion through a comparative analysis of Near Eastern cultual practices, this study shows how each time Israel was submitted to a new foreign power its exclusive deity underwent a visible transformation. *Baal Berith* would have first been venerated beside the Canaanite deities inherited from the Babylonian pantheon. As Canaan became a vassal of Egypt, a nation fond of compounded deities, *Baal Berith* would have taken on the attributes of *El, Baal* and *Asherah* and morphed into a new super deity: *Yahweh*. Initially venerated alongside the former pagan deities, theological and political struggles would have compelled the Israelites to monolatrism and the refutation of lesser *Baals*. It would finally be in the aftermath of the Babylonian Exile, under Assyrian influence, that the religion of *Yahweh* would adopt its final ontological concepts. Modern monotheism would therefore be the result of this slow evolutionary process.

The quest to identify the Lord of the Covenant enables us to show that the chronologies reported in the Bible can be surprisingly accurate, but only after the errors introduced by Nabonidus' scribes while converting them from the Babylonian sexagesimal system are corrected. Using archeological, chronological and dendrochronological (i.e., tree rings) evidence, the lives of Abraham and king Hammurabi can be correlated in order to show how the later could very well prove to be the mythical Lord of the Bible. In what is more than just a stream of coincidences, the long chain of biblical events line up with astonishing accuracy with the history of the region. The dates and events, people's tradition and cultual practices, laws and structure of governance all come together to give this biblical story a rational interpretation. Common sense finally prevails in the meeting of myth and history.

Structure of this book

This book is organized into four main sections: The first part focuses on the textual evidence found in the biblical text. A survey of past researches is conducted to frame the questions that help compare the relative efficiencies of the narrative when Abraham's Lord is perceived as either divine or mortal.

The second part of this book provides historical references, as well as a contextual overview of the situation prevailing during the Middle Bronze Age, when Jewish tradition claims Abraham lived. This information helps explain the syncretic evolution of the faith, and serves as the foundation for the third part of the book, where the quest for the historical figure of Abraham's Lord takes place.

The last part of the book explores what might have become of the historical descendants of Abraham in relation to the biblical text. Finally, the various Annexes extend the research in more speculative ways and offer supplemental reference material. To help you keep track of the various characters and geographic locations, I have included an explanatory chart with a distribution of roles (p. 381), a revised and amended family tree of the Patriarchs (p. 386), as well as a geographical map of the region (p. 387).

Unless otherwise stated, all dates cited in this book (in years or in centuries) are Before the Common Era (BCE).[16] Moreover, I have

---

[16] The traditional method involves expressing dates as either BC or AD (Before Christ or Anno Domini, meaning "in the year of our Lord"). But, since Christ was supposedly born in the year 4 or 5 BC, and because many historical events do not concern Christians, the use

tried to draw attention to the fact that many dates in antiquity are still the subject of debate among experts. I have used middle chronology for dates related to the reigns in the Ancient Near East, and believe that you will find a justification for this choice. In order to characterize the submissive relationship between Abraham and *Yahweh*, I have allowed myself to apply the concepts of *lord*, *overlord*, *suzerain* and *vassal*—terms that normally refer to social realities in the feudal middle Ages—to this period of antiquity.

Finally, the many Bible verses I have quoted are extracted from the familiar Authorized King James's version of the Old Testament (see Genesis 12-25 p. 357). But, in order to remain more faithful to the original Hebrew texts, I have substituted the terms *Lord* and *God* with *Yahweh* and *Elohim* respectively. Wherever appropriate, I have included references to the Masoretic Hebrew text[17].

---

of BCE (Before the Common Era) and CE (Common Era) is now recommended.

[17] While there are many known old textual witnesses of the Bible, the Masoretic text, which was used and maintained by the Masoretes, is perceived within the biblical scholar communities as one of the oldest and most reliable sources of the Bible.

We are all atheists about most of the gods that humanity has ever believed in. Some of us just go one god further.
Richard Dawkins

Part I - A Divine or Mortal Lord?

The first part of this investigation brings us to evaluate the coherence and plausibility of the Abrahamic Covenant narrative when approached from the traditional perspective of a divine Lord, followed by a quick review of past academic research that has led us to where we are today. We will then engage in an in-depth analysis of the same narrative, but this time through the perspective of a mortal lord.

Religious interpretation of the Covenant

As tradition and past research have always considered the story of Abraham from the perspective of a divine Lord, there are plenty of theological texts on the subject. We shall therefore focus our attention on the important questions and concerns that such a perspective raises. Among them, why do some biblical texts portray God with a divine and loving character, while others paint Him with a war-like personality and an unsavory moral record? And, perhaps more importantly, why is He so often referred to by two different names?[18]

---

[18] While God is occasionally referred to in the Bible by other names, "*Yahweh*" and "*Elohim*"

Yahweh/Elohim, two names for one God

Most modern translations of the Bible have preserved the dualistic nature of God that is found in the Hebraic Bible, which refers to Him as both *Yahweh* (rendered as "Lord" in English) and *Elohim* (plural Hebrew term for "gods" rendered as singular "God" in English). For Judaism, Christianity and Islam, there can be no doubt that *Yahweh* and *Elohim* are one and the same divine entity, as it is a *sine qua non* condition to their very faith. And while Islam recounts the Abrahamic story in a slightly different way, it clearly builds on the Judaic and Christian presuppositions. So much so, that it has replaced the two divine names in the Qur'an with a single one, *Allah*, therefore losing sight of His original dualistic nature. These changes are symptomatic of the recurring need to adjust the text so it fits a particular context and theology. This is why in the field of Textual Criticism, the more difficult reading of two variants is often, although not always, preferred and seen as an indication of the older and more genuine source (*Lectio difficilior potior*).[19]

Below is a diagram of the traditional biblical story that can be summarized as "God makes a Covenant with Abraham." All the key elements of the narrative are presented below:

---

are by far the two most common ones.

[19] Using this principle, we can better understand how Islam has eliminated many problematic portions of the Bible in its desire to "make it perfect." For instance, it has eliminated significant portions of the story of Sodom for which it has only preserved its homophobic component (nowhere even present in the Abrahamic narrative, as it developed much later in the Bible).

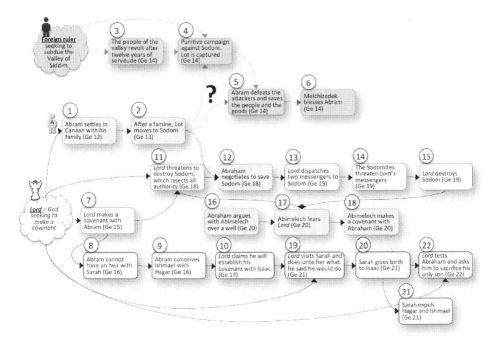

4: Traditional religious interpretation

In the above diagram, the cloud shapes denote the external forces that are influencing the actions. Key structural elements of the story are summarized in the boxes and the links between them represent their causalities.

In this diagram, one can see the two external forces that are behind the story: the first one is obviously God who makes a covenant with Abraham and the second one is the foreign ruler who is seeking to subdue the valley of Siddim. Both of these forces influence how events unfold. Many scholars have commented on the fact that some elements (darker in the diagram) are only loosely connected to the main story and do not reinforce its religious interpretation. This is why Chapter 14 of Genesis is often referred to as "anecdotal" and even "erratic" and is believed by many biblical scholars to be a late addition to the text. Several other elements in the narrative are either missing or do not contribute to strengthening the story. When trying to make sense of the story, the following observations can be made:

While the narrative indicates to the reader that God asked Abraham to settle in Canaan with his family (1), the text doesn't explain why this destination was chosen. It seems that the purpose of God's request is simply to show that Abraham is capable of blind faith. The narrative doesn't explain why the famine is important or why it is critical that Lot settle in Sodom instead of another place (2). Neither does the text explain why it is critical that the people of Sodom revolt (3) nor why it is critical that four foreign kings launch a punitive campaign (4). Of course, when Lot is captured, the reader understands why Abraham engages in a military campaign (5). However, the narrative does not explain what becomes of the foreign kings, or how this episode ties in with the overall religious theme. We are not told why God chooses to make a Covenant with Abraham (7), or why the issue of the heir is so important (8) to Him. This said, God seeks to sanction (10) Abraham for having a child with Hagar, Sarah's maiden wife (9) by stating that the heir will come only from Sarah. However, the text doesn't explain why Ishmael is not worthy enough to inherit the Covenant. In addition, other than claiming that the Sodomites are wicked, the text doesn't explain why God wants to destroy their city (11) and why Abraham audaciously dares negotiating with Him to save the people of Sodom (12). It is only after God sends some messengers (13) that a motive is provided (14) for the destruction of Sodom (15). The purpose of Abimelech's encounter (16-17-18) is unclear. We understand that God's spirit visits Sarah so she can bear a child to Abraham (19) and that Isaac is the child of the promise (20). From a monotheistic perspective, it also makes sense for God to test Abraham's faith by asking him to sacrifice his only child (22).

When looking at the tensions within the narrative, the climax doesn't build around the main theme of the Covenant, as one would anticipate, but rather around the expectation of the heir through God's promise of a son and then the test of faith through the sacrifice of Isaac.

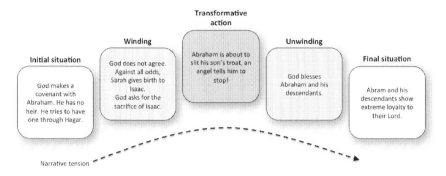

5: Narrative tension in the religious interpretation

The above questioning is intradiegetic, meaning that answers are sought within the storyworld itself. Of course, one could easily suggest a multitude of answers by drawing upon other portions of the Bible or upon Jewish tradition. However tempting, this would render the exercise futile. Indeed, if one is interested in testing the internal logic of a given story, one should not seek answers outside the story, as this would defeat the purpose.

Puzzling questions

Given the many shortcomings highlighted above, it is no wonder that the Abrahamic story is presented as incoherent and that it is believed to have originated from multiple oral sources that were integrated and consolidated around the Babylonian Exile period.

Several additional questions can be drawn from the story that cast doubt over the sacred or moral nature of the scriptures:

- *If there truly is only one God, why is He sometimes referred to as Elohim (God) and other times as Yahweh (Lord)?*

- *If God loves us all equally, why did He give the "Promised Land" exclusively to the Jewish people (Ge 17:7)?*

- *Why was Ishmael, even as a very young child, not considered worthy by God to inherit the Promised Land (Ge 17:19)?*

- *Why did Lot offer up his two virgin daughters to the angry mob of Sodomites? And why did the latter refuse them (Ge 19:8)?*

- *If God is merciful, why did He slaughter the Sodomites instead of trying to save them (Ge 19:24)?*

- *If God forbids incest, why was Abraham allowed to marry his half sister (Ge 20:2)? And why did Lot's sons, born of Lot's incestuous relations with his own daughters, become the fathers of the Moabite and Ammonite nations (Ge 19:34)?*

- *Why did God order Abraham to sacrifice his own son to prove his loyalty (Ge 22:2)?*

These questions, and many others, to which all kinds of clever theological answers have been provided, can certainly confuse the novice because responses cannot be found within the text itself.

But hasn't history always been experienced, reported and taught very differently from the perspectives of the oppressor and the oppressed, the believer and the nonbeliever, the nationalist and the federalist? As for the Bible, our thought processes have been so tainted, and even obscured, by thousands of years of indoctrination that we simply dare not question the words we read.

This is precisely why few have challenged the traditional image of Abraham, the humble shepherd peacefully tending to his sheep and with whom God decided to make a Covenant. But, wouldn't the fact that a line of kings succeeded him seem to indicate that Abraham was already a powerful man at the time of the Covenant?

- *During his trip to Egypt, Abraham is officially welcomed by Pharaoh (Ge 12:14).*

- *Abraham was already rich in cattle, silver and gold (Ge 13:2).*

- *Abraham pursues four kings with an army of more than three hundred men (Ge 14:14).*

- *King Abimelech fears Abraham; he offers him gifts and invites him to settle on his land (Ge 20:14).*

- *Abraham buys the cave of Machpelah for several kilograms of silver (Ge 23:14).*

These actions are not those of a simple shepherd, but rather of a powerful man, a diplomat and a well-respected and talented negotiator. Another paradox begs even more questions. The chapter on the War of Kings is often overlooked by tradition because it has little or no theological value. In fact, it is so perplexing that the author of the Qur'an chose to skip it altogether by making no reference to it. That is the chapter where we find the people of Sodom victims of a punitive campaign and Lot is taken away (Ge 14). After Abram defeated these Eastern Kings, it would have been only natural for them to seek revenge. Therefore, is it not surprising that we find "God" destroying the city of Sodom (Ge 19) in a rage, but not until He made His covenant with Abraham (Ge 15)? Why does God seem so aligned with these bloodthirsty Eastern Kings? While the Sodomites refused to submit to His will, the rest of the story shows their gratitude toward Abraham, who even pleads with God to spare them. Can a connection be established between these four Eastern Kings and Abraham's "Lord"?

As the above questioning is somewhat subjective, there are those who will object to the proposed exercise and will be tempted to resort to external data such as theology and tradition for answers. But again, when one looks to the storyworld for answers, one is left dubitative.

At this point, it would be useful to turn to the scientific community to better understand what scholars know of the Abrahamic narrative, and what can be learned from past research. Particular attention should be made to the questions that remain unanswered in the current research paradigm (i.e., Abraham's Lord is a divine entity) in order to see how the new hypothesis we are developing (i.e., Abraham's Lord was a mortal) can help address them.

In summary

- The notion of God's Covenant with Abraham is a fundamental tenet to the monotheistic faiths.

- God is sometimes referred to as *Elohim* and other times as *Yahweh* in the narratives.

- Two independent and external forces, namely *"God"* and the *"foreign Mesopotamian ruler,"* are driving the actions within the Abrahamic narrative.

- The Abrahamic narrative raises important questions that aren't answered by the storyworld itself.

- Scholars believe that the current Abrahamic narrative results from an amalgam of multiple sources inherited from oral traditions.

An ongoing scholarly debate

While many believers are keen to accept the supernatural events reported in the Bible, critical thinking brings us to acknowledge that it is rather unlikely that any human has ever spoken to God or experienced theophany in a literal sense.

The historico-critical research on the origins of the Pentateuch (i.e., Torah) has fuelled two centuries of fierce debate between proponents of the *maximalist* position on one hand—for whom some sections of the Bible are reliable historical documents—and the *minimalists* who view it as little more than a collection of myths and fables. The maximalists long believed they held the lead, but since the second half of the last century the discoveries of modern archaeology have gradually forced them to cede ground that minimalists have rushed to occupy. Countless archaeological digs have failed to turn up any trace of the Patriarchs. And while a few leads might have sparked the interest of the scientific and religious communities, initial excitement quickly gave way to disappointment. Some twenty years ago the controversy seemed to be over: most scholars were resigned to accept the idea that the Pentateuch had no real historical ground.

William G. Dever expresses the ambivalence that has characterized the historico-critical debate:

> *Originally, I wrote to challenge the biblical minimalists and then I became one of them, more or less.*[20]

One of the books that has considerably contributed to strengthening this minimalist view is *The Bible Unearthed* from archeologist Israel Finkelstein, published a little more than a decade ago. In this monograph, Finkelstein does a great job of explaining why so many generations of scholars *"have been convinced that the patriarchal narratives were at least in outline historically true."*[21] He does so by reviewing most of the material reported in the Bible that could lead someone to believe in the historicity of the Patriarchs. Then, using several examples, he thoroughly demonstrates that this material is too vague to be reliable and that none of the chronologies or key events it reports accurately match known historical ones:

> *... the search for the historical patriarchs was ultimately unsuccessful, since none of the periods around the biblically suggested date provided a completely compatible background to the biblical stories.*[22]

This observation brings him to reconsider the contribution and the role of the Patriarchs as founding fathers of Israel:

> *The main problem was that the scholars who accepted the biblical accounts as reliable mistakenly believed that the patriarchal age must be seen, one way or the other, at the earliest phase in a sequential history of Israel.*[23]

---

[20] Shanks, Hershel. "Losing Faith: Who Did and Who Didn't." http://www.basarchive.org (retrieved October 12, 2007).
[21] Finkelstein, Israel and Neil Asher Silberman. 2001. *The Bible Unearthed: Archaeology's New Vision of Ancient Israel and the Origin of its Sacred Texts.* New York: Free Press. p. 33
[22] Ibid. p. 33
[23] Ibid. p. 33

Ever since this assessment, it was established that the figures of the Patriarchs must have been fictitious characters created as part of a historical retro-projection effort meant to legitimize the Jewish identity in the aftermath of the Babylonian Exile.

The debate is not over, however, as Garfinkel more recently attempted to show that minimalism had been undermined by the recent archaeological discoveries of the Tel Dan and Mesha steles dating from the 9th century that make reference to the "House of David," thus substantiating the historicity of this king.[24]

In *Ancient Israel, What do we Know and How do we Know It*, Grabbe expresses his frustration on the hardening of stances that characterize the modern scholarly debate when he writes:

> *One has the sense that it has ceased to be a matter of academic disagreement and has become an emotive and personal issue.* [25]

And while Grabbe would like to see more nuances when it comes to arguing on the historicity of the Pentateuch, he nevertheless agrees with Finkelstein with regards to the patriarchal period:

> *Almost all scholars are minimalists in certain parts of history. That is, most scholars have now abandoned the picture of the biblical text for the 'patriarchal period' and the settlement in the land.*[26]

Robert David, tenured professor in the Faculty of Theology and Religious Sciences at Université de Montréal, eloquently expresses the state of modern thinking:

> *For several decades now, research on the book of Genesis has deviated from the historicity of the narrative of the Patriarchs, an approach that was popular from the 1950s to the 1970s. It appears increasingly clear within the scientific community that the narratives of the Patriarchs were not written before the 7th century, and perhaps not*

---

[24] Garfinkel, Yosef. 2011. "The Birth & Death of Biblical Minimalism." *Biblical Archaeology Review,* 30(03), http://www.basarchive.org (retrieved October 12, 2007).
[25] Grabbe, Lester L. 2009. *Ancient Israel: What do we Know and How do we Know It?* New York: Continuum. (Orig. pub. 2007.). p. 34
[26] Ibid. p. 23

even before the 5th century BCE (some even postulate the 2nd century). They are studied today not for what they might reveal about the Bronze Age (whether Middle or Recent), but for what they might tell us about the Jewish community during the Assyrian era, and during the exilic and post-exilic eras.[27]

When considered from the traditional perspective of a *Religious Covenant with a divine Lord*, the story of Abraham does indeed appear disjointed and completely out of context with the known historical background of the Bronze Age. No wonder so many scholars are in agreement with Finkelstein and believe that the Abrahamic story cannot possibly have originated from such an early polytheistic background, and must therefore have originated from a myth or legend fabricated at a much later date. They naturally believe that this story would have been imprinted with a *historical flavor* and passed down orally within a small community before being weaved into the largest biblical corpus in the aftermath of the Babylonian Exile, along with other Near Eastern myths, in order to establish continuity with the region's distant past.

---

[27] Authorized excerpt from a personal communication (translated).

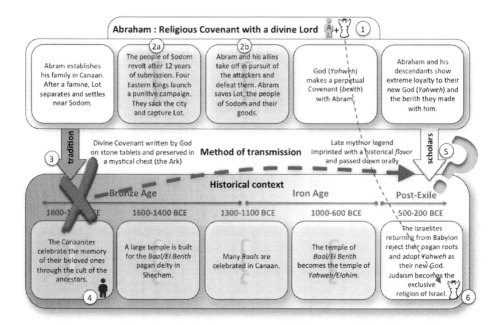

6: Abrahamic faith as a retro-projection of a mythical past

Scholars and critical thinkers are faced with considerable challenges when approaching the patriarchal narratives from the historical perspective of a divine Lord. In addition to the allegorical nature of the event, many elements of the story appear somewhat disjointed (2a) & (2b), and archaeology has demonstrated that such an account (1) could not have possibly taken place during the Bronze Age (4), as suggested by tradition (3), because the background and dates do not fit. This is why the story of Abraham is believed by modern scholars (5) to be a post-exilic fiction (6), a time when monotheism developed.

Isn't it telling, however, that we haven't yet been able to identify a specific period of time in history when the religion of *Yahweh* developed? It just seems to be fading into the distant past. Meanwhile, it is becoming increasingly clear for anyone taking an earnest look at the available data that the roots of *Yahwism* are strongly intertwined with paganism. Grabbe pinpoints the deadlock that characterizes the state of modern research:

> *Perhaps the most significant new finds were the Kuntillet 'Ajrud and Khirbet el-Qôm inscriptions which implied that Yhwh had a consort. A perennial question is when*

monotheism developed in Israel, and also whether
aniconism was always a feature of Yhwh worship.[28]

In Egypt, Mesopotamia and elsewhere, power and authority had long held a sacred dimension; they were a privilege granted to the king by a local divinity.[29] In return, the king acted as the head priest of the cult. But the line between the deity and the deity's representative was very fine. It's therefore not surprising that a number of pharaohs and kings in Antiquity didn't hesitate to cross that line by fashioning themselves into living gods. This is why the titles *lord*, *demi-god* and *god* attributed to them can sometimes cause confusion.

Could one of the primary reasons we have failed to identify the specific moment in time when the religion of *Yahweh* developed in Israel be because we have been culturally programmed to value *Yahwism* as opposed to *Baalism*? Blinded with such a strong presupposition, it is only natural to be puzzled by evidence that pleads for a cultual evolution of *Baalism* rather than a religious revolution.

If Abraham's Lord were indeed a powerful king, rather than a divine being, would it not then be necessary to reread the Scriptures in search of new clues and wouldn't it change the way we look at past hypotheses? Raising these questions prompts us to re-examine the available data from a new angle. With Pandora's box half open, will the apparent inconsistencies reveal a different picture? One of the "apparent inconsistencies" that has puzzled generations of scholars and directed biblical studies over the past century relates to the origin and use of the names *Yahweh* and *Elohim*. Indeed, why two names for one God?

The Documentary hypothesis

Tradition has long attributed the writing of the Pentateuch (i.e., Torah) to Moses. But in the late 19th century CE, based on textual criticism, Julius Wellhausen lays the foundation for the

---

[28] Grabbe, Lester L. 2009. *Ancient Israel: What do we Know and How do we Know It?* New York: Continuum. (Orig. pub. 2007.). p.35
[29] Vestiges of these practices can be found in modern society, when institutions, in order to legitimize their power, swear in their leaders before God or on the Bible.

Documentary hypothesis, which claims source material from different regions were collated to form the Bible, thereby giving substance to an idea that Witter and Astruc had foreseen a century before him. Wellhausen develops his hypothesis by investigating places of worship, sacrifices, festivals, clergy and tithing. The tensions and variations he detects in the text leads him to conclude that the Pentateuch is the by-product of four different sources he identifies as J, E, D and P. Underlying this hypothesis rests an old question: why is God sometimes referred to as "*Yahweh*" and at other times as "*Elohim*" in the Hebrew Bible? For Wellhausen, the Abrahamic narrative is a product of JE assembly, for which source J originates from the kingdom of Judea in the south, staging *Yahweh* as an anthropomorphic god (usually rendered as "Lord"), and source E from the northern kingdom of Israel that refers to *Elohim*, a more immaterial deity (usually rendered as "God"). Source D stands for Deuteronomy, and predates the priestly laws of P, the main legislative document of the Leviticus priesthood. Over time, the Documentary hypothesis of Wellhausen evolved and gave birth to several variants, including the theory of *fragments* and that of *supplements*.

A century and a half later, the hypothesis that once appeared to yield fertile ground for exegesis[30], has lost its shine. No sources for J, E, D or P texts were ever found outside the Bible and even their existence remains highly speculative. And while there is consensus on the fact that the Pentateuch is a product of assembly, scholars are still far from agreeing on the *history of the writing* that led to its composition. Great progress has nevertheless been made because there is now wide consensus that the Bible could not have been assembled before the post-exilic period, i.e., at the earliest in the 6th century BCE. However, the question of the *literary project* that gave birth to it and the origin of its many sources remain largely unexplained. For a while, the scientific community overwhelmingly rallied behind the idea of a mythical and oral tradition as the only hypothesis capable of explaining the ancient source of the tradition, but even this view is now challenged. Unfortunately, the puzzle remains incomplete. The scientific

---

[30] An exegesis is a critical analysis of a (religious) text.that is aimed at understanding its evolution and meaning.

community still does not know *where*, *when* and *why* the Abrahamic tradition was born, nor how it evolved over time. Ever since Wellhausen, generations of researchers have attempted to tackle these puzzling questions with mitigated success.

At the beginning of the 20th century CE, with the School of History of Religions, H. Gunkel promotes in-depth analysis of the texts to better understand the origin of this oral tradition.[31] He posits the theory that the stories found in Genesis are variations of ancient Babylonian myths. But there remains the question of the process leading to the assembly of these different stories. G. von Rad offers a response, and becomes the architect of the "final form." According to him, the Pentateuch contains traditions of the Hebrew people: a father's descent into Egypt, the sojourn in Egypt, the Exodus and the gift of the land. For von Rad, the characters of Abraham, Isaac and Jacob are used to flesh out the story while the early chapters relating the creation of the world serve as a prologue. With the help of "archaeological evidence," W.F. Albright seeks to entrench these myths in the history of the Middle Bronze Age. But his enthusiastic attitude is not universally shared, since there is very little evidence supporting his claims. Indeed, no trace of a monotheistic religion whatsoever can be found during that period. The work of Albright[32] only finds partial support through A. Alt's work on the "God of the Father," which presupposes the traces of a pre-*Yahwistic* nomadic religion.

During the first half of the last century, maximalist researchers thought that the people of Israel were born out of a group that developed under the influence of Canaanite society, but on the fringe of it. The idea of a fringe group helped explain why no trace of a monotheist people had been found within the Canaanite society. If this historico-critical reasoning held sway for some time, it stagnated in the 1950s before entering into crisis in the 1970s. At that time, some started to question the origins of the

---

[31] Jones, Gareth. 2004. *The Blackwell Companion to Modern Theology*. Malden: Blackwell Publishing. p.373
Johnson, Luke Timothy. 1998. *Religious Experience in Earliest Christianity: A Missing Dimension in New Testament Studies*. Minneapolis: Fortress Press. p. 16
[32] Römer, Thomas. 1996. La formation du Pentateuque selon l'exégèse historico-critique. In *Les premières traditions de la Bible*, eds Amphoux, C.-B. and Margain, J., 17-55. Paris: Éditions du Zèbre.

promises and the cults: were *Yahwistic* sources pre-dating or post-dating the Deuteronomic literature? Critics, including Rolf Rendtorff, started to question the little challenged Documentary hypothesis as they felt it was relying too much on a subjective and abusive segmentation of the texts. Furthermore, advances in archaeology came to contradict widely accepted beliefs by showing that no society has ever lived on the fringes of Canaan before conquering the land. The so-called *peasant revolt* theory developed by the biblical scholar George Mendenhall and the sociologist Norman Gottwald was thus refuted.

These new minimalist findings called for a revised interpretation of past assumptions. B.J. Diebner claims that the concept of the "God of the Father" can be explained in literary terms. He argues that this concept serves to strengthen the link between the various patriarchal figures. T.L. Thompson reasons that the analysis of the institutions of Israel does not lead to the Early Bronze Age, but rather to the Iron Age. For his part, Van Seters argues that the traditions related to Abraham only date from the period of exile.[33]

It will therefore come as no surprise that many conservative scholars are in total disagreement with this minimalistic vision of such "late events." They insist: the priests and regulations regarding worship and sacrifice existed in a pre-exilic period.

Despite their minimalistic stance, Finkelstein and Dever have revived the debate somewhat by showing that some archaeological traces of early Jewish settlements can be dated back to the monarchic period (around the 10th century BCE). Although the facts do not match the story purported in the Bible, these findings nevertheless confirm an older historical reality than most minimalist scholars had come to accept. According to Finkelstein, Israelite villages were created in the highlands as early as the Iron Age, in the wake of the settlement of nomadic Canaanites, but bear no resemblance to the descriptions found in the Bible.[34]

While there is occasionally a new impetus to rekindle the "historicizing" flame, the modern and liberal views continue to

[33] Ibid.
[34] Finkelstein, Israel and Neil Asher Silberman. 2001. *The Bible Unearthed: Archaeology's New Vision of Ancient Israel and the Origin of its Sacred Texts*. New York: Free Press.

dominate the debate, although they have failed to formulate a new synthesizing theory for explaining the origins of Israel. Thomas Römer, a leading authority teaching at Collège de France, claims there is only consensus among modern scholars on the significance of the period between the sixth and fourth century BCE (exilic and Persian periods) for the formation of the Pentateuch.

The minimalist perspective called into question

It goes without saying that the conservative Jews suffered a serious blow as the scientific community relegated their cherished historical claims to the realm of myth and legend. This minimalist conclusion has created a lasting chasm between biblical scholars holding conservative views and those holding liberal ones. Research projects on the origins of monotheism that focused on the Middle Bronze Age have virtually come to a halt because those *seriously* interested in this topic have come to grips with reality and are now focusing their attention on the Babylonian Exile and Persian periods (c. 600-500 BCE). As a result, only a handful of fringe researchers have continued to look into the Middle and Late Bronze Ages for traces of early Israelites. Needless to say, they have been largely ostracized from the right-thinking scientific community and labeled as conservatives or fundamentalists. But even the modern minimalist view is not a panacea, as it leaves a number of important unanswered questions that simply won't go away. Among other things, it can't explain the origin of the Abrahamic faith or the intriguing links that appear to exist between *Yahwism*, *Baalism* and the cult of the ancestors.

This lack of evidence for early monotheism is the primary reason scholars have given up on any historicizing research related to the Abrahamic narrative. They have instead retrenched behind the convenient and elusive claim of "oral tradition" some two decades ago, for which no evidence can ever be found and have since considered the case closed.

History nevertheless teaches us that social realities do not evolve through drastic steps, but rather through incremental ones. And much like Pasteur eventually dispelled the once popular notion of *spontaneous generation* for living organisms, we should not accept the idea that the religion of *Yahweh spontaneously* emerged out of a vacuum during the Babylonian Exile, just for the sake of fulfilling the need of strengthening the Jewish identity. Religions, much like other cultural mores, evolve slowly through intercultural exchange and syncretism. Already in the 4th century BCE, a period when the Bible was still being written, the Greek mythographer Euhemerus alleged that many gods developed from the deification of powerful men, usually kings.[35]

Historians regularly revisit the pages of our history, but oddly enough, it seems that no one has earnestly envisioned that such a possibility could explain the anthropomorphic nature of *Yahweh*, with some no doubt relying on their faith and others on tradition to rationalize the presence of this humanistic figure in the Abrahamic narrative. If such an earthly alliance had really taken place in the distant past, would we still be able to trace its process of mythification?

As it will be shown, the hypothesis and analysis put forth in this essay support the latest archaeological findings. By taking a fresh look at the available data, it is possible to straddle the minimalist and maximalist positions and offer a holistic, rational and coherent explanation for elements that have been perceived up to now as discrepancies. If the Bible is based on extrapolation of historical facts, we need to rely on its sociocultural context to grasp its deeper meaning.

The need for a new hypothesis

Some twenty years ago, a number of publications sounded the death-knell of the Documentary hypothesis developed by Wellhausen.[36] Scholars came to the realization they had reached a dead-end and accepted the inevitable conclusion that they had failed to identify the original sources J, E, D and P that had purportedly led to the formation of the Pentateuch. They nevertheless formulated the questions that any new theory would

---

[35] De Angelis, Franco De Angelis and Benjamin Garstad. 2006. "Euhemerus in Context." *Classical Antiquity* 25(2): 211-42.

[36] De Pury, Albert and Thomas Römer. 2002. *Le Pentateuque en question: les origines et la composition des cinq premiers livres de la Bible à la lumière des recherches récentes*. 3e ed. Genève: Labor et Fides. (translated)

need to answer. The failure of the Documentary approach forces everyone to rethink the problem. The slate must be wiped clean and a fresh and objective look must be taken at the available data. But to supplant existing theories, any new approach must meet the *principle of economy* and provide a simpler, more logical and more rational explanation for the questions left unanswered. To further our quest, let's draw on a few reflections in search for new clues.

Rendtorff, of the University of Heidelberg, considers that the Documentary hypothesis has occupied too much space and has virtually been consecrated:

> *Research on the Pentateuch has been in crisis for just over ten years. For nearly a century, the field has been dominated by the new Documentary hypothesis that Julius Wellhausen had helped to emerge. Apart from a few marginal, it is largely within this framework that the discussion has evolved. We can witness here, as Thomas Kuhn would put it, a classic example of how a given 'model' gets accepted to the point of becoming a 'paradigm' within which all research is conducted without ever again being questioned or subject to assessment.*[37]

Rendtorff rejects the idea that multiple sources were assembled and calls instead for a unique, coherent source:

> *... I doubt it is plausible to accept the existence of independent written 'sources,' which have each existed first for themselves, and that would have been assembled during a secondary editorial stage.*[38]

> *I advocate in favour of a new approach where we would not distribute, on the outset, the texts in predefined 'sources' or 'strata,' but where the exegesis would take the text in its present configuration. ... This view is rather based on the belief that the latter authors have written the current draft, as it presents itself to us, in obedience to a*

---

[37] Rendtorff, Rolf. 1989. L'histoire biblique des origines (Gen 1-11) dans le contexte de la " rédaction sacerdotale " du Pentateuque. In *Le Pentateuque en question*, eds De Pury, Albert and Römer, Thomas. Paris: Labor et Fides. p.83 (translated)
[38] Ibid. p.84

definite intention, and that the primary task of exegesis is to identify this intent and interpret the text accordingly.[39]

Römer and de Pury emphasize that such an approach would open the door to recognizing the texts as being much older than was previously thought. They raise new questions:

> *The approaches put forward by Rendtorff, Blum and Crusemann argue in fact for a kind of revised fragment hypothesis. In this perspective, nothing would oppose the presence in the Pentateuch of ancient literary sets and even of very ancient sets. But the Pentateuch as such would only be the result of a drafting exercise of the post-exilic period. This raises the question: What is the intent of this wording? To what end, and after which 'model' was the Pentateuch formed?*[40]

All these observations suggest that the historico-critical approach is proceeding along an incomplete dialectic trajectory. Despite the initial enthusiasm expressed towards Wellhausen's hypothesis, his model has gradually lost ground. Any new synthesis should attempt to reconcile previously opposing positions. The problem must be visited with a systemic perspective, calling into question past premises and articulating new hypotheses. But which method should be used to meet this challenge and what criteria should be applied to test the new hypotheses?

Werner G. Jeanrond, of the University of Glasgow, favors the *hermeneutic circle*, a comprehensive approach that uses the initial set of responses to feed a deeper analysis. He says:

> *If we do not ask questions, we will not be able to structure our reading.*

And

> *We cannot understand a whole without understanding the individual parts it is made of; and we do not comprehend the individual parts if we can't see how they all fit together.*[41]

---

[39] Ibid. p.93

[40] De Pury, Albert and Thomas Römer. 2002. *Le Pentateuque en question: les origines et la composition des cinq premiers livres de la Bible à la lumière des recherches récentes.* 3e ed. Genève: Labor et Fides. p.66 (translated)

No progress can therefore be achieved without first abandoning the prevailing presuppositions, because any new hypothesis must necessarily oppose the previous ones, despite the risk of sounding heretical. In addition, time continuously changes the horizon: research concerns and expectations are much greater today than they were yesterday. If we ask different questions, we must accept that the answers *will* be different. In this context, will the new proposal be received and taken at face value and not according to its intrinsically heterodox value? David J. A. Clines, University of Sheffield expresses his doubts:

> *Rational debate still happens in the academy, I allow, and issues are sometimes settled purely on their merits. But when it comes to grand theories like the Documentary Hypothesis there is too much investment in the power that world-views and grand theories accumulate to themselves for that to happen. I do not mean that there is no longer any place for rational argument, but only that rationality is subordinate to the exercise of power. It is naïve to think otherwise or to act as if our decisions on such matters were not bound up with where we stand in a world of power... The physicist Max Planck said: 'A new scientific truth does not triumph by convincing its opponents and making them see the light, but rather because its opponents eventually die, and a new generation grows up that is familiar with it.*[42]

Aware of the difficulties associated with such an approach, Römer and de Pury call for caution:

> *The exploration to which we are invited, as we have said in the introduction, is a task of major importance; since it is from these results that will depend not only our understanding of the formation of the Pentateuch, but also our renewed vision of Israel's theology, history, traditions and history itself. This undertaking, however, only has a*

---

[41] Jeanrond, Werner. 1995. *Introduction à l'herméneutique théologique: développement et signification*. Paris: Éditions du Cerf. (translated)
[42] Clines, David J. A. 2006. "What Happened to the Yahwist? Reflections after Thirty Years." *SBL Forum*, SBL Forum, SBL Forum, http://sbl-site.org/Article.aspx?ArticleID=551 (retrieved June 4, 2006).

chance of success if it preserves the freshness of its look and if it is careful not to replace the yoke of old theories by a brace of new slogans, be them of the New Criticism.[43]

But twenty years later, it is clear that the *New Criticism* interpretation has failed to meet these expectations. And if scientific interest in historico-critical research has been considerably weakened, the questions on the origins of monotheism it was trying to answer remain perfectly valid.

In summary

- In claiming a late historical origin for Judaism (c. 600 BCE), the minimalist scholars continue to maintain a stronghold, despite many indications in the texts that are pointing to a Middle Bronze Age origin.

- New archaeological evidence is surfacing on a regular basis that shows traces of proto-Judaism well before the dates articulated by the liberal minimalists. These findings are challenging, incrementally, the late historical claims.

- The JEDP hypothesis suggests the names *Yahweh* and *Elohim* originate from different geographical locations has brought scholars to distribute the biblical texts in predefined 'sources' or 'strata.' This approach is now seriously contested because it has proven incomplete and flawed.

- Many scholars are advocating in favor of a new approach where the text would no longer be distributed, but kept in its present configuration. However, this takes scholars back to the original question: why is God sometimes referred to as *Yahweh* and other times as *Elohim*? And how can we explain some of the obvious contradictions found in the text?

---

[43] De Pury, Albert and Thomas Römer. 2002. *Le Pentateuque en question: les origines et la composition des cinq premiers livres de la Bible à la lumière des recherches récentes.* 3e ed. Genève: Labor et Fides. p.80 (translated)

Earthly interpretation of the Covenant

Acknowledging the failure of the Documentary hypothesis brings us to suspect the presence of a fundamental error committed in its basic premise. Do U. Cassuto[44] and more recently Rendtorff foresee a solution when they refuse to admit the prior existence of independent "sources" or "layers" and advocate a coherent text and an original intent? But in this case, the age-old question that brought Wellhausen to develop his hypothesis remains: how to explain the presence of the terms *Yahweh* and *Elohim* side-by-side in the text?

If Wellhausen and his followers sought a solution by attributing various elements of the text to different sources or authors, they never doubt that the terms *Yahweh* and *Elohim* referred to divine entities. It is obvious that within the theology of Israel, the unicity of God (*Yahweh=Elohim*) is a *sine qua non* condition, and the cornerstone upon which all beliefs stand. By promoting the idea that these terms were derived from a blend of sources, and therefore potentially of polytheistic origin, Wellhausen had significantly bruised egos and offended sensibilities. And while A.T. Chapman[45] and S.R. Driver[46] emphasize early on that the use of these terms is not random, but depends on the context (the *God of nature* as opposed to the *God of revelation*, two sides of the same god), it seems that nobody has ever seriously challenged the fundamental principle of unicity, preferring to rely on tradition. But if the principle of unicity still applies to large portions of the Pentateuch, it will be argued that the separation of the terms *Yahweh* and *Elohim* into two distinct figures in the Abrahamic narrative is a prerequisite to understanding and solving the thorny problem of the Pentateuch's redaction.

---

[44] Cassuto, Umberto, Joshua Berman and Israel Abrahams. 2006. *The Documentary Hypothesis and the Composition of the Pentateuch: Eight Lectures.* Jerusalem [Israel]; New York [N.Y.]: Shalem Press.

[45] Chapman, Arthur Thomas. 1911. *An Introduction to the Pentateuch.* Cambridge: University Press. p. 53

[46] Driver, Samuel Rolles. 2005. *An Introduction to the Literature of the Old Testament.* Tenth ed. Whitefish: Kessinger Publishing. p. 13, note

Daring to distinguish two entities in this traditionally unified figure is a bit like applying Plato's cave allegory to expose a new reality: the dialogue between *Yahweh/Elohim,* one and the same God, and *Abraham* now becomes a trialogue between *Yahweh, Abraham* and *Elohim.* If nobody has ever seriously entertained this possibility, maybe it is because it can only be applied to the story of the Patriarchs, itself embodied in a much larger corpus. All those who followed Wellhausen into this cave enchained themselves to the Documentary hypothesis *in perpetuum,* being thereby distracted and preoccupied by the endless possibilities and the many implications it entails.

Do the terms *Yahweh* and *Elohim* then refer to separate gods, as the Documentary hypothesis could lead one to believe? In this case, how and why would anyone come to merge these two terms? Fortunately, it is not necessary to understand the *process* that has led to the merger of the two terms to make sense of the text. However, it is important to understand its *evolution*: is the *unification* of the terms *Yahweh* and *Elohim* predating or postdating the *writing* of the narrative? Wellhausen clearly assumes it is *predating* its final redaction. Otherwise, he would not have foreseen the final product as the result of an assemblage of separate sources where the terms *Yahweh* and *Elohim* designate one and the same god for the people of Israel.

Exploring a different hypothesis is therefore in line with the current post-Documentary trend, which, as seen earlier, suggests that the unification of the two terms does not result from the assembly of separate sources, as presupposed by Wellhausen, but is instead the result of a slow cultural evolution. The gradual amalgamation of the terms *Yahweh* and *Elohim* would eventually take place in the minds of the Hebrews as they sought to merge two powerful figures into a single entity. In this view, both terms naturally coexisted within the same original text, each with its own meaning. The *tensions* and *variations* that exegetes have surmised in the story of the Patriarchs through the alternative use of the terms *Yahweh* and *Elohim* would be pure delusion and the entire issue should be approached differently, with regard to both the *history of the writing* as well as the *literary project* that gave birth to the Pentateuch.[47]

Yahweh, the anthropomorphic figure

If we posit that the unification, or amalgam between the names *Yahweh* and *Elohim* took place a very long time ago, can one still trust the terms "*Yahweh*" and "*Elohim*" as they appear in the biblical texts that have survived to us? Wouldn't it be reasonable to believe that, over time, some scribes or copyists would have favored the use of one term over the other (i.e., *Elohim* rather than *Yahweh*)?[48] It does seem as if this was the case, because, while most textual witnesses of the Bible exhibit a high degree of consistency among them and with respect to the Masoretic text, a few transcription errors can nevertheless be found.[49] If these "errors" have no impact on a theological perspective where *Yahweh* and *Elohim* are perceived as one and the same divine entity, they conversely accumulate and become misleading in the context of an exegesis where each term must be understood as a different character in the story. Thus, despite an overall cohesion, a careful analysis of the narrative leads us to postulate that the initial clarity must have gradually given way to some digressions. But can we detect and correct these "mistakes" in order to restore the original terms? How can we steer towards the original intent rather than stray away from it? To avoid digression, an objective measure is needed, but which one?

Wellhausen attributes the anthropomorphic nature of *Yahweh* to his southern Judaic origin and the immaterial one of *Elohim* to its northern equivalent. However, if the term "*Yahweh*" *mostly* appears in the context of an earthly relationship, it is not *always* the case. In a few verses, "*Elohim*" is also portrayed with such characteristics. We postulate that initially, only the term "*Yahweh*" had an *anthropomorphic* connotation and that any discrepancies result from later substitutions, perhaps by the so-called "*Elohist*" redactor.[50] The nature of the first-degree relationship between

---

[47] De Pury, Albert, Thomas Römer, Jean-Daniel Macchi, Christophe Nihan and Philippe Abadie. 2004. Ge 12-36. In *Introduction à l'Ancien Testament*. Genève: Labor et Fides.139
[48] The Qur'an as well as the English translation of the Living Bible (TLB) are two examples of texts where the authors have chosen to abandon the dualistic nature of Yahweh/Elohim and have opted to refer to Him simply as Allah in the first case and God in the second.
[49] For example, compare: Ge 6:5 between King James and John Nelson Darby or Ge 15:6 between Bible in Basic English and American Standard Version, etc.
[50] See Joffe, L. "The Elohistic Psalter : What, How and Why?" *Scandinavian Journal of the*

Yahweh/Elohim and Abraham can help detect these discrepancies. Rather than trusting the term in place, it is necessary to insert, where the semantic context calls for it, the term that best fits. For example, when encountering an earthly relationship, the term "*Yahweh*" should be used. In contrast, "*Elohim*" is the term that should be used when Abraham addresses an immaterial deity.

Below are two verses that illustrate the problem. The first (Ge 15:18) indicates an earthly relationship, since *Yahweh* is speaking to Abraham. As *Yahweh* appears as an anthropomorphic figure, there is no inconsistency here:

> *Ge 15:18 In the same day* **"Yahweh" made a covenant** *with Abram, saying, Unto thy seed have I given this land, from the river of Egypt unto the great river, the river Euphrates:*

However, a few verses later, when this same figure takes his leave of Abraham, he is referred to as *Elohim*:

> *Ge 17:22 And he left off talking with him, and* **"Elohim" went up** *from Abraham.*

This appears to be an "error" since the term *Elohim* should refer exclusively to an immaterial pagan divinity and not an anthropomorphic figure.

In this next verse, Abraham prays to a pagan god for healing. In this case, the term *Elohim* seems appropriate:

> *Ge 20:17 So* **Abraham prayed unto Elohim: and Elohim healed Abimelech**, *and his wife, and his maidservants; and they bear children.*

The above example is interesting in several respects; in fact, it is one of only two verses in the Bible in which Abraham actually "prays" to God using the verb (פלל) *palal* ("to pray"). Everywhere else, the use of the Hebrew term (נא) *na* ("please") – merely represents a form of politeness, for example:

Ge 12:13 Say, **I pray (אָ) thee**, *thou art my sister: that it may be well with me for thy sake; and my soul shall live because of thee.*

Conversely, several other verses provide better insight into the origins of the misunderstanding. In the following verse, *Yahweh* is perceived as an *Elohim*.

Ge 28:21 So that I come again to my father's house in peace; then shall **"Yahweh" be my "Elohim"**:

The Patriarchs implicitly acknowledge a certain "divine" dimension to this great lord. As illustrated in the previous chapters, a number of kings during Antiquity bestowed these honorifics on themselves.

While the terms are used appropriately in the majority of cases, it appears that a number of substitutions have nevertheless made their way into the Scriptures over time. A textual analysis reveals the passages in which the terms *Yahweh* and *Elohim* have been distorted.

The diagram below represents the number of occurrences of the terms *Yahweh* and *Elohim* in each of Chapters 12 to 25 of Genesis—the story of Abraham—and their contextual use.

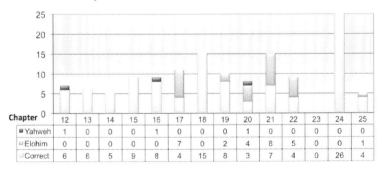

Chapter	12	13	14	15	16	17	18	19	20	21	22	23	24	25
Yahweh	1	0	0	0	1	0	0	0	1	0	0	0	0	0
Elohim	0	0	0	0	0	7	0	2	4	8	5	0	0	1
Correct	6	6	5	9	8	4	15	8	3	7	4	0	26	4

7: Contextual use of the terms Yahweh and Elohim

Taking Chapter 16 as an example, the terms *Yahweh* and *Elohim* are used correctly eight times according to the above chart. Only one occurrence of *Yahweh* in this chapter raises doubt:

Ge 16:2 And Sarai said unto Abram, Behold now, **Yahweh** *hath restrained me from bearing: I pray thee, go in unto my* *maid; it may be that I may obtain children by her. And Abram hearkened to the voice of Sarai.*

Indeed, it is difficult to understand how a mortal lord, however powerful he may be, could be responsible for Sarai's inability to bear a child. In this case, the term *Elohim* should have been transcribed, rather than *Yahweh*. Hence this occurrence is flagged as an "error."

Out of 135 occurrences of the terms *Yahweh* and *Elohim* in Chapters 12-25 of Genesis, we find *Yahweh* in 63% (85/135) of the cases and *Elohim* in 37% (50/135), that is, a ratio slightly exceeding 3:2. Overall, the terms are used appropriately 78% of the time (105/135). If they had been used interchangeably, as one might expect if these two names were truly equivalent, the error rate of 22% (30/135) should be much closer to 50% (flip coin theory). Note that almost half of the Chapters (i.e., 13, 14, 15, 18, 23 and 24) contain no obvious "errors." In these chapters, the use of the term *Yahweh* fits the context of an earthly relationship, whereas the use of the term *Elohim* refers to an intangible divine one.

Chapters containing "errors" should be understood as having been altered, intentionally or not, by scribes. Remarkably, and despite the fact that there are fewer overall instances of *Elohim*, in almost all cases where an error is detected, it is the term *Elohim* that appears where one would expect to find the term *Yahweh* – and not the other way around. In 54% (27/50) – slightly more than half of the instances where *Elohim* appears, we find it is used in the improper anthropomorphic context. However, we only find *Yahweh* used in the improper immaterial context in 3.5% (3/85) of the cases. This remarkable ratio of 10:1 (27/3) errors in favor of *Elohim* indicates an explicit intention to replace the original term *Yahweh*. This change is not unique to the Abrahamic story as there are other known biases towards the name *Elohim* in the Bible. A similar substitution is believed to have taken place in Ps 42-83, where the so-called *Elohistic Psalter* is suspected to have also replaced the name *Yahweh* with that of *Elohim*.[51] We can therefore conclude that the "real" errors – i.e., those resulting from

---

[51] See ibid.

accidental transcriptions as opposed to a name preference – should be those where *Yahweh* is found instead of *Elohim*, which only represents 2.2% (3/135) of the occurrences. Such an extremely low error rate is quite astonishing and testifies to how meticulously the original material must have been preserved, despite the countless transcriptions that the text has undergone over a period of almost 3,500 years. This impressive consistency can only attest to the historical accuracy of this narrative and the resolute desire to maintain its authenticity. [52]

As a result of this observation, the use of these terms – and especially that of *Elohim* – should be closely monitored and eventually substituted to fit the contextual nature of the relationship with Abraham. When the 27 erroneous occurrences of *Elohim* and 3 erroneous occurrences of *Yahweh* are properly substituted, we find that the occurrences of the term *Yahweh* in the narrative raises to 81% ((27-3+85)/135) and that of *Elohim* reduces to 19% ((50-27+3)/135) in the narratives. This 5:1 ratio in favor of *Yahweh* in the original narratives attests to the overwhelming presence of this humanistic figure; something that should be expected within the context of an earthly covenant.

If the terms *Yahweh* and *Elohim* were originally meant to refer to one and the same entity, their replacement would not affect the dynamic of the story or its deep narrative cohesion.[53] Given Greek mythology also depicts anthropomorphic gods, is it really fair to assume that the anthropomorphic nature of *Yahweh* necessarily refers to a *mortal* figure as we have suspected up until now? Couldn't it simply refer to a distinct, yet anthropomorphic deity? In Greek mythology, the stories do not hold up when humans replace gods, because their deeds remain eminently "fantastic" and "allegorical." This is why *Zeus*, despite his anthropomorphic characteristics, has to be a "god" so that the attributes bestowed upon him are coherent with the story that is being told. A parallel can be made with *Elohim*: this figure cannot take a human

---

[52] As this exercise is somewhat subjective, one should allow for a decent margin of error when quantifying these contextual "errors." The conclusion nevertheless remains overwhelmingly clear.

[53] When reading the Bible through the perspective of a divine Lord, randomly interchanging the terms Yahweh and Elohim does not affect the dynamic of the Biblical story.

dimension without the whole story's integrity collapsing. However, it will be shown that in the case of *Yahweh*, the opposite happens: the new dimension induced by this "human" presence, reveals a hidden meaning that, surprisingly, flushes out many inconsistencies that resulted from the amalgamation of the terms *Yahweh* and *Elohim*.

There will be no freedom for Sodom

When picturing the anthropomorphic figure in the story of Abraham as a mortal lord, a true historical record is suddenly revealed in which "*Yahweh*" appears to be seeking control over the entire region of Canaan. It should therefore no longer come as a surprise that the story rapidly leads to a military action: the War of Kings (Ge 14). Abraham courageously engages in a fight that only concerns him indirectly. While one would normally expect that the tension induced by such an early and dramatic action serves as a preamble and a foundation for the continuation of the story, it only plays an anecdotal role in the traditional religious interpretation.[54] However, the dissociation of *Elohim* and *Yahweh* into two distinct characters, along with the mapping of human characteristics to the figure of *Yahweh* allows restoring the preponderant role of an event that will prove critical in the context of an earthly covenant. A careful contextual and inclusive reading of the story featuring a mortal "*Yahweh*" can be summarized as follows:

> *To subdue the inhabitants of Sodom who revolt after 12 years of servitude, four Eastern Kings loot the city and take away men and booty (Ge 14:5). Hearing that Lot was taken prisoner, Abraham chases them with three hundred and eighteen men, defeats them, and recovers the goods and his nephew (Ge 14:16).*

One would naturally expect the four Eastern Kings to seek revenge, but surprisingly, they don't. Is it therefore pure coincidence that "*Yahweh*" destroys Sodom *again* shortly after? Shouldn't this rather be taken as evidence that these two events are

---

[54] A. de Pury does not hesitate to qualify Ge 14 as an "erratic block" (translated). See De Pury, Albert, Thomas Römer, Jean-Daniel Macchi, Christophe Nihan and Philippe Abadie. 2004. Ge 12-36. In *Introduction à l'Ancien Testament*. Genève: Labor et Fides. p.152

related to the insubordination of this city? The story definitely supports such an interpretation:

After undergoing a military defeat, "Yahweh" seeks to maintain control over this remote area. He has no choice but to retaliate against Abraham or turn him into an ally (Ge 15:1). As he knows he will need a reliable and devoted man to enforce his law and maintain order, he chooses to make a covenant with him. As a good diplomat, Abraham agrees to submit to this new master, and in return, he and his descendants shall enjoy the land and protection (Ge 15:18).

Sensitive to rumors suggesting that the citizens of Sodom are still trying to rebel, Yahweh tells Abraham about his intention to destroy the city and make an example of it (Ge 18:20). Abraham, who had also likely entered a covenant with the Sodomites, tries to dissuade Yahweh by appealing to his sense of justice, but in vain (Ge 19:24).

Considering that Ancient Israel was practicing the cult of the ancestors and history abounds with megalomaniacs who sought to deify themselves, *Yahweh*'s human characteristics beg this question: could a relationship exist between a mortal *Yahweh's* actions and those of the four Eastern Kings? Let's also remember that archaeology has found no trace of a monotheistic people living in the pagan land of Canaan until well after the United Monarchy period (9th century). [55]

In league with the four Eastern Kings

Given that the punitive campaign in Ge 14 and the destruction of the city of Sodom in Ge 19 are both aimed at punishing its people for disobeying and refusing to submit, it appears that the four Eastern Kings and *Yahweh* operate under one and the same objective, namely to subdue the Sodomites. If the logic of the narrative allows us to propose such a connection, is there any evidence within the Hebrew text itself that allows linking *Yahweh*

---

[55] For quite some time, biblical scholars thought that the Israelites were a different people living on the fringe of Canaanite society. This offered a convenient way to explain why no trace of monotheism had been found in the mainland. However, archaeological digs made by Finkelstein have clearly demonstrated that this could not have possibly been the case.

to the four Eastern Kings? Such a connection would strengthen our case. Of course, one shouldn't expect such an obvious link, as others before us would have obviously clued into it a long time ago. We should therefore lower our expectations to little more than subtle traces. Remarkably, it appears that verse Ge 14:22 of the Masoretic text does hold the vestiges of such a connection. We find this verse when Abram returns victorious from having defeated the four Eastern Kings and meets to negotiate with the king of Sodom:

ויאמר אברם אל־מלך סדם הרימתי ידי אל־יהוה אל עליון

קנה שמים וארץ:

*Ge 14:22 And Abram said to the king of Sodom, **I have lift up mine hand unto Yahweh**, the most high God, the possessor of heaven and earth,*

In the traditional interpretation, the expression "*I have lift up mine hand unto Yahweh*" is understood in the literal sense of "I lifted my hand to swear." Many translations simply assume this action as they literally translate in English using the verb *to swear,* which in Hebrew would be (שבע) *sheba* ("to swear"). However, in the Masoretic text, it is the Hebrew verb (רום) *ruwm* ("lift") – that is used to the perfect H tense (Hiphil) (הרימתי) *harimti* ("I have lift up") to indicate a completed action to the first person. While there are plenty of instances where the verb (שבע) *sheba* ("to swear") is used in the Pentateuch, there are no other instances where lifting the hand is used as a means to swear. *A contrario*, the image of the (יד) *yad* ("hand") fits perfectly and is commonly used in the Bible in the context of military actions. In fact, it is used in the figurative sense of "strength, power" in the same breath, just two verses earlier by Melchizedek when he blesses God for delivering the enemies into Abram's *hand*:

*Ge 14:20 And blessed be the most high God, **which hath delivered thine enemies into thy hand**. And he gave him tithes of all.*

There are multiple other instances in the Bible where the idiom "*to raise hand against*" is used in the sense of hitting or striking someone (see 2 Sam 18:28, 2 Sam 20:21, 1 Kings 11:26, 1 Kings 11:27, Psalm 106:26). I would therefore like to suggest that it is much more likely that we are here in the presence of this familiar idiom: Abram is telling the King of Sodom that he raised his army against the powerful *Yahweh*, and has therefore put them in a precarious position in order to save the people of Sodom, and that this act of bravery justifies paying tribute.[56] The text remains ambiguous as to who is actually making the payment. It therefore seems far more plausible that *Melchizedek* is the one paying tribute to Abram, and his men, for their dedication and courage, rather than the other way around as is always assumed.

The interpretation of this critical sequence provides us with some textual evidence supporting the idea that *Yahweh* could have been involved in this conflict and that the king of Sodom sought to thank Abraham for his efforts. But before we further this textual analysis, let's verify if there is any archaeological evidence supporting the idea of an earthly covenant.

A tradition culturally entrenched

Although factual analysis has now led a majority of scholars to accept the idea of a late composition for the story of Abraham, it remains difficult to understand how such a "myth" would have become so foundational, pervasive and intimately connected with the teachings of all the biblical prophets. What if Finkelstein rightfully understood that the early Israelites were no different than Canaanites, but his conclusions were precipitated because he didn't take his reflection far enough on the possible implications that such a critical observation entails?

I believe Finkelstein failed to grasp two[57] critical notions that would have changed his understanding of how biblical accounts

---

[56] In this context, the causative verb H fits perfectly since it is not the first subject - Abram - but the second implied subject - his men - who fought the battle.
[57] Finkelstein also failed to grasp these two additional notions that will be demonstrated later: the irreconcilable biblical chronologies and "extraordinarily long life spans" of the patriarchs are not embellished figures, but result from erroneous mathematical conversions; and finally, no masses of people ever had to leave Egypt in order to give birth to the myth of Exodus, but Egypt simply had to cease exercising its dominion over Canaan.

actually relate to the cultural, political and religious history of Canaan. First, he failed to fully appreciate how the religion of *Yahweh* is not a unique and distinct religion, but one that has its roots deeply intertwined with the Bronze Age pagan cult of the ancestors; second, he did not grasp from the narratives that the Sodomites weren't wicked people, but that they were revolting against a foreign power and that this is the reason an overlord sought to make a covenant with a Abraham, a trustworthy individual.

When approaching the Bible without these notions, the question of its historicity can be *tossed* aside, but it cannot be *resolved.* There is therefore little doubt in my mind that Finkelstein's conclusion would have differed significantly had he approached the problem with these notions. For one, curiosity might have brought him to investigate possible connections between *Yahweh* and the pagan deity *Baal Berith*...

Indeed, we know from the Bible (Jug 8:33) and from archaeological digs performed near Nablus in the Occupied Territories, that the ancient Israelites living around Shechem during the Late Bronze and Iron Age periods (c. 1600-1000 BCE) worshipped a pagan deity called *Baal Berith*, which in Hebrew literally means "Lord of covenant." This deity's name not only implies a covenantal form of worship, but also bears a striking resemblance to *Yahweh*'s epithet. We also know from the Bible that Abraham and his descendants lived near Shechem (Ge 12:6; 33-18; 37-12; Num 36:31; Josh 17:2). And while many scholars have been intrigued by their similarities, it appears that no one has ever investigated the extent of the connections that can be established between *Yahweh* and this pagan deity. This oversight is most apparent when reading about the history of Judaism and when reviewing scholarly literature on the Patriarchs. But in their defense, why would anyone who has always been taught to oppose abhorrent and primitive pagan deities with the only true God even suspect there could be a link between the two?

By acknowledging that *"the Bible's patriarchal narrative was initially woven together from earlier sources,"*[58] Finkelstein

---

[58] Finkelstein, Israel and Neil Asher Silberman. 2001. *The Bible Unearthed: Archaeology's*

implicitly recognizes that this story wasn't born out of thin air, but that it must have had a legacy. In fact, it appears that this religious concept is rather unique, as no other instances of a God making a covenant with a man have been found elsewhere. And given the abundance of cultual practices and religious themes surrounding the authors of the Bible during their exile to Babylon, they clearly had no shortage of inspiration for shaping their own religious concepts. It is therefore more likely that this story was already entrenched in the Israelite's cultural background and tradition. We should therefore pay very close attention to the *Sitz im Leben* – i.e., the sociological milieu from which these "earlier sources" might have evolved – when looking for answers. And given the patriarchal narrative contains multiple references to "the God of your father," an expression that points to remnants of the cult of the ancestors, perhaps it is time we stop looking for the vestiges of a religious covenant made with a "new God," and instead consider that the "divine" character in the Abrahamic story could have been a mortal Lord that got fashioned into a god a long, long time ago.

In regard to ancestor worship, the Jewish Encyclopedia early on held the following view:

> *Many anthropologists are of opinion that this was the original form of religion (H. Spencer, Lippert); the school represented by Stade and F. Schwally argues that it was the original religion of Israel before Jahvism was introduced by Moses and the Prophets. According to them, much of the priestly legislation was directed against the rites connected with Ancestor Worship. At present the view that the original religion of the Israelites was some form of Ancestor Worship is the only one that has been put forward scientifically or systematically, together with an explanation of the changes made by the later and true religion of Israel.[59]*

New Vision of Ancient Israel and the Origin of its Sacred Texts. New York: Free Press. p. 33
[59] Jacobs, Joseph "Ancestor worship." Jewish Encyclopedia. http://www.jewishencyclopedia.com/articles/1488-ancestor-worship (retrieved September 10, 2015).

One could not accuse the Jewish Encyclopedia of having a negative bias towards Judaism. It therefore shows that early biblical scholars have long suspected that the early form of *Yahwism* somewhat evolved out of the cult of the ancestors. However, they have never been able to connect the dots and have been left with suppositions. At a time when Semitic nomads were still practicing a form of primitive ancestor worship, the late Herbert Spencer, one of the most influential philosophers of his time, raised the all-important question:

> *If this person to whom Abraham salaams as his lord, with whom he has made the covenant, is a terrestrial ruler, as implied by the indirect evidence, the conclusion is reached that the ancient Semitic idea of a deity was like the modern Semitic idea cited above. And if, otherwise, Abraham conceives this person not as a local ruler but as the Maker of All Things, then he believes the Earth and the Heavens are produced by one who eats and drinks and feels weary after walking: his conception of a deity still remains identical with that of his modern representative, and with that of the uncivilized in general.*[60]

Although he was not able to offer additional evidence supporting his reflection, the above rationale brought Spencer to conclude that, whatever the case may be, Abraham must have been practicing a form of ancestor worship. Fortunately, and thanks to modern biblical and archaeological research, we now know a lot more about ancient Israel. It is therefore regrettable that all research on the historicity of the Patriarchs came to a halt and, as such, no further investigation regarding possible ties with ancestor worship was ever made.

We are only taking Spencer's questioning a step further by suggesting that Abraham made a territorial covenant with a powerful ruler, and that this covenant has given rise to the deification and worship of this overlord through the cult of the ancestors. Such a strategic alliance, made in regard to the land that Abraham's descendants would later occupy, helped turn this cult

---

[60] Spencer, Herbert. 1893. *The principles of sociology Vol. 1.* New York: Appleton and Company. p. 409

into idolatry and then monolatrism. It naturally follows that, instead of rejecting their pagan roots by adopting an entirely new religious model during the Babylonian Exile, as is currently believed, the Israelite priests simply sought to consolidate their identity around the vestiges of their ancient pagan cult – namely the cult of *Baal*, (i.e., lord), and the territorial covenant, or "*berith*," once made with their forefather Abraham – by grafting some new ontological concepts onto it.

In addition to suspecting ties between the Abrahamic Covenant and ancestor worship, scholars have long suspected that the religion of *Yahweh* also has ties with the ancient pagan cult of *Baal*, as even the New World Encyclopedia comments:

> *It has been suggested by modern scholars that the Lord of the Hebrews and the Baal of the Canaanites may not always have been so distinct. Psalm 82:1 states: "God presides in the great assembly; he gives judgment among the gods." Many commentators believe this verse harkens back to a time when the Hebrew religion was not yet monotheistic. Some suggest that Yahweh and Baal were originally both thought of as sons of El, while others claim that the worship of Yahweh and Baal may once have been nearly indistinguishable.*[61]

So, there we have it: on the one hand, a covenant suspected to be tied to ancestor worship; and on the other, early *Yahwism* suspected to be linked to the pagan cult of *Baal*. All we are missing is the secret ingredient that links all this together, which would allow us to establish with certainty that an earthly covenant led to the worship of *Baal* and that the worship of *Baal* slowly evolved into the religion of *Yahweh*. Could *Baal Berith* prove to be this missing link? Most likely, but unfortunately, we do lack reliable information on this pagan deity. Thankfully, and as this work demonstrates, the solution can also be found in the patriarchal narrative itself, and in the understanding that its Covenant (*Berith*) was initially referring to a territorial land grant made with a mortal

---

[61] New World Encyclopedia Contributors. "Baal." *New World Encyclopedia*, http://www.newworldencyclopedia.org/p/index.php?title=Baal (retrieved August 30, 2015).

Lord (*Baal*) who would later be celebrated and deified as *Baal Berith*.

How Yahweh became Elohim

The valuable data we have been able to cumulate thus far allows us to revisit the narrative under the perspective of a secular covenant established with a mortal lord, rather than the traditional perspective of the religious fervor for a new God. So what happened over the course of history? How could the cult of the ancestors have given rise to the cult of *Baal Berith* and then to *Yahwism*? What traces of such an early evolution remain and where can we find them?

As *Yahweh/Elohim* is perceived as a unified figure and the *foreign ruler* as a distinct force in the traditional religious interpretation (figure 4), it is necessary to go back in time in order to adopt the perspective of an earthly covenant. To do so, we simply need to transpose our basic presupposition and view *Yahweh* (i.e., *Baal Berith*) as a *foreign ruler* in league with the four Eastern Kings instead of a god.

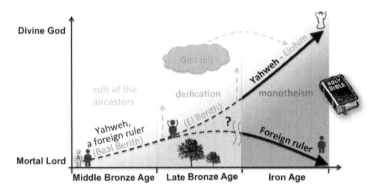

8: Evolution of "*Yahweh*" in the psyche of the early Israelites

The above diagram depicts how Yahweh (i.e., Baal Berith), a foreign ruler, was initially deified. His "mortal" attributes would have slowly receded into the background before being forever lost. This last step, exemplified by the literal vs. figurative interpretation of Ge 14:22 would have been instrumental in allowing Yahweh to be elevated to the rank of the supreme god Elohim.

Such a shift in presupposition would have taken place a long time ago when this foreign ruler was elevated from the ranks of mortal lord to that of a divine god in the psyche of the early Israelites. Here is an interesting question: did *Yahweh* stop being perceived as a mortal lord *after* the Israelites lost sight of his connection with the four Eastern Kings, or did it became *necessary* to conceal his humanistic nature once he was perceived as a god? Either way, that is eminently the point in time after which tradition would forever lose sight of the fact that it was once with a mortal that Abraham made his Covenant, and that is also likely when the Israelites would start viewing *Yahweh* and *Elohim* as one and the same divine entity.

As soon as one adopts such a perspective and views *Yahweh* as a powerful overlord and *Elohim* as a pagan deity, it becomes apparent through the biblical text that this Covenant (*Berith*) was made with Abraham in order to put an end to the unrest in the valley of Siddim and secure control over the region of Canaan, and that *Yahweh* (*Yhwh*) is just another name for *Baal Berith* that became necessary in order to help differentiate Him from lesser pagan gods. With this perspective, the Abrahamic narrative flows with no deterrent to understanding the origin, transmission and evolution of the Covenant in light of the Jewish historical claims and as part of the historical context of the Bronze Age.

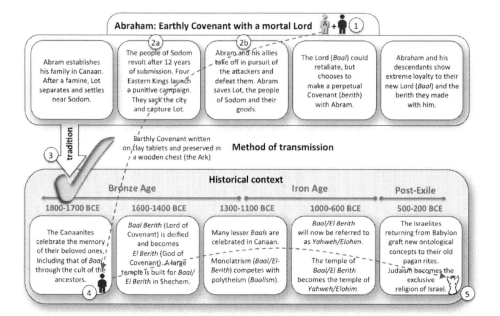

9: Abrahamic faith as natural evolution of an Earthly Covenant with a mortal Lord

When considering the story of Abraham from the perspective of a mortal Lord (1), unexpected elements of the story (2a) & (2b) now fit perfectly. In addition, such an earthly covenant (1) could have very well taken place during the Bronze Age (4), as suggested by tradition (3). The cult of Baal Berith would have evolved into monolatrism and eventually monotheism over time through syncretism (5).

While the above diagram shows how the perspective of a mortal Lord fits perfectly within the historical context of the Bronze Age and helps explain the evolution of the Covenant, what evidence supporting such a suggestion can be found inside as well as outside the biblical texts? To answer this question, one must venture beyond the realm of theology to explore sociology, anthropology and etymology. It is necessary to go back to the early Near East civilizations of the Middle and Late Bronze Ages, at a time when the cult of the ancestors was prominent and the concepts of god and demi-god were still vague, and revisit the Abrahamic narrative anew; through the perspective of a strategic alliance with a powerful overlord instead of a religious experience with a new God. By legitimizing their "right" to their forefather's land, such an earthly covenant would have certainly fostered hope and unity among the Israelites in exile. The scope of the *exilic reform* could then be better understood as an adaptation of the ancient pagan cult to the more modern Persian religious concepts, with the goal of reinforcing the unique Israelite identity.

A secular origin for Abraham's Covenant

To help put things into perspective, it would now be useful to adopt the paradigm of an earthly covenant and revisit the Abrahamic narrative through the eyes of the inhabitants of Sodom. This is achieved by performing what I refer to as a *dissociative exegesis*, an exercise of textual analysis that invites you to assess the story of Abraham in the Bible while:

1) Identifying and *dissociating* the humanistic *Yahweh* from the immaterial *Elohim*.

2) Picturing *Yahweh* as a powerful Mesopotamian overlord (i.e., *Baal Berith*) in league with the four Eastern Kings.

Meant to cancel and reverse the slow evolutionary process that led the early Israelites to unify *Yahweh* and *Elohim* in their psyche, this simple, yet extremely powerful exercise reveals a whole new meaning of the text that not only dramatically increases its coherence and psychological plausibility, but also attests to its authenticity.

These two steps expose the new dynamic of the story and can help you filter out some of the remnant editorial "noise" that inevitably resulted from the countless transcriptions that this biblical text has undergone over thousands of years. To perform this exercise, I recommend that you start by copying and pasting the biblical text of Ge 12-25 into a Word document (see Annex C), as this will allow you to re-read the story and substitute the name "God" for "Lord" (or vice-versa) wherever you feel it's applicable (as discussed on page 60). You can then compare your notes with the analysis provided below and detailed in Part III.

Below is a diagram of the biblical story that can be summarized as *A Foreign Ruler Seeks to Subdue the Valley of Siddim*. In this diagram, the figures of *Lord (i.e., Yahweh)* and that of the *Foreign ruler* have been merged in order to illustrate what happens at the macroscopic level as a result of a dissociative exegesis, where all actions are derived from a single, external and unified force.

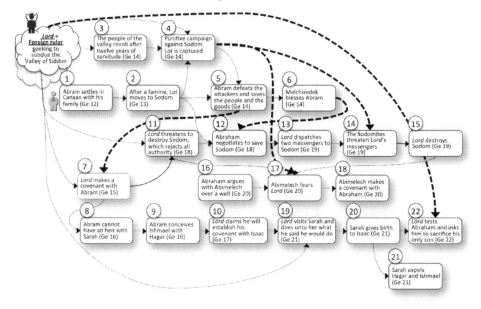

10: Dissociative exegesis interpretation

The key difference between the usual unified exegesis (figure 4) and the proposed dissociative exegesis (above) is that in the latter case the figures of Yahweh and Elohim are dissociated. The two external forces representing Lord (i.e., Yahweh) and the Foreign ruler can then be aligned and Elohim's role relegated to that of a pagan god bearing no influence on how the story unfolds.

It is helpful to compare the above diagram with figure 4 in order to fully realize that none of the boxes have moved or been altered. That's because virtually nothing in the text of Ge 12-25 needs to change in order to reveal a completely different story (only a few name substitutions are required to properly reflect the contextual relationship between *Yahweh/Elohim* and Abraham).[62] The earthly

---

[62] A handful of fantastic verses, such as those of the Sodomites going blind (Ge 19:11) or of Lot's wife turning into a pillar of salt (Ge 19:26), must have been inserted into the Scriptures by late redactors. These inserts are easily identified because they add a supernatural dimension to the text, but do not alter the flow of the story. While they most likely originate from legends or myths that developed around these stories, and were later added to the text to add a dose of mystique in support of the theological interpretation, they could also more simply result from a scribe's inability to decipher an original text. It would therefore be

interpretation relies exclusively on a new understanding of the roles and intentions of the characters. The only difference is to be found in causal relationships. Once the association is made between the foreign ruler and Abraham's Lord, it is no longer necessary to revert to allegory or theophany to make sense of the text. This new interpretation not only makes more sense, it tightens the relationship between the elements and improves the story's psychological plausibility.

The increased number of links reflects the stronger causal relationships between the various events in the story and testifies to the improved coherence of this interpretation. A new analysis of the *structural* elements and *causal* links pertaining to the narrative in light of the association between *Yahweh* and the *Foreign ruler* confirms that many *anecdotal* elements have now become *structural*. The number of *causal* links is also significantly higher, reflecting stronger interrelationships between elements of the story and a higher level of complexity. Such a higher level of organization cannot be attained by mere chance, as the detailed narrative analysis performed in the third part of this book demonstrates.

When re-reading the story of Abraham in the Bible under the perspective of an earthly covenant, one realizes that the story starts with Abraham moving into Canaan with his family (figure 10-1). The choice of this destination will prove important, as it is the area over which the Lord seeks control. The famine forces Abraham and his nephew to separate, which brings Lot to settle in the luxuriant valley of Sodom (2). This decision will prove crucial as the people of Sodom are about to revolt (3) and this rebellion triggers a punitive campaign that results in Lot being taken away (4). This event naturally engages Abraham in the battle (5). By successfully defeating the attackers he becomes a hero in the eyes of the people of Sodom (6), which makes them feel indebted to Abraham (12). While he could retaliate, the Lord opts to make a Covenant with someone who appears to be a loyal, powerful and respected man (7). It is therefore no surprise that this core event

interesting to perform a detailed etymological and morphological textual analysis of these verses in order to eventually shed additional light on their possible origin.

takes place immediately after Abraham was given the opportunity to reveal himself as a valiant and dependable ally (5).

The issue of the heir is critical for this covenant, as it is needed to ensure long-term stability of the region. By rejecting Ishmael, the Mesopotamian overlord indicates that he has an issue with an heir born of Egyptian blood (10). The fact that the Sodomites continue to send signals of unrest is of concern to the Lord, who wants to make an example of them (11). Abraham is in a difficult situation and negotiates to save the city because he cares for the people of Sodom (12). The Lord agrees to send messengers to inquire about the situation (13), but the aggressive response from the Sodomites (14) leaves him no choice but to destroy the city (15). Abraham's ability to rely on the Lord to impose respect is demonstrated through his encounter with Abimelech (16-17-18). Given that Abraham is unable to conceive a child with his half sister Sarah, the Lord himself takes care of fathering the child (19). After Isaac is born (20), Ishmael is seen as a threat and is sent away by Sarah (21). To make sure that Abraham won't betray him, the Lord demands the sacrifice of Abraham's only son (22), but this is only a test.

Projected to the historical context of the Bronze Age, this exercise completely transforms the religious story of Abraham (Ge 12-25) that we thought we knew into a secular one that exposes a nation vanquished, betrayed and annihilated for standing up and refusing to submit to a foreign ruler. Here's how I believe the story of Abraham[63] unfolded some 3,500 years ago[64]:

> *Bera was the respected king of Sodom, a small and prosperous kingdom located in the Siddim valley of Canaan (modern Israel). As an important trade route between Mesopotamia (modern Iraq) and Egypt, the economy of the region flourished. Kingship was usually entrusted by a*

---

[63] Abram will become Abraham (Ge 17:5) and Sarai will become Sarah (Ge 17:15).

[64] It will be shown in "Part III - Abraham ", that although additional details have been added to "fill the gaps," the main characters, their actions, motivations and the order in which they appear, accurately respect the biblical story described in figure 10.

local pagan divinity, and the king himself was often seen as the representative of this deity. The king's daily activities included resolving conflicts and organizing justice and the life of the small community of a few hundred souls. The land was fertile and there were always merchants passing through, willing to buy, trade or sell goods. Bera had established reciprocal covenants with neighboring kingdoms to ensure territorial security, as was then customary among respectful leaders.

Things took a turn for the worse when Chedorlaomer, a powerful ruler of far away Mesopotamia, ventured deep into Canaan with his army, with the objective of subduing the entire valley and securing the trade route for himself. The offensive proved successful, as it did not meet much resistance: no organized force could be mobilized against them and so the foreigners marched over the entire valley and subdued it.

Life proved much harder for the inhabitants of Sodom in the aftermath of the attack. Not only had they lost their livestock and had their goods taken away, but it would now also be necessary to pay a steep annual tribute to king Chedorlaomer, their new overlord, as failing to do so would spell bitter reprisals.

***

Twelve years had passed since the terrible attack and things were slowly returning to normal in the little kingdom of Sodom. A new generation of children was playing in the fields and laughter could be heard again. At that point, the people of the valley felt they had endured enough pain and sacrifice and that it was time to regain their freedom. They jointly made the decision that they would not pay any tribute to Chedorlaomer this year. There were plenty of young men around who could easily defeat the lord's representatives the next time they would show up to collect the tithe. The inhabitants estimated the chances of retaliation to be pretty slim, as in all those years, Chedorlaomer had never ventured back into the valley. The overlord was also getting old. If the people of the valley stood together, Chedorlaomer would most likely not venture this far out as it would hardly be worth it.

When Chedorlaomer's men showed up to collect the tribute, the villagers did exactly as they said they would. Chedorlaomer's men were easily put to flight. Everyone in Sodom was ecstatic: the vassals stood up to their overlord! From now on, they would be a free people... and that freedom tasted wonderful.

***

A few months later, a cloud of dust was seen rising from the horizon. A wave of panic was in the air. Everyone feared Chedorlaomer was retaliating. The most courageous young men were sent to the front to prepare an ambush. As they got closer, they weren't met by armed horsemen, but by a small group of herdsmen walking in their direction with their flock of sheep. What a relief!

The herdsmen set up their tents near Sodom while their leader, a man called Lot, was escorted and introduced to the king. Bera was curious to find out what had brought them to the valley. Lot explained that they were nomads and that they had been traveling with his uncle's family until recently, but that their flocks had grown too large. A recent famine had forced them apart and he was now trying to find sufficient pastures to feed his herd. Lot had heard of the fertile valley of Siddim and was seeking permission to settle in the area. After successful negotiations, which involved trading and gifts, Lot and his followers were allowed to settle in the valley.

It didn't take long for Lot to learn about Chedorlaomer and the most recent events that had taken place. It was therefore not a complete surprise when, a few months later, the rumors of a possible punitive campaign reached the valley. Within days, reports of terrible attacks were confirmed. Chedorlaomer, the bloodthirsty overlord of Mesopotamia, was on his way along with three of his allies

— Amraphel, Arioch and Tidal. Their troops were destroying villages, killing people, and plundering all the goods. It seemed that despite all odds, the aging overlord would not let this revolt go unpunished.

***

Bera, Birsha and three other local kings of the valley assembled all men of age to engage in combat. Bera would lead the attack. Unfortunately, these men were unable to counter the proficient Mesopotamian army. Ill prepared and inexperienced, they simply did not know how to fight effectively. Bera and Birsha hid among the tar pits while others fled toward the mountain. The four Eastern Kings took everything they could on the battlefield before heading to the villages to sack them. They enslaved the people and took them away with all their goods.

As one man managed to escape, Lot urged him to go find his uncle Abraham who dwelt by the oaks of Mamre. When the uncle heard of his nephew's capture, he went to get Eshcol and Aner, his two nearby allies, and gathered three hundred trained mercenaries before pursuing the Eastern Kings towards the North. Abraham divided his troops against them by night, smote them, and pursued them as far as Hobah, which is to the left of Damascus. He brought back his nephew and all the people and their goods.

Bera went out to meet them. Abraham was blessed before the gods and celebrated as the new national hero by the king and his priest. To thank Abraham, Bera gave him a tenth of all the goods that had been saved and made him an ally. Although everyone was rejoicing, Bera remained anxious and didn't sleep well over the following weeks. He was concerned that the Eastern Kings would come back. Chedorlaomer had shown that he wasn't the kind to let go easily. Clearly, the situation wouldn't remain indeterminate...

***

Back in Mesopotamia, Chedorlaomer, infuriated and thirsty for even more power, conspired to seize one of his allies' kingdoms, but Amraphel successfully defeated the treacherous man. Empowered by this victory, Amraphel consolidated his forces and quickly rose as the new Mesopotamian ruler. After a short period of time, he established himself as a respected and just ruler. Securing control over the far-away trade route to Egypt through Palmyra, a caravan stop for travelers crossing the desert, nevertheless remained a priority. The defeat suffered in Damascus at the hands of Abraham was a bitter blow and, with Chedorlaomer no longer representing a threat, lord Amraphel knew he had both the momentum and the power to retaliate. However, as an astute diplomat, he also knew that a display of force would not have a long lasting impact and that it would be much better to establish an enduring peace covenant with a powerful, trustworthy and respected ally who already had influence in the region... and Abraham stood out as the perfect candidate!

***

The new lord sent a messenger to reveal his true intentions: the lord would be Abraham's protector in exchange for absolute and unwavering loyalty, and as his very great reward, Abraham would inherit control over the land of Canaan for generations to come. As a semi-nomadic people living at a time when this lifestyle was increasingly threatened by emerging civilizations, this covenant represented an amazing opportunity, as it would ensure that Abraham's name would be esteemed and his descendants would be able to reap the benefits of the land.

A perpetual covenant was established between the two parties.

When Bera heard that Abraham did an about face and became the lord's right-hand man, he became livid: Abraham, the man he so admired, the man who had saved the valley had now joined the ranks of the enemy! How could this be? Abraham saw things differently and tried to explain the situation: by making a covenant with this foreign lord, he was securing the entire valley's future. As long as the inhabitants obeyed the rules and the laws, they would benefit from this great lord's protection. If anyone were to attack them, the lord would defend them. But Bera cherished his newly acquired freedom more than anything else and he wasn't prepared to let it go.

***

In order for the covenant to perpetuate itself over time, Abraham needed offspring who would maintain it. Failing to provide a legitimate heir would automatically put an end to the covenant, and Abraham's family would lose its prestigious standing. Unfortunately, Abraham had no heir. Endogamy was a popular practice of the Bronze Age that allowed maintaining one's heritage within the family. It was therefore common for a wealthy man to marry his cousin or sister. Abraham had married his half sister, Sarah, with whom he shared the same father. Sarah was believed to be barren as she hadn't been able to give him any children. Given the significance of this covenant, it became imperative for Abraham to get an heir. Considering the critical outcome, Sarah eventually offered Abraham to have a child with her Egyptian maid Hagar... This was not such an unusual practice at the time, and this is how Ishmael was born to Abraham.

Hagar quickly gained status within the household. After all, she was the one who had given an heir to Abraham. Sarah grew jealous, but she wasn't the only one concerned. The lord wasn't pleased either, as an heir from Hagar could open the door to foreign Egyptian claims on the land of Canaan. To maintain control over this important trade corridor, it was imperative it remained under the exclusive control of Mesopotamia... The lord gave Abraham no choice: the heir of the covenant must be born from Sarah.

***

Given his new role and political status, Abraham tried to convince the Sodomites that things would be different and that life would improve under their new ruler, if only they would oblige. While a few were inclined to give the lord a chance, many refused to subdue their freedom. The Sodomites had been vassals for too long and weren't prepared to accept any foreign control! No offense to Abraham, but they would continue to reject the authority he was now representing.

When the lord heard of the ongoing unrest in Sodom, he grew very impatient: not clamping down on these rebels would send the wrong message across the empire. In order to avoid having other regions dispute his authority, it became imperative to make an example of these wicked people...

The lord was very aware that Abraham held a special status within the Sodomite community. He was therefore reluctant to share his grim plan with his right-hand man... but in the end, he knew he had little choice. Abraham found himself caught between a rock and a hard place because he had made himself an ally of king Bera and swore that he would protect the people of Sodom. He therefore could not allow his old allies to be annihilated! Abraham invoked his lord's sense of justice: would he kill the innocents who are prepared to accept him, just as he would kill those who reject him? After a skillful and diplomatic negotiation, the lord eventually agreed to spare the city if only a handful were willing to submit.

The lord sent two of his messengers to inquire about the situation in the city. When they arrived in Sodom, an angry mob surrounded them. The mob adopted a bold and defiant attitude. The inhabitants wanted to send a clear message to this Mesopotamian lord. They wanted the messengers to feel the pain of submission that they had themselves endured as vassals during twelve grievous years. They therefore did what conquerors often do to the vanquished in order to add insult to their injury, and "sodomized" them… Realizing that the city would never submit, the lord was left with no other choice but to send his troops and destroy the city, sparing only Lot and his family as a favor to Abraham.

The desired effect was immediately achieved and everyone in Canaan took notice. Abraham's authority had a newfound legitimacy that would never be questioned.

***

A few more years passed before the lord would visit Abraham again. What he found was of great concern to him: his right-hand man had still been unable to get an heir from Sarah. Abraham and Sarah were aging and the situation was becoming critical. Enough time had been wasted! The lord had a heart-to-heart discussion with Abraham before he visited Sarah in the tent and impregnated her with his own seed, thereby doing to Sarah exactly what Abraham had done to Hagar. Before taking his leave, the lord insisted that this son be named Isaac. He also confirmed that it would be through this son that the covenant would be fulfilled. Nine months later, Sarah gave birth to Isaac, Abraham's new son. The solution was perfect: as Sarah was Abraham's half sister, Isaac duly carried Abraham's family bloodline, and so he ended up adopting and raising Isaac as his own son.

The lord wanted to ensure that Isaac would truly inherit after his death, and he was uncertain of Abraham's loyalty. He therefore decided to kill two birds with one stone by ordering the sacrifice of Abraham's only son, Ishmael. [65]

There was so much wealth and reputation at stake that Abraham had no choice but to carry out the horrific request. He traveled with his beloved son to the sacrificial mountain as he was instructed to do, and just as he was about to slit his son's throat, from a nearby hill the voice of

---

[65] Although Jews and Christians believe Isaac was the son that God ordered to be sacrificed, they disagree with Muslims who believe it was Ishmael instead. The logic of the earthly covenant gives credence to the Muslim tradition.

the lord's messenger ordered him to stop. Abraham had successfully passed the test! Entrusted, he would forever be thankful to his new lord for having spared the life of his only son.

* * *

After this great lord died, Abraham's descendants sought to commemorate their genitor's memory. The cult of the ancestors was common practice in ancient Israel. The great king and benevolent man he once was would soon be remembered as the Lord of Covenant (Baal Berith). Through deification, he would become the God of the Covenant (El Berith). A temple would be erected in Shechem to honor Him. Many generations later, Israel had adopted many lesser gods that they also referred to as Baals. It therefore became important to dissociate Him from all these pseudo-gods, and that's when Israel started referring to Him by the Tetragrammaton Yhwh, as well as Elohim, Israel's exclusive deity that, to this day, we still call "God."

As demonstrated by the above rendering of the Abrahamic story, the characters, their quests and motivations can all be linked, in one way or another, to the unrest in Sodom and the need to ensure long-term control over this important region. Events that appeared irrelevant or loosely connected in the religious interpretation now come to life and are intimately contributing to building the intrigue and climax, and drive the progression towards the resolution of the plot. It can also be observed that the sequence of these events cannot be interchanged without introducing incoherence or losing significant plausibility.

We can feel the tension winding up through the story until Lot is taken captive. A transformative action takes place when Abraham defeats the four Eastern Kings. The climax is reached at that point, as there is uncertainty about the outcome of the situation. While some form of retaliation is expected, a solution is found instead through the making of a long lasting covenant. The tension then unwinds and returns to normal.

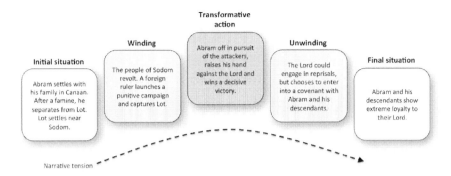

11: Narrative tension in the Earthly Covenant

While it is often possible to come up with a new metaphor when considering the story at a second-degree level, what are the chances of finding a more plausible, more realistic first-degree literal interpretation of the story by dissociating its key figure into two (i.e., *Yahweh/Elohim* ➔ *Yahweh + Elohim*) and then establishing a connection between one part of its main character (*Yahweh*) and some remote characters (*four Eastern Kings*)? I think we can safely say that the chances of finding a better solution are nil… implying that the story was originally written to be interpreted this way.

Well-reasoned answers

From this point on, the story of Abraham takes on true historical meaning, and this re-analysis finally yields answers to the questions asked by perplexed readers.

In the wake of these observations, listed below are answers to questions raised in the traditional theological interpretation section (see p. 39):

- *If there truly is only one God, why is He sometimes referred to as Elohim (God) and other times as Yahweh (Lord)?*

  - *In the story of Abraham, Yahweh represents a mortal lord, whereas Elohim refers to the pagan god El. Successive priests, scribes and copyists invariably used one or the other of these "recognized" names.*

- *If God loves us all equally, why did He give the "Promised Land" exclusively to the Jewish people (Ge 17:7)?*

  o *The lord made a covenant with Abraham, giving him and his descendants, exclusive control over the land of Canaan. As such, this agreement was necessarily limited to Abraham's immediate family, and their heirs.*

- *Why was Ishmael, even as a very young child, not considered worthy by God to inherit the Promised Land (Ge 17:19)?*

  o *It was inconceivable that the son of an Egyptian slave woman should be appointed heir to such wealth, as this would have paved the way to possible Egyptian claims to the succession. By fathering a suitable heir to Sarah, the lord secured greater influence over the region and granted exclusive power to his own bloodline.*

- *Why did Lot offer up his two virgin daughters to the angry mob of Sodomites? And why did the latter refuse them (Ge 19:8)?*

  o *He did so to appease the rebels, and to save himself and the messengers sent by the lord. But these men wanted nothing to do with Lot's daughters. They cherished their right to honor, freedom and independence, and their only intention was to humiliate these government representatives as revenge for having been enslaved.*

- *If God is merciful, why did He slaughter the Sodomites instead of trying to save them (Ge 19:24)?*

  o *Abraham's armed intervention during the War of Kings spared the rebellious Sodomites from punishment. As they kept rebelling, the lord had little other choice than to make an example of them. After they offended his messengers, the lord decided to annihilate the city.*

- *If God forbids incest, why was Abraham allowed to marry his half sister (Ge 20:2)? And why did Lot's sons, born of Lot's incestuous relations with his own daughters, become the fathers of the Moabite and Ammonite nations (Ge 19:34)?*

  ○ *Endogamy, which was already common practice among royal families, served to preserve noble bloodlines and limit claims to the throne or the dynasty.*

- *Why did God order Abraham to sacrifice his own son to prove his loyalty (Ge 22:2)?*

  ○ *The lord felt it necessary to ensure Abraham's loyalty by ordering him to sacrifice his son Ishmael (born of Egyptian blood from Hagar), who represented a threat to the dynasty. However, this was merely a tactic to test Abraham's loyalty.*

These questions are answered in a logical and psychologically plausible manner. Those versed in the practice of a theological reading of the Bible will naturally find it difficult to accept this new formulation, but in science, whenever we are faced with diverse points of view, which rest on verifiable facts, we eventually find a theory that can unify all the facts because they are only expressing the many facets of one and the same reality. Albert Einstein also once said, *"In the confusion, we must find simplicity."*[66] In this case, the fact that a theological interpretation can *also* be obtained from the same narrative seems quite remarkable too. It is therefore only through the comparison of the respective plausibility of the two interpretations that one can decide which interpretation better fits the original author's intent.

In summary

- One can easily detect anthropomorphic and immaterial figures behind the names *Yahweh* and *Elohim*. In most cases, *Yahweh* can be found associated with the

---

[66] Frank, Philipp and Shuichi Kusaka. 2002. *Einstein: His Life and Times*. Cambridge: Da Capo Press.

anthropomorphic figure, and *Elohim* with the immaterial one.

- Scholars acknowledge that there has always been a preference for the name *Elohim* among the scribes and that evidence of substitution of *Yahweh* for *Elohim* has been found elsewhere in the Bible.

- If *Yahweh* is systematically to be associated with the anthropomorphic figure and *Elohim* with the immaterial one, a few name substitutions must take place within the Abrahamic narrative. In most cases, we find that it is the name *Elohim* that replaces *Yahweh*, which would be expected given that some scribes prefer the name *Elohim*.

- Daring to dissociate *Yahweh* and *Elohim*, so they can be perceived as two distinct figures in the text rather than one unified God, leaves little doubt about the nature of *Elohim*, but brings one to wonder if *Yahweh* has to be identified with a mortal or a divine figure.

- If we understand the expression "Abraham raised his hand towards *Yahweh*" as the figurative idiom meaning "he fought against him" instead of the traditional "he swore an oath to him," we then have textual evidence linking *Yahweh* to the punitive campaign and the four Eastern Kings.

- Linking *Yahweh* and the four Eastern Kings to the same foreign Mesopotamian ruler helps to explain that the main quest of the story is to maintain control over Sodom.

- The revisited story provides *Yahweh* with a clear motive for wanting to make a covenant with Abraham.

The truth will set you free.
But first, it will p*ss you off.

Gloria Steinem

Part II - The Bronze Age

When divine intervention is ruled out in favor of a mortal lord, it becomes possible to review the available data in search for a historical character. However, since no historical proof of Abraham's existence has ever been found outside of the Bible, how can we possibly identify the mysterious "*Yahweh*" among all the powerful men who lived in the Fertile Crescent at the turn of the second millennium? While a great many kings, conquerors and other important men shaped this part of the world over thousands of years, most of the insignificant ones have been long forgotten, leaving very few traces behind. Only the greatest, those who roused the collective imagination or who left behind monuments and accounts of their glory, were assured a place in the annals of history. Given the major influence that this lord had on Abraham and his descendants, it wouldn't be surprising if *Yahweh* turned out to be one of these great men. If this were indeed the case, there should be widespread and clear evidence of this relationship.

Before we can identify such a lord, we first need a better understanding of the historical context of the Bronze Age; the period in which the Jewish tradition claims Abraham lived. A clearer understanding of the State dynamics and Middle Eastern history would also come handy. Since our collective memory is so deeply imprinted with the image of a nomadic, tent dwelling shepherd roaming the desert, it's highly likely that to some extent this picture is rooted in reality. But, what do we truly know about the people who inhabited the "Promised Land" at the turn of the second millennium BCE? Was their religion, culture and law consistent with those of the Patriarchs? How did the systems of government develop in these regions? How could a man such as

Abraham have come to be appointed governor of Canaan, in what conditions and by whom? And finally, how can we explain the process of mythification that would have eventually led to the religion of *Yahweh*?

The Fertile Crescent

The story told in the Bible begins approximately 6,000 years ago in the Garden of Eden.[67] While scholars cannot agree on the exact location of this earthly paradise, most believe that it was located in Mesopotamia, at the confluence of the Tigris and the Euphrates, in the region of Sumer, cradle of the world's first civilizations. Mankind's transition from a nomadic to a sedentary lifestyle is consistent with the myth of the Garden of Eden, since the transition from one way of life to another marks the beginning of a new era.

The Creation theme, already recurrent some four thousand years ago, is a topic humanity has always been pondering over. It's therefore consequent for Genesis to draw upon it. In fact, certain passages in the first chapters of Genesis bear a striking resemblance to the well-known ancient texts of the *Enûma Eliš*, the Babylonian creation myth.[68] While its date of origin is unknown, we know that its final version was written by the 12th century BCE. However, the concept of creation it puts forth is much older, predating the tablets by almost a millennium. The creation sequence it describes resembles that in Genesis: darkness gives way to light; the oceans and continents are formed; plants and animals are created; and, finally, man appears.

Is it any surprise that almost all cultures explain the origins of life in virtually the same way? This conception most likely stems from the development of agriculture and the realization of what we now call the "food chain", namely that man could not exist if plants, water and sunlight had not preceded him on this Earth.

---

[67] A literal reading of the Scriptures yields a genealogy that can be traced from Jesus back to Adam and Eve.
[68] Bottéro, Jean and Samuel Noah Kramer. 1989. *Lorsque les dieux faisaient l'homme: mythologie mésopotamienne*. Paris: Gallimard.
Heidel, Alexander. 1963. *The Babylonian Genesis: The Story of Creation*. University of Chicago Press. p. 129

Water and sunlight are the only elements over which humans have no control. If sunlight follows a regular and predictable cycle, the same does not hold true for rain, which man depends on completely for his survival. Ignorant of the evaporation-condensation cycle, the rain appeared to man to fall magically from the sky. He naturally believed that this element was controlled by a higher being. Whether known as *Baal*, *Hadad*, *Thor* or *Teshub*, these "rain gods" occupied a central place in the pantheons of all plains- and mountain-dwelling societies. They helped fill the larders of the people, who attempted to stay in their good graces and earn their favor.[69]

The city of Ur, Abraham's birthplace, is located not far from the mythical Garden of Eden. However, Abraham's story unfolds largely in the land of Canaan, in the Levant, a region nestled between the two vast Near Eastern empires of Egypt and Mesopotamia. The geographic area that encompasses these three regions is called the Fertile Crescent.

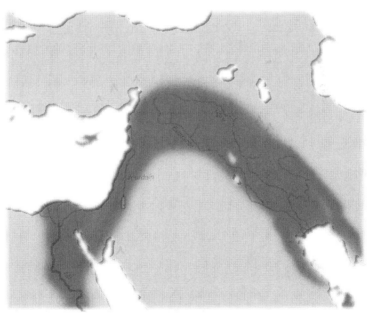

12: The Fertile Crescent

---

[69] Green, Alberto Ravinell Whitney. 2003. *The Storm-God In the Ancient Near East.* Winona Lake: Eisenbrauns. p.10

Intimately connected, these regions form the background of our investigation. Unfortunately, we do not even know where or when this lord lived. We do not even have a precise date. All we know is that the Jewish tradition claims Abraham lived sometimes between 2200-1750 BCE. The only other sources of information we have at our disposal are the Bible and the available historical data. Searching for this lord is therefore a bit like searching for a needle in a haystack. We must first take a step back, open the aperture of our lenses, and look at the "big picture" of the Bronze Age: How do these three geographical regions relate and differ from each other? How do they relate to the information available in the Bible? Can we see the pieces of the puzzle converging towards a common timeframe, location and target that we can then analyze and scrutinize in greater details?

We know from the Scriptures that Abraham lived in the Levant and traveled to Egypt to escape famines and to Mesopotamia to find a daughter for Isaac. We also know that most of the story of Joseph took place in Egypt. Given that the Patriarchs had an ongoing relationship with this country and its pharaohs; it would be unwise to rule out the possibility that Abraham's Lord be an Egyptian pharaoh despite textual evidence pointing to a relationship with the Eastern Kings of Mesopotamia. Many pharaohs upheld their authority by deifying themselves in order to achieve immortality.

It is therefore useful to learn more about Egypt in this investigation as it is intimately linked with the Levant and Mesopotamia. More specifically, what can we learn of this region during the Bronze Age?

Egypt

Thanks to countless archaeological digs, we know quite a bit about Egypt. Inscriptions, documents, pyramids, mummies, tombs and publications are just some of the elements that have contributed to our knowledge of this people. The Egyptians left behind innumerable accounts of their rich culture and the development of their society. In many respects, the Egyptian civilization was one of the most sophisticated in Antiquity; no other civilization managed to achieve and maintain such stability over a period of three thousand years.

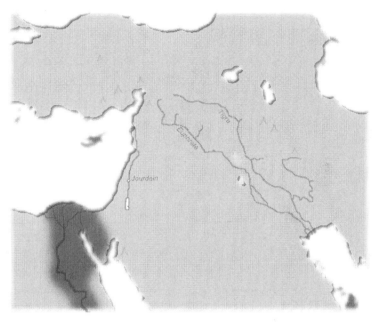

13: Egypt

Egypt truly flourished in the 4th millennium, upon contact with the Sumerian civilization. It acquired writing and perfected the clay brick construction technique.[70] It also developed a very rich local culture and a specific art form that still distinguishes it today. This omnipresent art, which was realistic, rich and structured, reflected the important social, political and religious concepts of the era; it expressed thoughts through symbols called hieroglyphs.

---

[70] While the oldest traces of writing still come from Mesopotamia, the most recent archaeological discoveries have closed the gap between Egyptian hieroglyphics and the oldest known Sumerian cuneiform tablets.

14: Step pyramid of Djoser

The architect Imhotep erected the first pyramid to King Djoser around 2600 BCE. It was a multi-level mastaba, or step pyramid. These immense structures were used as funeral complexes for the kings of Ancient Egypt. Clearly, these "new" constructions later influenced the ziggurats of Mesopotamia. It will later be shown that Abraham's ancestors began their migration from the Levant to Mesopotamia precisely as the first ziggurats were erected.

The Egyptian compounded deities

Unlike the inhabitants of Mesopotamia, who had to build vast irrigation systems, the Egyptians could rely on the annual flooding of the Nile to sustain their crops. The natural silt from the river, which fertilized the land, helped shore up the population against famine and contributed to the wealth that also trickled down to neighboring populations. The fertile lands of the Nile delta were particularly conducive to abundant crops.

Since access to water was not a daily concern for most Egyptians, they naturally didn't grant the same level of importance to the rain gods as other people did. Hundreds of gods would represent various phenomena, such as natural elements, geographical locations or even perceptions. Many Egyptian "super gods" were the result of compounded deities, that is, a new deity taking on the names and attributes of existing deities. In discussing this particular form of syncretism, Becking, refers to the work of late Hans Bonnet and explains:

> *Deities receive each other's names and qualities without becoming merged or lost in one another, that is without dissolving the identity of the deities, who lie behind a new deity. Gods may adopt each other's names and epithets, that is absorb each other's essence and qualities and develop into a new divinity by convergence and differentiation, or even a new type of deity.*[71]

Pointing to the *Amun-Re* deity as a noticeable example, Becking explains that, although it had developed its own cult in Egypt, both the gods *Amun* and *Re* continued to exist as independent deities with their own temple and cult.

While the Egyptians had many gods, some were clearly more important than others, especially in regards to the ruling class. The kings of Egypt exerted remarkable influence over their people, blessed as they were with specific powers passed on by the gods in the mythical *Horus-Osiris* cycle. According to tradition, Osiris was a legendary king who ruled Egypt with justice and passion.[72]

> *Jealous of his position as king, Osiris' brother, Set, kills him in a great battle. But Isis, Osiris' wife, magically breathes enough life back into her husband's dead body to conceive a child with him.*[73] *After burying Osiris, she flees to the Delta, where she gives birth to a son, Horus. On reaching manhood, Horus decides to avenge his father by confronting his uncle. Set rips out one of his eyes but the battle rages on and Horus emerges the victor. He reclaims his eye and offers it to Osiris, who is restored to life and appoints his son Horus as Pharaoh.*

---

[71] Becking, Bernhard, Engelbert, Jan and Hendrik. 2001. *Only One God? : Monotheism in ancient Israel and the veneration of the goddess Asherah.* London; New York: Sheffield Academic Press. p. 96

[72] Eliade, Mircea and Willard R. Trask. 1979. *A History of Religious Ideas: From the Stone Age to the Eleusinian Mysteries.* Vol. 1 of 3. London: Collins. p. 97

[73] Shahrukh, Husain. 2003. *The Goddess: Power, Sexuality, and the Feminine Divine.* Ann Arbor: University of Michigan Press. p. 86

Following this pattern, upon the death of his father, each new king of Egypt ascended to the throne in a ceremony that recreates the Osirian cycle. The new king becomes Horus while his deceased father represents *Osiris* by taking his place in the heavens. This cycle legitimized the power of the Pharaohs and brought rare stability to the area over a period of time that spans over several thousands of years, which have been classified by historians into several periods; each encompassing a number of ruling dynasties.

The periods that corresponds to the Bronze Age extends from the end of the Middle Kingdom to the New Kingdom, and include the Second Intermediate Period, during which tradition suggests that the Patriarchs have lived.

The Middle Kingdom

During this era (28th-20th century BCE), Ancient Egypt was divided into two regions, Upper Egypt bordering Africa and Lower Egypt, where the Nile Delta stretched out to the Mediterranean Sea. An unavoidable corridor between Africa and the Near East, it was the gateway to the precious resources of far-off countries.

While there had been several previous attempts, it was Mentuhotep II, Pharaoh of the 11th Dynasty (20th century), who succeeded in unifying Upper and Lower Egypt after a number of military campaigns mounted during the first 30 years of his reign.[74] But, once unification was achieved, the pharaohs of the Middle Empire turned their backs on Lower Egypt, preferring instead to reign from Thebes, in Upper Egypt.

A nomadic Amorite population, most likely issued from the Levant, began to settle in the Delta region of the Lower Egypt, where they built up several cities. Avaris became an important city with far-reaching influence.

The term *pharaoh*, or *per aâ* in Egyptian, means *great house*, and is believed to be in reference to the unification of the two territories. This term emerged only in the New Empire, that is, after the time of the Patriarchs. But, during the Middle Empire, the

---

[74] Valbelle, Dominique. 1998. *Histoire de l'État pharaonique*. Paris: Presses universitaires de France. p. 127

"king of Egypt" was already more than just a simple king—he was a god and the son of a god.

In *The King-God and the God-King in ancient Egypt*, professor Jan Zandee demonstrates how Amon-Ra and the pharaoh are presented as both king and god.[75] Passages VI.3, VI.10 and VIII.1 listed on the recto of the same papyrus are highly revealing:

> *VI.3 Lord of the Gods*
>
> *VI.10 Homage to you, Horus of Horuses, regent of regents, power of powers, great of the great (eldest), prince of eternity, lord of lords, god of gods, king of the kings of Southern Egypt, king of the kings of Northern Egypt.*
>
> *VIII.1 as for royalty, which is without end. To many jubilees over countless years; he reigns for centuries upon centuries.* [76]

This notion of a "living god" dates from the Ancient Empire (5th Dynasty – 26th to 24th century) and fits particularly well with the possible description of Abraham's suzerain.

The Hyksos of the Second Intermediary Period

At the turn of the second millennium (18th to 16th century), a large number of foreigners travelled through Egypt to settle in the lands located at the mouth of the Delta, in Lower Egypt.

Perhaps through negligence or simply out of slackness, the Egyptians did not keep a very close watch over their borders. These foreigners took advantage of the weakening central power to gradually establish themselves. The term *Hyksos* refers to the people who inhabited Lower Egypt in the late Middle Empire and during the Second Intermediary Period, precisely at the time Abraham would have lived according to tradition.

The Semitic origins of their names and the archaeological digs at Avaris indicate that the Hyksos were likely to have been Amorites

---

[75] Zandee, J. 1956. "Le Roi-Dieu et le Dieu-Roi dans l'Egypte ancienne." *Numen Numen* 3(3). p. 230

[76] Gardiner, Alan H. 1990. *The Admonitions of An Egyptian Sage: From a Hieratic Papyrus In Leiden (Pap. Leiden 344 recto).* Hildesheim: Georg Olms. (Orig. pub. 1909.).

descended from Canaan who gradually took possession of lands they already occupied. It is interesting to note that, in the entire history of Egypt, the Hyksos were one of very few foreign invaders who managed to seize power.

Started by Josephus Flavius, a Jewish Roman general who became an historian in the 1st century CE, the controversy surrounding the origins of the term *Hyksos* continues to fuel some discussions.[77]

> *This whole nation was styled Hycsôs, that is, Shepherd-kings: for the first syllable Hyc, according to the sacred dialect, denotes a king, as is sos a shepherd; but this according to the ordinary dialect; and of these is compounded Hycsôs: but some say that these people were Arabians. Now in another copy it is said that this word does not denote Kings, but, on the contrary, denotes Captive Shepherds, and this on account of the particle Hyc; for that Hyc, with the aspiration, in the Egyptian tongue again denotes Shepherds, and that expressly also; and this to me seems the more probable opinion, and more agreeable to ancient history.* [78]

Flavius' preferred expression "captive shepherds" better corresponds to the image of the children of Israel that he saw in these men. He also maintains that the Egyptians who lived alongside the Hyksos referred to the latter as *heka khasewet*, meaning "rulers of foreign lands".

According to Manetho of Sebennytos[79], an Egyptian priest and historian who lived in the 3rd century BCE, the Hyksos were barbarians who pillaged Egypt. But, the few historical traces that remain paint a portrait of a people much more concerned with absorbing and preserving Egyptian knowledge and culture than destroying it. It seems more likely that it was the Egyptians who disparaged the Hyksos in an attempt to forget this rather inglorious episode of their past.

---

[77] Falk, Avner. 1996. *A Psychoanalytic History of the Jews.* Madison: Fairleigh Dickinson University Press. p. 53
[78] Josephus, Flavius. 2006. *Against Apion.* Portland: Read How You Want p. 17
[79] Long since disappeared, the writings of Manetho were revealed to us solely through Flavius.

Flavius believed that the Hyksos were the ancestors of the Hebrews. Many popular authors have since been intrigued by the phonetic and historical correspondence between the Hyksos king Yakub-her and the biblical Jacob.[80] Tradition suggests Jacob lived in Egypt at around the same time and was no doubt an important man. And, if we accept that the Patriarchs and the Hyksos were both Amorite, and therefore of common ancestry, then the potential for speculation abounds.

Armed with new weapons (axes, iron daggers and horse-drawn chariots), the Hyksos began to rule Avaris around 1730 BCE. At the zenith of their power, even the king of Upper Egypt bowed before them.

The famous Papyrus Leiden I.344, housed in the Leiden museum in Netherlands, also dates from the Second Intermediary Period and is better known as the Admonitions of Ipuwer—the name of the scribe who wrote it. This ancient manuscript describes plagues much like those that Moses inflicted on Pharaoh in the book of Exodus. While there is no way to establish a direct link between these two texts, they could both refer to the natural disasters caused by the explosion of the island of Thera, one of the largest volcanic eruptions in the history of the world. The following correspondences are obvious in the natural disasters listed on the verso of this papyrus :

---

[80] In "Hiram Key", Christopher Knight and Robert Lomas suggest potential links between the Hyksos and the patriarchs. Also see the documentary entitled The Exodus Decoded , by Simcha Jacobovici

Disasters	Bible verse	Papyrus I.344
Rivers turned to blood	Ex 7:20	II.10
Crops decimated	Ex 9:31, 10:15	VI.3, VI.1
Livestock diseased	Ex 9:3	V.6
Fire and hail	Ex 9:23	II.11
Darkness	Ex 10:22	IX.11
Widespread death	Ex 12:30	II.3, IV.4, VI.16
The people grieve	Ex 12:30	III.14

The reign of the Hyksos lasted until the Pharaohs of the 17th Dynasty, when Seqenenre Tao II and Kamose, chased them out of Egypt.

The New Kingdom

The expulsion of the Hyksos marked the end of the Second Intermediary Period and the beginning of the New Kingdom, which will extend from the 16th to the 11th century BCE. This period was ruled by the Pharaohs of the18th, 19th and 20th Dynasties. According to the Jewish tradition, this was a period when the Hebrew people were slaved in Egypt, and when Moses led them out of the country. And while some have tempted to link the expulsion of the Hyksos with Exodus, dates simply do not match.[81]

The New Kingdom provided us with some of Egypt's most famous Pharaohs, including Thutmose III, Akhenaten, Tutankhamun and Ramses II.

Thutmose III (1481-1425) was nicknamed the "Napoleon of Egypt" because he was a great conqueror. He vanquished Israel and Canaan in the 15th century BCE, shortly after the Hyksos were booted out of the country. For most of the New Kingdom, many cities of the Levant will remain vassals of Egypt.

Amenhotep IV (c. 1380-1332) is better known as Akhenaten, for this is the name he took in recognition of the god *Ra-Horus-Aten* or just *Aten* that he adopted in lieu of the *Amun-Re* god of Thebes that had been elevated to the rank of supreme god of Egypt. *Aten* embodies many ancient gods, viewed in a new and different way and is considered to be both masculine and feminine. Akhenaten is called the heretic Pharaoh because he is regarded as a monotheist Pharaoh that abandoned the polytheist gods of Thebes in a new form of monotheism. He built the city of Amarna, which would be abandoned shortly after his death (c. 1332 BC) while the old state religion of *Amun-Re* would quickly get re-enacted. A significant collection of vassal correspondence with the Levant has been found in this city that helps us better understand the relationship that united these two regions. Ever since Sigmund Freud, the father of Psychoanalysis, published a study on the biblical Moses and the origins of Judaism[82] in 1938, many popular authors such as Jacq[83] and Sabbah[84] have investigated possible links and resemblances between the religion of Akhenaten and that of biblical Moses.

Tutankhamun (c. 1332-1323), although well known for his well-preserved tomb and mummy that was discovered in 1922, died at a young age and didn't leave much of interest to us behind him.

Ramses II (1303-1213), on the other hand, is another well-known figure of Egypt often associated with the biblical Pharaoh of

---

[81] See The Exodus Decoded (2006) by filmmakers Simcha Jacobovici and James Cameron.
[82] Freud, Sigmund and Katherine Jones. 2013. *Moses and monotheism.* Milton Keynes: Lightning Source UK Limited. (Orig. pub. 1939.).
[83] Jacq, Christian. 1976. *Akhenaton et Néfertiti : le couple solaire.* Paris: R. Laffont.
[84] Sabbah, Messod and Roger Sabbah. 2004. *Secrets of the Exodus : the Egyptian origins of the Hebrew people.* New York: Helios Press.

Exodus because he built the city of Pithom. Ramses II, who lived to the age of 90, is also best known for the Battle of Kadesh that is dated to 1274 BCE. This battle was fought in the north of the Levant, with the bordering Hittites. It is also the earliest battle for which military tactics and formations have been recorded. It was a memorable battle that involved thousands of chariots. More than a decade later, the battle was ended with no clear winner. Ramses II and Hattusili III signed the first Peace treaty known to historians that is proudly displayed on a wall at the United Nations' headquarters.

This brief overview of Egypt shows that the notion of living-god was a popular notion in a country familiar to the Patriarchs. We also know that Amorite kings—the Hyksos—ruled Egypt in the 18th century BCE and adopted the local customs. It would certainly be interesting to further explore the potential connection that Flavius foresaw between the Hyksos and the Patriarchs. Egyptians continued to exercise significant influence over the Levant in the aftermath of the Hyksos expulsion and for most of the New Kingdom.

We shall now turn to the Levant in order to better understand how the people of Canaan, and ultimately the Patriarchs, lived during the Bronze Age period.

In summary

- Egyptian gods were many and could also be created as compounded deities. Such "super gods" would take on the names as well as attributes of their original deities, which would continue to be celebrated. One such example is *Amun-Re*.

- The notions of living-god and king-god were familiar ones throughout the Bronze Age in Egypt.

- The Middle Kingdom saw the unification of the two regions.

- The Second Intermediary period of the Middle Bronze Age was ruled by the Hyksos, which were an Amorite people with ties to Mesopotamia.

- The Admonitions of Ipuwer papyrus relates plagues similar to those found in Exodus.

- The New Kingdom saw many great pharaohs that exercised significant control over the Levant, including Akhenaten the "monotheist" and Ramses II that is often believed to be the pharaoh of Moses.

- The Battle of Kadesh marked the end of the war between Egypt and the Hittites. From there on, Egypt would slowly lose its hegemony over the Levant.

Levant

The Levant is the vast region that extends along the Mediterranean coast from Egypt in the south to the tip of the Euphrates in the north. A subregion of the Near East, the Levant encompasses modern Israel, Palestine, Jordan, Lebanon and Syria.

Inside the Promised Land

Canaan is the coastal area of the Levant located on the Mediterranean Sea, where the Patriarchs settled and where most of their story takes place. It is also where the future nation of Israel would eventually be created. As a key corridor between two major powers, this region is both strategically and historically significant. Whether for reasons of war or trade, one has no choice but to travel through Canaan to get from Egypt to Mesopotamia and vice versa.[85]

---

[85] Lemche, Niels Peter. . 1991. *The Canaanites and Their Land: The Tradition of the Canaanites.* New York: Continuum International Publishing Group p.154

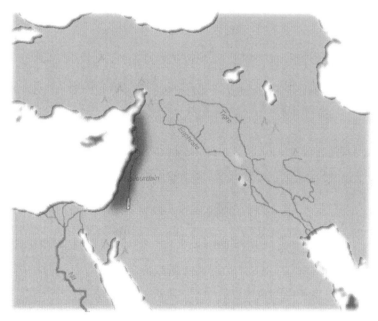

15: Region of Canaan

From the third millennium onwards, traces of a Semitic people that settled in the region are found; these were essentially the first "Canaanites." Sustained by a flourishing agriculture, they founded several cities. At the turn of the second millennium, a new wave of Semitic invaders, the nomadic Amorite people, settled in the region.[86] The "Amurru" are mentioned on Akkadian cuneiform tablets dating as far back as 2400 BCE.[87] While this marks the start of a tumultuous period, their successive attacks and frequent interactions with the local populations gradually prompted them to embrace the regional lifestyle and put down permanent roots. Through their encounters with the local people, the Amorites sired several different bloodlines and, today, are considered the ancestors of not only the Arameans, but also the Phoenicians, the

---

[86] "Amorrite," Hooper, Franklin Henry. 1909. *The Encyclopaedia britannica: Eleventh Edition*. London: Cambridge University Press.
Cluzan, Sophie. 2005. *De Sumer à Canaan: l'Orient ancien et la bible*. Paris: Éditions du Seuil. p.31

[87] Westermann, Claus. 1995. *Genesis 12-36*. Minneapolis: Fortress Press. (Orig. pub. 1985.). p. 64
Van De Mieroop, Marc. 2004. *A History of the Ancient Near East: ca. 3000-323 B.C.* Oxford: Blackwell Publishing. p. 82

Chaldeans, the Hebrews, the Hyksos and the Israelites—in short, most of the people who would later occupy the territory of Canaan.

16: Bronze statue of the Ur Dynasty

The archives of Nuzi (in Mitanni), which date from the 15th century BCE, contain enlightening information on Amorite customs of the time. They describe a society in which infertile couples could adopt a child slave as their descendant. Another custom involved offering a female slave to a man whose wife was infertile, as was the case with Hagar in the Bible (Ge 16:1-4; 30:1-13). The ambiguous inheritance rights resulting from these unions are also described in the documents of the time.

Some major discordant voices have also been heard. Through a comparison of the Nuzi texts with those of Genesis, Thompson has come to the conclusion that although nothing prevents the patriarchal narratives from fitting the second millennium, they much better fit the 7th century:

> ... aside from the still enigmatic Gen 14, I have tried to show that what we know about the history of Palestine in

the Second Millennium seems to argue definitively against such historicity.[88]

But if Thompson – who acknowledges not understanding the critical role of Ge 14 with regards to the Covenant – managed to convince a majority that the texts of Genesis could also "fit" the Neo-Assyrian period (7th century), he failed – at least in my opinion – to show that they didn't fit the second millennium. Kitchen has more recently refuted much of Thompson's claims by presenting a strong case for dating the patriarchal narratives to the second millennium based on a wealth of external and internal data. In his conclusion, Kitchen states:

> *We have here the Canaan of the early second millennium and not of the Hebrew monarchy period, in any wise. The oft-stated claim of a 'consensus' that the patriarch never existed is itself a case for self-delusion on the data presented here.*[89]

Kitchen shows that if some of these cultural elements can also be found during the Neo-Assyrian period, they clearly better fit the second millennium. He nevertheless also acknowledges some limitations:

> *... high ages at death, etc. are the only unusual features, and this may be in part the result of long-term transmission of numbers, a matter subject to change through time.*[90]

Kitchen's argumentation spans well over 600 pages where he does an extensive investigation of all the archeological data, compiles arguments for the various historical periods, and compares how each period supports the patriarchal narratives. Among other things, Kitchen compares the price of slaves throughout history to show how it perfectly matches that reported in the Scriptures. While Kitchen is somewhat biased and ruthless in his approach, he does provide valuable insights and data that are too often blindly dismissed.

---

[88] Thompson, Thomas L. 1992. *Early History of the Israelite People: From the Written and Archaeological Sources.* Leiden: E.J. Brill. p.296
[89] Kitchen, Kenneth Anderson. 2003. *On the Reliability of the Old Testament.* Cambridge: Eerdmans. p.372
[90] Ibid. p.361

A mix of sedentary and nomadic lifestyles

We are taught that Abraham is the father of modern monotheistic religions, but even if he had bestowed upon his mortal lord a certain divine dimension, in no way could he have thought of him as a god in the spiritual or religious sense. How could he possibly have? *Yahweh*'s humanistic nature betrays his true identity. Throughout Genesis, Abraham maintains a man-to-man relationship with him. Only the verses where the immaterial *Elohim* deity gets invoked can give us some insight into the real worship practiced by the Patriarchs. Once the distinction between Abraham's relationship with his suzerain, *Yahweh*, and his worship of the pagan god *Elohim* is made, it is astonishing to realize the extent to which Abraham's religion takes a back seat to his life as a governor who fulfills his duties with earnestness, deference and diplomacy.

With this premise put forward, it becomes possible to compare the *Elohistic* verses with the known practices of the time. This reveals a framework consisting of a mix of sedentary pagan religion and nomadic cults that are perfectly coherent with the local culture and has absolutely nothing to do with our traditional image of the father of a revolutionary monotheistic religion.

In *Ancient history of Israel: from its origins to its settlement in Canaan*[91], Father Roland de Vaux, one of the original authorities on the subject, emphasized the strong similarities between the story of the Patriarchs and the Middle Bronze period in Canaan.[92] He clearly illustrates the duality of this period, during which the predominant sedentary city lifestyle still coexisted with the nomadic one. However, like many others before him, Father de Vaux accepts the dogma of *Yahweh*'s divine nature without question and fails to consider Abraham's religious practices strictly on the basis of his relationship with *Elohim*, as an immaterial deity.

The social and religious duality illustrated by de Vaux rests on a blend of concepts related to nomadism, superimposed on a set of sedentary pagan rituals to local gods. Like any good nomad,

---

[91] De Vaux, Roland. 1971. *Histoire ancienne d'Israël, des origines à l'installation en Canaan*. Paris: Lecoffre.
[92] Ibid.

Abraham was naturally first and foremost influenced by the values of his nomadic clan, and then by those of the neighboring people.

Religion of *El*, *Baal* and *Asherah*

During the Bronze Age, the predominant religious practices of the Canaanites were sedentary and unequivocally pagan. The absence of monotheism has been proven by countless archaeological digs, which have only revealed widespread pagan activities at the time. The city of Ugarit, gateway between the Mediterranean basin and Mesopotamia, was a major capital that reached its pinnacle during the Middle Bronze Age, under the control of the Amorites.

Since farming in Canaan depended so heavily on the rain, the area's gods naturally dwelt in the sky, granting or denying this heavenly gift—bringer of life or death—at will. The archaeological site of Ugarit offers up vast documentary evidence of this in the form of cuneiform tablets. These texts date from the 14th and 12th centuries BCE and, although most are rather literary in nature, some describe the rituals, offerings and myths that reveal a number of parallels with passages in the Old Testament. This is the sedentary environment that surrounded the early Israelites, and within which they evolved.

The "*Baal* cycle" stands out from this famous collection. It was written in the 14th century, but as with many other ancient documents, the concept it puts forth most likely existed long before it was written and offers significant parallels with the *Bel* deity of Mesopotamia.[93] It describes *Baal* (בעל) – which in Hebrew means "lord" or "master" – as the son of the primary god *El* and the god of rain and thunder, who reigned over Ugarit with his sister, *Asherah*, goddess of fertility (also known throughout the Near East as *Ishtar, Anat, Astarte, Baalat* or *Zaparnit*). *Baal* is generally depicted as a calf or a bull (many representations of *Baal* feature horns) because they are a universal symbol of fertility.

---

[93] Driver, Godfrey Rolles and John C. L. Gibson. 1978. *Canaanite Myths and Legends*. Edinburgh: T. & T. Clark. (Orig. pub. 1956.).

Smith's observation on the role of death in the Baal Cycle gives further credence to our working hypothesis:

> *"[I contend] that the royal concern for the deceased kings and Rephaim has intensively influenced the longest piece of Ugaritic literature, the Baal Cycle. Baal is cast in the role of dead king and hero in the final two tablets of the cycle. Indeed, nowhere else in the ancient Middle Eastern literature is Death so prominent a divinity as in the Baal Cycle."*[94]

Baal was worshipped on mountaintops, ideally beneath pine trees. Cult members attempted to get closer to the heavens through earthly offerings and sacrifices made on an altar.

Discovered at Gezer, one of the most explored sites in Palestine, the High Place is a raised area perfect for worship, where archaeologists have discovered the bones of young children, perhaps the victims of sacrifice much like the one demanded of Abraham. This city was built up considerably during the Middle Bronze Age, as indicated by the many traces of Amorite civilization found there. What appear to be vestiges of similar human sacrifices found at Ta'anakh and Tel Megiddo suggest that this practice might have been widespread at the time.[95]

Likely written much later, when the inhabitants of Jerusalem were taken into captivity, the following passage condemns this archaic practice:

> *Jer 7:31 And they have built the high places of Tophet, which is in the valley of the son of Hinnom, to burn their sons and their daughters in the fire; which I commanded them not, neither came it into my heart.*

Craigie and Wilson describe the "fertility ritual," which consisted of the sacred union of male and female with the goal of stockpiling fertility energy, which ensured the continuing stability of agricultural as well as human and animal productivity.[96]

---

[94] Smith, Mark S. 2001. *The Origins of Biblical Monotheism : Israel's polytheistic background and the Ugaritic texts*. New York: Oxford University Press. p.70
[95] Vincent, Hugues. 1907. *Canaan d'après l'exploration récente*. Paris: J. Gabalda. p. 13
[96] Bromiley, Geoffrey William. 1979. *The International Standard Bible Encyclopedia*. Grand

Archaeological digs in Canaan have unearthed temples containing rooms where sexual practices are believed to have taken place. Several representations of fertility goddesses have also been found. And, while such rites were widespread, they were later nevertheless strongly opposed by Israel, since they were believed to violate God's commandments.

It was more recently shown by Dever and Hadley that, through syncretism, there was a time when *Asherah* eventually became the consort of *Yahweh*.[97] The Kuntillet 'Ajrud *pithos* ("storage jar") inscriptions that speaks of "*Yahweh of Shomron (Samaria) and his Asherah*" and the one carved into a wall of the Khirbet el-Kom tomb where someone is blessed "by *Yahweh*" and "by his *Asherah*" are dated to the 8th century BCE and continue to steer controversy. Scholars cannot agree on the description of the pictures or if one should see in the word "*Asherah*" the goddess deity or the "*asherah*" cult symbol. For J. Glen Taylor, the answer lies in the Taanach cult stand of late 9th century BCE on which one can find two representations of the goddess flanked by two lions; one *Asherah* is depicted as the naked goddess herself, and the other as a tree of life. For Taylor, there is little doubt that *Asherah* was perceived as both a consort to *Yahweh* and a cult object.[98]

Rapids: W.B. Eerdmans. p. 101
[97] Dever, William G. 2005. *Did God Have a Wife?: Archaeology and Folk Religion in Ancient Israel.* Grand Rapids: Eerdmans.
Hadley, Judith M. 2000. *The Cult of Asherah in Ancient Israel and Judah: Evidence for a Hebrew GoddessUniversity of Cambridge Oriental Publications.* Cambridge: Cambridge University Press.
[98] Taylor, J. Glen 1994. "Was Yahweh Worshiped as the Sun? Israel's God was abstract, but he may also have had a consort." *Biblical Archaeology Review* 20(03): 53-61, 90-91.

17: Taanach cult stand

When one is aware of this relationship between *Yahweh* and *Asherah*, it is very difficult to read the 8th century BCE prophet Hosea and not see in his tirade a clear condemnation of the cults of *Asherah*, consort of *Yahweh* and mother goddess of Israel:

> *Ho 2:2 Plead with your mother, plead: for she is not my wife, neither am I her husband: and let her put away her whoredoms from her face, and her adulteries from between her breasts;*
>
> *...*
>
> *Ho 2:11 And I will cause all her mirth to cease: her feasts, her new moons, and her sabbaths! and all her solemnities.*
>
> *Ho 2:12 And I will make desolate her vine and her fig-tree, whereof she hath said, These are my rewards which my lovers have given me; and I will make them a forest, and the beasts of the field shall eat them.*
>
> *Ho 2:13 And I will visit upon her the days of the Baals, wherein she burned incense to them, and decked herself*

with her rings and jewels, and went after her lovers, and forgot me, saith Yahweh.

Two centuries later, the Israelites continued to show their attachment to *Asherah*, the *queen of heaven*:

Jer 44:16 As for the word that thou hast spoken unto us in the name of the Lord, we will not hearken unto thee.

Jer 44:17 But we will certainly do whatsoever thing goeth forth out of our own mouth, to burn incense unto the queen of heaven, and to pour out drink offerings unto her, as we have done, we, and our fathers, our kings, and our princes, in the cities of Judah, and in the streets of Jerusalem: for then had we plenty of victuals, and were well, and saw no evil.

Jer 44 : 18 But since we left off to burn incense to the queen of heaven, and to pour out drink offerings unto her, we have wanted all things, and have been consumed by the sword and by the famine.

These few verses support the idea that *Asherah* had indeed become *Yahweh*'s consort in the eyes of the early Israelites.

Unlike the book of Exodus, which contains a wealth of ecclesiastical detail, Genesis provides very little information on the Patriarch's worship. Nevertheless, traces of the cult of fertility can be found within, as can be seen in this passage:

Ge 49:25 Even by the Elohim of thy father, who shall help thee; and by the Almighty, who shall bless thee with blessings of heaven above, blessings of the deep that lieth under, blessings of the breasts, and of the womb:

There are also explicit mentions of sacrifice and the art of divination...

Ge 15:9 And he said unto him, Take me an heifer of three years old, and a she goat of three years old, and a ram of three years old, and a turtledove, and a young pigeon.

> *Ge 15:10 And he took unto him all these, and divided them in the midst, and laid each piece one against another: but the birds divided he not.*

> *Ge 15:11 And when the fowls came down upon the carcasses, Abram drove them away.*

…most often practiced on a mountain:

> *Ge 22:2 And he said, Take now thy son, thine only son Isaac, whom thou lovest, and get thee into the land of Moriah; and offer him there for a burnt offering upon one of the mountains which I will tell thee of.*

The many analogies between these social sedentary mores and certain passages in the patriarchal story have already been underlined, but so far, these have always been presented as "resemblances" because we have been unable to dissociate *Yahweh* from *Elohim* and therefore didn't realize they were much more than just one aspect of the Patriarch's religion.

Now that we have a better understanding of sedentary worship, we can turn to the nomadic rituals.

Idolatry, necromancy and the cult of the ancestors

Whereas each region or area in Antiquity worshipped its own god, traditional nomadic religion could not be based on local gods since nomads were constantly on the move. Instead, a nomadic son recognized his filiation by invoking the memory of the "god of his father" and by praying to his ancestors. As Mircea Eliade points out in *A History of Religious Ideas*, the concept of worshipping the god of one's immediate ancestor is a primitive one that is especially well suited to this lifestyle.[99] Foltz also reports that devotion to ancestors is certainly the most archaic form of religion in the world.[100] Although this practice was predominant among nomadic people, it was also widespread throughout the Near

---

[99] Eliade, Mircea and Willard R. Trask. 1979. *A History of Religious Ideas: From the Stone Age to the Eleusinian Mysteries.* Vol. 1 of 3. London: Collins. p. 172
[100] Foltz, Richard. 2007. *L'Iran, creuset de religions: de la préhistoire à la République islamique.* Québec: Presses de l'Université Laval. p.12

Eastern region. Remnants of this practice can still be found today. Who has never spoken to a deceased loved one? And it's not uncommon for people to call on the spirits of their ancestors and departed loved ones to protect them and watch over them.

The Talmud[101] claims that Terah, Abraham's father, was an idolater worshipping twelve divinities, one for each month of the year.[102] In the Talmud, Abraham's beliefs are opposed to those of his father. And yet, nothing in Genesis indicates that this was the case. These affirmations appear only much later, when the rabbis sought to interpret the Scriptures; in studying the texts and the oral traditions, they attributed the Patriarchs with a number of monotheistic characteristics that appear nowhere—and were not even implied—in the Pentateuch. This is most likely why the Talmud, as well as the Qur'an[103], written much later, claim that Abraham was offended by idol worship. These affirmations became necessary to re-enforce a theological interpretation that was clearly at odds with the biblical text:

> Ge 31:19 And Laban went to shear his sheep: and Rachel had stolen the images that were her father's.

The word (תרפים) *teraphim*, which is found more than a dozen times in the Bible, is generally translated as "idols" or "images." The passage in which Rachel steals her father's *teraphim* demonstrates how important these "idols" were to the Patriarchs. Jacob – who will later take on the name of Israel – even demands the death penalty for the thief:

> Ge 31:32 With whomsoever thou findest thy gods, let him not live: before our brethren discern thou what is thine with me, and take it to thee. For Jacob knew not that Rachel had stolen them.

---

[101] The Talmud is a collection of precepts and teachings by the great rabbis, written between 200 BCE and 500 CE. The Mishna, a basic text of the Talmud describing Jewish traditions, was written in the early 3rd century CE. The Gemara, written at the end of the 5th century CE, contains commentary and analysis of the Mishna. The Mishna/Gemara together make up the Talmud. For more details, see The Jewish Encyclopedia, Funk and Wagnalls, 1906
[102] Pinches, Theophilus G. 2002. *The Old Testament in the Light of the Historical Records and Legends of Assyria and Babylonia.* New York: Elibron Classics. (Orig. pub. 1902.). p. 198
[103] Qur'an Sourates 21:51-70

And when Laban addresses Jacob, he does not speak of a local god, but rather the god of Jacob's ancestors:

> *Ge 31:29 It is in the power of my hand to do you hurt: but the god of your father spake unto me yesternight, saying, Take thou heed that thou speak not to Jacob either good or bad.*

Although the question of whether the dead were deified in West Semitic traditions is still debated today, Lewis is affirmative:

> *Would any anthropologist who documents the widespread use of divination in the ancient Near East (including Israel, where liver omens were found) conclude that Iron Age Israel waited until Dtr to concoct its notions about necromancy? Could any historian of religions who studies tomb amulets in western Asia dispute that there was belief in the dead and in their power? Could any archaeologist who inspects burial vaults beneath private homes in Ugarit deny that their owners venerated the dead?* [104]

Lewis hereby makes reference to the Book of Deuteronomy, which clearly prohibits the Israelites to engage in necromancy, a by then popular practice that consisted of talking to the spirits of the deceased ones::

> *Dtr 18:10 There shall not be found among you any one that maketh his son or his daughter to pass through the fire, or that useth divination, or an observer of times, or an enchanter, or a witch.*

> *Dtr 18:11 Or a charmer, or a consulter with familiar spirits, or a wizard, or a necromancer.*

> *Dtr 18:12 For all that do these things are an abomination unto the Lord: and because of these abominations the Lord thy God doth drive them out from before thee.*

Lewis also points out that the term "*Elohim*" is occasionally used to refer to the dead in the Bible itself:

---

[104] Lewis, Theodore J. 1999. "Israel's Beneficent Dead: Ancestor Cult and Necromancy in Ancient Israelite Religion and Tradition by Brian B. Schmidt." *Journal of the American Oriental Society* 119(3): 512-14.

1 Sa 28:13 And the king said unto her, Be not afraid: for what sawest thou? And the woman said unto Saul, I saw Elohim ascending out of the earth.

1 Sa 28:14 And he said unto her, What form is he of? And she said, An old man cometh up; and he is covered with a mantle. And Saul perceived that it was Samuel, and he stooped with his face to the ground, and bowed himself.

The (מרזח) *marzéah* ceremony referred to in Amos 6:7 and Jer 16:5 is a ritual banquet for the deceased. It corresponds to the Mesopotamian *kispu* ceremony, which was for the royal class.[105] The *kispu* consisted of three parts: invocation of the deceased's name, presentation of food, and libation of water. The Genealogy of Hammurabi Dynasty (BM 80328) shows that the *kispu* ceremony for the dead was already common practice at the turn of the second millennium.[106]

The religion of the nomads conceded greater importance to idols; to some extent, the iconography of these objects embodied their "dead" and "gods," which they could then carry along on their travels.

Isa 46:1 Bel boweth down, Nebo stoopeth, their idols were upon the beasts, and upon the cattle: your carriages were heavy loaden; they are a burden to the weary beast.

There are many passages in the Bible insisting on the importance for the descendants to keep the ancestors' bones with them (Ge 50:25; Ex 13:19; Josh 24:32; 1 Sam 31:13; 2 Sam 21:12-14; etc.). The most prominent example is certainly that of Joseph, whose bones have been preciously kept as a relic for generations:

Ge 50:25 And Joseph took an oath of the children of Israel, saying, Elohim will surely visit you, and ye shall carry up my bones from hence.

---

[105] King, Philip J. and Lawrence E. Stager. 2001. *Life in Biblical Israel.* Louisville: Westminster John Knox. p. 380
[106] Finkelstein, J. J. 1966. "The Genealogy of the Hammurapi Dynasty." *Journal of Cuneiform Studies* 20(4): 95-118. p.115

Exodus and the book of Joshua were written many generations later according to Jewish tradition:

> *Ex 13:19 And Moses took the bones of Joseph with him: for he had straitly sworn the children of Israel, saying, God will surely visit you; and ye shall carry up my bones away hence with you.*

> *Josh 24:32 And the bones of Joseph, which the children of Israel brought up out of Egypt, buried they in Shechem, in a parcel of ground which Jacob bought of the sons of Hamor the father of Shechem for an hundred pieces of silver: and it became the inheritance of the children of Joseph.*

These nomadic practices contrast with the concept of local gods, but given their close contact with the sedentary local populations, the Patriarchs and the ancient Israelites naturally lived with this religious duality.

Emergence of the *Baal Berith* deity

Among the many pagan gods referred to as the *Baals*, one deity deserves special attention. *Baal Berith* (בעל ברית), which literally means "Lord of Covenant"—was an important pagan deity worshiped at Shechem during the Late Bronze Age and Iron Age periods. Regrettably, little is known about this deity. Some believe local covenants gave rise to this cult. In addition to archaeological findings, there are a few references to it in the Bible, where the same deity is sometimes called *El Berith* (אל ברית), which means "God of Covenant."

According to Wright, the strongest period of settlement at Shechem was from around 1800-1100 BCE. The early Israelites had built a temple in Shechem where they venerated the *Baal/El Berith* deity. In Judges, we learn that Abimelech kills all the Israelites that had found refuge in this temple. This reported killing matches the temple and sacred area destruction that was dated through archeological digs to the late 12th century: [107]

Jud 8:33 And it came to pass when Gideon was dead, that the children of Israel turned again, and went a whoring after the Baals, and set up Baal-Berith as their god.

...

Jud 9:46 And all the men of the tower of Shechem heard that, and they entered into the stronghold of the house of Baal Berith.

Jud 9:49 And all the people likewise cut down every man his bough, and they followed Abimelech, and put them to the hold, and burned the hold with fire upon them. And all the men of the tower of Shechem died also, about a thousand men and women.

Commenting on this critical passage, the New World Encyclopedia underlines the intriguing similarities that exist between *Baal Berith* and *Yahweh* with regards to their name, function and place of worship:

After Gideon's death, according to Judges 8:33, the Israelites started to worship a Baal Berith ("Lord of the Covenant"), and the citizens of Shechem supported Abimelech's attempt to become king by giving him 70 shekels from the temple of Baal Berith (Judges 9:4). The scene involving this "Lord of the Covenant" appears eerily similar [sic] one described in Joshua 24:25 as involving a covenant with Yahweh. Judges 9:46 goes on to say that these supporters of Abimelech enter "the House of El Berith"—apparently the same temple earlier referred to as belonging to Baal. Thus, all three names—Baal, El, and Yahweh—refer to a Covenant Deity at Shechem; and possibly to one deity referred to by three different names. The fact that altars devoted to Yahweh, even in the Temple of Jerusalem itself, were characterized by horned altars could also indicate a carryover from more primitive days with El and Baal (both of whom were sometimes portrayed

---

[107] Purvis, James D. 1966. "Shechem: The Biography of a Biblical City by G. Ernest Wright." *Journal of Near Eastern Studies* 25(2): 140-42.

as bulls) were not worshiped on common hilltop altars with Yahweh.[108]

By indicating that *Yahweh*, *Baal* and *El* could refer to one and the same deity, the authors suggest that there was a point in time when the Israelites made, in effect, no distinction between these various figures. Smith more recently noted:

> *Traditions concerning the cultic site of Shechem illustrate the cultural process lying behind the Yahwistic inclusion of old titles of El, or stated differently, the Yahwistic assimilation of old cultic sites of El. In the city of Shechem the local god was 'ēl bĕrît, "El of the covenant" (Judge. 9:46; cf.8:33;9:4). This word 'ilbrt appears as a Late Bronze Age title for El in KTU 1.128.14-15. In the patriarchal narratives, the god of Shechem, 'ēl, is called 'ĕlōhê yiśrā'ēl, "the god of Israel," and is presumed to be Yahweh. In this case, a process of reinterpretation appears to be at work. In the early history of Israel, when the cult of Shechem became Yahwistic, it inherited and continued the El traditions of that site. Hence Yahweh received the title 'ēl bĕrit, the old title of El.*[109]

Smith's observations are accurate although he failed, in my opinion, to understand that *Yahwism* did not "assimilate" or "reinterpret" the ancient cult of *El Berith*, but that it rather perpetuated it.

And while this may come as a surprise for those holding *Yahweh* as the only True God, it makes perfect sense when adopting the logic of a mortal Lord. But is there any evidence pointing to a possible deification of *Baal Berith* (i.e., nomadic practice of the cult of the ancestors) into *El Berith* (i.e., sedentary practice of a local deity)? Given the Bible is silent on this topic, it might be helpful to turn to other documents.

---

[108] New World Encyclopedia Contributors. "Baal." *New World Encyclopedia*, http://www.newworldencyclopedia.org/p/index.php?title=Baal (retrieved August 30, 2015).
[109] Smith, Mark S. 2002. *The Early History of God: Yahweh and the Other Deities in Ancient Israel*. Grand Rapids: Mich. : Eerdmans. (Orig. pub. 1990.). p. 41

Deities were commonly invoked as witnesses in Near-Eastern treaties and it seems that *Baal Berith* bore unique characteristics. After surveying the role played by deities in known Akkadian, Babylonian and also Neo-Assyrian treaties, Lewis made this critical observation that confirms our suspicions:

> *All of the expressions cited above of ba'al/bēl + treaty term (Gen 14:13 included) involve human agreements and sometimes refer to divine witnesses elsewhere in the text.*[110]

Lewis hereby confirms that the term *"Baal"* (i.e., *"Bel"* in Akkadian) is often found in Ancient Near-Eastern treaties. However, in all known examples, the term is always associated with the human counterpart, rather than the divine witness. Lewis therefore underlines the surprising and unexpected nature of *Baal Berith* that he understands to be a deity playing a human role as a treaty partner instead of the traditional divine witness. Unfortunately, Lewis fails to understand that this *Baal Berith* "deity" most likely evolved from the deification of an original mortal being, and carries on with his analysis. When he later discusses the strange dualistic nature of the names *Baal Berith vs. El Berith*, that some perceive as two independent deities, he makes yet another important observation:

> *Can two deities play the role of the patron deity or covenant partner in one locality? Probably not. ...A priori we cannot decide which of these two deities would better head the clan groups (both El and Baal Hamon head confederacies elsewhere) at Shechem except for Israelite tradition which prefers El.*[111]

Although he does recognize that the Israelite tradition has always favored the *El* name over *Baal*, Lewis fails to understand that the *Baal* component of the name has been elevated to *El* through a deification process. Lewis also fails to make any association between *"Yahweh"* and *"Baal,"* despite the dualistic nature of *Baal/El* having clear parallels with the *Yahweh/Elohim* one, which

---

[110] Lewis, Theodore J. 1996. "The Identity and Function of El/Baal Berith." *Journal of Biblical Literature* 115(3): 401-23. p.414

[111] Ibid.

both carry this unusual *lord/god* component in their respective names.

In the conclusion of his monograph, he makes yet another significant observation:

> *Eventually the Canaanite religion at Shechem gave way to the monolatrous and exclusivist tendencies in early Israelite religion. The same exclusive vision that transformed a Canaanite polytheism into a monolatrous worship of the god El was responsible for developing the notion of the deity as a treaty partner to a far greater degree than that found among Israel's neighbors.*[112]

Is it truly pure coincidence that Abraham, Isaac and Jacob in the patriarchal narratives are so intimately connected with Shechem? Is it also pure coincidence that we find with this *Baal/El Berith* pagan divinity the same duality of the *lord/god* component in their alternative names? Can further connections be made between the covenant (i.e., "*berith*") that Abraham made with "*Yahweh*" and this "*Baal Berith*" deity? While believers who have always known *Baal* as the bloodthirsty pagan god of the cult of the golden calf might resent such an association as blasphemous, it is important to note that this "negative" view of *Baal* emerged only at a later date. During most of Antiquity, the term *Baal* had the same meaning as "master" or "lord"—a purely honorific title applicable to powerful men of that era. The use of this term confirms the confusion that can exist between the statuses of "god," "demi-god" and "man of power."

---

[112] Ibid. p.423

18: Ruins of Bronze Age temple of Baal Berith in Shechem (near Nablus)

While commenting on the type of fatherhood attributed to Abraham in the patriarchal traditions, Claus Westermann, considered by many as one of the premier Old Testament scholars of the 20th century, wrote:

> *There has as yet been no study of the relationship of the patriarchal story to the cult of ancestors. It is possible, however, that some expressions of ancestor cult are linked with narratives about the ancestors. Parallels to the patriarchal stories, therefore, should not be excluded. Such a study would be worthwhile.*

> *A variant is the divinization of the ancestor; he becomes God and is venerated as such; the fact that he was the ancestor generally recedes into the background. The third possibility, on the other hand, seems to occur only in the patriarchal stories: the ancestor takes on the character of one who is unique, of the father par excellence; he remains, nevertheless, a man without the slightest trace of divinization or ancestor worship. It is clear from the nature of the traditions in Israel that the father of the people could not, in retrospect be divine or semi-divine, nor could there be any cult of the ancestors. This is based on the great importance of history in these traditions and on the confession of the one God. It is more difficult, however, to*

> *explain why the old, pre-Israelite patriarchal traditions*
> *also show no trace of ancestor worship or of divinization of*
> *the ancestor.*[113]

Westermann hereby confirms that a study of the relationship between the Abrahamic narrative and the cult of the ancestors would be worthwhile, and that it is difficult to explain why the Israelite traditions show no trace of divinization of the ancestor. However, by focusing his attention entirely on Abraham, and his role as a father for Israel, Westermann misses the mark and neglects to consider the eventuality that Abraham's Lord himself could result from the deification of a powerful ancestor.

Given that the cult of the ancestors prevailed throughout the Levant during the Bronze Age, it seems that Isaac, Jacob/Israel and Joseph, would have had every reason in the world to celebrate their lord's benevolent memory. Is the book of Wisdom not providing explicit insights about these celebrations?

> *Wis 14:17 And those whom men could not honour in*
> *presence, because they dwelt far off, they brought their*
> *resemblance from afar, and made an express image of the*
> *king whom they had a mind to honour: that by this their*
> *diligence, they might honour as present, him that was*
> *absent.*
>
> *Wis 14:18 And to worshipping of these, the singular*
> *diligence also of the artificer helped to set forward the*
> *ignorant.*
>
> *Wis 14:19 For he being willing to please him that employed*
> *him, laboured with all his art to make the resemblance in*
> *the best manner.*
>
> *Wis 14:20 And the multitude of men, carried away by the*
> *beauty of the work, took him now for a god that a little*
> *before was but honoured as a man.*

As Theodore Lewis rightfully pointed out just a few years ago:

---

[113] Westermann, Claus. 1995. *Genesis 12-36.* Minneapolis: Fortress Press. (Orig. pub. 1985.). p.25

> *The Shechemite deity (or deities?) El/Baal Berith (Jud 8:33; 9:4, 46) has attracted far too little attention from the scholarly community, especially when one considers that here we have data that are intimately connected to the development of ancient Israelite religion, not to mention the reconstruction of the concept of covenant in ancient Israel.[114]*

It appears that the dualistic lifestyle of the Patriarchs – partially nomads and sedentary – presented a unique set of conditions that have led to the emergence of *El Berith*, a new local deity for the Canaanites living near Shechem. Indeed, it seems likely that the practice of the cult of the ancestors, inherited from their nomadic origin, would have fostered the deification of Abraham's Lord shortly after his death, while the gift of the land through the covenant would have provided Abraham's descendants with the sedentary lifestyle that would have been conducive to the emergence of a local god and its associated worship.

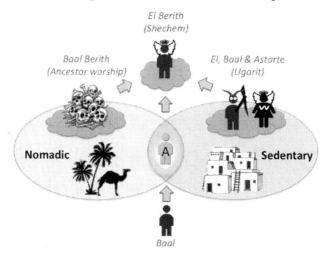

19: Conditions that have led to the emergence of El Berith

Important questions must nevertheless still be answered: why was the name *Baal/El Berith* abandoned in favor of *Yahweh*? And how

---

[114] Lewis, Theodore J. 1996. "The Identity and Function of El/Baal Berith." *Journal of Biblical Literature* 115(3): 401-23. p. 401

did a hodgepodge of nomadic and sedentary practices give birth to such a comprehensive religion as Judaism?

From *Beliya* to *Yahweh*

While there have been many suggestions made for the origin of the Tetragrammaton (יהוה) *Yhwh* over the last century, there now seems to be growing acceptance among biblical scholars that this name, most often transliterated as *Yahweh* or even *Jehovah*, might actually originate from a Late Bronze (LB) name place called *Yahu*, in Judea.

Grabbe explains:

> *Some Egyptian inscriptions of LB mention what may be a geographical name Yhwh, with reference to 'the land of the Shasu Yahu' (§ 2.2.1.4). Although the name Yhw seems to be geographical, it is possible that there is a connection with the divinity Yhwh, perhaps the region giving its name to the god worshipped there, or even possibly the deity giving its name to the region. However, arguments have been advanced from several quarters that Yhwh arose out of the context of El worship (see next section); this does not rule out a geographical origin (since the two theories could be combined), but it illustrates the difficulties.* [115]

Rather than seeing in *Yhwh* the late appearance of a new god, mysteriously issued from a place called *Yahu* in Judea, which for all intents and purposes there is no textual or archaeological evidence, perhaps it is time for us to consider the Tetragrammaton to be the result of a slow and natural evolution that finds its root in the covenant that Abraham made with *Baal*. Indeed, the *Baal/El Berith* deity is not only tied to the development of the ancient Israelite religion, but is also intimately tied to the story of the Patriarchs, as seen in previous sections, and given that the early amalgam of *Baal/El (i.e., lord/deity)* appears to have been carried over to *Yahweh/Elohim*, one can easily foresee how the term

---

[115] Grabbe, Lester L. 2009. *Ancient Israel: What do we Know and How do we Know It?* New York: Continuum. (Orig. pub. 2007.). p. 151

"Baal/El Berith"—Lord/God of Covenant—will eventually become an epithet for *Yahweh*.

In *A Reassessment of Biblical Elohim*, Burnett suggests that the morphologically plural term (אלוהים) *elohim* ("gods") used as singular – in lieu of the singular (אלוה) *eloah* ("god") – likely finds its origin in several Late Bronze Age documents from Syria-Palestine. Burnet makes a case for what he calls "concretized abstract plural" and cites the Amarna letters and vassal correspondence of the 14th century BCE, where the plural terms *ilanu* ("gods") and *ilaniya* ("my gods") were used as a form of plural of majesty when addressing Pharaoh. Written on clay tablets, these correspondences were written in Akkadian using a cuneiform script that remained in use throughout the Babylonian and Assyrian empires. Akkadian is a Semitic language that shares many similarities with Hebrew and was popular for diplomatic correspondence, much like English is today. One particular characteristic of cuneiform, as well as ancient Hebrew writing is the absence of spaces to delineate words, which opens the door to additional interpretations. In the cited Amarna letters, the following expressions are found:[116]

Akkadian	English
*sarri beliya samsiya **ilaniya***	the king, my lord, my sun-god, **my god(s)**
*ana sarri beliya **iliya** samsiya*	the king, my lord, **my god**, my god-sun
*belu **ilanu** napistaka lissur*	may the lord, **god(s)**, protect your life

---

[116] Burnett, Joel S. 2001. *A Reassessment of Biblical Elohim*. Atlanta: Society of Biblical Literature. p. 183

Given the terms *Yahweh* and *Elohim* are so intimately related to each other as they both refer to the one God of Israel, and given Akkadian sources could explain the origins of the peculiar use of the plural term *Elohim* to refer to a singular majesty, shouldn't we also consider these same Akkadian sources for a better understanding of the origins of the term *Yahweh*?

As exemplified by the popular expression (הללויה) *hallelujah* ("praise *yah*"), the divine element (יה) *yah*, is often used in the Bible as a diminutive for *Yahweh* (יהוה). It is first used in Exodus as part of a song in Ex 15:2, then in Ex 17:16, and then mostly in Psalms thereafter (Pss 68:5, 19; 77:12; 89:9; 94:7, 12; 102:19; 105:45; 106:1, etc.). It is also well known that many Hebrew proper names use the divine element *yah* as a suffix, and occasionally as a prefix (e.g., *Ahaziah, Bealiah, Elijah, Jeremiah, Nehemiah*, etc.). The proper name (בעליה) *Bealiah* (see 1 Chr 12: 5) clearly stands out and deserves special attention because it combines the two uniquely critical elements (בעל + יה) "*baal* + *yah*" [117], and as such could very well represent *the* missing link to our understanding of their pairing.

Given there is no solid explanation for a Hebrew origin of the divine element *yah*[118], it would seem reasonable to consider that it could have originated from the Akkadian *beliya*, which actually means "my lord" or "my *baal*," as the Akkadian ending *-yâ* (or *-ia*, *-iya)* marks the 1st singular possessive adjective. The expression *beliya* is actually found alongside the *ilaniya/ilanu* plurals in the Akkadian sources that refer to Pharaoh as a king-god. Again:

---

[117] Although Bealiah grammatically means "yah is baal," it is most often translated as "yah is Lord."

[118] In the Enûma Eliš, *Marduk* is presented as the son of *Ea*, the Mesopotamian god of the sea. The Canaanite equivalent of *Ea* is *Yam*. Some scholars, including Hommel, Gray and Smith have suggested a possible connection between *Yam, Ea* and *Yah*. Such a connection could help explain the hastiness of the Canaanites to adopt "*Yah*" as a name for their God.

Akkadian	English
sarri beliya *samsiya ilaniya*	the king, my lord, my sun-god, my god(s)
ana sarri beliya *iliya samsiya*	the king, my lord, my god, my god-sun
belu ilanu napistaka lissur	may the lord, god(s), protect your life

Just over a century ago, Professor Morris Jastrow suggested that the ending (יה) *yah* found in many Hebrew proper names does not systematically represent the divine element, as is assumed by tradition, but instead often originates from the Akkadian ending -*yâ* (i.e., the one found in the expressions cited above).

> *Instead of this I would propose an identification of Babylono-Assyrian ia with Hebrew יה and regard both as one of the many afformatives in Semitic substantives that give emphatic force to the noun to which they are added.*[119]

And while Jastrow understands that the Babylono-Assyrian ending -*yâ* operates as an afformative substantive, rather than a possessive adjective, there is no doubt in his mind that *Bealiah* perfectly matches the *beliya* found in the Amarna letters. Jastrow analyzes and classifies well over a hundred Hebrew proper names containing "*yah*" (or "*yahu*") as being either theophoric or non-theophoric. He finds that the vast majority of these proper names are non-theophoric and should therefore be understood as carrying the Akkadian termination, rather than the divine name. While commenting on his experiential classification, he explains:

> *The obstacle in the way of an entirely satisfactory and complete division lies in the natural confusion that arose between yâ as afformative and as the divine name, and which just as naturally led to slight modifications in the vocalization of the names in order to find in them a*

---

[119] Jastrow, Morris. 1894b. "Hebrew Proper Names Compounded with יה and יהו." *Journal of Biblical Literature* 13(1): 101-27. p. 108

suggestion of the deity, and to adapt them to such as contained this name.[120]

Jastrow hereby stresses the perennial confusion that has existed between the divine element *yah* and the Akkadian ending *–yâ*. However, it appears that his presuppositions prevented him from foreseeing that the emergence of the divine name *yah* could actually have arisen from this confusion. Given all the evidence pointing towards a direct connection between *Baal* and *Yah/Yahweh*, and given the quasi-absence of any references to a deity called "*yah*" during the Middle and Late Bronze Ages, I would like to suggest that the divine proper name *yah* finds its origin in the Akkadian *beliya*, that would have first been understood by Hebrew descendants as "*baal yah*." They would have therefore naturally adopted *yah* as the proper name for *Baal*, their deity, as this corresponds to the proper Hebraic reading of the Akkadian *beliya*.[121] The same expression would have later given rise to the proper name *Bealiah*. Such a suggestion would help explain the appearance of the divine element *yah* in theophoric names and also help explain the confusion surrounding non-theophoric Hebrew proper names ending in *–yah*. Although we know that Babylonian/Assyrian was used for diplomatic correspondence in Canaan, there remains the question of how, when and why this confusion came to be. And while we might never figure it out precisely, we do know this confusion has existed for a long time and that the Hebrew tradition – as demonstrated by Jastrow – continues to systematically view *yah* as a divine element in its proper names, often in lieu of the Akkadian possessive adjective.

There appears to be further evidence supporting this hypothesis. The name *Belial (בליעל)*, literally *Beli-Yaal* is another biblical Hebrew name having its etymology clearly connected to *baal yah*, *bealiah* and *beliya*. Its meaning remains ambiguous as some see it as a proper name, while others see it as an adjective[122]. In the

---

[120] Ibid. p. 126
[121] The Hebrew possessive equivalent of beliya would be baali.

Hebrew bible, the word is written (בליעל), beli- (בלי "without-") and ya'al (יעל "value"), which proves to be a clever heteronym meant at concealing the meaning of the word without affecting its vocalization.

I would therefore also like to suggest that the name *Belial* originates from the Akkadian *beliya iliya* meaning "my lord, my god" or from *beliya ilu* meaning "my lord, god," which are expressions associated with the Pharaoh king-god and found in the Amarna letters. Certainly, the expressions "children of *Belial*" (Dtr 13:13), "son of *Belial*" (Jug 19:22) and "men of *Belial*" (1 Sam 25:25) betray an origin, an attachment, or even some form of loyalty to an ancient tradition that might have been banned, but that nevertheless maintains the remnants of an archaic formula related to *baal yah (baal yah ≈ beliya ≈ Bealiah)*. The use of the proper name *Bealiah* and its confusion with the expression *beliya* offers a plausible explanation for the origin of the divine proper name (יה) *Yah/yh*.

We are therefore left to explain the origin of the last two letters of the Tetragrammaton (וה) *weh/wh*. This is where understanding the concept of syncretism and the idea that *baal* had a consort might come in handy. The *we/w* is the Hebrew letter (ו) *wav* that often stands for the conjunction "and." The *h* is the Hebrew letter (ה) *he*, which is often used as a feminine termination.

As seen before, there was a time when *Baal/Yahweh* is believed to have had a consort named *Asherah*.[123] As *Baal*'s consort, *Asherah*

---

[122] *Běli-yaal* (ב֗ ל֗ י֗ ע֗ ל֗)

[123] Dever, William G. 2005. *Did God Have a Wife?: Archaeology and Folk Religion in Ancient Israel.* Grand Rapids: Eerdmans.
Hadley, Judith M. 2000. *The Cult of Asherah in Ancient Israel and Judah: Evidence for a Hebrew GoddessUniversity of Cambridge Oriental Publications.* Cambridge: Cambridge University Press.
Grabbe, Lester L. 2009. *Ancient Israel: What do we Know and How do we Know It?* New York: Continuum. (Orig. pub. 2007.). p. 157

would naturally adopt the title (בעלה) *Baalah* ("goddess," "mistress," "spouse"), the Hebraic feminine form of *Baal*.[124]

In discussing the problem associated with *Yahweh* having a consort, Smith underlines some important similarities with *Baal*:

> *"The name designation of Astarte and her martial character and special relationship to the warrior god Baal approximate the martial character of the name and its special relationship to Yahweh the warrior god.*[125]

Given *Astarte*[126] is referred to as *"name of Baal"* (*šm b'l*) in some Ugaritic texts, we should not be surprised to see it associated with *Yahweh* in a similar manner:

> *"Accordingly, Athtart's designation as šm b'l marks her in manner similar to a person with the name "name of Baal." This name perhaps then denotes her relationship to the god in a manner analogous to the human person who would bear such a name. One might presume that a worshipper with such a name is dedicated to or associated with the deity named; an analogous sentiment may lie behind Athtart's title and thus her relationship to Baal in Ugaritic texts."*[127]

Smith also provides an extensive list of various pairings of deities found in Ugaritic ritual and myths, which include:[128]

'*il w 'atrt*   (*El* and *Athirat*)
'*dgn w b'l*   (*Dagan* and *Baal*)

---

[124] Kittel, Rudolf. 1925. *The Religion of the People of Israel.* New York: Macmillan. p. 20

[125] Smith, Mark S. 2001. *The Origins of Biblical Monotheism : Israel's polytheistic background and the Ugaritic texts.* New York: Oxford University Press. p.75

[126] Asherah is generally associated with Astarte/Ishtar/Athtart.

[127] Smith, Mark S. 2001. *The Origins of Biblical Monotheism : Israel's polytheistic background and the Ugaritic texts.* New York: Oxford University Press. p.75

[128] Ibid. p.70

When characterizing the various types of pairing pertaining to divinities, Smith emphases the role of family relationships in the above example (divine couple vs. father and son). Smith continues:

> *"[The] binomial pattern is so common that it is used also to denote single deities with two names, as in Kothar wa-Hasis and Nikkal wa-Ib. In these two cases, the second term characterizes the deity named with the first term."*[129]

As indicated with the above examples, pairing of divinities was not unusual in Ugaritic ritual and myths. Also note the presence of the conjunction *wav* (ו) "and", that is characteristic of such pairings.

As *Asherah* was commonly associated with *Baal* and *El,* it seems fair to suggest that the name *Yahweh* may result from such a pairing. Indeed, by extracting the proscribed term (בעל) *b'l* from the expression (בעליה ו בעלה) *b'l yh w b'lh* ("*Baal Yah* and *Baalah*" or "Lord *Yah* and goddess"), we obtain the Tetragrammaton (יהוה) *yhwh*; the divine name that shall not be pronounced.

In addition to textual pairing found in Ugaritic texts, we can turn to Egyptian religious practices for supporting this suggestion. When Butler discusses the practice of syncretism, we learn that it was not unusual for the Egyptians to combine two, three or even four deities into a molecular compound deity. He provides the examples of *Amun-Re, Ptah-Sokar-Osiris* and *Harmachis-Khephri-Re-Atum,* and then explains:

> *The most important feature of this practice is that, as Hornung has explained, it does not mean that the deities in question have "'fused,' 'equated,' or 'identified'."*[130]

This henotheistic form of worship means that although a new deity is created, the original deities continue to exist in their own right.

---

[129] Ibid. p.70
[130] Butler, Edward P. 2012. *Essays on a polytheistic philosophy of religion.* New York: Phaidra Editions. p. 107

Now, given Canaan was vassal of Egypt at that time, isn't it possible that Akhenaten, the heretic pharaoh who attempted to establish the sun-god *Ra-Horus-Aten* (aka *Aten*) as the nation's super deity, could be responsible for influencing a new form of syncretism? The timing would certainly support such a hypothesis and would allow us to situate the appearance of the Tetragrammaton *Yhwh* somewhere during, or shortly after Akhenaten's reign (1332-1323 BCE).[131] Such an interpretation would also help us understand why *Yahweh* was occasionally depicted using solar iconography as demonstrated by Taylor[132], and why so many authors since Freud have been investigating possible ties between Moses and Akhenaten. One only needs to compare Psalm 104 in the Bible with Akhenaten's *Great Hymn to the Aten* to understand the extent of possible influences.

It therefore appears, especially in light of the fact that in these Amarna letters "lord" is also perceived as a "god," that the names *Yahweh* and *Elohim* would have found their origins in the expression *beliya ilaniya* ("my lord, my god-s") found in old Babylonian and Assyrian sources. The Tetragrammaton *Yhwh* would have been introduced as a contraction of the expression *Baal Yah and Baalah* sometime during the Iron Age period, by priests now wanting the sacred text to refer to both the male and female counterparts of their deity and perhaps also wanting to combine the attributes of *Baal, Baalah* and *Baal Berith* together.

As it will be shown in the next section, the term (בעל) *baal* will eventually be repudiated, proscribed and obliterated from the sacred texts. It should therefore not come as a surprise that the priests would have sought to remove it.

Isn't it then telling that whenever Jewish rabbis see the Tetragrammaton when reading the Torah, they do not pronounce "*Yahweh*" or "*Jehovah*" aloud, but instead say "*Adonai,*" which

---

[131] Refer to the section Slaves in Egypt p. 370 in order to understand how the event referred to as Biblical Exodus likely took place shortly after the reign of Akhenaten.

[132] Taylor, J. Glen 1994. "Was Yahweh Worshiped as the Sun? Israel's God was abstract, but he may also have had a consort." *Biblical Archaeology Review* 20(03): 53-61, 90-91.

actually means "my master," "my lord," the Hebraic expression that corresponds to the original meaning of the Akkadian *beliya*?

The question that stands before us, however, is whether the original compounded deity was named "*Baal Yah we Baalah*" or whether the term "*Baal*" was dropped from the outset to create the contracted form "*Yah/we/h*"? The latter case could further help explain why the *Baals* would be later repudiated, but poses the question of the motivation that would have led to such a contraction. Was it done in order to facilitate the transcription process of the sacred tablets by maintaining a similar character count per line, thereby minimizing the risks of transcription errors?

I wasn't able to find similar contractions in the names of other ancient Near East deities. This being said, the case of wanting to refute the lesser deities of a compounded deity also appears quite unique. Either way, we know that the later repudiation of the *Baals* did take place, and this established fact should be sufficient to account for the process that has led to the contraction of the name, which would also help explain why the Tetragrammaton is deemed unpronounceable.

Further support to this suggestion may be found within the Ugaritic context. When comparing Ugaritic and Mesopotamian conceptions of divinities, Smith stresses the importance of family relationships:

> "*On the whole, Mesopotamia does not use the divine household as a means of achieving conceptual unity to the same extent as Ugaritic myth. ... In general, it is my impression that the root metaphor of the family, although well attested for specific relationships between deities, does not extend as strongly to the collectivity of divinities in Mesopotamia.*

He therefore views the status of *Yahweh* as exceptional because it has lost the middle tiers of the pantheon:

> *What generally remained is a system headed by the chief god, possibly his consort, lesser or subordinate deities (some members of his retinue), astral bodies, and servant-*

> *messengers. In short, a single assembly with Yahweh as its*
> *head is the conceptual unity of Israelite polytheism. ..."*[133]

But because Smith does not understand *"Yahweh"* to be a compounded deity embedding the characteristics of the older pantheon, his conclusion is biased:

> *"Yahweh not only lacks peers within the pantheon; with his*
> *genealogy largely erased from the biblical record, he*
> *becomes a god not only without peer but also without*
> *precedent."*[134]

Indeed, if our analysis is correct, *Yahweh* was a product of its time. What started out as polytheistic worship of Israel's distinct pagan deities eventually gave rise to a compounded "super deity," which bore the contracted name *"Yahweh."* This "super deity" would have been exclusive to the Israelites, as it would have combined the unique attributes of all its chief deities. This would further explain why *Yahweh* is systematically referred to, and associated with *Elohim*, a term that refers to a plurality of deities.

It therefore appears realistic to suggest that the Akkadian expression *"beliya ilanu"* ("My Lord, Gods") would have led to the Hebrew equivalent *"baal yah elohim"* ("Lord Yah, Gods"), and the *plural majesty* that Burnet saw as a sign of reverence might have instead referred to the compounded deities associated with Pharaoh. Such an interpretation would seem to elegantly close the loop on this investigation.

Given the significance of *Baal Berith* with regards to the possession of the land of Israel, it would naturally be necessary for the priests to acknowledge his historical continuity through *Yahweh*. Perhaps this is why the author of Exodus confirms that God was not known by the name *Yahweh* in Abraham's time:

---

[133] Smith, Mark S. 2001. *The Origins of Biblical Monotheism : Israel's polytheistic background and the Ugaritic texts*. New York: Oxford University Press. p.77

[134] Ibid. p.77

> *Ex 6:3 And I appeared unto Abraham, unto Isaac, and unto Jacob, by the name of God Almighty, but by my name Yahweh was I not known to them.*

By stating that Abraham did not know *Yahweh*, is the author of Exodus not indicating that he substituted this name?

In Ex. 3:13-15, when answering Moses who was inquiring under what name to present Him to the children of Israel, God responds with a puzzling statement: (אהיה אשר אהיה) *ehyeh asher ehyeh,* which can be translated by "I Am That I Am." Countless speculative – and even mystical – explanations have been offered in order to explain this strange response, but perhaps the authors of the Bible were simply trying to say that although His name had changed, He continued to be the same?

> *Ex 3:15 And Elohim said moreover to Moses, Thus shalt thou say unto the children of Israel: Yahweh, the Elohim of your fathers, the Elohim of Abraham, the Elohim of Isaac, and the Elohim of Jacob, hath sent me unto you. This is my name forever, and this is my memorial unto all generations.*

By identifying the Tetragrammaton with the God of the Patriarchs, the priests would have facilitated the adoption of their new "super deity."

I have attempted to demonstrate how the divine name *yah* can be better understood as a linguistic confusion that arose from the use of the term *beliya* in Akkadian diplomatic correspondence, and how the Tetragrammaton *Yhwh* can be better explained as a contraction of the expression *Baal Yah we Baalah*. As this explanation appears sound from a linguistic, grammatical, contextual and historical perspective, it should be at least as valid as those previously postulated. It is nevertheless important to realize that this is not fundamental to our research, as whichever explanation one wishes to embrace, the fact remains that it is now almost universally accepted by the scientific community that there was a time in the history of Israel when *Yahweh* and *Baal* were considered to be one and the same deity. One critical question nevertheless remains: if *Baal* was such an important deity for the early Israelites, what could have led to its repudiation?

The repudiation of the *Baals*

There is no doubt that a number of *Baals* were important deities in Israel and Samaria during most – if not all – of the Bronze Age, as well as part of the Iron Age.[135] There is also little doubt that the super deity *Yahweh* remained associated with *Baal* during the early Monarchy period. But while in Egypt the cult of the individual deities continued to be celebrated alongside that of the new super deity, it seems that Israel eventually began the repudiation process of its lesser *Baals*. Perhaps the fact that the name *Yahweh* did not carry the root *Baal* contributed to establishing a distance; but we cannot be certain of this. What we definitely know is that it would eventually become necessary, for theological and political reasons, to dissociate *Yahweh* from the other *Baals*.

The Bible offers numerous examples of the desire to get rid of the word "*Baal*" in the Scriptures. As Professor Lester Grabbe puts it "*Considering the biblical polemic against Baal, one might have expected not to see such names, but they are found in surprising contexts.*"[136] Two well-known examples are those of *Esh-Baal*, son of Saul, and *Merib-Baal* his grandson through Jonathan. Their names still appear with the suffix "*Baal*" in 1 Chr 9:39 and 1 Chr 9:40 respectively, but appear with the suffix "*Boseth*" in 2 Sam 2:10 and 2 Sam 4:4. In Hebrew, the word "*Boseth*" means "abashed," which conveniently serves the theological interpretation. However, Jastrow explains that the Hebrew word בשת should probably be pronounced "*beseth*," which would accordingly correspond to an Assyrian *baštu*, which means "possession" and possibly "power."[137] In both cases, the Hebrew consonants בשת are the same since the Masoretic only introduced

---

[135] A study exploring the eventual deification of other historical figures of the Bronze Age that had an ascendant on the Levant and these lesser Baals would certainly be worthwhile.
[136] Grabbe, Lester L. 2009. *Ancient Israel: What do we Know and How do we Know It?* New York: Continuum. (Orig. pub. 2007.). p. 156
[137] Jastrow, Morris. 1894a. "The Element בשם in Hebrew Proper Names." *Journal of Biblical Literature* 13(1): 19-30.

modern Hebraic punctuation for vowels between the 7th and 10th centuries CE.

The Bible also provides indication that *Yahweh* and *Baal* were once thought of as one and the same. The last verse of Hosea's tirade previously cited becomes even more telling:

> *Ho 2:16 And it shall be in that day, saith Yahweh, that thou shalt call me, My husband, and shalt call me no more, my Baal*

Here we find *Yahweh* pleading with his consort to no longer call him (בעלי) *baali* ("my *Baal*"), but to call him (אישי) *'ishi* ("my husband") instead. This reading is in perfect accordance with archaeological finds confirming that *Asherah* was perceived as *Yahweh's* consort during this period.[138] By then, many lesser *Baals* were celebrated throughout the land and it had therefore become important for the priests to stop associating their "super deity" *Yahweh* with all other pagan gods and this is why it became necessary to no longer refer to Him as *Baal*.

It is interesting to compare the above interpretation of Hosea's tirade with that of the Jewish tradition that claims that this passage must be interpreted as a metaphor where *Yahweh* is speaking to the people of Israel.[139] According to this tradition, the word "*Baal*" should be understood as meaning "husband" in this particular context. In other words, *Yahweh* would no longer want Israel to call him (בעלי) *baali* ("my lord," "my husband") – in the sense of "my husband," but to call him (אישי) *'ishi* ("my husband") instead. While offering an interesting play on words, this interpretation lacks some logic.[140] Of course, acknowledging that the term *Baal*, clearly associated with *Yahweh* in the above verse, refers to a pagan god, would certainly pose a significant ontological challenge in the context of a monotheistic religion that abhors paganism and

---

[138] See previous section on the Religion of El, Baal and Asherah

[139] Rallis, Irene Kerasote. 1986. Nuptial Imagery in the Book of Hosea: Israel as the bride of Yahweh.

[140] It is said that the metaphor of Yahweh being married to Israel mirrors that of Hosea's marriage to Gomer. Yahweh is presented metaphorically as a husband to Israel, which in turn is presented as the mother of the Israelites.

would seem a good enough reason for the Jewish tradition to retain the alternative play on words instead.

Nocquet recently conducted an extensive study of the evolution of the religious ideas of Israel during the first millennium BCE. He stresses that Hosea was indeed a key witness to this important transition period:

> *Hosea is an implicit witness of this time when the worship of Baal had an official place in Israel and the time when Jehu put an end to its cult in Samaria. ... Hosea would find himself at the beginning of this movement that differentiates Yahweh and Baal, until then considered as one and the same deity by the people.*[141]

Violence and killings of the pagan infidels also contributed to eradicating *Baalism*. While still celebrated as a great and righteous man of God, prophet Elijah would be better regarded today as a fanatic, vehement and obsessive predicator because he didn't hesitate to revert to the use of extreme violence to forcefully impose the worship of *Yahweh* over that of *Baal*, which was then supported by King Ahad:

> *Things become even more problematic, however, during the reign of the King Ahab in the Kingdom of Israel. His Phoenician wife, Jezebel, introduces Baal worship in her court and attempts a purge of the prophets of Yahweh, who vehemently oppose Baal worship. The struggle reaches its climax in the dramatic struggle between the prophet Elijah and the prophets of Baal for control of the high place at Mount Carmel. Baal's prophets fail to produce a sign that Baal has accepted their sacrifice, while Elijah succeeds powerfully when Yahweh consumes his sacrifice with fire from heaven. Elijah then incites the onlookers to massacre all 450 of the Baal's representatives (I Kings 18).*[142]

---

[141] Nocquet, Dany. 2004. *Le livret noir de Baal: la polémique contre le dieu Baal dans la Bible hébraïque et l'ancien Israël.* Genève: Labor et Fides. p.298

[142] New World Encyclopedia Contributors. "Baal." *New World Encyclopedia*, http://www.newworldencyclopedia.org/p/index.php?title=Baal (retrieved August 30, 2015).

Nocquet draws important parallels between the condemnation of *baalism* and that of the Omride dynasty (which was sympathetic to the cult of *Baal*):

> *In terms of the [narrative] contexts of the polemic against Baal, the same structure links the controversy against Baal to the rivalry against all forms of royalty submitted to this deity.*[143]

He also shows how prophet Elijah and King Jehu exploited the growing polemic between *Yahweh* and *Baal* to King Jehu's advantage. By posing as the hero of the fight against *Baal*, and by establishing the supremacy of *Yahweh* over *Baal*, Jehu justified his overthrowing of King Ahad:

> *The Jehu cycle embodies a panegyric of the coup and of the religious revolution in favour of Yahweh, initiated by the usurper king. It is a discourse of the legitimation of the king and the power exercised by his family over Israel.*[144]

Since the texts of Exodus confirm that Abraham did not know *Yahweh* (Ex 6:3), and that *Yahweh* pleaded with *his consort Asherah/Baalah* to no longer call him *Baal* (Ho 2:16), it would be fair to hypothesize that *Yahweh* is indeed a late designation that came to replace the more likely equivalent name of *baal* (or *beliya)* that was found in the Abrahamic narrative. Given the above, *Yahweh* and *Baal* would fundamentally mean the same thing, and the essence of the text remains unchanged.

Therefore, instead of writing:

> *Ge 15:18 In the same day "Yahweh" made a covenant with Abram, saying, Unto thy seed have I given this land, from the river of Egypt unto the great river, the river Euphrates:*

The original author of the Covenant could have written:

> *Ge 15:18 In the same day "Baal" made a covenant with Abram, saying, Unto thy seed have I given this land, from the river of Egypt unto the great river, the river Euphrates:*

---

[143] Nocquet, Dany. 2004. *Le livret noir de Baal: la polémique contre le dieu Baal dans la Bible hébraïque et l'ancien Israël*. Genève: Labor et Fides. p.283
[144] Ibid. p.337

Such a substitution doesn't change the nature of the text, but, by taking us one step closer to the original covenant, it definitely helps supplant the traditional image of the divine Lord, with that of a mortal one.

Baal Berith, *Baal Zebub*, and the scarab amulets

For additional evidence of the close ties that exist between Egyptian religious practices and the religion of *Yahweh* as well as the repudiation of the *Baals*, one might turn to Egyptian amulets and Christian demonology. In the New Testament, *Beelzebub (*or *Belzebuth)* is a demonic creature depicted as a beastly humanoid with large wings. The name *Beelzebub* results from the transliteration of the Hebrew *Baal Zebub* (בעל זבוב) "Lord of the fly" is the pagan god of Ekron (2 Kings 1:2-3, 6, 16) whom king Ahaziah, victim of serious injuries after a fall, inquires to find out if he was going to recover. Given the negative connotation associated with *Beelzebub*, contemporaries are not surprised to find prophet Elijah condemning king Ahaziah. However, why would Ahaziah look positively upon the demon? Ahaziah's attitude only makes sense when considering the contextual background and perspective painted above, where the *Baals* were perceived as positive deities. So, what do we really know of *Baal Zebub*?

Because it is somewhat difficult to explain how one would come to associate a "fly" with a "god," it has long been suggested that *zebub* (זבוב) "fly" was in fact a pun intended to replace an original *zebul* (זבל) "elevated" because this term has also been associated with the title of "prince" frequently attributed to *Baal* in Ugaritic mythological texts. The expression *Baal Zebul* is usually rendered as "Lord of the manor" because the term *zebul* is most often associated with a dwelling place (1 Ki 8:13, 2 Ch 6:2). The repudiation process that was already underway under king Ahaziah, helps us better understand why Christian demonology further developed the derogatory traits by portraying *Beelzebub* as the "Prince of Darkness."

The Talmud of Babylon, a Late Antiquity compilation of texts containing the teachings and opinions of rabbis on a variety of subjects related to the Hebrew Bible, informs us that small amulets were used to represents *Baal Zebub*:

> *Even an idol the size of a fly, like the idol of the Ekronites, which was called Zebub (fly) is also prohibited; for we are taught it is written in the passage [Judges, viii. 33]: "And they made themselves Baal-berith for a god"; by Baal-berith is meant the Zebub (fly) idol of Ekron, and every idolater (at that time) made an image of his idol in miniature in order to keep it constantly at hand and to be able at any time to take it out, embrace, and kiss it; hence there is no question as to size.*[145]

We hereby learn from the Talmud that *Baal Zebub* was used as a synonym for *Baal Berith* and that the idols representing him could be the size of a fly. Could these "images" or "idols" prove to be nothing more than Egyptian scarabs?

Scarab amulets were extremely popular in Egypt as well as in the Levant throughout the Bronze and Iron Ages and remained popular until after the Babylonian Exile. With the exception of the larger "heart scarabs" destined to funerary rites, these amulets were very small and inscribed at their base with names, good wishes or mottos.

The Egyptians believed that scarabs held special significance because of the way these insects are born. The adult beetle forms a dung ball with its back legs into which it lays eggs. When young beetles hatch, they appear to emerge somewhat magically out of the dung ball. Very early on, the Egyptians associated this process with that of the sun god Re rising in the east and setting in the west, which symbolized daily rebirth. *Kheper*, the Egyptian name for these scarabs, means "to come into being," and thus, the Egyptian god *Khepri*, depicted as a scarab (or a man with a scarab-like head) is associated with the rising sun and the mythical creation of the world.

---

[145] Rodkinson, Michael Levi, Godfrey Taubenhaua and Isaac Mayer Wise. 1918. *Tract Sabbath.* Vol. 1 of 9 *New edition of the Babylonian Talmud.* Second ed. Boston: The Talmud Society. p.154

According to Elaine A. Evans, Curator/Adjunct Assistant Professor at McClung Museum:

> *The name of a particular person, king, or official title was inscribed on their flat bases to ensure protective powers would be given to the owner and to the owner's property. Interestingly, some scarabs with royal names were worn after the king was deceased, in the saintly sense, similar to the holy medals of Christian saints. In all probability, no matter what their category, scarabs represented sacred emblems of Egyptian religious belief.[146]*

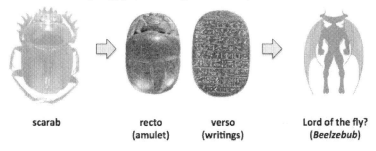

scarab   **recto (amulet)**   **verso (writings)**   **Lord of the fly? (*Beelzebub*)**

20: Egyptian scarab amulet: Lord of the fly?

Carved in speckled green serpentine, this large heart scarab (inch and a half long) is believed to date from the reign of Thutmose III (1490-1436 BCE). It was recovered from Tomb D120 at Abydos during excavations directed by Sir W. M. Flinders Petrie.

Couldn't the demonic figure *Beelzebub*, and its associated iconography, originate from the widespread use of scarab amulets in the Levant that would later be repudiated along with the *Baals* they represented? The term *zebul* could refer to the distinguished figure they once represented, while the name *zebub (i.e., "fly")* could refer to the shape and look of these small objects – rather than the proper name of a specific god – and this would explain the association made between *Baal Zebub, Baal Zebul* and *Baal Berith*. Certainly, the appearance, function, and popularity of these small fly-shaped amulets are pointing in this direction and would be further evidence of the influence of Egyptian religious practices over the Levant during this critical period.

---

[146] Evans, Elaine A. "The Sacred Scarab." McClung Museum.
http://mcclungmuseum.utk.edu/sacred-scarab (retrieved August 17, 2015).

At this point in our research, we have found a wealth of evidence supporting the idea that the Patriarchs were pagans. When approaching the Abrahamic narrative from the historical perspective of the Middle Bronze Age, we saw that the *Elohistic* verses – rather than the *Yahwistic* ones – reveal practices that are perfectly consistent with the pagan customs of the time. The many references to *Yahweh* muddy the waters somewhat; because in using these two terms interchangeably, one loses sight of the fact that the religion of *Elohim* corresponds perfectly to the pagan religions of the time and that, through a blend of sedentary and nomadic rituals, their dualistic lifestyle provided the fertile grounds for the emergence of the cult of *Baal Berith.* Grown out of a deified mortal lord, this new deity would slowly adopt the sedentary attributes of the local gods *El, Baal* and his consort *Asherah.* It would be this unique combination of pagan worship that would have led to the compounded creation of the super deity "*Yahweh,*" benefactor of the land of Israel, and would soon command the rejection of all other *Baals*, as well as the idols representing them.

Sarah, mother goddess of Israel?

As one comes to accept the idea that Isaac was fathered by Abraham's Lord, and that the memory of this lord was elevated to the rank of deity, one naturally starts wondering what might have happened to his mother Sarah.

We know that in the eyes of the Canaanites, *Asherah* was the consort of *Baal* and the mother goddess of Israel. Can a connection be established between *Asherah* and *Sarah*? Was the memory of Isaac's mother also elevated to the rank of deity?

From an etymological standpoint, the only difference between the names *Asherah* (אשרה) and *Sarah* (שרה) is the letter aleph (א) that assumes a leading position in the name of the goddess. What do we know of this letter and where does it come from?

The precursor to the modern alphabet was invented by a Semitic people who worked in the turquoise mines of Serabit.[147] Sir

William Matthew Flinders Petrie is the Egyptologist who led an archaeological expedition in this region in 1905.[148] He discovered a sphinx with strange Egyptian hieroglyphs. It was later found that these symbols were not all hieroglyphs. Unlike cuneiform, which is made up of an assortment of straight lines, these inscriptions expressed letters through symbols that would be referred to as Proto-Sinaitic.[149]

21: The goddess Hathor

This sphinx, like a mini Rosetta stone, spelled out a simple inscription in both Egyptian and Canaanite. The hieroglyphic inscription reads *"Beloved of Hathor, lady of the turquoise"* while the Proto-Sinaic inscription simply reads *"Lady"* or *"Baalat"*, the feminine construct equivalent of *Baal*.

The Serabit sphinx suggests that this alphabet was born through close proximity to Egyptian pictograms. The meaning of the pictograms was key to the Canaanites as they served as an important mnemonic tool. For instance, the letter *aleph* is the *'alp*, the word for "ox" or "bull"; the letter *bêt* is the *beit* or "house"; the letter *'ayin*, "eye", etc.

The very word "alphabet" comes from *"aleph beit"*, the first two

---

[147] Desroches Noblecourt, Christiane. 2006. *Le fabuleux héritage de l'Egypte*. Paris: Pocket. p. 131
[148] Gardiner, Alan H. 1964. *Egypt of the Pharaohs: An Introduction*. London: Oxford University Press. p. 25
[149] Desroches Noblecourt, Christiane. 2006. *Le fabuleux héritage de l'Egypte*. Paris: Pocket. p. 127

letters, which eventually became *"alpha beta"* in Greek. This Proto-Sinaitic alphabet predated Modern Hebrew and Aramaic by more than a thousand years. The number and names of the letters have been somewhat preserved, but their associated pictograms have evolved.

T	Ch	Z	V, W	H	D, Th	G	B,V	Vowel
ט ⊗	ח ◪	ז =	ו ף	ה ✿	ד ◖	ג ◟	ב ◻	א ४

	S	N		M	L		K	Y
ס ↟	נ ן ◝		מ ם ∿	ל ∕		כ ך ϣ		י ◟

Th, T	Sh, S	R	Q		Ts		P, F	'
ת ✗	ש ◠	ר ◤	ק ◐	צ ץ ↓		פ ף	ף ◠	ע ◠

22: Latin alphabet, Modern Hebrew and Proto-Sinaitic

Meanwhile in Egypt, the falcon pictogram ( ) was commonly used to represent Horus, the god of the Kings. This symbol would often accompany the name of Pharaoh, much like the Akkadian dingir ( ) would precede the name of a Babylonian god to indicate his divine status. Were the Canaanites using a similar pictogram to represent their king god *Baal*? It appears that Genesis 36 contains the remnants of such a practice. This chapter relates Esau's genealogy—the most detailed of any in Genesis. We learn that the descendants of Esau are referred to as "aluf" (אלוף) in Hebrew, which is most often translated to "duke" or "chief" in English.

> *Ge 36:40 And these are the names of the dukes[150] that came of Esau, according to their families, after their places, by their names; duke Timnah, duke Alvah, duke Jetheth,*
>
> *Ge 36:41 Duke Aholibamah, duke Elah, duke Pinon,*
>
> *Ge 36:42 Duke Kenaz, duke Teman, duke Mibzar,*
>
> *Ge 36:43 Duke Magdiel, duke Iram: these be the dukes of Edom, according to their habitations in the land of their possession: he is Esau the father of the Edomites.*

The term *aluf* (אלוף) is closely related to *aleph* (אלף), the name of

---

[150] Hebrew אלוף(aluf) - chief

the Hebrew letter "א", which derives from an ox's head.[151] Its numerical value is "1". Not only is it the first letter of the alphabet, it is also the most important: it is the symbol for God, the only God, the Absolute. There can be no doubt, then, that it has always been a term associated with power and uniqueness. Is it then pure coincidence if, to this day, the title *Aluf* still refers to the highest-ranking officials of the Israelite army?

Given the close ties between Canaan, Egypt and Babylonia, it would therefore seem reasonable to suggest that the Canaanites would have used the pictogram of a bull-head (𒀭) as a symbol for representing their god-king, and that the function of this symbol would have eventually been conflated with the letter it was also representing through the adoption and evolution of the Proto-Sinaitic alphabet. [152] This pictogram evolved into the Greek letter α (a sideways bull's head) and the modern A (an upside-down bull's head):

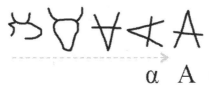

23: Evolution of the letter "A"

In her quality of mother of Isaac and stepmother of Ishmael, *Sarah* (שרה) could have been referred to as "*Baalat*" or "*Baalah*", the feminine form of *Baal* that signifies princess or consort. As such, her name written "✶◖ᨾ" in Proto-Sinaitic could have been preceded by a bull-head pictogram "✶◖ᨾ𒀭". What was once meant to be pronounced "*Ballah Sarah*" (שרה א) would have eventually been assimilated into "*Asherah*" (אשרה.)[153]

---

[151] Lamm, Norman. 1999. *The Religious Thought of Hasidism: Text and Commentary.* Hoboken: KTAV Publishing House. p. 32

[152] Menninger, Karl Augustus and Paul Broneer. 1992. *Number Words and Number Symbols: A Cultural History of Numbers.* New York: Dover. p. 122

[153] In Hebrew, "s" and "sh" are both represented by the consonant shin "ש". Also there was no vowels or spaces between letters in Proto-Sinaitic as well as in ancient Hebrew. The

Sarah, the head of the pantheon *Baalah Sarah*, mother goddess of Israel, would have been closely associated, and maybe even conflated with the Babylonian goddess *Astarte/Ishtar* through syncretism. She would have inherited much of her qualities, in much the same way *Baal Berith* became associated with *Bel*.

Yahweh, the deified progenitors

If we are correct in our analysis, *Yahweh* would be more than just a compounded deity integrating the masculine and feminine qualities of *El, Baal* and *Asherah*. It would also prove to be the deified progenitors of Israel's lineage: *Abraham's Lord (i.e. Baal Berith)* and *Sarah*.

Smith reports that the Canaanite pantheon is structured like an earthly family.[154] If *Abraham's Lord* and *Sarah* were indeed presiding this divine assembly, one has to wonder if some of their descendants, in light of the use of the title "duke", did not also came to be regarded as part of it. A survey of possible ties linking some of their names to lesser gods of the Levant would be interesting.

Let's now turn to Mesopotamia, homeland of the four Eastern Kings and of the suspected foreign ruler. Extended to these far borders, will this investigation reveal even more similarities to the culture and history of the Patriarchs?

In summary

- Many passages of the patriarchal narratives offer striking similarities to known social mores of the Middle Bronze Age.

- The Levant was characterized by a mix of sedentary and nomadic lifestyles.

---

etymological match is therefore perfect.

[154] Smith, Mark S. 2001. *The Origins of Biblical Monotheism : Israel's polytheistic background and the Ugaritic texts*. New York: Oxford University Press. p.77

- While *El, Baal* and *Asherah* were the main deities, each local city also celebrated its own deity.

- The cult of the ancestors was a popular practice among nomadic people.

- The *Baal Berith* ("Lord of covenant") would have first been celebrated as part of the cult of the ancestors, and then deified through the sedentariness of the covenant. This pagan deity had a temple and was celebrated in Shechem during the Late Bronze and Iron Ages.

- *Baal* had a consort named *Asherah*. Coincidentally, archaeological evidence shows that *Yahweh* also had a consort named *Asherah*.

- It is possible to obtain the Tetragrammaton (יהוה) *Yhwh* by extracting the proscribed term (בעל) *baal* from the expression (בעליה ו בעלה) *baal yah we baalah* ("*baal yah and baalah*").

- This form of compounded syncretism could date from the 14th century and have been influenced by Akhenaten.

- *Beelzebub* is the Christian demonic version of *Baal Zebub*, a repudiated name derived from the small scarab amulets representing *Baal Berith*.

- Goddess *Asherah* appears to have evolved from the name "*Baalah Sara*". Together with *Baal*, they would perfectly represent the divinized earthly couple.

Mesopotamia

Mesopotamia, in Greek (μεσο ποταμός) which means "land between the rivers", is located on the far eastern side of the Fertile Crescent, more specifically between the Euphrates and the Tigris rivers. This region largely corresponds to modern Iraq. Anthropologists call it the "cradle of civilization" because it is the site of one of the most extraordinary revolutions in human history. Between 12500 BCE and 7500 BCE, people began gathering in small communities, and agriculture developed alongside hunting, gathering and fishing. In *Guns, Germs, and Steel*, Jared Diamond explains why certain animal species are more suited to breeding than others.[155] He also tells how, of the 14 species that have been domesticated, the five most conducive to breeding—goat, sheep, cow, swine and horse—were all indigenous to the Fertile Crescent. This abundance of ideal species significantly helped to ease the transition to this new way of life.

With the shift to a sedentary lifestyle, nomadic encampments were transformed into the first communities and cities. The appearance of pottery and metallurgy was the impetus for the development of numerous trades. Large-scale irrigation systems were built around 6000 BCE to enhance the region's natural fertility.

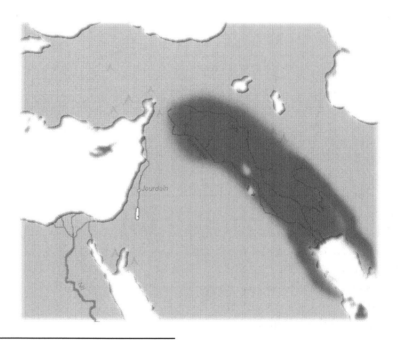

---

[155] Brown, F., S. Driver and C. Briggs. 2007. *The Brown-Driver-Briggs Hebrew and English Lexicon: Coded with Strong's Concordance Numbers*. Peabody, Mass.: Hendrickson Pub. Inc. (Orig. pub. 1907.). p. 158

24: Mesopotamia

Writing developed in Mesopotamia around 3000. The Sumerians were the first to carve cuneiform symbols into soft clay tablets using sharpened reeds. Initially, writing served a purely administrative purpose, namely counting and taking inventory of the property in the kingdom. As such, it became necessary to devise a system of numbering and identifying objects. However, the Mesopotamians quickly realized that this new form of "memorization" could also be used to help stimulate cultural development. It naturally follows that the first known literary works date from this era. Whereas stories in the past were passed on orally, writing established the literary form of storytelling. Genealogy also emerged during this time, as evidenced by the *Sumerian King List*, an ancient cuneiform text that provides valuable insight into the chronology of these ancient kingdoms.

Writing, reserved for the privileged few, was also invested with magical qualities; once a name, a policy or even a religious rite was committed to writing, it was considered "fixed for eternity"[156]. But, very few people at the time could decipher a message engraved on a clay tablet. "Revealed" by the scribe much like the way in which an oracle interprets a vision, cuneiform writing became an object of interest and curiosity and, naturally, the exclusive domain of kings, priests, and wealthy and privileged men.

But, the peak of the revolution was yet to come. At the time, Mesopotamia—like virtually every other civilization in the world—was made up of a multitude of small "city-states" for the very simple reason that it was difficult for a conqueror to manage and run a larger territory without the means to quickly send orders and reports from a distance. In this sense, the emergence of writing would open up doors to the foundation of vast empires, allowing rulers to oversee the expansion of their territories from their own "city-states". Such conquests gave rise to the Sumerian, Akkadian, Babylonian and Assyrian empires. Writing represented the next giant leap in the evolution of mankind.

---

[156] Simonnet, Dominique and Pascal Vernus. "Graver le nom du roi, c'était le rendre immortel." *L'Express* (July 13, 2006).

If so many similarities can be drawn between the Bible and older known Sumerian texts, that's because the Bible truly tells us the story of these people, who would later have a profound influence over the Hebrews.

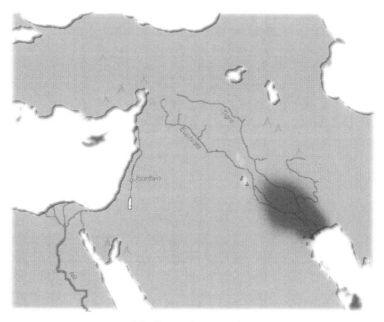

25: Sumerian empire

The Flood revisited

In the Bible, Abraham's story immediately follows that of the Great Flood, in which God orders Noah to build an immense ark. The ark must be filled with a pair of each living species to save them from a terrible flood that will wash over the world, submersing it for several weeks. Since the genealogy in the Bible dates back as far as Adam and Eve, Abraham is naturally listed as a descendant of Noah.

One version of this story, which pre-dates the Bible, was revealed to the modern world on December 3, 1872 CE by George Smith, a young British scholar of Assyria, before the Society of Biblical Archaeology in London. Smith had succeeded in translating the

Sumerian text—an excerpt from the *Epic of Gilgamesh*—from 3,700-year-old clay tablets. While these tablets had been unearthed a few years earlier at the palace of Nineveh by Henry Laylard, Smith was the first to be able to decipher them,[157] effectively rediscovering a story that had been forgotten for some 2,000 years:[158]

> *Man of Shuruppak (Utnapishtim), son of Ubar-Tutu,*
> *Tear down (this) house, build a ship!*
> *Give up possessions, seek thou life.*
> *Despise property and keep the soul alive.*
> *Aboard the ship take thou the seed of all living things.*
> *The ship that thou shalt build,*
> *Her dimensions shall be to measure.*
> *Equal shall be her width and her length.*
> *Like the Apsu (subterranean waters) thou shalt ceil her.[159]*

Today, over 200 fragments of cuneiform tablets exist that contain slight variants on this story; only the names of the heroes and certain details vary. In Sumer, around 1700 BCE, it was known as the story of Ziusudra; in Akkad, around 1600 BCE, that of Athrasis; and finally, in Babylon, around 1200 BCE, while the city was under Assyrian control, the Epic of Gilgamesh took the form in which we know it today. Often described as the first known bestseller in humanity, it tells the stereotypical story of the man who never wants to die, a recurring theme in this part of the world throughout Antiquity.

> *I am the one you call Gilgamesh. I am the pilgrim who roams all roads within the Country and beyond the Country. I am the one to whom all things have been revealed, truths hidden, mysteries of life and death, and especially death. I have known Inanna in the sacred Marriage bed; I have slain demons and I have eaten with gods; I myself am two-thirds god, and just one-third man.[160]*

[157] The palace of Nineveh of Ashurbanipal (669-627) is located on the eastern shore of the Tigris, in northern Mesopotamia.
[158] Foucart, Stéphane. "Gilgamesh l'immortel." *Le Monde* (July 13, 2007).
Damrosh, David. 2007. *The Buried Book: The Loss and Rediscovery of the Great Epic of Gilgamesh*. New York: Macmillan. p. 5
[159] Bottéro, Jean. 1992. *L'épopée de Gilgames: le grand homme qui ne voulait pas mourir*. Paris: Gallimard.

In most of the texts discovered, the name Gilgamesh is accompanied by a star symbol that the Sumerians liked to attribute to divine beings: the ✳ dingir.[161] And, while Gilgamesh was no doubt a ruler with divine aspirations, it seems he was not actually worshipped during his lifetime. This ideogram may have been added to his name only much later, after the myth took on greater proportions.

As Robert Best explains in *Noah's Ark and the Ziusudra Epic: Sumerian Origins of the Flood Myth*, many parallels can be drawn between the stories of Noah and Gilgamesh. The finer details, such as the number of days spent on the ark and the bird that never returned, heralding the presence of land in the distance, provide evidence that these two stories are intimately linked.[162]

Given this story's status and its immense popularity with Mesopotamian societies at the time, we can easily understand how, by establishing a bloodline between Noah and Abraham, the Bible legitimized the latter's role as a Patriarch, assigning him a place in the historical timeline of this region.

Was Abraham's "Lord" also part of this timeline?

The Akkadian empire

The Akkadian empire was the first true empire in Mesopotamia. Since Abraham's family originally hailed from the city of Ur, not far from Akkad, we shall examine how this empire was born and how it progressed, in the hope of establishing possible links between the Patriarchs and the conquerors of this region.

[160] Ibid.
[161] Green, Margaret Whitney. 1975. Eridu in Sumerian Literature. University of Chicago. p. 224
[162] Best, Robert M. 1999. *Noah's ark and the Ziusudra Epic: Sumerian Origins of the Flood Myth*. Fort Myers: Enlil Press.

26: Sargon of Akkad

Sargon of Akkad

While scholars do not always agree on the historical authenticity of Gilgamesh, that of Sargon of Akkad (2334-2279 BCE), who has the distinction of being the first conqueror of Mesopotamia[163], is generally not questioned.

Founder of the city of Akkad (Agade) and of the Akkadian dynasty, Sargon united the regions of Elam and Sumer in the south and Akkad in the north.

With new and more destructive weapons of war, such as javelins, bows and arrows, Sargon of Akkad successfully defeated the vast Sumerian army to conquer a large territory.

---

[163] Van De Mieroop, Marc. 2004. *A History of the Ancient Near East: ca. 3000-323 B.C.* Oxford: Blackwell Publishing. p. 60

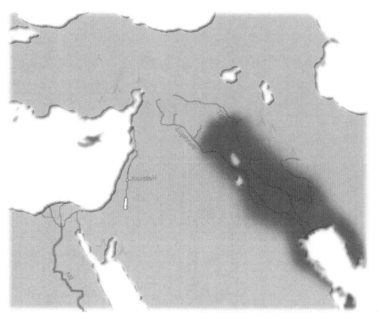

27: The empire of Sargon of Akkad

In order to reign over such a far-reaching empire, Sargon created an efficient management and communication system that included a network of outposts located every 50 km.

It is said that Sargon was born to a mother who was unable to care for him. When a gardener found him floating on the river in a reed basket, he rescued him and raised him as his own son. The myth of the birth of Sargon of Akkad is strikingly similar to that of Moses in Exodus:

> *Ex 2:3 And when she could not longer hide him, she took for him an ark of bulrushes, and daubed it with slime and with pitch, and put the child therein; and she laid it in the flags by the river's brink.*

> *Ex 2:5 And the daughter of Pharaoh came down to wash herself at the river; and her maidens walked along by the river's side; and when she saw the ark among the flags, she sent her maid to fetch it.*

Freud maintains that this is a basic myth aimed at legitimizing the hero. The myth in question traces the struggle back to the very dawn of the hero's life, by having him born against his father's will and saved in spite of his father's evil intentions.[164]

After rising to the position of cupbearer for the king of Kish, Sargon dethroned the latter before overthrowing the king of Uruk and conquering this southern Sumerian city, thus creating the first true empire. He attributed his success to his patron goddess, Ishtar, who invested him with royalty.

While the size of his kingdom was considerable in many respects, it seems that Sargon's influence did not extend as far as the Levant. Moreover, he reigned well before the time of Abraham. Once again, the story of the birth of Moses supports the link between the Bible and the history of this region.

Sargon died an old man and was succeeded by his sons, Rimush and Manishtushu. But, the great conqueror's death heralded a period of unrest in the kingdom and Rimush was forced to wage war to reassert his power. His reign lasted only nine years, although a number of inscriptions describe epic battles involving a massive army. Manishtushu succeeded his brother and reigned for some 15 years, continuing his brother's efforts to build up the military and the government.

Expansion of the empire

It was Naram-Sin, Sargon's grandson, who would once again make history.[165] After the death of his father, Manishtushu, Naram-Sin reigned for 36 years, from 2254 to 2218 BCE. His military prowess allowed him to further expand the borders of the Akkadian empire.

Bolstered by his political popularity and remarkable military exploits, King Naram-Sin ruled over an immense empire that encompassed a large portion of the Fertile Crescent, appointing his

---

[164] Segal, Robert Alan. 1996. *Psychology and Myth.* New York: Taylor & Francis. p.262

Freud, Sigmund and Katherine Jones. 2013. *Moses and monotheism.* Milton Keynes: Lightning Source UK Limited. (Orig. pub. 1939.). p.15
[165] Van De Mieroop, Marc. 2004. *A History of the Ancient Near East: ca. 3000-323 B.C.* Oxford: Blackwell Publishing. p. 61

sons as governors and his daughters as priestesses; the rulers who preceded him no doubt did the same.

So, it was without any false modesty that Naram-Sin christened himself "King of the Four Regions"; he was even so bold as to proclaim himself "God of Akkad" and to add the divine symbol ✳ to his name.

Naram-Sin was the first Mesopotamian sovereign to bestow this title upon himself while living, but many others soon followed suit, and it quickly became a custom. This new interpretation of royal power would be embraced by the kings of the Third Dynasty of Ur and by many other royal families thereafter.

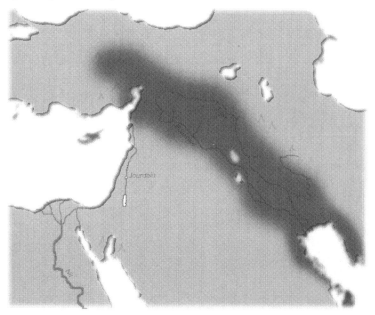

28: The empire of Naram-Sin

Since Naram-Sin's reign is known to have taken place before the era generally attributed to Abraham, there is very little chance that they were contemporaries. However, Naram-Sin adds new perspective to our research. The size of his territory would have, in fact, allowed him to make an alliance with the ruler of the neighboring Levant. Also, his self-proclaimed title of "god" left no doubt as to his ambitions. This display of narcissism easily allows us to imagine him as a megalomaniac king drunk with power.

These titles and this image of a "living king" would make him an excellent "lord".

An empire in decline

While Naram-Sin was the first ruler of Mesopotamia to proclaim himself a "living god", he also bears the distinction of being the last great king of the Akkadian empire. The Gutians, a nomadic tribal people from the Zagros Mountains in the northeast and probably the ancestors of the Kurds, appeared on the scene, pillaging villages, robbing travelers and terrorizing the population.[166] These raids had a direct impact on the economy of Sumer. Trade slowed down, famine set in and the empire eventually collapsed.

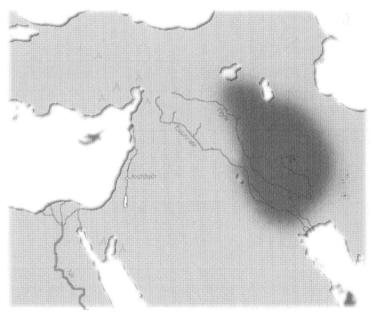

29: The Gutian empire

The Gutians rose to power and controlled this territory for some 100 years before finally being pushed out by Utu-hegal, the king of Uruk, who defeated the Gutian ruler Tirigan in 2130 BCE.

With Akkad crumbling, the centre of power gravitated further south to Sumer. It was at this point that Utu-hegal proclaimed himself king of Sumer, although his victory would be short-lived

---

[166] Ibid. p. 67

as the Third Dynasty of Ur emerged amidst a power struggle between the regions of Uruk and Ur. After eight years as governor of Ur, Ur-Nammu (2112-2095 BCE) was crowned the new king of Sumer.[167]

The arrival of the Third Dynasty ushered in the 600-year period during which most early biblical scholars tried to situate Abraham, namely 2100 to 1500 BCE.

Ur-Nammu was a great statesman; not only did he found the Third Dynasty of Ur, but he also restored order to the chaos left behind by the Gutians. His best-known legacy remains his famous code of laws, the *Code of Ur-Nammu*, the oldest legal document in existence and reminiscent of Moses' ten commandments. During his reign, Ur-Nammu also rebuilt roads, and renovated and expanded one of the largest temples in Antiquity. He is also credited with having built a number of terraced structures—the famous ziggurats, as iconic to Mesopotamia as the pyramids are to Egypt.[168] The death of Ur-Nammu, left to perish on the battlefield by his army after a battle with the Gutians, was immortalized in a poem.

The ancient ziggurats were made up of two to seven receding tiers with a shrine or temple at the summit, where priests officiated over religious ceremonies. Access to the shrine was provided by a series of ramps. Incidentally, the word *ziggurat* means "to build on a raised area".

Ziggurats were built throughout Mesopotamia. The discovery of foundations dating from the 18th century BCE indicate that construction of the Etemenanki ziggurat ("temple of the foundation of heaven and earth") probably began during this era. It was seven stories high and believed to be measuring close to one hundred meters. This impressive structure no doubt captured the collective imagination of the local people. Perhaps this ziggurat, whose last level permitted man to reach the heavens, inspired the expression "seventh heaven".

---

[167] Ibid. p. 69
[168] "ziggurat", Hooper, Franklin Henry. 1909. *The Encyclopaedia britannica: Eleventh Edition*. London: Cambridge University Press.

30: Ziggurat of Nanna (2100-2050 BCE)

As Babel and Babylon are the same city, the "tower of Babel" most likely alludes to this ziggurat. In any case, no other construction at this time, with the exception of another ziggurat, could have rivaled it in height.

> *Ge 11:4 And they said, Go to, let us build us a city and a tower, whose top may reach unto heaven; and let us make us a name, lest we be scattered abroad upon the face of the whole earth.*

> *Ge 11:5 And Yahweh came down to see the city and the tower, which the children of men builded.*

A Sumerian text from the Enûma Eliš whose similarities with the creation myth have already been pointed out, draws another interesting parallel with this passage in the Bible. However, in this case, it is not men who irritate the gods, but rather their own progeny:

> *Their ways are truly loathsome to me. By day I find no relief, nor sleep at night. I will destroy, I will wreck their ways, so that quiet may be restored. Let us have rest![169]*

---

[169] Bottéro, Jean and Samuel Noah Kramer. 1989. *Lorsque les dieux faisaient l'homme: mythologie mésopotamienne.* Paris: Gallimard. (translated)

For his code of law and the construction of ziggurats, Ur-Nammu joins the long list of men who marked the history of Mesopotamia, and, consequently, that of the Bible.

Besides, Ur-Nammu appears to be the first possible candidate for the title of "Abraham's lord", since both men came from the same city and could have lived at the same time.

The Amorites take power

Ur-Nammu was succeeded by his son, Shulgi (2094-2047 BCE), who began his reign with a series of punishing wars against the Gutians to avenge his father's memory.[170] Shulgi then undertook a series of projects to rebuild the kingdom's roads, along which he built rest stops where weary travelers could partake of fresh water and a place to sleep.

Having reached its peak, the Akkadian empire found itself weakened by its decades-long efforts to fend off the Gutian invasions. However, there would be no respite, as a new threat was looming on the west, prompting Shulgi to build a protective wall on the northwestern border to protect against fresh attacks by a nomadic Amorite tribe that the Assyrians called the "Martu".

After some twenty years as king, Shulgi proclaimed himself a "god" and ordered temples to be built in which he erected statues in his effigy so that his people could come and worship him and present him with offerings. While this personality trait could make him another "suspect" in our investigation, Shulgi clearly sought to protect himself against these tribes rather than develop a relationship of trust with them.

His brother, Shu-Sin, who ruled until 2029 BCE, succeeded Shulgi. He held on to the reins of power, ordering the construction of a 275-km wall to protect the kingdom against the Amorites, who had migrated to Mesopotamia from the Levant. It will be argued that these Amorite people would also become the ancestors of Abraham.

---

[170] Van De Mieroop, Marc. 2004. *A History of the Ancient Near East: ca. 3000-323 B.C.* Oxford: Blackwell Publishing. p. 73

During the reign of Ibi-Sin (2028-2004 BCE), the Amorite nomads finally managed to breach the protective wall.[171] Amid the chaos and panic that ensued, Ibi-Sin still managed to maintain control over his provinces.

The Amorites took full advantage of the confusion to gain a foothold. Their status as nomads no doubt played an important role in their success; their many local contacts and their excellent knowledge of the area helped them to gradually shore up their power. They were also already well entrenched in Canaan and in the Nile Delta. At the time, Egypt had a rich culture and a flourishing trade system. Upper and Lower Egypt were governed from Thebes, in the south. This peaceful, hospitable empire in no way sought to expand or even to protect itself.

While Ur's influence was eroding, that of the Amorites of Babylon was increasing, to the point that Hammurabi (1792-1750 BCE), sixth king of the Dynasty of Babylonia, succeeded in expanding his power over all of Mesopotamia, thus earning himself the distinction of being the first king of the Babylonian empire.[172]

Hammurabi inherited the throne from his father, Sin Muballit, in 1792 BCE. Since most early biblical scholars believe that Abraham lived during the 18th century BCE, and since the history of Hammurabi's ancestors appears to correspond with that of Abraham's ancestors, it seems appropriate to focus on this important character in Antiquity.

Could he be Abraham's "lord"? What does history have to say about this?

Hammurabi spent the first years of his reign improving his kingdom, specifically by reinforcing the fortifications and erecting a number of temples. Hammurabi's diplomatic correspondence reveals that, around 1767 BCE, following a series of provocations intended to expand his territory, Hammurabi's neighbor, the king of Elam, invaded the low-lying plains and hatched a plan to inflame the rivalry between the kings of Babylonia and Larsa.

---

[171] Ibid. p. 77
[172] Van De Mieroop, Marc. 2005. *King Hammurabi of Babylon: a Biography*. Malden: Blackwell

However, these two rulers were no fools and they quickly formed an alliance to oust this scoundrel. Unfortunately, Larsa did not keep its end of the bargain, leaving Hammurabi alone to fight and defeat the king of Elam. Offended by his new ally's indifference, Hammurabi subsequently invaded Larsa. By 1763 BCE, he had succeeded in conquering the entire Mesopotamian basin.

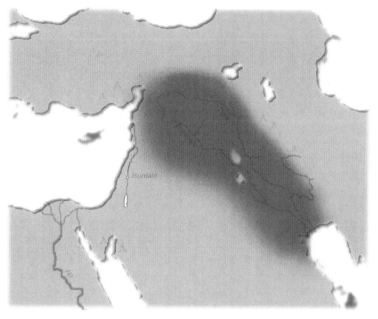

31: Hammurabi's Babylonian empire

Flushed with victory, Hammurabi quickly expanded his influence to the west as far as Canaan and Syria, with support from Amorite dynasties already governing a number of Mesopotamian and Syrian cities, including Uruk, Mari and Alep.

An excellent military strategist and a talented diplomat, Hammurabi was a great statesman. Curiously, however, these qualities shone through only towards the end of his reign.

32: Presumed head of Hammurabi

An inscription discovered on a stele near Diyarbakir refers to Hammurabi as "king of the land of the Amorites". According to Van De Mieroop:

> *Perhaps the highest esteem awarded to him was his inclusion among the gods during his lifetime. He is called the god Hammurabi, the good shepherd, in one song that celebrates how the gods of the south respect him. At the same time people named their children after Hammurabi. The name Hammurabi-ili, meaning 'Hammurabi is my god,' appeared, something unparalleled in his dynasty.*[173]

This is certainly a qualifier that draws our attention. At this juncture, it might be a good idea to further examine the culture and, specifically, the religion practiced by this Babylonian people.

The gods of Babylon

The pantheon of Babylonian gods was also densely populated, with over twenty divinities.[174] But what comparisons can we draw between the Babylonian gods and the gods of the Levant?

The Amorites adapted naturally to local religious rites, which were very similar to those practiced throughout this vast region. They

---

[173] Ibid. p.127
[174] Green, Alberto Ravinell Whitney. 2003. *The Storm-God In the Ancient Near East*. Winona Lake: Eisenbrauns. p. 36

used religion to help them through their daily lives, mainly to reap favors from nature.

Marduk was the patron deity of the city of Babylon.[175] His origins are uncertain, although we know that he was worshipped as early as the Third Dynasty of Ur. Son of Anu and Enki, he is often simply called "Bel", the equivalent of the Canaanite god "*Baal*". In fact, there are many similarities between the Babylonian god Marduk and the Canaanite deity *Baal*. Both were gods of storms and thunder. The Enûma Eliš tells of the characteristics of Marduk:

> *He raised the club, in his right hand he grasped (it), the bow and the quiver he hung at his side. He set the lightning in front of him, with burning flame he filled his body. He made a net to enclose the inward parts of Tiamat, the four wind he stationed so that nothing of her might escape; ... He sent forth the winds which he had created, the seven of them; To disturb the inward parts of Tiamat, they followed after him. Then the lord raised the thunderbolt, his mighty weapon, he mounted the chariot, the storm unequalled for terror, he harnessed and yoked unto it four horses, destructive, ferocious, overwhelming, and swift of pace.* [176]

Ishtar, the goddess of fertility, is the Babylonian equivalent of the goddess Asherah/Astarte, described in the chapter on the Levant. She was also deeply revered by the Babylonians. The god Tammuz sacrificed himself for her by agreeing to spend several months every year in the underworld in exchange for her freedom. In the spring, the king, acting as the embodiment of the god Tammuz, would enter into a sacred carnal union with Ishtar, herself incarnated by the high priestess of the temple.

The religious tenets of Babylon are fundamentally the same as those of the Levant. In both cases, the acting out of the fertility rite was intended to celebrate and perpetuate the renewal of life and energy, in both nature and in the kingdom.

---

[175] Frankfort, Henri. 1978. *Kingship and the gods : a study of ancient Near Eastern religion as the integration of society & nature.* Chicago: University of Chicago Press. p. 321
[176] King, Leonard William. 2004. *Babylonian Religion and Mythology.* Kila: Kessinger Publishing. (Orig. pub. 1903.). p.71

In Babylon, the men sought to ingratiate themselves with the gods through sexual intercourse with the goddesses of the temple, which were prostitutes. Each temple also had its "favorites"—male prostitutes—who were often castrated. Homosexuality was tolerated.

The modern celebration of Easter (*Ishtar*) appears to be a transposition of this springtime pagan feast, in which eggs; a symbol of new life, already played a pivotal role.[177] Because Ishtar is none other than the daughter of Sin, the moon god, calculating the date of this holiday remains a challenge as it relates to the moon cycle.

Hammurabi is better known for his famous code of law, the best preserved in Antiquity. Written circa 1760, *Hammurabi's Code* contains 282 laws governing various aspects of society.

Hammurabi claimed to have been granted his royal capacity by the god Marduk:

> *I am Hammurabi, the efficient king. I have not been careless with the mass of mankind, which Enlil has entrusted to me and which Marduk has made my flock; I have not been lazy.*[178]

[177] Jobes, Gertrude. 1962. *Dictionary of Mythology, Folklore and Symbols.* New York: Scarecrow Press. p. 487
[178] Richardson, M. E. J. 2004. *Hammurabi's Laws: Text, Translation, and Glossary.* New York: Continuum International Publishing Group. p. 119

33: Marduk gives the rod and the ring to Hammurabi

On the top portion of his Code, we see him accepting the emblems of sovereignty from Marduk: the rod and the ring. Like Sargon of Akkad and many other kings before him, he also invokes the protection of his goddess, Ishtar.

> *O Ishtar, lady of war and conflict, the one who draws out my weapons, my gracious Protecting Spirit, who loves me to rule,*[179]

Not wanting to question established values, Hammurabi instead adopted and institutionalized them.

A flourishing culture

Thanks to their nomadic roots, the Amorites—ancestors of Abraham—were quick to adopt and embrace local values. Unburdened by any heavy cultural baggage, they assimilated the local culture with ease, enriched their own culture through contact

---

[179] Ibid. p. 131

with others and contributed to the development of the outlying regions.

But, the Amorites also managed to preserve traits of their nomadic origins. The concept of "shepherd king" is applied to Mesopotamian sovereigns even in the earliest historical texts. According to this nomadic concept, the king is the "shepherd" of the people who guides their actions.

The prologue to Hammurabi's Code describes this "shepherd" king:

> *It is the great gods that have nominated me so that I am the shepherd who brings peace, with a staff that is straight. My protective shadow has been spread over my city, I have set the people of the land of Sumer and Akkad securely on my knees. They have come to prosper Under my protection; I have always governed them in peace, I have always guided them by my wisdom.*[180]

In light of this, the uncertainty over the origins of the name "Hyksos", begun by Flavius in *Against Apion*, fades away. Recall that the Hyksos were foreign kings of Amorite descent who ruled the entire Egyptian empire in the 17th century BCE.

Whether Hyksos is translated as "shepherd kings" or "captive shepherds", or *heka khasewet* as "rulers of foreign lands", these various interpretations clearly refer to the Amorite leaders of Babylon, the "shepherds of the people".

This argument is supported by another piece of information: a scroll attributed to the Hyksos king Khyan, found on a Babylonian site, attests to contact between the Babylonians and the Hyksos.[181]

Since the term "shepherd" is an Amorite cultural concept according to which the king is the "shepherd" of his people, it is appropriate to wonder about the true nature of Abraham. Shouldn't

---

[180] Ibid. p. 121
[181] Crew, P. Mack, I. E. S. Edwards, J.B. Bury, C. J. Gadd, Nicholas Geoffrey, N. G. L. Hammond and Edmond Sollberger. 1973. *History of the Middle East and the Aegean Region c.1800-1380 B.C.* Vol. 2 of *The Cambridge Ancient History*. Cambridge: Cambridge University Press. p. 60

the use of this term instead confirm his role as a guide with links to the Amorite leaders of Babylon?

Beyond the borders

While this information provides better insight into the context in which the Babylonian empire developed under Hammurabi, we still need to clarify the nature of his potential ties to the Patriarchs. This will enable us to confirm whether this information supports the hypothesis that Abraham also espoused the values and gods of the era, contrary to our typical image of him.

New territories were conquered either by force or by forming alliances with the local kings. Interpersonal relationships were extremely important to the nomadic Amorite people. Power was shared amongst members of the same family or clan.

While the Sumerian empire was an agglomeration of independent and autonomous city-states, the Babylonian empire was made up of a dozen cities, all ruled by a monarch invested with divine powers. At his zenith, Hammurabi's sphere of influence extended over most of the Fertile Crescent.

Since most of the region was now being controlled by Amorites, Hammurabi managed to consolidate his empire by multiplying alliances. To maintain order and control over this immense territory, new methods of administration were needed within the Empire: conscription, taxation and centralization of powers. Laws were enforced and upheld by local governors.[182]

---

[182] Cohen, Ronald and Judith D. Toland. 1988. *State Formation and Political Legitimacy.* New Brunswick: Transaction Books. p. 97

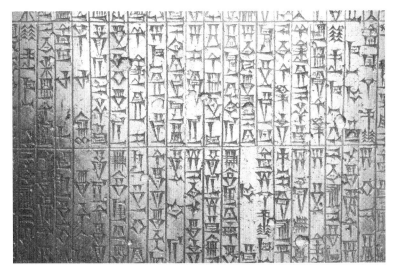

34: Detailed view of Hammurabi's Code

Hammurabi's new code of law was much stricter on offenders than previous laws. In Hammurabi's view, law and order took precedence over human life. In his Code, he imposed the death sentence for crimes other than murder, for example for offenses that would have warranted a simple fine under Ur-Nammu's code.

> *So that the mighty might not exploit the weak, and so that the orphan and the widow may be treated properly, I have written these very special words of mine on this stone; I have set them together with the image of me, the king of justice.*[183]

In her book *De Sumer à Canaan*, Sophie Cluzan compares several laws in the Bible with those in Hammurabi's Code. She explains:

> *The similarities between Hammurabi's Code and the texts in the Bible reveal the existence of common origins—probably Semitic—and a sharing of norms common to the entire region and which each generation embraced, reinforcing them through new realities and practices.*[184]

---

[183] Richardson, M. E. J. 2004. *Hammurabi's Laws: Text, Translation, and Glossary*. New York: Continuum International Publishing Group. p. 121

[184] Cluzan, Sophie. 2005. *De Sumer à Canaan: l'Orient ancien et la bible*. Paris: Éditions du Seuil. p. 210 (translated)

Cluzan then compares several laws:

Hammurabi's Code (18th century BCE)	Exodus (13th century BCE)
§ 250. If an ox has tossed a man while walking along the road and caused his death, there is no cause for complaint.	Ex 21:28 If an ox gore a man or a woman, that they die: then the ox shall be surely stoned, and his flesh shall not be eaten; but the owner of the ox shall be quit.
§ 251. If a man has an ox which tosses and his council have informed him that it tosses and he has not covered its horns and has not tied the ox up and the ox tosses a man's son and causes his death, he shall pay half a shekel of silver.	Ex 21:29 But if the ox were wont to push with his horn in time past, and it hath been testified to his owner, and he hath not kept him in, but that he hath killed a man or a woman; the ox shall be stoned, and his owner also shall be put to death. Ex 21:30 If there be laid on him a sum of money, then he shall give for the ransom of his life whatsoever is laid upon him. Ex 21:31 Whether he have gored a son, or have gored a daughter, according to this judgment shall it be done unto him.
§ 252. If it was a man's slave he shall give a third of a mana of silver.	Ex 21:32 If the ox shall push a manservant or a maidservant; he shall give unto their master thirty shekels of silver, and the ox shall be stoned.

In both cases, the same general principles govern the situation. If an animal causes harm, its owner is not held responsible the first time. Conversely, if the owner is aware that his animal is problematic, but does not intervene, then the owner is held accountable on the animal's first offense and is punished.[185]

It seems unlikely that these similarities should be nothing more than coincidence.

Sarah's behavior toward Hagar, Rebekah's receipt of a dowry from her young husband's father, and the conditions surrounding the sale of the Cave of Machpelah are all examples of the application of these laws.[186] In the epilogue to the Code, there is also another interesting parallel with the eternal promise made to Abraham in the Covenant, in exchange for the observance and enforcement of the laws:

> *Then they will say: "Hammurabi is a ruler, who is as a father to his subjects, who holds the words of Marduk in reverence, who has achieved conquest for Marduk over the north and south, who rejoices the heart of Marduk, his lord, who has bestowed benefits for ever and ever on his subjects, and has established order in the land."[187]*

Engraved on a magnificent block of basalt, Hammurabi's Code is now on display in the basement of the Louvre Museum. Discovered in Iran in 1901 CE, it comes from the Babylonian temple at Sippar, where it had been taken as plunder in the 12th century BCE by the Elamite king Shutruk-Nahhunte.

Hammurabi had several copies of his code engraved, which he distributed judiciously throughout his empire in order to maintain his rule over the outlying regions.[188] Babylonian became the official language of trade and literature, where cuneiform writing was taught in school. The governors made sure that every city paid its just tribute to the central government.

---

[185] Ibid. p.210 (translated)
[186] Ibid p.160 (translated)
[187] King, Leonard William. 1996. *The Code of Hammurabi.* Edition Richard hooker ed. Washington: Washington University. (Orig. pub. 1910.).
[188] Pinches, Theophilus G. 2002. *The Old Testament in the Light of the Historical Records and Legends of Assyria and Babylonia.* New York: Elibron Classics. (Orig. pub. 1902.). p. 165

35: Hammurabi's Code

Bolstered by their extensive knowledge of the regions, strong clan unity and advanced methods of war, the Amorites took advantage of local alliances and betrayals to expand their power over all of Mesopotamia, the Levant and Egypt. The kingdom of Ekallatum is a prime example of the type of relationships fostered by Hammurabi. When the Elamites attacked Ekallatum around 1765 BCE, King Ishme-Dagan sought refuge with Hammurabi. After defeating the Elamites, Hammurabi helped Ishme-Dagan take back the throne. The price? Ekallatum became a vassal city subservient to the king of Babylon.[189]

Hammurabi seems to fit the profile of Abraham's lord: he was the first Amorite to control the entire geographic area comprising Mesopotamia. He was also a natural ally of the Hyksos, who ruled Egypt at the same time. But, while several kings before him

---

[189] Charpin, Dominique and Nele Ziegler. 2003. "Mari et le Proche-Orient à l'époque amorrite: essai d'histoire politique." *Mémoires de NABU 6* Florilegium marianum 5

apposed the Akkadian (⟐) or Sumerian (✳) dingirs to their names, it appears this was not the case with Hammurabi.

Was Abraham a vassal of Hammurabi, much like the neighboring kings, who were also subservient to him? While no archaeological evidence have been found that confirms he had an ascendant over the Levant, we will soon find out that the Bible contains the chronological data allowing us to make such a case. However, we first need to better understand how the Mesopotamians were keeping track of time, as this will allow us to properly decode the biblical chronologies and ultimately compare them with known historical events of Hammurabi's reign.

In summary

- The stories of Enûma Eliš and Gilgamesh show important similarities with the biblical stories of the Creation and that of Noah's flood.

- The tower of Babel most likely refers to the ziggurat of Babylon.

- Hammurabi is the first Amorite king to have seized power in Mesopotamia and to have established the large Babylonian Empire.

- Hammurabi was a just and beloved king. Children were named after Hammurabi, and he was considered a god by some; something unparalleled in his dynasty.

- Hammurabi's code of law has significant parallels with the Mosaic laws.

- He relied on governor and alliances to maintain control over the region.

Calculating time

To fully appreciate the historical context in which Abraham and his "Lord" lived, one must examine another important aspect of Mesopotamia's prolific culture that has too often been neglected by historians: the calculation of time.

Originally, time was counted in order to predict the harvests and major religious feasts. Artefacts dating from the Upper Palaeolithic age show that the lunar cycle was already being used as a means of calculating time over 10,000 years ago.[190]

The Babylonians made remarkable contributions to the development of mathematics and astronomy. One year was made up of 12 lunar cycles of 29.5 days each, for a total of 354 days. But, because the lunar year is approximately 11 days shorter than the solar year, one month was added every three or four years, in the same way that we now add an extra day in February during leap years.

The Islamic calendar (Hijri calendar) is a 354-day lunar calendar that is still used in Saudi Arabia. However, the Qur'an specifically forbids the use of the extra month, since *"The count of months, as far as Allah is concerned, is twelve"* (Sura 9:36).

During Hammurabi's era, there was no absolute benchmark for time; it was measured by the number of years in a sovereign's reign. For example, a specific event was noted as having taken place during the 15th year of Hammurabi's reign. Obviously, this system was valid only for a particular location. Elsewhere, time was calculated differently, and each region—or even each city— had its own way of measuring it.[191]

[190] Rudgley, Richard. 2000. *The Lost Civilizations of the Stone Age*. New York: Simon & Schuster. p. 86
[191] Trigger, Bruce G. 2003. *Understanding Early Civilizations: A Comparative Study*. Cambridge: Cambridge University Press. p. 612

The number 12 was highly significant to the Babylonians. It represents the number of new moons in a year; as such, it is a way of governing both time and the seasons.

Since the earliest days of Antiquity, humans have observed a few specific groupings of stars—among the billions that dot the heavens—along the path followed by the moon. Today, these are known as the constellations of the zodiac. While these constellations appear to orbit the Earth, we know that it's actually the Earth, with its moon in tow that orbits the Sun along the ecliptic plane. This is why a different constellation can be seen with each new moon and why some are visible only during the winter, and others only during the summer.

To better understand and predict the inner workings of these heavenly movements, the Babylonians developed the sexagesimal system (base of 60).[192]

This system can be used to easily calculate time and angles. The number 60, a divisor of 360, is an obvious choice for the base, as it provides a good approximation of the number of days in a year (1 degree ≈ 1 day). The number 60 is also a natural complement of the number 12 and is divisible by as many factors, which is three more than the number 100 (1, 2, 3, 4, 5, 6, 10, 12, 15, 20, 30, 60 versus 1, 2, 4, 5, 10, 20, 25, 50, 100). This high degree of divisibility supports the use of reverse multiplication tables, used for rapid and accurate mental calculations.

In *A geometrical link between the circle and sexagesimal system,* Jaime Vladimir Torres-Heredia Julca brilliantly demonstrates the natural relationship between the geometry of a circle and the numbers 6, 12, 24, 30, 60 and 360.[193] He postulates that this relationship probably forms the foundations of the sexagesimal system invented by the Babylonians. The number 12 can be achieved by juxtaposing three layers of perfect circles.

---

[192] Katz, Victor J. and Annette Imhausen. 2007. *The Mathematics of Egypt, Mesopotamia, China, India, and Islam: A Sourcebook.* Princeton: Princeton University Press. p. 73
[193] Torres-Heredia Julca, Jaime Vladimir. 2005-2006. "Un lien géométrique entre le cercle et le système sexagésimal." *Université de Genève,* Université de Genève, Université de Genève, http://halshs.archives-ouvertes.fr/docs/00/03/44/42/PDF/Un_lien_geometrique_entre_le_cercle_et_le_systeme_s exagesimal.pdf (retrieved January 23, 2009).

This highly practical system, which we still use today to calculate time and solve geometrical equations, was likely to have been developed by observing the movements of these celestial bodies.

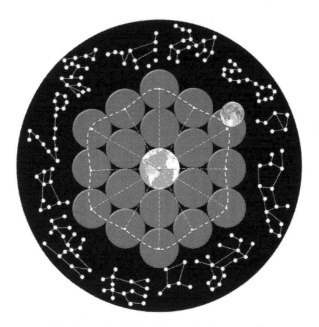

36: A constellation for each lunar cycle

This diagram represents the 12 constellations of the zodiac. During each lunar cycle, a different constellation appears in the night sky along the ecliptic. It takes one year to complete the cycle. Jaime Vladimir Torres-Heredia Julca points out that six circles arranged around a same-sized nucleus would surround it perfectly, and that the same would apply for the next layer of 12 circles, followed by 18 circles, and so on. He suggests that this relationship was likely to be at the origin of the sexagesimal system.

The perfect relationship between the number 12 and the geometric shape of a circle was no doubt fascinating to the Babylonians, since it corresponds well to the movements of the planets and the moon along the ecliptic. According to Bartel Leendert Waerden, the oldest known astronomy texts in Mesopotamia date from the time of Hammurabi.[194] It is therefore reasonable to presume that

Abraham and his kin were already aware of these dating and notation systems.

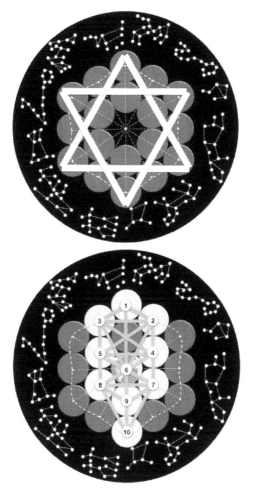

37: The Star of David and the Kabbalah tree of life

At the center of these figures, one can see the Star of David, the preeminent symbol of Judaism that encompasses the curved outlines of the 12 circles; as well as the mystical Kabbalah tree of life. Could both symbols attest of the close relationship between the Hebrew people and astronomy, the sexagesimal system and the "perfect" number 12 of the Bible?

---

[194] Van Der Waerden, B. L. 1961. *Science Awakening*. New York: Oxford University Press.

There was no distinction between "astrology" and "astronomy" at the time. This new ability to accurately predict the movements of heavenly bodies revolutionized the practice of astrology. The Mesopotamians defined the first-ever zodiacs, which much later evolved into the study of personal horoscopes as the ability to predict complex celestial movements, such as lunar eclipses, led the Babylonians to believe they could also predict an individual's future.

38: Beth Alpha Synagogue in Jerusalem (6th century CE)

The names of these constellations are simply a memory aid to identify the months corresponding to each of the lunar cycles in a year: Aries, Taurus, Gemini, Cancer, Leo, Virgo, Libra, Scorpio, Sagittarius, Capricorn, Aquarius, Pisces. Since certain constellations are much larger than others, the division of the zodiac into twelve equal segments of 30° helps bring some regularity to the calendar. The Serpens constellation is also located on the ecliptic, although it is not used in astrology.

Chronological conundrum

While a number of past attempts at chronological dating have tried to situate the Patriarchs within an historical timeframe, none has lined up in a satisfying and complete manner with the data available. At most, only a few events in the Bible have been linked to historical data, although, each time, this led to contradictions with other events. This is why many scholars have concluded that the dates given in the Bible are incorrect.[195] Indeed, no mater how hard one tries; biblical chronologies simply do not match historical data. It is therefore not surprising that expressions of time in the Bible are believed by many scholars to only hold prophetic or spiritual significance. For instance, number "7" and "12" represents perfection and number "40" represents a generation. While this interpretation has merits in regards to the prophetic literature, it probably came as a late development.

Below are the biblical references most often used when trying to establish a link with known archaeological evidence:

Source	Event
Ge 14:1	Amraphel, king of Shinar, has often been identified as Hammurabi, king of Sumer (1792-1750)
Ge 12:4	Abraham is 75 years old when he leaves Harran (enters Canaan)
Ge 21:5	Abraham is 100 years old when Isaac is born
Ge 25:26	Isaac is 60 years old when Jacob is born
Ge 47:28	Jacob dies at the age of 147

[195] Cluzan, Sophie. 2005. *De Sumer à Canaan: l'Orient ancien et la bible*. Paris: Éditions du Seuil. p.161
Cline, Eric H. 2007. *From Eden to Exile: Unraveling Mysteries of the Bible*. Washington, D.C.: National Geographic. p. 45

Ge 50:26	Joseph dies at the age of 110 (Jacob's age at the time he fathers Joseph is unknown)
Ex 1:11	Ramses II (1279-1213) is generally identified as the Pharaoh of the Exodus because he ordered the construction of Pithom
Ex 12:40	The children of Israel spend 430 years in Egypt
1 Ki 6:1	480 years elapse between the Exodus and the construction of King Solomon's Temple

According to the Bible, the Exodus should have taken place under the reign of Ramses II (1279-1213 BCE). History indeed teaches us that Ramses II is the pharaoh who ordered the construction of the city of Pithom. It is also generally recognized that Solomon reigned around the year 970 BCE.

As many experts have shown, these dates do not correspond with historical teachings:

> *Ex 1:11 Therefore they did set over them taskmasters to afflict them with their burdens. And they built for Pharaoh treasure cities, Pithom and Raamses.*

> *1 Ki 6:1 And it came to pass in the four hundred and eightieth year after the children of Israel were come out of the land of Egypt, in the fourth year of Solomon's reign over Israel, in the month Zif, which is the second month, that he began to build the house of Yahweh.*

If construction of Solomon's Temple began in the fourth year of his reign, then the Exodus should have taken place 480 years earlier in the middle of the 15th century BCE, namely in 1446

(= 970 – 4 + 480). This period does not correspond to the rule of Ramses II, which took place almost two centuries later.

Another method of calculation consists of determining the date of the Exodus based on the recognition that Abraham was Hammurabi's contemporary. This involves adding the span of the generations of Patriarchs to the number of years the Hebrews spent in Egypt:

> *Ex 12:40 Now the sojourning of the children of Israel, who dwelt in Egypt, was four hundred and thirty years.*

Knowing that Abraham was 100 years old at the birth of Isaac (Ge 21:5), that Isaac was 60 years old at the birth of Jacob (Ge 25:26), and that Jacob died at the age of 147 (Ge 47:28), we can conclude that the generations spanned close to 300 years.

If their descendants dwelt for 430 years in Egypt, then the Exodus should have taken place in the mid-11th century BCE, or 730 years after Hammurabi, i.e. sometimes after c. 1062 (= 1792 –300 – 430). But, once again, there is nothing in the Bible or in the historical records to indicate that a mass exodus of the Jewish people from Egypt took place at this time.

Others, such as filmmaker Simcha Jacobovici, have tried to match the Exodus with the explosion of Mount Santorini and the expulsion of the Hyksos. However, other than by seriously bending chronologies, none of these dates work. This is why most scholars have now abandoned the idea of a historical timeframe in the Bible.

However, let's start with the premise that the dates in the Bible are accurate, but that they were misinterpreted, whether intentionally or unintentionally. There is nothing natural about the reported life spans of Adam (930 years) and Noah (950 years), prompting some to even speculate about the involvement of aliens! Even Abraham's lifespan (175 years) and the age at which Sarah gave birth to Isaac (90 years) are clearly exaggerated. Scholars speculate that these unbelievable life spans are the product of myth, or of the sacred nature of the characters. However, they become much easier to understand when considered from the perspective of the time.[196]

While it is now completely natural to keep track of time in 365-day years, this was not always the case. In fact, what is time to an observer, if not the observation and measurement of recurring cycles?

The shortest cycle is that of the day, although it is not very practical as it is difficult to keep track. In the *Sumerian King List*, certain antediluvian rulers are reported to have lived more than 28,800 years.[197] Substituting the concept of years for that of daily cycles adds a dose of realism to the chronology. So, by dividing 28,800 cycles by 365 days, we get a much more believable life span of 79 years.

Sedentary people were first to observe and accurately calculate the annual cycle of 365 days. For nomads who travelled from city to city, it was much easier to keep track of the cycles of the moon, which could be seen in the sky without any complex instruments.

In the *Sumerian King List*, rulers of the First Dynasty of Kish are reported to have lived anywhere between 300 and 1500 years. These are similar to the life spans of Adam (930 years) and Noah (950 years) that are found in the Bible. Were these calculated in lunar cycles rather than in days or years? Based on 12.4 lunar cycles per year (365 divided by 29.5), Adam and Noah would have been 75 (930/12.4) and 77 (950/12.4), respectively.

Whatever the case may be, the scribes who compiled the various texts of Genesis were clearly influenced by similar lists and transcribed this information out of context. These implausible life spans are clear evidence that the precise origins and nature of these texts must have been unknown to the scribes and that they were intended only as a preface, to explain the origins of Creation.

The age of the Patriarchs

Given their many parallels with the Enûma Eliš and the Epic of Gilgamesh, it is probably fair to assume that the stories of Creation

---

[196] It is interesting to see Young applying interesting algebraic formula to the Sumerian King List in: Young, Dwight W. 1988. "A Mathematical Approach to Certain Dynastic Spans in the Sumerian King List." *Journal of Near Eastern Studies* 47(2): 123-29.

[197] Cluzan, Sophie. 2005. *De Sumer à Canaan: l'Orient ancien et la bible*. Paris: Éditions du Seuil. p. 167

and the Great Flood originate from earlier sources that were later adapted. While Abraham's bloodline in the Bible can be traced back to Adam and Eve, his family tree becomes relevant only once we begin to see a significant drop in people's ages, that is, after Noah and the Flood.

Interestingly, a comparison of antediluvian and postdiluvian dates reveals that the kings in the *Sumerian King List* had a similar life span drop to the characters in the Bible.[198] This further supports the idea that the Bible was partially based on the same sources.

Whether they were naïve or simply unable to explain this shift, the authors of Genesis nevertheless seemed a little embarrassed in having to point out and justify this change by reporting that people now had more "normal" life spans:

> *Ge 6:3 And Yahweh said, My spirit shall not always strive with man, for that he also is flesh: yet his days shall be an hundred and twenty years.*

While still somewhat exaggerated, the Patriarchs' life spans are nowhere near those of Noah and previous generations. This more human scale is most likely due to the availability of more recent sources and more reliable data. This reframing would appear to indicate that the lunar cycle was no longer in use.

The cuneiform writing and the sexagesimal system

It is important to recall that mathematical calculations in Mesopotamia had long been based on the number 60. Is it possible, therefore, that an error of interpretation occurred during transcription?

The cuneiform writing (Latin cuneus: wedge-shaped) is a mark printed by a reed stylus into clay. The Babylonians in the Middle Bronze Age used this form of writing.

---

[198] Ibid. p. 167

39: The Plympton tablet (Bronze Age)

Numbers were recorded using an additive decimal system formed with nails « Ͳ » to express units (1 to 9) and chevrons « ❬ » for the tens (10 to 50). The combination of these symbols allows representation of the numbers 1 to 59.[199]

1	2	3	4	5	6	7	8	9
Ͳ	ͲͲ	ͲͲͲ						

10	20	30	40	50
❬	❬❬	❬❬❬		

40: Cuneiform numbers

Thus the cuneiform inscription « ͲͲͲ❬❬ » reads "3:45". Note that it is common practice today to use a colon symbol to separate the sexagesimal numerals; much as is done with time.

Considering this notation, it appears that the ages of the Patriarchs reported in the Genesis narratives cannot be expressed in the sexagesimal base, for the very reason that the last two digits are often occupied by a figure greater than 59. And unless one accepts the idea that Abraham actually lived 175 years, common sense leads us to conclude that his age cannot be expressed in base 10 either. This is why we posit that the scribes, who assembled the

[199] Boucher, Claude. 2009. *Une brève histoire du Proche et du Moyen-Orient.* [Montréal]: Fides. p. 154

Bible out of ancient texts were dealing with sexagesimal numbers, but weren't familiar with this notation. As such, they introduced a conversion error. Is it possible to understand what went wrong and what is the cognitive process that led to it?

The 6/10 multiplier

Thanks to the Babylonians, modern clocks are still divided into twelve hours of sixty minutes. How would one go about creating a new clock for which each hour would contain 100 minutes? This is possibly the kind of question that Nabonidus' scribes asked themselves when faced with the need to convert ages from the sexagesimal to the decimal notation. One would find an equivalent ratio between the bases so that a quarter of an hour, or 15 "old" minutes become 25 "new" minutes:

$$\frac{15}{60} = \frac{25}{100} = \frac{1}{4}$$

Using this method, one converts 3 hours and 45 minutes, or "3:45" as:

$$\frac{3*60 + 45}{60 \quad 60} = \frac{3*100 + 75}{100 \quad 100} = 75$$

or 3 hours and 75 "new" minutes, that we could also write as "375"

And since "years" is a measure of time, much like minutes and hours, it would seem natural for a scribe to use this approach when converting sexagesimal numbers representing years. As such, he could have transcribed 15 "old" years into 25 "new" years and it seems that this is exactly what they did.

Unfortunately, this is wrong. Why? Because a minute is a *fraction* of an hour, and an hour is a *fraction* of a day. But years are not fractions. They are *whole numbers* that must be accounted as such.

More than fifty years ago, George Sarton wrote:

> *The Greeks inherited the sexagesimal system from the Sumerians but mixed it up with the decimal system, using the former only for submultiples of the unit and the latter for*

multiples, and thus they spoiled both systems and started a disgraceful confusion of which we are still the victims. They abandoned the principle of position, which had to be reintroduced from India a thousand years later. In short, their understanding of Babylonian arithmetic must have been very poor, since they managed to keep the worst features of it and to overlook the best. This must have been due to deficient tradition rather than lack of intelligence, or else, to the fact that, as we should remember, intelligence is always relative.[200]

Although Sarton underlines clearly that this error was common with the Greeks, he also acknowledges it was most likely inherited from a deficient tradition.

To understand how the sexagesimal system actually works, it is useful to refer to the decimal system. In decimal notation, each digit (0-9) is multiplied by 10 to the power of the position it occupies within the number. Similarly, in the sexagesimal notation, each numeral (1-59) is multiplied by 60 to the power of the position it occupies within the number.

To convert sexagesimal "3:45" into decimal, the following calculation must be made:

$$3 * 60^1 + 45 * 60^0 = 225$$

We do find that "225" is the proper conversion.

Thankfully, it is possible to correct any mis-conversion using the constant multiplier 6/10. It is indeed possible to fix the erroneous 375 by multiplying it by 6/10 in order to get 225; just like it is possible to fix the erroneous "25 years" by multiplying it by 6/10 in order to get "15 years".

The 6/10 correction factor should therefore systematically be applied to all biblical numbers in order to rediscover the "correct" numbers. For instance, based on the information in 1 Kings 6:1, if, instead of taking place 480 years before the construction of Solomon's Temple in 966 BCE, we presume the Exodus occurred

[200] Sarton, George. 1993. *Ancient Science Through the Golden Age of Greece*. Harvard: Harvard University Press. (Orig. pub. 1952-59.). p.118

288 years (= 480 x 6/10) before, we should then place the Exodus in 1254 BCE—exactly during the reign of Ramses II.

Solving biblical chronologies with the 6/10 multiplier

It is probably useful at this point to compare two sets of chronologies. The first one reflects standard biblical chronology in relation to major historical events. The second shows the effect of submitting the biblical chronology to the 6/10 multiplier. It is easy to see how this simple correction provides an elegant solution to the otherwise difficult problem of biblical chronologies.

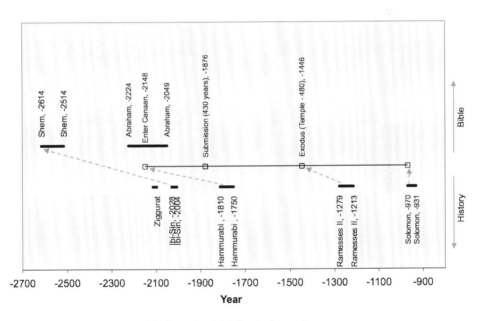

41: Standard biblical chronology

When working dates back from the construction of the Solomon temple, the Exodus does not fall anywhere near the kingship of Ramses II. When making Abraham contemporary with Hammurabi, neither their ancestors, nor their descendants fit a proper historical timeline.

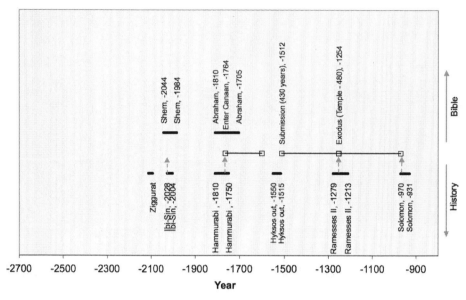

42: Corrected biblical chronology

Once corrected using the 6/10 multiplier, all biblical dates line up perfectly with the available historical data and it is not only possible, but also logical to see Hammurabi and Abraham as contemporaries.

Can we find similar conversion errors outside of the Bible? If so, it would certainly give credence to this model.

Nabonibus' conversion error

In his book *King Hammurabi of Babylon: A Biography*, Marc Van De Mieroop, refers to an inscription that is found on the Nabonidus cylinder (c. 556-539 BCE), which refers to a tablet of King Burnaburiash (c. 1359-1333 BCE) that speaks of Hammurabi as having *"lived 700 years before him."* Marc Van De Mieroop claims that King Burnaburiash's calculations are *"substantially off"*.[201]

Nabonidus was defeated by Cyrus the Persian and was the last Babylonian king of the Exile. He was therefore ruling Babylon precisely at the time when the Bible is believed to have been

---

[201] Van De Mieroop, Marc. 2005. *King Hammurabi of Babylon: a Biography*. Malden: Blackwell p.131

collated. That was a time when the sexagesimal system had been abandoned in favor of the decimal system.

43: Nabonidus' cylinder (6th century BCE)

If we apply the 6/10 multiplier to the number reported by Nabonidus, we find that Hammurabi would not have lived 700 years, but rather 420 (700*6/10) years before Burnaburiash, hence:

c. 1779-1753 = (c. 1359-1333)+420

…whereas Hammurabi actually reigned from 1792-1750.

We therefore have a perfect match. This proves that Burnaburiash was not off, but instead, that Nabonidus could not properly convert the sexagesimal number into decimal. It seems that Van De Mieroop was mislead by the "erroneous" dates and hastened to put the blame on Burnaburiash.

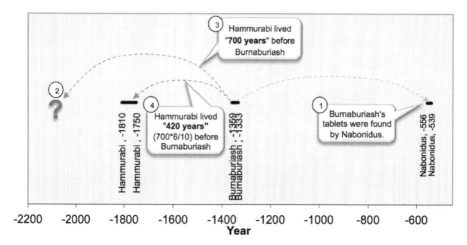

44: Solving Nabonidus' conversion error using the 6/10 multiplier

Some believe that Burnaburiash was "substantially off" in his calculations. In reality, it was Nabonidus (1) that did not know how to convert (2) the sexagesimal numbers (3) found on Burnaburiash's ancient tablets. Applying the 6/10 multiplier (4) allows us to correct this mistake.

This external and completely independent source offers confirmation that the conversion errors found in the Bible are not unique to this period of history and can be corrected with a simple multiplier. The fact that the same error is found in the Bible and on the Nabonidus cylinder is remarkable and shows that the same scribes, or at least scribes sharing the same knowledge, were involved in making the same conversion errors. This external evidence offers additional support to the hypothesis put forth in this book.

It is now time to see if it is possible to correlate the lives of Abraham and Hammurabi.

In summary

- Time is relative and relates to cycles. The way people have kept track of it varied and evolved.

- The amazing life spans of the early biblical characters can be better understood when considered from the perspective of lunar cycles.

- The more realistic, yet still abnormal lifespans of the patriarchal characters are likely the result of a poor conversion of old sexagesimal numbers.

- It is possible to "fix" these erroneous biblical dates by applying the 6/10 multiplier.

- Example of the same "error" can be found outside of the Bible; as the cylinder of Nabonidus, a man that lived at the time the Bible was collated, demonstrates.

The truth is incontrovertible, malice may attack it,
ignorance may deride it,

but in the end; there it is.

Winston Churchill

Part III – Abraham's Lord

By examining the historical context of Egypt, the Levant and Mesopotamia at the turn of the second millennium, we have gained some insight into the situation prevailing at the arrival of the Patriarchs. This information enables us to construct a new "interpretative framework" which, when applied to Genesis, reveals the story of the Amorites, ancestors of the Jewish people.

Armed with this new historical knowledge, will the rereading of Genesis confirm that Abraham's relationship with *Yahweh* is effectively one of a vassal and a lord? We know that the Amorites took control of Mesopotamia during the reign of Ibi-Sin, shortly after the construction, under Ur-Nammu, of the first ziggurats. When compared to the many historical characters and ancient texts that shaped this region, the Bible does reveal many parallels:

- The ancient Sumerian texts of the Enûma Eliš are reflected in the stories of the Garden of Eden and the Tower of Babel.

- The account of Noah and the Great Flood finds its origin in the myth of Gilgamesh.

- The story of the infant Moses, who was abandoned on the river in a basket of bulrushes, is very similar to the description of the birth of Sargon of Akkad.

- The incredible lifespans of Adam and Noah are paralleled in the Sumerian King List.

- Moses' Ten Commandments bear a significant resemblance to Hammurabi's Code.

We now have a better understanding of how a number of Mesopotamian kings, in proclaiming themselves "living gods", in fact dulled the notions of "god", "demigod" and "lord".

It was only during the 18th century BCE, under the powerful Hammurabi, "king of the land of the Amorites", that this civilization reached its zenith. A man of strong convictions and a keen sense of justice, Hammurabi had a profound influence over the entire Fertile Crescent. Whilst he expanded his territory and enforced his laws with diplomacy, he did not hesitate to use force when necessary. The administration of such a vast kingdom required the assistance of trusted and dedicated men. Since many past scholars have suggested that Abraham and Hammurabi were contemporaries and that they shared a common cultural background, the question can be asked: Is it likely that Hammurabi appointed Abraham governor of Canaan? Could Hammurabi be Abraham's "*Baal*"? And could this covenant have given rise to the *Baal Berith* cult?

When viewed from this new perspective, will the Abrahamic narrative emerge as the story of the relationship between these two men?

Working hypothesis

Since no documents exist to support the historical authenticity of Abraham, how can we prove he even existed? Much like modern scientific theories that build on logical assumptions to develop a coherent mathematical model that is then confirmed through practical tests, our approach will follow a similar process. However, confirmation for our assumptions will not come from "tests" but, rather, from the study of existing (and eventually upcoming) historical and biblical data.

How can such a mathematical model be applied to this literary research? The story of the Patriarchs contains many clues about the age of its main characters at various events. It is therefore possible to situate one event in relation to another by using the age of the characters, and thereby construct a fairly detailed timeline of the story. One simply needs to note the age of a character at a precise event and situating it in relation to previous events and generations. Since the story of the Patriarchs revolves around Abraham, it is possible to use this character's birth date as an *anchor point* to accurately align the *historical events* around his timeline.

Our hypothesis rests on two key postulates:

- Hammurabi is *Baal Berith*, or Abraham's Lord (*events*)

- Abraham and Hammurabi were born c. 1810 BCE (*anchor point*)

Since the purpose of this essay is to establish "evidences" confirming our hypothesis, the following pages will demonstrate that these two basic postulates provide an exclusive, complete and coherent framework for interpreting the biblical narratives in the historical context of the Bronze Age. Of course, these postulates are in no way random; they were deduced from collected data. While the 1810 BCE date may first seem arbitrary, the reader will come to see that it is actually very precise as the evidence is laid out.

In following the biblical story of Abraham, we will focus on three types of evidence: logical, chronological and dendrochronological.

We will first confirm the relationship that existed between the two men by conducting a detailed dissociative exegesis of the texts, where King Hammurabi will take on the role of *Baal Berith* (i.e. *Yahweh*). We will therefore be sensitive to the contextual relationship between *Yahweh/Elohim* and Abraham. The anthropomorphic figure will now exclusively be referred to as "*Baal*" (as opposed to "*Yahweh/Elohim*") and the immaterial one by "*Elohim*". These substitutions are meant at restoring the original terms[202]. Dendrochronological data will provide further evidence by allowing us to accurately date periods of drought.

---

[202] The verses quoted from the Bible have already had their terms Yahweh/Elohim replaced when applicable. A footnote indicates the original term.

To minimize the risk of random errors, it is essential to first define the period in which this research takes place. It will be argued that, not only did Abraham and Hammurabi lived at the same time, but also that the two men probably shared common ancestors. This will confirm that the selected "anchor point" does fall within a plausible historical range.

Following this initial demonstration, a critical analysis of Ge 14, the Chapter on the War of Kings that has preceded the Covenant, will provide the foundation for our argumentation, as well as confirm the relationship between these two men.[203] This analysis will allow further refining the date of the *anchor point* and confirm its accuracy.

An analysis of the subsequent chapters of Genesis will yield a certain amount of circumstantial evidence to support these initial observations and validate the interpretation of the earthly covenant.

Abraham's ancestors settle in Mesopotamia

What do we know about Abraham's ancestors? The Torah (Ge 25:20, De 26:5) states that the Patriarchs were (ארמי) *Arammiy* ("Aramean"), which are believed to have evolved from the Amorites stem.[204] Their culture was influenced by that of the Amorites during the Bronze Age, as well as the Neo-Hittites who would control Canaan between the 14th and the 12th centuries BCE.

A majority of early scholars also claim that "if" Abraham ever lived, it would have been during the 18th century BCE. Can this hypothesis be confirmed through an analysis of biblical texts and the dates they contain?

According to Genesis, they were part of a group of people that migrated from the East to Mesopotamia, to eventually settle in

---

[203] The Qu'ran doesn't make mention of the twelve years of servitude of the Sodomites and of the attack of the four Eastern Kings. The only logical conclusion is that most of the chapter was conveniently ignored as it didn't offer much theological value and was therefore seen as a problem. In fact, the whole perspective adopted by the Qu'ran on Sodom, is solely based on Jewish's theological presuppositions.

[204] It would be appropriate to expand upon this demonstration if scholars weren't already unanimous on the subject.

Shinar (Sumer). These people could therefore be of Indo-European origin, which corresponds to what we know of the Amorites.

> *Ge 11:2 And it came to pass, as they journeyed from the east[205], that they found a plain in the land of Shinar; and they dwelt there.*

Incidentally, the Bible confirms that the *"land of Shinar"* corresponds to Sumer, since this region encompasses the cities of Babylon, Uruk and Akkad:

> *Ge 10:10 And the beginning of his kingdom was Babel, and Erech, and Accad, and Calneh, in the land of Shinar.*

We also know that the migration of these Amorites took place simultaneously with the construction of the Tower of Babel:

> *Ge 11:4 And they said, Go to, let us build us a city and a tower, whose top may reach unto heaven; and let us make us a name, lest we be scattered abroad upon the face of the whole earth.*

Although a nomadic people, they were nevertheless exposed to and influenced by the growing trend of sedentariness. The development of agriculture, the increasing occupation of territories and the expansion of new empires were all factors that prompted them to settle in order to avoid the threat of a diaspora. Therefore, it's only natural that they sought to "build a city" and "make themselves a name before they get scattered."

The first ziggurat was erected during the reign of Ur-Nammu (2112-2095 BCE) and many others followed it. It is often believed that Babylon's Etemananki ziggurat was the inspiration for the myth of the Tower of Babel. Unfortunately, the start date of its construction is unknown. But, because it was built on the site of the temple of Marduk, we can surmise that it was already standing during Hammurabi's time.[206]

As seen previously, the first nomadic Amorite tribes entered Mesopotamia during the reign of Shulgi, but it was only during Ibi-

---

[205] Hebrew (קֶדֶם) qedem ("East", "front"). Chouraqui translates this term by "Levant".

[206] Talbott, Strobe. 2008. *The Great Experiment : The story of Ancient Empires, Modern States, and the Quest for a Global Nation.* New York: Simon & Schuster.

Sin's reign, in the 21st century BCE, that they finally managed to penetrate the city walls and conquer Ur.

If Abraham was indeed one of Hammurabi's governors, then his family tree could mesh naturally with the history of this land. Chapter 11 of Genesis (verses 10-27) lists his ancestors as far back as Sem, the first of his bloodline to settle in Mesopotamia, as well as the ages at which each one fathered his son.

If we convert the biblical data[207] from the sexagesimal system (based on the 6/10 calculation), we obtain the following results:

Source	Event	Bible	6/10
Ge 11:10	Age at which Sem begets Arphaxad	100	60
Ge 11:12	Age at which Arphaxad begets Salah	35	21
Ge 11:14	Age at which Salah begets Eber	30	18
Ge 11:16	Age at which Eber begets Peleg	34	20
Ge 11:18	Age at which Peleg begets Reu	30	18
Ge 11:20	Age at which Reu begets Serug	32	19
Ge 11:22	Age at which Serug begets Nahor	30	18
Ge 11:24	Age at which Nahor begets Terah	29	17

---

[207] The genealogy of Sem to Abraham Sem provides realistic dates when considering the ages at which the sons were begat. However, lifespans appears to have been grossly exaggerated. We therefore need to careful when using this data.

Ge 11:26	Age at which Terah begets Abram	70	42
	Total	390	234

According to the Bible, Abraham was born some 390 years after Sem.[208]

If Hammurabi reigned between 1792 and 1750, and Abraham was his contemporary, then Sem would have lived 390 years before Hammurabi, around 2182 (= 1792 + 390). However, if we apply the 6/10 multiplier, then Sem would have only lived 234 years before, or around 2026 (= 1792 + 234).

Recall that the nomadic Amorites managed to breach the wall surrounding the city of Ur during the reign of Ibi-Sin, who came to power c. 2028.

Sem, Abraham's ancestor, possibly skirmished with Ibi-Sin for a few years before defeating him, seizing control of the region and settling in Ur.

The sum of the generations of Abraham's nine ancestors—234 years—corresponds perfectly with the time elapsed between the Amorites' rise to power in Mesopotamia and Hammurabi's ascent to the throne. We also know that the Amorites rose to power shortly after the construction of the first ziggurats, at the time of the migration. Completed just a few years before, these ziggurats were no doubt an inspiration to any fortunate enough to witness them.

More than just simple coincidences, these arguments tend to confirm that Abraham was very likely a contemporary of Hammurabi. The migration and rise to power are further evidence that these two powerful men probably belonged to the same ethnic group.

---

[208] It is possible that the author was attempting to identify the lineage based on years of reign. In this case, "beget" would have meant "to transfer power".

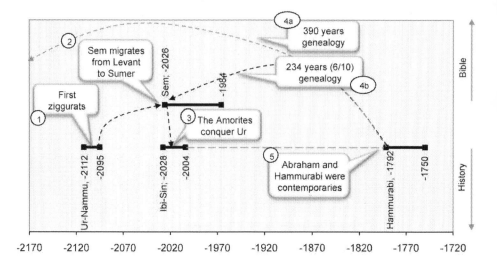

45: Migration of Abraham's ancestors

Once we posit that Abraham and Hammurabi were contemporaries (5), the timeline of 390 years (4a) becomes anachronistic (2) since it would imply that Abraham's ancestors migrated well before the construction of the first ziggurats (1). However, the Bible tells us that this migration took place shortly before construction of the Tower of Babel (Babylon's Etemananki ziggurat), which could not have been built before the ziggurat erected by Ur-Nammu. Conversely, the timeline of 234 years (4b) shows that the biblical Sem migrated and rose to power during the reign of Ibi-Sin, precisely when history teaches us that the Amorites conquered Ur (3).

An Earthly Covenant

We shall now turn to the Abrahamic narrative in search of new clues that would allow us to establish a historical connection between Abraham and Hammurabi.

The governance of Canaan

Abraham's story truly begins when his father, Terah, leaves Ur to go to Canaan:

Ge 11:31 And Terah took Abram his son, and Lot the son of Haran his son's son, and Sarai his daughter in law, his son Abram's wife; and they went forth with them from Ur of the Chaldees, to go into the land of Canaan; and they came unto Haran, and dwelt there.

If Terah was dispatched to Haran, a city located in the far northwest sector of the Babylonian empire, perhaps he may have already been appointed to govern this remote region. If this were the case, Abraham would have been in an excellent position to learn the basics of diplomacy from his father. Once the situation in the area stabilized, this experience would most certainly have made him an excellent ambassador in the expansion of the empire.

The Bible tells us that Abraham was directed to Canaan. At this point, there was no mention of an alliance *per se*. He was simply promised a bright future:

Ge 12:1 Now Baal had said unto Abram, Get thee out of thy country, and from thy kindred, and from thy father's house, unto a land that I will show thee:*

Ge 12:2 And I will make of thee a great nation, and I will bless thee, and make thy name great; and thou shalt be a blessing:

The above two verses could very well represent a challenge to the proposed deification hypothesis as it is difficult to explain how "*Baal*" would have talked to Abram prior to engaging on the battlefield… It is nevertheless possible that a) *Baal* was related to Abraham and knew him beforehand b) it was a different *Baal* that spoke with him (as *Baal* simply means lord) or c) that it wasn't *Baal*, but rather Elohim that appeared to Abraham in a vision or an omen. However, given hindsight is always 20/20, the most logical explanation for these two verses might be that they have been introduced at a later date, in order to support the theological view.

---

* Yahweh in the Bible

Lot settles near Sodom

A severe drought in Canaan brings Abraham and his family to head south, and settle in the fertile region of the Delta for some time. We learn that Abram was already a rich man.

> *Ge 13:1 And Abram went up out of Egypt, he, and his wife, and all that he had, and Lot with him, into the south.*

> *Ge 13:2 And Abram was very rich in cattle, in silver, and in gold.*

Given Lot and Abram had sizeable herds to feed with pasture, Abram offers to separate:

> *Ge 13:9 Is not the whole land before thee? separate thyself, I pray thee, from me: if thou wilt take the left hand, then I will go to the right; or if thou depart to the right hand, then I will go to the left.*

> *Ge 13:10 And Lot lifted up his eyes, and beheld all the plain of Jordan, that it was well watered every where, before Baal* destroyed Sodom and Gomorrah, even as the garden of Baal*, like the land of Egypt, as thou comest unto Zoar.*

Although their construction only started in the first millennium BCE, the hanging gardens of Babylon were one of the Seven Wonders of the Ancient World. As previously seen, and much like Egypt, the area was already fertile during the Bronze Age, as testified by the mythical reference to the Garden of Eden and thanks to many irrigation works.

> *Ge 13:12 Abram dwelled in the land of Canaan, and Lot dwelled in the cities of the plain, and pitched his tent toward Sodom.*

The region of Sodom was thus fertile and only suffered occasional periods of drought. If Lot knew that the people of Sodom were truly wicked and sinners, why would he have chosen to settle in this valley?[209]

---

* Yahweh in the Bible
[209] It is very likely that verses Ge 13:13-18 are either late editorial additions aimed at

No trace of Sodom and Gomorrah has ever been found. Tradition places these cities in the south of the Dead Sea, in a deserted and salty area not far away from modern *Jebel Usdum*. Rast and Shaub have led significant digs in this area that unearthed the ruins of two cities, *Bad edh-Dhra* and *Numeira* — two possible candidates for Sodom and Gomorrah. [210] However, these cities, and other suggested ones, were reportedly destroyed at the end of the Early Bronze Age, some hundreds of years before Hammurabi. The only matching evidence seems to be the known presence of bitumen on the eastern side of the Dead Sea.[211]

The War of Kings

Abraham's story quickly progresses to what is often presented as an anecdotal event in regards to the traditional theological teachings: the War of Kings.

As seen before, the Bible tells us that the city of Sodom was "attacked" on two occasions. During the first attack, four Eastern kings sought to repress the people of Sodom. Since they were only partially successful, retaliation would be expected. But, strangely enough, it was by God's "fire and brimstone" that the inhabitants of Sodom were destroyed for not respecting "divine" laws and for committing homosexuality.

It seems that the destruction of Sodom had nothing to do with divine intervention but, rather, that these two events addressed the same commercial needs, namely the importance of collecting taxes, and of controlling the territory's resources and ensuring their free circulation throughout the empire.

The description of the first battle, commonly called the War of Kings, can be summarized as follows:

---

reinforcing the divine theology; or that they originally belonged to Chapter 15 or 17, both of which describe the actual terms of the Covenant. See the section entitled "Lost tablets".
[210] Hattem, Willem C. Van. 1981. "Once Again: Sodom and Gomorrah." *The Biblical Archaeologist* 44(2): 87-92. p. 87-88
[211] Forbes, Robert James. 1936. *Bitumen and Petroleum in Antiquity.* Leiden: E.J. Brill. p. 16

During twelve years, Chedorlaomer, king of Elam, kept the distant cities of Sodom and Gomorrah in a state of servitude (Ge 14:4). When their residents rose up against him, threatening to jeopardize the trade route with Egypt, Chedorlaomer convinced his allies, Amraphel, Arioch and Tidal, to help him suppress this rebellion. The four kings sacked the two cities and abducted a number of their inhabitants, including Lot, Abraham's nephew (Ge 14:12).

Upon learning this news, Abraham pursued the attackers and smote them, recovering the plunder and releasing the prisoners (Ge 14:16). Melchizedek celebrated the victory by blessing and thanking Abraham (Ge 14:23).

Did these four kings who attacked Sodom and Gomorrah really exist? How does this story fit into our analysis?

Let's analyze the story in detail in order to grasp its full meaning:

> *Ge 14:1 And it came to pass in the days of Amraphel king of Shinar, Arioch king of Ellasar, Chedorlaomer king of Elam, and Tidal king of nations;*

> *Ge 14:2 That these made war with Bera king of Sodom, and with Birsha king of Gomorrah, Shinab king of Admah, and Shemeber king of Zeboiim, and the king of Bela, which is Zoar.*

> *Ge 14:3 All these were joined together in the vale of Siddim, which is the salt sea.*

> *Ge 14:4 Twelve years they served Chedorlaomer, and in the thirteenth year they rebelled.*

The real motive for this first war is clear: to suppress all signs of rebellion.

After twelve years of servitude, the king of Sodom and his allies revolted in an attempt to deliver their people to freedom, but retaliation soon followed:

> *Ge 14:5 And in the fourteenth year came Chedorlaomer, and the kings that were with him, and smote the Rephaim in*

Ashteroth Karnaim, and the Zuzims in Ham, and the Emins in Shaveh Kiriathaim,

Ge 14:8 And there went out the king of Sodom, and the king of Gomorrah, and the king of Admah, and the king of Zeboiim, and the king of Bela (the same is Zoar;) and they joined battle with them in the vale of Siddim;

Ge 14:9 With Chedorlaomer the king of Elam, and with Tidal king of nations, and Amraphel king of Shinar, and Arioch king of Ellasar; four kings with five.

Can Amraphel, Arioch, Chedorlaomer and Tidal correspond to men who lived in the 18th century BCE?

Although most modern scholars have now given up on trying to identify these men, no one has been able to offer a decisive rebuttal. In Ge 14:1, the Bible says that Amraphel was the king of Shinar, and it correctly describes the region of Sumer in Ge 10:10. This is why some are still keen to identify Amraphel as Hammurabi, thereby agreeing with late professors Eberhard Schrader and Fritz Hommel.[212] According to the latter, the name Hammurabi comes from Hamu(m)-rabi, meaning "my family is widespread". A more recent tablet mentions "Ammurapi", which more closely resembles the Amraphel found in the Bible. To some experts, the final "l" is difficult to explain, but it most likely represents the divinity "el", attached to the name *Ammurapi-ilu*.[213] Van De Mieroop also confirms that the name *Hammurabi-ili*, meaning *"Hammurabi is my god"*, appeared during Hammurabi's lifetime.

Although some early biblical scholars had come to accept the idea that Hammurabi could have been involved in this war, none has ever proposed that he was also Abraham's "lord", a fact we will try to demonstrate by the unfolding of events.

What about the three other kings? There are two possibilities for Arioch. According to inscriptions found at Gasur/Nuzi he could

---

[212] Pinches, Theophilus G. 2002. *The Old Testament in the Light of the Historical Records and Legends of Assyria and Babylonia*. New York: Elibron Classics. (Orig. pub. 1902.). p. 209
[213] Ibid. p. 211

have been the Hurrian king Ariukki, who also ruled during the 18[214] century BCE.[214] However, we will see that "Eriaku, king of Larsa", generally associated with Rim-Sin, who reigned from 1822-1763, does appear to be a more likely candidate for "Arioch, king of Ellasar".[215]

As for Tidal, he could have been the Hittite king Tudhaliya, great-grandfather of Hattusili I, who also reigned during the 18th century BCE.[216] In fact, several Hittite kings bore the same name. Since the Hittites and the Amorites maintained close ties throughout history, it's not surprising that Tidal and Hammurabi may have had contact.

Finally, there is very little information to identify Chedorlaomer.[217] At best, this name could be a transliteration of "Kudur-Lagamar", a reference to Lagamaru, an Elamite deity mentioned by Assurbanipal. This link would confirm that the name truly came from the region of Elam. However, the king of Elam during Hammurabi's time was Siwe-Palar-Khuppak.[218] If we are to believe the Bible, Chedorlaomer would simply be another name for Siwe-Palar-Khuppak (or his successor, Kuduzulush I, who could have fought this war in the name of Siwe-Palar-Khuppak).

But, why did the powerful Hammurabi need the support of three other kings in this venture? And, why were the people of Sodom vassals to Chedorlaomer and not Hammurabi?

---

[214] Freedman, David Noel , Allen C. Myers and Astrid B. Beck. 2000. *Eerdmans Dictionary of the Bible.* Grand Rapids: W.B. Eerdmans. p. 100

[215] Van De Mieroop, Marc. 2005. *King Hammurabi of Babylon: a Biography.* Malden: Blackwell p. 31
Bromiley, Geoffrey William. 1979. *The International Standard Bible Encyclopedia.* Grand Rapids: W.B. Eerdmans. p. 127
Arendzen, John. 1907. *The Catholic Encyclopoedia.* New York: Robert Appleton Company.

[216] Pinches, Theophilus G. 2002. *The Old Testament in the Light of the Historical Records and Legends of Assyria and Babylonia.* New York: Elibron Classics. (Orig. pub. 1902.). p. 366
Hoffner, Harry A., Gary M. Beckman, Richard Henry Beal and John Gregory Mcmahon. 2003. *Hittite Studies In Honor of Harry A. Hoffner Jr.* Winona Lake: Eisenbrauns. pp. 16, 20

[217] Pinches, Theophilus G. 2002. *The Old Testament in the Light of the Historical Records and Legends of Assyria and Babylonia.* New York: Elibron Classics. (Orig. pub. 1902.). p. 209

[218] Crew, P. Mack, I. E. S. Edwards, J.B. Bury, C. J. Gadd, Nicholas Geoffrey, N. G. L. Hammond and Edmond Sollberger. 1973. *History of the Middle East and the Aegean Region c.1800-1380 B.C.* Vol. 2 of *The Cambridge Ancient History.* Cambridge: Cambridge University Press. p. 265

Recall that, during the first 25 years of his reign, Hammurabi focused primarily on improving local infrastructures and only began expanding his kingdom in the later years of his reign. If this war took place at the beginning of, or just after, the expansion of his kingdom, that is, before he became so powerful, then it's only natural that he would seek out allies for a military operation. However, the history books tell us that before the expansion of the Babylonian empire by Hammurabi, the king of Elam was—or considered himself to be—more powerful than the king of Babylon. It would therefore not be surprising that the distant cities of Sodom and Gomorrah were under Elam's yoke—despite the lack of archaeological evidence suggesting this.

Following the major offensive by this foreign coalition, the kings of Sodom and Gomorrah fled, abandoning their spoils—and Lot, Abraham's nephew—to their attackers:

> Ge 14:10 And the vale of Siddim was full of slime pits[219]; and the kings of Sodom and Gomorrah fled, and fell there; and they that remained fled to the mountain.

Bitumen, used for boats, lighting and home construction, was a highly coveted resource at the time[220], one that those in power sought to control. Bitumen is to this day a valuable commodity.

Some scholars suggests that the kings of Sodom and Gomorrah must have died, but as the author is not explicit, it seems equally reasonable to conclude that terrified, they took refuge in an area full of tar pits and holed up[221] there to escape the massacre.

> Ge 14:11 And they took all the goods of Sodom and Gomorrah, and all their victuals, and went their way.

> Ge 14:12 And they took Lot, Abram's brother's son, who dwelt in Sodom, and his goods, and departed.

---

[219] Hebrew חמר- bitumen, asphalt (Strong H2564 - chemar)
[220] Lurton Burke, Madeleine and Paule Jarre-Chardin. 1963. *Dictionnaire archéologique des techniques: (1-2. A- Z)*. Paris: Éditions de l'Accueil.
Forbes, Robert James. 1936. *Bitumen and Petroleum in Antiquity*. Leiden: E.J. Brill. p. 23
[221] As the case is not clear, it may be wise to compare the Hewbrew verb naphal with the Assyrian verb palāhu that offers similar consonance through the assimilation of the nan ןat perfect tense H (yi-pelu). The term palāhu is employed in the sense of fear, of being terrified and of being reverent.

Once Abraham learned that his nephew, Lot, was among the prisoners, he sprang into action, amassing an army and heading off in pursuit of the four kings.

> *Ge 14:13 And there came one that had escaped, and told Abram the Hebrew; for he dwelt in the plain of Mamre the Amorite, brother of Eshcol, and brother of Aner: and these were confederate with Abram.*

> *Ge 14:14 And when Abram heard that his brother was taken captive, he armed his trained servants, born in his own house, three hundred and eighteen, and pursued them unto Dan.*

For Abraham to have had access to a few hundred men "trained" and "born in his own house", he was obviously a very powerful man.

> *Ge 14:15 And he divided himself against them, he and his servants, by night, and smote them, and pursued them unto Hobah, which is on the left hand of Damascus.*

> *Ge 14:16 And he brought back all the goods, and also brought again his brother Lot, and his goods, and the women also, and the people.*

But, if the Sodomites had truly sinned in God' eyes, why didn't Abraham simply content himself with rescuing his nephew, Lot? Why did he so generously return the stolen goods?

> *Ge 14:17 And the king of Sodom went out to meet him after his return from the slaughter of Chedorlaomer, and of the kings that were with him, at the valley of Shaveh, which is the king's dale.*

> *Ge 14:18 And Melchizedek king of Salem brought forth bread and wine: and he was the priest of Most High God.*

In his capacity as "priest of the Most High God", the mysterious Melchizedek is puzzling to many believers, since traditional theology describes him as a high-ranking official who already accepted and served the "new" god of Abraham. But, if Abraham was indeed the father of a new religion, how could Melchizedek have already been a priest of this faith?

"Most High" is a translation from the Hebrew *Elyon*, which could also be a proper name. It is therefore more likely that Melchizedek is instead a priest of the pagan god *Elyon*. In fact, it has been shown earlier that the concept of "sacrifice" was already very deeply rooted in local pagan rites.

> *Ge 14:19 And he blessed him, and said, Blessed be Abram of the Most High God, possessor of heaven and earth:*

> *Ge 14:20 And blessed be the Most High God, which hath delivered thine enemies into thy hand. And he gave him tithes of all.*

After congratulations for Abraham's victory, thanks are given to the god Elyon and his priest.

> *Ge 14:21 And the king of Sodom said unto Abram, Give me the persons, and take the goods to thyself.*

> *Ge 14:22 And Abram said to the king of Sodom, I have lift up mine hand unto Baal*, the most high Elohim, the possessor of heaven and earth,*

> *Ge 14:23 That I will not take from a thread even to a shoe-latchet, and that I will not take any thing that is thine, lest thou shouldest say, I have made Abram rich:*

> *Ge 14:24 Save only that which the young men have eaten, and the portion of the men which went with me, Aner, Eshcol, and Mamre; let them take their portion.*

As seen before, Ge 14:22 is important because this passage is traditionally interpreted as Abraham lifting up his hand to his God and swearing that he will never attempt to profit from the Sodomites. However, this interpretation warrants questioning, since even the king of Sodom believes that this campaign deserves a just reward (Ge 14:21).

Given the military context it appears far more appropriate to interpret the expression "lift up one's hand" as having its usual aggressive meaning of "to smite"? In fact, the image of the hand to

---

* Yahweh in the Bible

describe use of force is pervasive in the Bible and other ancient texts.

Abraham clearly is the hero of the day. Not only did he save his nephew Lot, but he also saved the inhabitants of Sodom by *raising his hand* on the foreign kings. This is why Westermann raises the all-important question:

> *... should the victorious liberator establish a dynasty for himself out of the struggle or not?*[222]

to which Glissmann responds :

> *Abram, being the hero of the people, could easily crown himself, yet he refused to establish any political or governmental hold on the land. Perhaps, as the war hero, he could have become the predominant leader of an alliance of Canaanite city-states.*[223]

While Abraham may have refused to establish a political hold on the land, evidence shows he most likely entered a local covenant with the King of Sodom, much like he had already done with his allies Aner, Eschkol and Mamre (Ge 14:13). The role of *Melchizedek* sheds important light on this question. The Hebrew transliteration for "King of Salem" (מלך שלם) is *mlk šlm*. However, the Masoretic vocalization is subject of much debate because Salem can hardly be associated with Jerusalem.[224] The very same *mlk slm* consonants can be read *milki šalim*, which in Assyrian means "advisor of peace".[225] Even the name *Melchizedek* (מלכי־צדק) is quite telling as it literally means "my King (is) righteous". It then becomes quite evident from this new context that *Melchizedek* is acting as a peace advisor, whose role is to

---

[222] Westermann, Claus. 1995. *Genesis 12-36.* Minneapolis: Fortress Press. (Orig. pub. 1985.). p. 201

[223] Glissmann, Volker. 2009. "Genesis 14: A Diaspora Novella?" *Journal for the Study of the Old Testament* 34(1): 33-45. p. 41

[224] Elgavish, David. 1999. The Encounter of Abram and Melchizedek King of Salem: A Covenant Establishing Ceremony. In *Studies in the Book of Genesis : Literature, Redaction and History,* ed. Wénin, André, 495-508. Leuven; Paris; Sterling: Leuven University Press ; Uitgeverij Peeters.

[225] Oppenheim, A. Leo and Erica Reiner. 1999. *The Assyrian Dictionary of the Oriental Institute of the University of Chicago* 27. Chicago: Oriental Institute.

officiate a covenant between Abraham and the righteous King of Sodom.

On the topic of the tithe (Ge 14:20), the Hebrew syntax is also ambiguous. And despite most translations claiming Abraham is giving the tithe to *Melchizedek*, there is no such evidence in the Hebraic text, as it simply says:

ויתן־לו מעשר מכל

And he gave him tithes of all.

When considering the plot leading to this sequence of events, wouldn't one naturally expect to find *Melchizedek* offering Abraham the tenth of the returned Sodomite possessions, for which the later had just risked his life?

The last few verses depict a negotiation. It is useful to compare the structure of this dialog with the purchase of the cave of Machpelah in Ge 23 as can be seen in the following table:

Comparison of two public negotiations	
The goods of Sodom	The cave of Machpelah
Step 1 – Acknowledge status of acquirer The owner of the goods acknowledges the status of the acquirer by making a very generous offer	
Ge 14:21 And the king of Sodom said unto Abram, Give me the persons, and take the goods to thyself.	Ge 23:11 No, my lord: hear me. The field give I thee; and the cave that is in it, to thee I give it; before the eyes of the sons of my people give I it thee: bury thy dead.
Step 2 - Balance of power: The acquirer establishes his position in the eyes of the witnesses	

Ge 14:22 And Abram said to the king of Sodom, I have lift up mine hand unto *Baal*, the most high *Elohim*, the possessor of heaven and earth,	Ge 23:12 And Abraham bowed down before the people of the land; Ge 23:13 and he spoke to Ephron, in the ears of the people of the land, saying,
Step 3 – Acknowledge generosity of owner: The acquirer pretends to be insulted as accepting such a generous offer would make an abuser of him.	
Ge 14:23 That I will not take from a thread even to a shoelatchet, and that I will not take any thing that is thine, lest thou shouldest say, I have made Abram rich:	But if only thou wouldst listen to me, I give the money for the field: take it of me, and I will bury my dead there.
Step 4 - Fair proposal: A fair offer is made.	
Ge 14:24 Save only that which the young men have eaten, and the portion of the men which went with me,	Ge 23:14 And Ephron answered Abraham, saying to him, Ge 23:15 My lord, hearken to me. A field of four hundred shekels of silver, what is that between me and thee? bury therefore thy dead.
Step 5 - Conclusion: The settlement.	
Aner, Eshcol, and Mamre; let them take their portion.	Ge 23:16 And Abraham hearkened to Ephron; and Abraham weighed to Ephron the money that he had named in the ears of the sons of Heth -- four hundred shekels of silver, current with the merchant.

In the end, Abraham feels he has already been treated fairly by receiving the tithe. Only his allies will take their part.

In summary

- There were two attacks upon Sodom. The first was motivated by purely commercial reasons. But, according to traditional theology, the second was an act of "God". It seems more logical that both attacks were driven by the same motivations.

- The people of Sodom and Gomorrah revolted after 12 years of servitude under Chedorlaomer.

- Amraphel, Arioch and Tidal allied with Chedorlaomer to suppress them, fleeing with plunder and prisoners.

- These kings may have been, respectively, Hammurabi, Eriaku (Rim-Sin), Tudhaliya and Siwe-Palar-Khuppak, who all lived during the 18th century BCE.

- Abraham amassed an army of 318 men and went after the kings with his allies. He "struck" *Baal* and recovered the prisoners and the goods of Sodom.

- In the traditional interpretation, the expression "I have lift up mine hand unto" is taken literally as meaning "I swear", but wouldn't it be more logical to understand it as the idiom "I struck him"?

- Melchizedek blesses Abraham and officiates a local covenant with the righteous King of Sodom.

- Melchizedek gives Abraham a tenth the recovered goods

- The king of Sodom shows extreme gratitude towards Abraham, but the later prefers not to take advantage of the situation.

Hammurabi's rise to power

It seems that the War of Kings was only a prelude to Hammurabi's rise to power. Here is how events might have taken place:

> Upon returning to Babylon after participating in the War of Kings, Hammurabi faces a conspiracy: Chedorlaomer, the king of Elam, is attempting to overthrow him. A talented diplomat, Hammurabi allies with the king of Larsa to outwit this conspirator. However, this ally is undependable and Hammurabi gets rid of him. Swept up into the battle against his will, Hammurabi expands his control over the neighboring kingdoms, thus laying the foundations for the Babylonian empire.

Does this hypothesis mesh with what history teaches us?

After inheriting the throne, Hammurabi easily conquered the nearby kingdoms of Isin and Uruk (1786). He then turned his attention to improving the kingdom's infrastructures; it was only much later, during the 26th year of his reign, that he embarked on expansionist campaigns, no doubt following the maneuvers instigated by the king of Elam. During the 28th year of his reign, Hammurabi defeated Elam, and in his 29th year, he conquered Larsa after the defeat of RimSin (Eriaku). Continuing his expansion efforts, he seized the kingdoms of Assur and Mari to create the Babylonian empire, earning himself the prestigious title of "king of the four quarters of the world".[226]

The following dates are those taught to us by history:[227]

---

[226] Van De Mieroop, Marc. 2005. *King Hammurabi of Babylon: a Biography.* Malden: Blackwell
[227] Magill, Frank Northen. 1992. *Great Events from History II: Human Rights.* Pasadena: Salem Press. p. 2169

Event	Date	Year
Hammurabi is born	-1810	-18
Hammurabi becomes king of Babylon	-1792	0
Hammurabi conquers the kingdoms of Isin and Uruk	-1786	8
Period corresponding to the improvement of local infrastructures: 1786-1767		
The kingdom of Elam rules over the neighbouring plains	-1767	25
Hammurabi defeats the king of Elam	-1764	28
Hammurabi conquers the kingdom of Larsa (Rim-Sin)	-1763	29
Hammurabi conquers the kingdom of Mari	-1761	31
Hammurabi's Code is written (approximate date)	-1760	32
Hammurabi dies	-1750	42

Now, let's see how these dates compare to the information in the Bible.

Source	Event	Bible	6/10
Ge 12:4	Abraham's age when he leaves Haran (enters Canaan)	75	45
Period corresponding to the War of Kings: age 45-52			

Ge 16:16	Abraham's age at Ishmael's birth	86	52
Ge 17:25	Age difference between Ishmael and Isaac	14	8
Ge 17:17	Sarah's age at Isaac's birth	90	54
Ge 21:5	Abraham's age at Isaac's birth	100	60
Period corresponding to the ordered sacrifice of Ishmael: age 60-76			
Ge 23:1	Sarah's life span	127	76
Ge 25:07	Abraham's life span	175	105

Based on the timeline of the biblical story, we can deduce that the War of Kings took place after Abraham arrived in Canaan, but before the birth of Ishmael. Abraham would have been between the ages of 45 and 52 at the time.

By comparing Abraham's genealogy against the Amorites' rise to power in Mesopotamia, we discovered earlier that Abraham and Hammurabi were most likely contemporaries.

From a biblical point of view, we know that the War of Kings could not have taken place before Abraham arrived in Canaan, when he was 45 years old. If Abraham was born in 1810, we could date his arrival in Canaan in 1765 (= 1810 - 45).[228] And, since this war took place before the birth of Ishmael, it could not have carried on after the latter event. Since Abraham was 52 when Ishmael was born, this war should have ended before 1758 (= 1810 - 52). Therefore, if Abraham was born in 1810, the War of Kings would have taken place between 1765 and 1758.[229]

---

[228] It is necessary to subtract instead of add, because the period covering these events took place before the common era (BCE).

[229] Note that Hammurabi's reign dates are presented here as absolute dates based on middle chronology. This facilitates anchoring relationships across multiple generations. For the most part, this absolute reference can move without affecting our demonstration.

The years 1765 and 1758 correspond to the 27th and 34th years, respectively, of Hammurabi's reign, a period during which the ruler was expanding his empire.

While Elam may have allied with its adversaries in the War of Kings in the unprofessed goal of later attacking them, history does confirm that Hammurabi defeated the king of Elam in 1764. Existing information about Rim-Sin (Eriaku) points to a link with Arioch. In fact, in order for RimSin to fight in this war, it must have taken place before his 1763 defeat by Hammurabi. Since this defeat is well documented, this information seems reliable enough to be used. This further reduces the range of possibilities and allows us to date this war in 1764, or the 28th year of Hammurabi's reign.

While the resulting margin of error is very slim, it fits perfectly with the historical data. We will see that the conclusions related to this war and to the period in which it took place cannot deviate significantly.

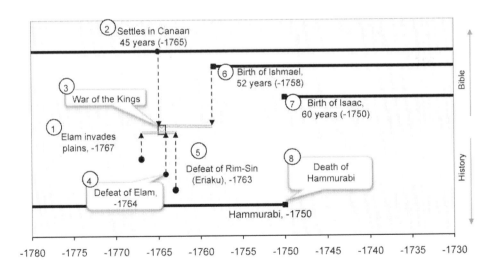

46: The War of Kings

Postulating that Abraham and Hammurabi were born in the same year, that is 1810, opens a very small window of possibilities for the War of Kings (3): Abraham had to be between the ages of 45 (2) and 52 (6). For his part, Hammurabi could only have been involved after the start of the new conquests by Elam (1) but before the latter's defeat (4) and the capture of Rim-Sin (Eriaku) (5).

In summary

- Hammurabi began his expansionist efforts only around the 25th year of his reign, following provocation by the kingdom of Elam.

- The king of Elam could not have participated in this war alongside Hammurabi after his defeat, which took place during the 28th year of his reign.

- Eriaku (Rim-Sin) could not have participated in this war alongside Hammurabi after his defeat, which took place during the 29th year of his reign.

- Abraham was 45 when he arrived in Canaan and 52 at the birth of Ishmael, resulting in a seven-year window during which he could have engaged in this war.

- If Abraham had been born six years earlier or one year later, he could not have been involved in a war with Hammurabi, since the chronologies would no longer line up. This means that he must have been born between 1816 and 1809. The rest of the story will corroborate that both men were in fact born c. 1810.

An everlasting treaty

Most historians would probably argue that Hammurabi's reach never extended over the Levant. However, the absence of evidence does not mean it didn't happen or that he wasn't influential over the region. We know his influence extended all the way up in the North, near Aleppo, but given he was at odds with the local kings it is unlikely he would have taken that route. It is therefore far more probable that he would have crossed through the desert via either *Ar-Rutbah* or *Tadmor* (modern day *Palmyra*), two oases situated halfway between Babylon and Damascus. While *Ar-*

Rutbah would appear as a better option, little is known about it during the Bronze Age. And while one can surmise that this oasis was already known back then, it is not certain. The *Tadmor* oasis, on the other hand, was already clearly attested in the early second millennium BC as a caravan stop for travelers crossing the Syrian Desert.[230] This main trade route would eventually become instrumental in connecting the Levant to the famous Silk Road.[231] It required several weeks of walk through the desert to cross, and this is why the *Tadmor* oasis represented such a critical rest area.

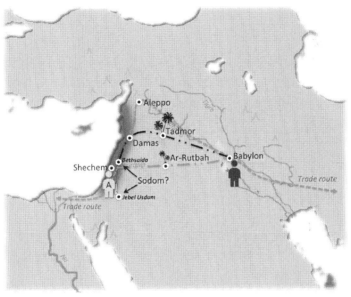

47: Trade route between Babylon and Canaan

Following the defeat of Chedorlaomer, Hammurabi either seized control or exerted greater influence over Elam's far-off territories, which, according to Ge 14 in the Bible, included Sodom (סדום) and Gomorrah (עמורה). Considering the information in the Bible, it would seem that Sodom's description of Ge 13:10, portraying a flourishing and luxuriant valley, would better fit that of the New

[230] Stoneman, Richard. 1994. *Palmyra and its Empire : Zenobia's revolt against Rome.* Ann Arbor: University of Michigan Press. p. 54
[231] Gardner, Chris and BaşAk GüNer Gardner. 2014. *Flora of the Silk Road : an illustrated guide.* p. 145

Testament city of (בית צידה) *Bethsaida* ("House of Saida") that was located in the northern mouth of lake Tiberia.[232] This fertile valley extends all the way up to Damascus (Damas) to the north, and corresponds precisely to the route taken by the Four Eastern Kings on their way back home; where Abram and his men intercepted them.

Either way, Hammurabi would have certainly sought to turn this far away region over to a trusted individual, as it is difficult to believe that such a powerful man would not even look after this key region for trade. Having to deal with an unpredictable and rebellious Sodom on this important trade route would further justify the need to keep it under control.

No doubt impressed by Abraham's military skills, as well as the courage, loyalty and honor he showed in rescuing Lot, Hammurabi knew that rather than try to oppose him it was wisest to negotiate a solid agreement with this valuable man and to secure his absolute loyalty.

In *The Bible Unearthed*, archaeologists Israel Finkelstein and Neil Asher Silberman describe a 19th century BCE Egyptian carving that recounts the exploits of a general named Khu-Sebek and attests to the existence of the "lands" of Shechem and Hebron—the two main cities where Abraham lived. The authors point out that Shechem was already the economic seat of a vast territory.[233]

Hammurabi knew that he needed a strong ally in the region and that such an alliance was crucial to ensuring stable relations and trade routes between Sumer and Egypt.

> *Ge 15:1 After these things the word of Yahweh came unto Abram in a vision (חזה)[234], saying, Fear not, Abram: I am thy shield, and thy exceeding great reward.*

---

[232] This suggestion is made based on the geographical location, description and phonetic similarities between Sodom, Siddim and Saida. It is also much closer to Shechem, where Abram settled after his separation with Lot.

[233] Finkelstein, Israel and Neil Asher Silberman. 2001. *The Bible Unearthed: Archaeology's New Vision of Ancient Israel and the Origin of its Sacred Texts*. New York: Free Press. p. 155

[234] Hebrew (חזה) chozeh ("seer"), but can also read chazah ("see", "behold")

In this case, the term "vision", (חזה) *chozeh* "seer", but also *chazah* ("see", "behold"), should be understood as meaning a message on a tablet revealed by a scribe, rather than a "divine inspiration", as suggested by the traditional theological interpretation. In Assyrian, the word *rēṣu* shares the same root and means "helper" or "supporter"[235], which is exactly what a scribe would be expected to do.[236]

> *Ge 15:7 And he said unto him, I am Baal* that brought thee out of Ur of the Chaldees, to give thee this land to inherit it.*
>
> ...
>
> *Ge 15:18 In the same day Baal* made a covenant with Abram, saying, Unto thy seed have I given this land, from the river of Egypt unto the great river, the river Euphrates:*
>
> *Ge 15:19 The Kenites, and the Kenizzites, and the Kadmonites,*
>
> *Ge 15:20 And the Hittites, and the Perizzites, and the Rephaim,*
>
> *Ge 15:21 And the Amorites, and the Canaanites, and the Girgashites, and the Jebusites.*

While, to some Zionists, this alliance represented the "classic" expanded territory, there is no mention of the region of Shinhar (Sumer). Since his goal was simply to expand his influence over far-off lands, Hammurabi would never have entrusted the immediate territory over which he reigned to a governor. Instead, his objective was to expand his influence beyond his borders.

More details can be found a little further on:

> *Ge 17:8 And I will give unto thee, and to thy seed after thee, the land wherein thou art a stranger, all the land of*

---

[235] Biggs, Robert D., John A. Brinkman, Miguel Civil, Walter Farber, Ignace J. Gelb, A. Leo Oppenheim, Erica Reiner, Martha T. Roth and Matthew W. Stolper. 1999. *The Assyrian dictionary of the Oriental Institute of the University of Chicago.* Vol. 14 of. Chicago: The Oriental Institute, University of Chicago. p.268
[236] The Hebrew Het, transliterated as « ch » is a voiceless pharyngeal fricative that has a pronunciation similar to « r »
* Yahweh in the Bible
* Yahweh in the Bible

Canaan, for an everlasting possession; and I will be their Elohim.

Ge 17:9 And Elohim said, Sarah thy wife shall bear thee a son indeed; and thou shalt call his name Isaac: and I will establish my covenant with him for an everlasting covenant, and with his seed after him.

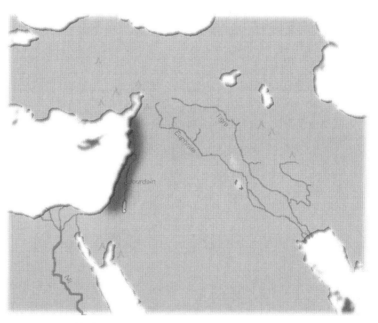

48: The Promised Land of the Covenant

It seems realistic to limit this covenant to the region of Canaan in the Levant, which corresponds to the description *"from the river of Egypt unto the great river, the river Euphrates"* and which was not directly controlled by Hammurabi.

The "Promised Land" would therefore be the territory managed by Abraham and his descendants, over which the tribes of Israel would attempt to regain control after the Exodus.

By securing this buffer zone, Hammurabi would have brought greater stability to the region. Abraham would have been charged with enforcing and applying his code of law and with collecting taxes.

The birth of Ishmael

Accordingly, Hammurabi offered his protection to Abraham in exchange for his loyalty. But, we still need to resolve the question of the legitimacy of the bloodline, since the Covenant between Abraham and Hammurabi would have been virtually meaningless without a legitimate and recognized heir. As such, it was important to make a pact that would transcend generations and guarantee stability in the region.

> *Ge 15:2 And Abram said, Baal* Elohim, what wilt thou give me, seeing I go childless, and the steward of my house is this Eliezer of Damascus?*

> *Ge 15:3 And Abram said, Behold, to me thou hast given no seed: and, lo, one born in my house is mine heir.*

> *Ge 15:4 And, behold, the word of Baal* came unto him, saying, This shall not be thine heir; but he that shall come forth out of thine own bowels shall be thine heir.*

Abraham never had any children with his wife, Sarah. We learn from his encounter with Abimelech about the true nature of his relationship with his half-sister:

> *Ge 20:12 And yet indeed she is my sister; she is the daughter of my father, but not the daughter of my mother; and she became my wife.*

By keeping the lineage within the same family, the practice of endogamy helps avoid inheritance claims by outside parties; this is why endogamy is common in royal families and other powerful clans.[237] Perhaps the consanguineous relationship between Abraham and his half-sister Sarah might have had a negative effect on the couple's fertility.

---

* Yahweh in the Bible
[237] Van Selms, A. 1954. *Marriage and Family Life in Ugaritic Literature.* London: Luzac. p. 18

As a result, Sarah suggests that Abraham produce an heir with a slave woman. At the time, it was acceptable practice for an infertile couple to use the "services" of a slave.

> *Ge 16:1 Now Sarai Abram's wife bare him no children: and she had an handmaid, an Egyptian, whose name was Hagar.*

> *Ge 16:2 And Sarai said unto Abram, Behold now, Elohim[238] hath restrained me from bearing: I pray thee, go in unto my maid; it may be that I may obtain children by her. And Abram hearkened to the voice of Sarai.*

> *Ge 16:3 And Sarai Abram's wife took Hagar her maid the Egyptian, after Abram had dwelt ten years in the land of Canaan, and gave her to her husband Abram to be his wife.*

> *Ge 16:4 And he went[239] in unto Hagar, and she conceived: and when she saw that she had conceived, her mistress was despised in her eyes.*

Since Abraham was 52 years old when Ishmael was born, we can deduce the lad was born in 1758, or eight years before Hammurabi's death. But, the child that Hagar bears for Abraham quickly becomes a source of dissent; the son of an Egyptian woman would indeed have been an unlikely candidate as heir to the Amorite dynasty.

> *Ge 16:5 And Sarai said unto Abram, My wrong be upon thee: I have given my maid into thy bosom; and when she saw that she had conceived, I was despised in her eyes: Baal* judge between me and thee.*

Hammurabi's Code contains a provision for just such a case:

> *§ 146. If a man has married a temple-woman and she has given a slave-girl to her husband and she has born sons, but afterwards that slave-girl takes over the position of her mistress because she has born sons, her mistress may not*

---

[238] Yahweh in the original text, but clearly refers to superstitions about God
[239] Hebrew (בא) bow' ("come", "go in"), means "to impregnate" in this context
* Yahweh in the Bible

sell her for silver. She shall put on her the mark of slavery and she shall be treated as a slave-girl.[240]

A child for Sarah

Hammurabi grants Abraham a few more years in which to produce an heir with Sarah, but unfortunately their blood relationship seems to have rendered them infertile. Seeing Sarah grow older, Hammurabi tells Abraham that he himself will father a child with her.

> *Ge 17:16 And I will bless her, and give thee a son also of her: yea, I will bless her, and she shall be a mother of nations; kings of people shall be of her.*

As a result, it is Sarah—and not Abraham—who produces the heir.

> *Ge 17:17 Then Abraham fell upon his face, and laughed, and said in his heart, Shall a child be born unto him that is an hundred years old? and shall Sarah, that is ninety years old, bear?*

This important passage tells us that Isaac's father was "an hundred years old", or rather, 60 years old (= 100 x 6/10). However, this verse can be interpreted in two very different ways:

- The traditional theological interpretation concludes that Abraham was "an hundred years old". Ge 21:5, announcing the birth of Isaac nine months later, confirms that Abraham was indeed this age at Isaac's birth, hence the source of the confusion.

- But, the proposed reinterpretation results in a very different conclusion. Since Abraham knows full well that Hammurabi is Isaac's genitor, then this verse is clearly referring to Hammurabi. Therefore, it is Hammurabi who is "an hundred years old" when he begets Isaac (100 x 6/10 = 60). Moreover, Ge 21:5 confirms that Abraham was also 100 years old at the time of Isaac's birth.

---

[240] Richardson, M. E. J. 2004. *Hammurabi's Laws: Text, Translation, and Glossary.* New York: Continuum International Publishing Group. p. 87

This interpretation is crucial, since it provides evidence that Abraham and Hammurabi were very likely the same age. If the latter was born in 1810, then Abraham was born the same year. Moreover, this cannot be a coincidence, since the timeline of numerous events confirms that Abraham was born c. 1810.

Realizing that Hammurabi is resolved to settle the matter himself, Abraham implores:

> Ge 17:18 And Abraham said unto Baal**, O that Ishmael might live before thee!

Clearly, Abraham is now worried about the fate of his son, Ishmael.

> Ge 17:19 And Baal** said, Sarah thy wife shall bear thee a son indeed; and thou shalt call his name Isaac: and I will establish my covenant with him for an everlasting covenant, and with his seed after him.

> Ge 17:20 And as for Ishmael, I have heard thee: Behold, I have blessed him, and will make him fruitful, and will multiply him exceedingly; twelve princes shall he beget, and I will make him a great nation.

> Ge 17:21 But my covenant will I establish with Isaac, which Sarah shall bear unto thee at this set time in the next year.

> Ge 17:22 And he left off talking with him, and Baal** went up from Abraham.

> Ge 17:23 And Abraham took Ishmael his son, and all that were born in his house, and all that were bought with his money, every male among the men of Abraham's house; and circumcised the flesh of their foreskin in the selfsame day, as Baal** had said unto him.

After Abraham agrees to seal the Covenant by being circumcised, Hammurabi inquires about Sarah.

> Ge 18:9 And they said unto him, Where is Sarah thy wife? And he said, Behold, in the tent.

** Elohim in the Bible

Ge 18:10 And he said, I will certainly return unto thee according to the time of life; and, lo, Sarah thy wife shall have a son. And Sarah heard it in the tent door, which was behind him.

Ge 18:11 Now Abraham and Sarah were old and well stricken in age; and it ceased to be with Sarah after the manner of women.

Ge 18:12 Therefore Sarah laughed within herself, saying, After I am waxed old shall I have pleasure, my lord being old also?

In Hebrew, verse 18:12 uses the word (אדני) *adonai* ("my lord", "my master")[241].

It is indeed Hammurabi who is insulted by Sarah questioning his virility.

Ge 18:13 And Baal* said unto Abraham, Wherefore did Sarah laugh, saying, Shall I of a surety bear a child, which am old?

Ge 18:14 Is any thing too hard for Baal*? At the time appointed I will return unto thee, according to the time of life, and Sarah shall have a son.

It is clear that this son will belong to Sarah, and not Abraham. The story continues a few verses later, although it appears that certain passages were transposed, as we will see later.

Ge 21:1 And Baal* visited[242] Sarah as he had said, and Baal* did unto Sarah as he had spoken.

Note the use of the euphemism "visit", which has the same meaning as the modern-day "went with", to signify "to impregnate".[243]

---

[241] Pronounce Adonai in English. It is interesting to note that this is also how the Tetragrammaton yhwh is to be pronounced in the rabbinic tradition (because His name is sacred and should not be pronounced out loud as "Yahweh").
* Yahweh in the Bible
[242] Hebrew (פָּקַד) paqad ("attend to", "visit", "muster", "appoint")
[243] See another example in Ge 16:4

Ge 21:2 For Sarah conceived, and bare Abraham a son in his old age, at the set time of which Baal** had spoken to him.

When interpreting theses verses from a theological perspective, one sees a miracle. However, the situation could not be clearer: Hammurabi visits Sarah in the tent and impregnates her. Isaac is born nine months later.

Ge 21:3 And Abraham called the name of his son that was born unto him, whom Sarah bare to him, Isaac.

Ge 21:4 And Abraham circumcised his son Isaac being eight days old, as Baal** had commanded him.

Ge 21:5 And Abraham was an hundred years old, when his son Isaac was born unto him.

Since Abraham was "an hundred years old" (100 x 6/10 = 60) when Isaac was born and since Hammurabi died in 1750, we can deduce that Hammurabi died during the year of Isaac's birth (= 1810-60). As a result, we cannot be certain that Hammurabi was still alive when Isaac was born.

The demise of Sodom

According to the traditional theological interpretation, God destroyed Sodom and Gomorrah to punish the "miscreants". But, why did "God" annihilate the city with such fury? Was it truly a coincidence that the city was annihilated shortly after Hammurabi and his allies suffered a humiliating defeat that left the rebel city unpunished? Or was it further evidence that Hammurabi, emboldened by a new covenant with Abraham, returned to Sodom to exert his authority over the still-rebellious inhabitants?

A quick review would be helpful to better understand the logical sequence of events.

As we saw earlier in the detailed analysis of the War of Kings, the four kings eventually retreated despite a successful "attack" against Sodom. Abraham pursued the king of Elam, Chedorlaomer, and his

---

allies, smote them and recovered the prisoners and the spoils, as well as his nephew, Lot. It was thanks to Abraham that the inhabitants of Sodom did not suffer a worse fate.

It seems that this defeat heralded Chedorlaomer's fall and Hammurabi's rise to power. No doubt, the kings of Sodom and of the distant territories of the Levant perceived this geopolitical reorganization of Mesopotamia as an ideal opportunity for emancipation.

However, the Covenant between Abraham and Hammurabi would enable the new king of Babylon to maintain his control over this distant region. The rumors drifting into Babylon confirmed that the unrest was threatening to engulf the entire area. As a result, it became a matter of urgency to organize a military campaign to crush any sign of an uprising; in short, Sodom had to be destroyed.[244]

At this point in the story, Hammurabi is campaigning and is preparing to annihilate the city. However, recalling Abraham's interests in this territory, he hesitates:

> Ge 18:16 And the men rose up from thence, and looked toward Sodom: and Abraham went with them to bring them on the way.

> Ge 18:17 And Baal* said, Shall I hide from Abraham that thing which I do;

> Ge 18:18 Seeing that Abraham shall surely become a great and mighty nation, and all the nations of the earth shall be blessed in him?

> Ge 18:19 For I know him, that he will command his children and his household after him, and they shall keep the way of Baal*, to do justice and judgment; that Baal* may bring upon Abraham that which he hath spoken of him.

---

[244] In the traditional chronological order of the Bible story, Sodom is obliterated after Isaac's birth. However, without affecting the value of this version, it seems that this event should logically have taken place earlier in the story, namely immediately after Abraham makes the Covenant. See the chapter on Isaac and the lost tablets for more on this topic.
* Yahweh in the Bible

Recall that in Ge 14, Melchizedek celebrated what can be understood as a covenant between Abraham and the King of Sodom. In light of the new covenant he has just made with Hammurabi, Abraham finds himself helpless. He therefore seeks a more diplomatic way of dissuading him from attacking his Sodomite ally. Aware of Hammurabi's sense of justice, he tries to reason with him: some of the city's residents still want to rise up (the wicked), while others (the righteous) are resigned to accepting the new king and his laws.

> *Ge 18:20 And Baal* said, Because the cry of Sodom and Gomorrah is great, and because their sin[245] is very grievous;*
>
> *Ge 18:21 I will go down now, and see whether they have done altogether according to the cry of it, which is come unto me; and if not, I will know.*
>
> *Ge 18:22 And the men turned their faces from thence, and went toward Sodom: but Abraham stood yet before Baal*.*

A skilled diplomat, Abraham knows that the excessive use of force risks giving the other cities a perception of ruthless central power. Would they also attempt to revolt?

> *Ge 18:23 And Abraham drew near, and said, Wilt thou also destroy the righteous[246] with the wicked[247]?*
>
> *Ge 18:24 Peradventure there be fifty righteous within the city: wilt thou also destroy and not spare the place for the fifty righteous that are therein?*
>
> *Ge 18:25 That be far from thee to do after this manner, to slay the righteous with the wicked: and that the righteous should be as the wicked, that be far from thee: Shall not the Judge of all the earth do right?*

Hammurabi is swayed by Abraham's arguments and promises not to destroy the city if he can find at least ten "righteous" ones. In

---

* Yahweh in the Bible

[245] Hebrew (חטא) chata' ("miss", "go wrong", "sin")

[246] Hebrew (צדיק) tsaddiyq ("just", "righteous")

[247] Hebrew (רשע) rasha` ("wicked", "criminal")

this context, the notions of "sin", "righteous" and "wicked" have no religious or moral connotations. The "righteous" accept this new authority, whereas the "wicked" reject it. In addition, the expressions "slay the wicked" and "the Judge of all the earth" fit perfectly with Hammurabi since they correspond to his description of himself in the prologue to his Code:

then Anu and Bel called by name me, Hammurabi, the exalted prince, who feared God, to bring about the rule of righteousness in the land, to destroy the wicked and the evil-doers; so that the strong should not harm the weak; so that I should rule over the black-headed people like Shamash, and enlighten the land, to further the well-being of mankind. [248]

Hammurabi then sends two messengers to inquire about the situation:

Ge 19:1 And there came two angels[249] to Sodom at even; and Lot sat in the gate of Sodom: and Lot seeing them rose up to meet them; and he bowed himself with his face toward the ground;

Ge 19:2 And he said, Behold now, my lords, turn in, I pray you, into your servant's house, and tarry all night, and wash your feet, and ye shall rise up early, and go on your ways. And they said, Nay; but we will abide in the street all night.

But, the rebels are aggressive with these strangers:

Ge 19:5 And they called unto Lot, and said unto him, Where are the men which came in to thee this night? bring them out unto us, that we may know them.

In this context, the verb (ידע) *yadā'* ("to know") is a euphemism meaning "to have sexual relations with".[250] But, far from seeking

[248] King, Leonard William. 1996. *The Code of Hammurabi*. Edition Richard hooker ed. Washington: Washington University. (Orig. pub. 1910.).
[249] Hebrew (מלאך) malach ("messenger"). The term "angel" comes from the Greek (ἄγγελος) angelos, meaning "messenger". The Pentateuch makes no mention of wings, which were added much later. See: 2008. *La Civiltà Cattolica* 3795-3796(2-16 August). pp. 327-328

carnal pleasure, it seems the inhabitants' goal was instead to humiliate these government representatives by forcing them into "submission", a state they themselves endured as vassals during twelve years.[251] Homosexuality was accepted and practiced in Sodom, as well as in most cities throughout Antiquity, including Babylon.[252]

> Ge 19:8 Behold now, I have two daughters which have not known man; let me, I pray you, bring them out unto you, and do ye to them as is good in your eyes: only unto these men do nothing; for therefore came they under the shadow of my roof.

> Ge 19:9 And they said, Stand back. And they said again, This one fellow came in to sojourn, and he will needs be a judge: now will we deal worse with thee, than with them. And they pressed sore upon the man, even Lot, and came near to break the door.

The villagers accuse Lot of being in league with Hammurabi and of wanting to enforce his laws.

> Ge 19:10 But the men put forth their hand, and pulled Lot into the house to them, and shut to the door.

What kind of man was Lot to offer up his daughters in sacrifice? While it appears he was only responding to higher political imperatives, the Sodomites wanted nothing to do with his daughters; what they wanted was their honor, freedom and independence. By "sodomizing" Hammurabi's messengers, their goal was to send a clear message in defiance of the central power to which they refused to submit.

Highly insulted by this affront, the messengers report back to their master on the state of the rebellion. Knowing it will be impossible to conquer the "wicked", Hammurabi realizes that he has no choice but to act forcefully. He urges Lot to flee with his family and destroys the city without further ado.

---

[250] Hamilton, Victor P. The Book of Genesis: Chapters 18-50. Grand Rapids: W.B. Eerdmans. p. 34
[251] War rapes have always been used as a way to humiliate the enemy.
[252] Greenberg, David F. 1988. *The Construction of Homosexuality*. Chicago: University of Chicago Press. p. 126

Ishmael poses a threat

As Isaac and Ishmael grow up, tension begins to mount in the household. No reason is given in the text as to why. The tradition tells us that Ishmael was a bad son, but there is no such evidence in the narratives.

But if Isaac has the "purer" bloodline, Ishmael is not only Abraham's real son, but also his firstborn, and, therefore, his legal heir. As such, Sarah, mother of the appointed heir, has every intention of protecting "her" son, Isaac, son of Hammurabi.

> *Ge 21:10 Wherefore she said unto Abraham, Cast out this bondwoman and her son: for the son of this bondwoman shall not be heir with my son, even with Isaac.*

> *Ge 21:11 And the thing was very grievous in Abraham's sight because of his son.*

Note that Hammurabi's Code clearly establishes the rights of heirs conceived with a slave girl:

> *§ 170. If the first wife of a man has borne him sons and also his slave-girl has borne him sons, and during his lifetime the father has said to the sons the slave-girl bore him, "My sons", they shall reckon them together with the first wife's sons. After the father has passed to his destiny the first wife's sons and the slave-girl's sons shall share out the treasures in the father's house equally. An heir, the son of a first wife, shall have the choice of which share to take.[253]*

Abraham is very attached to his only son and cannot bring himself to cast him out. But, Hammurabi lays down the rule. To reassure Abraham, he promises to take care of Ishmael.

> *Ge 21:12 And Baal[**] said unto Abraham, Let it not be grievous in thy sight because of the lad, and because of thy bondwoman; in all that Sarah hath said unto thee, hearken unto her voice; for in Isaac shall thy seed be called.*

---

[253] Richardson, M. E. J. 2004. *Hammurabi's Laws: Text, Translation, and Glossary*. New York: Continuum International Publishing Group. p. 95

[**] Elohim in the Bible

Ge 21:13 And also of the son of the bondwoman will I make a nation, because he is thy seed.

It is interesting to note the subtle difference in the choice of terms: in referring to Isaac, "in Isaac *shall thy seed be called*", whereas in speaking of Ishmael, "he is *thy seed*". Isaac is not Abraham's natural son; however, he is the son who will carry on the lineage.

The test of loyalty

In the history of monotheistic religions, this event represents the ultimate sacrifice attesting to Abraham's blind faith in and absolute submission to his God.

> *Ge 22:1 And it came to pass after these things, that Baal** did tempt Abraham, and said unto him, Abraham: and he said, Behold, here I am.*

> *Ge 22:2 And he said, Take now thy son, thine only son Isaac, whom thou lovest, and get thee into the land of Moriah; and offer him there for a burnt offering upon one of the mountains which I will tell thee of.*

This pivotal passage casts doubt over the proposed hypothesis. It doesn't make sense that *Baal* would order Abraham to sacrifice Isaac, the appointed heir. Therefore, this verse can only be referring to Ishmael, whose sacrifice would both prove Abraham's loyalty and ensure that the son of an Egyptian never rose to power.

Many Bible readers are perplexed by the expression "*Take now thy son, thine only son*" in reference to Isaac, since we know that Ishmael was born before Isaac. This expression makes more sense when applied to Ishmael, since Isaac was the son of Hammurabi and not Abraham. The only son born of Abraham's seed—his *only* son—is indeed Ishmael.

While Jews and Christians believe that Isaac is the son that Abraham is ordered to sacrifice, many other religious believers are convinced it is actually Ishmael. In fact, this is a tenet of the Muslim faith. A crucial point in the analysis, this disagreement between believers brings support to the proposed hypothesis. Of course, the Muslims are not aware of the whole truth either, since they also believe Abraham to be a pious man, devoted to his god rather than to his overlord. This is further evidence – if it still needed to be proven – that the Qu'ran naturally evolved out of Judaism. For this reason, I believe that Isaac's name was added to the text at a later date, for partisan reasons. Accordingly, the original text should read:

> Ge 22:2 And he said, Take now thy son, thine only son, whom thou lovest, and get thee into the land of Moriah; and offer him there for a burnt offering upon one of the mountains which I will tell thee of.

This is a damning observation. Abraham, archetype of the ultimate believer, now appears as a politically responsible father, willing to sacrifice the fruit of his loins in deference to his lord for the purpose of inheriting a "land".

How can we prove this? A more extensive analysis of the dates surrounding this event sheds additional light on the situation. When exactly did this test of loyalty occur? The Bible is not forthcoming. Chronologically, it took place sometime between the birth of Isaac and the death of Sarah. Keeping in line with our original postulate – Abraham was born in 1810; we find that Isaac was born in 1750, when Sarah was 54 years old (Ge 17:17). We also know that Sarah died 22 years later, in 1728, at the age of 76 (Ge 23:1). Ergo, the test of loyalty took place between 1750 and 1728.

What event prompted this extreme request? Did *Baal* order this human sacrifice simply to secure legitimacy for his own son, Isaac? All evidence points to the conclusion that Hammurabi put Abraham to the test immediately after Isaac's birth. Yet this demand seems overly harsh, given the Covenant between the two men, which was based on mutual respect and a strong sense of trust. In fact, this inhuman request could just as easily have backfired on Hammurabi if Abraham had performed an about-face.

Could there be a more plausible explanation?

According to history, Hammurabi died in 1750, the same year that Isaac was born. We also learn that his son succeeded him upon his death.

It seems much more believable, therefore, that it was Samsu-iluna, new king of the Babylonian empire, who sought to secure the absolute loyalty of one of his governors, namely Abraham.

Samsu-iluna, who, as we have seen is also Isaac's half-brother, rose to power after his father's death and reigned from 1750 to 1712. Recall that Hammurabi had complete trust in Abraham and relied on him to honour their agreement (Ge 18:19). But, since the Covenant was made between Hammurabi and Abraham, Samsu-iluna was not bound by its terms. When Samsu-iluna rose to the throne, it's therefore very likely that he sought to assert his authority through a show of force, and by testing the loyalty of a man who had been devoted to his father.

He faced a sizable challenge, namely ensuring that Canaan remained under the control of the Amorite royal family. When viewed from this angle, Ishmael's "Egyptian" blood could in fact have opened the door to claims from the outside, which were to be avoided at all costs. Samsu-iluna killed two birds with one stone: he tested the loyalty of his governor and he made sure that Isaac would succeed Abraham upon the latter's death.

Deeply shaken by this demand, Abraham obediently resigns himself to his fate and prepares to sacrifice his son:

> *Ge 22:3 And Abraham rose up early in the morning, and saddled his ass, and took two of his young men with him, and ~~Isaac~~ his son, and clave the wood for the burnt offering, and rose up, and went unto the place of which Baal** had told him.*

> *Ge 22:4 Then on the third day Abraham lifted up his eyes, and saw the place afar off.*

> *Ge 22:5 And Abraham said unto his young men, Abide ye here with the ass; and I and the lad will go yonder and worship, and come again to you.*

** Elohim in the Bible

Ge 22:6 And Abraham took the wood of the burnt offering, and laid it upon ~~Isaac~~ his son; and he took the fire in his hand, and a knife; and they went both of them together.

Ge 22:7 And ~~Isaac~~ (he) spake unto Abraham his father, and said, My father: and he said, Here am I, my son. And he said, Behold the fire and the wood: but where is the lamb for a burnt offering?

Ge 22:8 And Abraham said, My son, Elohim will provide himself a lamb for a burnt offering: so they went both of them together.

Ge 22:9 And they came to the place which Baal** had told him of; and Abraham built an altar there, and laid the wood in order, and bound ~~Isaac~~ his son, and laid him on the altar upon the wood.

Ge 22:10 And Abraham stretched forth his hand, and took the knife to slay his son.

Ge 22:11 And the angel of Baal* called unto him out of heaven, and said, Abraham, Abraham: and he said, Here am I.

Ge 22:12 And he said, Lay not thine hand upon the lad, neither do thou any thing unto him: for now I know that thou fearest Baal**, seeing thou hast not withheld thy son, thine only son from me.

Samsu-iluna must have ordered his messenger to spare Ishmael's life at the last minute if Abraham indeed proved that he was willing to follow orders. This was a shrewd display of generosity by a skilled diplomat, as it sealed the pact with a gesture of trust and mutual respect. From this point on, one can easily imagine that Abraham, both proud and relieved, would have become a dedicated and grateful governor to Samsu-iluna.

This interpretation fits perfectly the Scriptures, as Ge 22:16-18 confirms that the covenant with Abraham is renewed after successfully passing the test.

---

* Yahweh in the Bible

Ge 22:16 And said, By myself have I sworn, saith the Baal*, for because thou hast done this thing, and hast not withheld thy son, thine only son:

Ge 22:17 That in blessing I will bless thee, and in multiplying I will multiply thy seed as the stars of the heaven, and as the sand which is upon the sea shore; and thy seed shall possess the gate of his enemies;

Ge 22:18 And in thy seed shall all the nations of the earth be blessed; because thou hast obeyed my voice.

This governor-lord relationship continued well beyond Abraham's death, since Isaac, Jacob and Joseph also had submissive relationships with other "*Baals*", heirs to the dynasty.

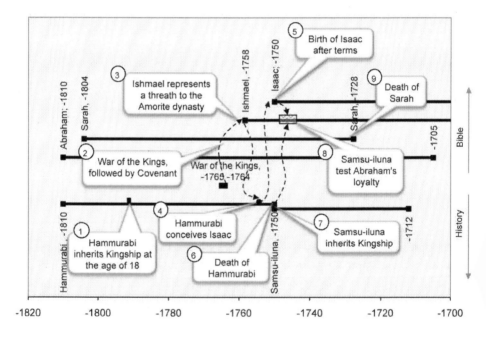

49: Samsu-Iluna secures Abraham's loyalty

This table illustrates the sequence of events that preceded the test of loyalty. Hammurabi makes a covenant with Abraham after the War of Kings (2). Ishmael is born shortly thereafter (3), but his birth is problematic, which is why Hammurabi fathers Isaac (4), who is born

---

* Yahweh in the Bible

nine months later (5), in the same year as his father's death (6). This death leads to the rise of Samsu-iluna (7), who has every reason to test Abraham's loyalty (8). Sarah dies a few years later still (9).

In summary

- The defeat of the king of Elam was a unique opportunity for the Sodomites to secure their freedom.

- To ensure control over this remote region, Hammurabi chose to ally with Abraham rather than to fight him.

- Given his previous alliance with the King of Sodom, Abraham finds himself "caught between the rock and the hard place".

- In returning to destroy the city of Sodom, "*Yahweh*" reveals to be Hammurabi.

- The blood relationship between Abraham and his half-sister, Sarah, negatively affected their fertility.

- Abraham's son with his Egyptian slave girl represented a threat to the dominion of the Amorite dynasty.

- Seeing Sarah grow older without an heir, Hammurabi realized that time was of the essence. He took it upon himself to father Isaac, Abraham's "new" son.

- Hammurabi died shortly after Isaac's birth.

- Samsu-iluna, Hammurabi's son, inherited the throne on his father's death. In a move to confirm Abraham's unwavering loyalty, he ordered him to sacrifice Ishmael, the "problem" son, but spares the kid when convinced of Abraham's loyalty.

- If Abraham had been born just one year later, the timelines would not have overlapped, and Hammurabi, who would have been dead by then, could not have conceived Isaac.

Joseph in Egypt

With Abraham portrayed as a powerful governor and a representative of the central government, it would be interesting to see how the rest of the story of the Patriarchs unfolds to shed more light on the history of this great region.

The Bible contains fewer details about Isaac than about his twin sons, Esau and Jacob, or about the latter's son, Joseph. Jacob's story can be summarized as follows:

> *Esau is the eldest, born before his twin brother, Jacob. But, Esau sells his birthright to Jacob for a plate of lentils. Later on, Jacob tricks his elderly blind father, Isaac, and steals the blessing intended to hand over power to his brother. An enraged Esau threatens Jacob, forcing him to seek refuge with his uncle, Laban, where he struggles for several years to win the heart of the beautiful Rachel. Upset by Laban's behavior— he changes Jacob's wages several times and forces him to marry his eldest daughter, Leah, before he can marry Rachel— Jacob grows rich at Laban's expense before fleeing with Rachel, Leah and his children. On the road home, Jacob wrestles with "God", after which he takes the name Israel. In the meantime, his brother Esau has settled in the region of Edom, where he has become wealthy. Jacob comes to visit him and Esau agrees to forgive his brother and allows him to settle in the region of Canaan.*

> *Jacob has twelve sons, who will later become the leaders of the Twelve Tribes of Israel. Only Joseph and Benjamin are Rachel's children; Jacob's other sons were born to Leah. Joseph, the eleventh son, is Jacob's favorite and the one destined to lead his elder brothers. In a fit of jealousy, Joseph's brothers sell him to some Ishmaelite merchants who take him to Egypt. Jacob believes his beloved son to be dead. Joseph's talent for interpreting dreams quickly finds him favor with Pharaoh. After predicting a devastating famine, he quickly*

becomes the most powerful man in Egypt, putting him in a position to send for his family in Canaan, thus sparing them from starvation.

Joseph's rise to power in Egypt and the terrible famine that ruins the land are more than just a simple anecdote; as proof of this, seven of the fifty chapters of Genesis are dedicated to this story (Ge 41-47). But, while Canaan was regularly hit by famine, Egypt had always been an abundant and fertile land thanks to the silt deposited by the annual flooding of the Nile. This famine, which affected even Egypt, was certainly exceptional; it lasted several years and "was grievous on the whole earth" (Ge 41:57). It must have been caused by a major natural disaster.

The eruption of Mount Thera

One of the largest volcanic eruptions in history occurred at this time: the catastrophic eruption of Mount Thera, better known today as Santorini,[254] a Greek island in the Mediterranean Basin, less than 1,000 km from Egypt and the Levant. According to estimates, this colossal volcano spewed some 30 km^3 of magma into the air and propelled a column of smoke 36 km into the Earth's atmosphere, in the process scattering a phenomenal amount of ash. The expulsion of such a huge amount of matter created a gigantic crater, causing the island to collapse and throwing ash high into the air, which then rained down on Turkey and the countries of the Mediterranean Basin. Volcanic residue settled up to two meters deep in the areas immediately surrounding the eruption, while lighter particles were carried to the east by the prevailing winds.

This explosion marked the beginning of a period of cooling in the Northern hemisphere, which had a major impact on a number of civilizations. It seems even China experienced famines in the aftermath of this event.

---

[254] Forsyth, Phyllis Young. 1997. *Thera in the Bronze Age.* New York: P. Lang.

50: Epicenter of the eruption of Mount Thera (Santorini)

Scholars do not seem to unanimously agree on the date of this event since different dating methods yield different results.[255] By using carbon-14 dating, Manning suggests that this eruption took place between 1622 and 1618 (although he agrees with the window of 1660 to 1613, with 95% certainty.)[256] However, carbon-14 dating is imprecise since carbon levels in the upper atmosphere vary with latitude and the solar cycle.

Dendrochronology analyzes the growth rate and number of rings in a cross-section cut through the trunk of trees. This data is used in archaeology to correct the errors of linearity introduced by the carbon-14 method. By studying wood samples (collected from ruins) to compile dendrochronological databases, Peter I. Kuniholm, Maryanne W. Newton, Carol B. Griggs and Pamela J. Sullivan, influenced by the work of Manning and Hammer, obtained the following growth rates:[257]

---

[255] Based on archaeological data, some experts claim instead that the eruption took place around 1550-1500. However, these dates are strongly contested by more recent and more accurate analyses.

[256] Manning, S. W., C. B. Ramsey, W. Kutschera, T. Higham, B. Kromer, P. Steier and E. M. Wild. 2006. "Chronology for the Aegean Late Bronze Age 1700-1400 B.C." *Science (New York, N.Y.)* 312(5773): 565-9.

[257] Kuniholm, Peter I., Maryanne W. Newton, Carol B. Griggs and Pamela J. Sullivan. 2005.

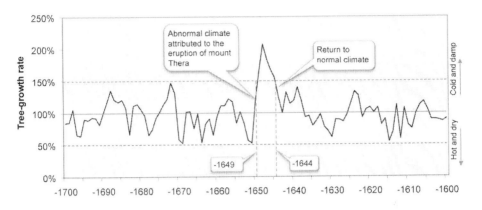

51: Dendrochronological data for the XVIIth BCE

This graph, which shows the growth rates measured on wood samples dating from 1700 to 1600, reveals an abnormal surge between 1649 and 1644. This growth, the most significant recorded in thousands of years, is evident in all samples collected. The authors of this study explain that it was caused by years of excessively cold and damp weather, which they attribute to the atmospheric disturbances that resulted from the eruption of Mount Thera.

The local inhabitants could have perceived this disaster as a sign from the heavens. Presented as a dream, the following passage seems to describe Pharaoh's riverside vision of a thick column of smoke rising high into the sky:

> *Ge 41:1 And it came to pass at the end of two full years, that Pharaoh dreamed[258]: and, behold, he stood by the river.*

> *Ge 41:2 And, behold, there came up out of the river seven well favored kine and fat-fleshed; and they fed in a meadow.*

Dendrochronological Dating in Anatolia: The Second Millennium BC. Ithaca: Cornell University. p. 42
[258] Hebrew חלם(chalam) - to dream

Christiane Desroches-Noblecourt explains that the seven fattened cows and the seven emaciated cows represent the benevolent cycles of the "good" and "bad" floods of the Nile.[259] The cows appear, starting in the 18th Dynasty, in the Egyptian Book of the Dead; they are associated with the fertile bull.

Historians are aware that local people had long known this cycle. However, the immense cloud formations looming on the horizon, above the reeds growing on the shoreline, appear as a harbinger of doom. The dream ends with the following verse:

> *Ge 41:6 And, behold, seven thin ears and blasted with the east wind sprung up after them.*

This verse is very interesting, and the New King James Version translation provides additional details:

> *Ge 41:6 Then behold, seven thin heads, blighted[260] by the east wind, sprang up after them.*

The term *blighted* refers to an extremely adverse environmental condition, such as air pollution that affects plants, as well as a technique used to blacken the metal.[261]

Was this in fact the massive cloud of ash, carried by the wind, and deposited on the crops of Egypt? If so, Joseph correctly interprets Pharaoh's dream and announces that a terrible famine will strike the entire land.

> *Ge 41:27 And the seven thin and ill favored kine that came up after them are seven years; and the seven empty ears blasted with the east wind shall be seven years of famine.*

In all likelihood, an enormous amount of particles hung suspended in the air for a long period of time, blocking out the sun's rays and affecting the crops. The ash that did fall to the ground also covered a vast area, causing additional problems for farmers.[262]

---

[259] Desroches Noblecourt, Christiane. 2006. *Le fabuleux héritage de l'Egypte*. Paris: Pocket. p. 201

[260] In the expression "דקות ושדופת קדים", the (דק) means "thin", "small", "fine"; while (שדף) means "scorch", "blight", and (קדים) means "East wind", "sirocco"

[261] Ross, Robert B. 1988. *Handbook of Metal Treatments and Testing*. London; New York: Chapman and Hall. p. 32

[262] The Ipuwer Papyrus tells of the devastation that affected Egypt, probably as a result of this eruption. Given the ensuing cold and damp climate, it's not impossible that the crops

Ge 45:6 For these two years hath the famine been in the land: and yet there are five years, in the which there shall neither be earing nor harvest.

If Joseph lived at the same time as this natural disaster, it should be possible to locate him on a timeline based on written documents, and on information already known about Abraham.

Information from the Bible:

Source	Event	Bible	6/10
Ge 21:5	Abraham's age at Isaac's birth	100	60
Ge 25:26	Isaac's age at Jacob's birth	60	36
Ge 35:28	Death of Isaac	180	108
Ge 41:46	Joseph's age when he appears before Pharaoh	30	18
Ge 47:9	Jacob's age when he appears before Pharaoh	130	78
Ge 47:28	Jacob's age at his death	147	88
Ge 50:26	Joseph's age at his death	110	66

Based on Abraham's age at Isaac's birth, Isaac's age at Jacob's birth, Jacob's life span, and on the premise that Abraham was born in 1810, we can deduce that Jacob lived from 1714 (= 1810 - 60 - 36) to 1626 (= 1810 - 60 - 88).

---

were also infected with eelworm, a parasite that attacks wheat crops. See: Davaine, Casimir-Joseph. 1857. *Recherches sur l'anguillule du blé niellé considérée au point de vue de l'histoire naturelle et de l'agriculture, mémoire couronné par l'Institut.* Paris: J.-B. Baillière.

With this information to hand, it now becomes possible to pinpoint Jacob's son, Joseph, and the famine on a timeline.

The Bible tells us that Joseph was 18 years old (= 30 x 6/10) when he stood before Pharaoh and interpreted the "dream" heralding the devastating famine:

> Ge 41:46 And Joseph was thirty years old when he stood before Pharaoh king of Egypt. And Joseph went out from the presence of Pharaoh, and went throughout all the land of Egypt.

Unfortunately, Genesis does not tell us how old Jacob was when he fathered Joseph. Joseph was the second-youngest child in a family of twelve. Had he been 47 years old when Joseph was born in 1667 (= 1714 - 47), the famine would have occurred 18 years later, when Joseph stood before Pharaoh in 1649 (= 1667 - 18), and this would fit perfectly with the eruption of Mount Thera.

How long did the famine last?

> Ge 41:30 And there shall arise after them seven years of famine; and all the plenty shall be forgotten in the land of Egypt; and the famine shall consume the land;

This verse tells us that, according to the 6/10 calculation, the famine lasted four years, or until 1645 (= 1649 - 4), much like the duration of anomaly we can observe on the dendrochronological data.

Below is a summary of known information:

Event	Date
Abraham's birth (premise)	-1810
Isaac's birth (when Abraham was 60)	-1750
Jacob's birth (when Isaac was 46)	-1714
Joseph's birth (if Jacob was 47)	-1667

Start of the famine (Joseph was 18)	-1649
End of the famine	-1645

For the first time, it seems possible to establish a causal link between the famine during Joseph's time and this terrible disaster. The perfect correspondence between the dendrochronological data and the years of the famine, calculated based on Abraham's family tree, is further confirmation that Abraham was indeed born in 1810.

In summary

- The Bible provides extensive details about the famine in Egypt, and Joseph's prominent role in that country in the years that followed.

- Joseph predicts a terrible famine to Pharaoh. If Abraham was born in 1810, then Isaac would be born in 1750 and Jacob would be born in 1667. If he had fathered Joseph at the age of 47, then Joseph would have been 18 when he would have interpreted Pharaoh's dream in 1649.

- Dendrochronological data indicates that Mount Thera erupted c. 1649 and that conditions returned to normal four years later; this corresponds to the length of the famine in the Bible.

- Joseph could have lived at the same time as this eruption.

- History tells us that the eruption of Mount Thera disrupted the world's climate, causing conditions similar those that the Bible describes in relation to this terrible famine.

The Hyksos rise to power

The state of famine and the various woes that plagued the local populations would have caused major political instability throughout the entire region. Did the Amorite Patriarchs benefit from this tumultuous period?

The Bible describes the powers Pharaoh granted to Joseph:

> *Ge 41:40 Thou shalt be over my house, and according unto thy word shall all my people be ruled: only in the throne will I be greater than thou.*
>
> *Ge 41:41 And Pharaoh said unto Joseph, See, I have set thee over all the land of Egypt.*
>
> *Ge 41:42 And Pharaoh took off his ring from his hand, and put it upon Joseph's hand, and arrayed him in vestures of fine linen, and put a gold chain about his neck;*
>
> *Ge 41:43 And he made him to ride in the second chariot which he had; and they cried before him, Bow the knee: and he made him ruler over all the land of Egypt.*
>
> *Ge 41:44 And Pharaoh said unto Joseph, I am Pharaoh, and without thee shall no man lift up his hand or foot in all the land of Egypt.*

As such, the most important affairs of Egyptian state were entrusted to Joseph. Does this surprising decision coincide with the Hyksos rise to power? The Amorite people had been living in the Delta for close to a century, from the time of Abraham's first travels. Given the wealth of cultural evidence tying the Patriarchs to the Hyksos and the Amorites, and indirectly to Hammurabi, it is logical to assume that a link existed between the Patriarchs and the Hyksos. And, while the story of the Patriarchs is vague about the precise nature of the positions held by Jacob and Joseph in Egypt, they were clearly high-ranking officials.

Pharaoh gives Joseph permission to send for his family:

> *Ge 47:6 The land of Egypt is before thee; in the best of the land make thy father and brethren to dwell; in the land of*

> *Goshen let them dwell: and if thou knowest any men of activity among them, then make them rulers over my cattle.*

The "land of Goshen" was located only a few kilometers south of Avaris.[263] The significance of being pronounced *"rulers over [my] cattle"* for a "shepherd king" is clear, given the fact that Hammurabi and other Amorite kings declared themselves "shepherds" or "pastors" of the people.

Jacob's arrival in Egypt and his appointment to a high-profile position seem to support the hypothesis already postulated by a number of popular authors that the Hyksos pharaoh, Yakub-her, and the biblical Jacob could in fact be one and the same person.[264] However, it has thus far proven impossible, based on any known dates, to establish this assertion.

The Bible tells us the following:

> *Ge 47:7 And Joseph brought in Jacob his father, and set him before Pharaoh: and Jacob blessed Pharaoh.*

> *Ge 47:8 And Pharaoh said unto Jacob, How old art thou?*

> *Ge 47:9 And Jacob said unto Pharaoh, The days of the years of my pilgrimage are an hundred and thirty years: few and evil have the days of the years of my life been, and have not attained unto the days of the years of the life of my fathers in the days of their pilgrimage.*

> *Ge 47:10 And Jacob blessed Pharaoh, and went out from before Pharaoh.*

> ...

> *Ge 47:28 And Jacob lived in the land of Egypt seventeen years: so the whole age of Jacob was an hundred forty and seven years.*

[263] Hirsch, Emil G. and W. Max Muller. "Goshen." Jewish Encyclopedia. http://www.jewishencyclopedia.com/articles/6819-goshen (retrieved September 10, 2015).
[264] Knight, Christopher and Robert Lomas. 2001. *The Hiram key : pharaohs, Freemasons and the discovery of the secret scrolls of Jesus.* Gloucester, MA: Fair Winds Press.
Bucaille, Maurice. 2008. *Moses and Pharaoh in the Bible, Qur'an and History.* Selangor: Islamic Book Trust. p. 39
Fatoohi, Louay and Shetha Al-Dargazelli. 1999. *History Testifies to the Infallibility of the Qur'an: Early History of the Children of Israel.* Kuala Lumpur: A.S. Noordeen. p. 26

Jacob was 78 years old (= 130 x 6/10) when he arrived in Egypt, where he lived another ten years (= 17 x 6/10), until the age of 88 (= 147 x 6/10). As such, he lived in Egypt from 1636 (= 1714 - 78) until his death ten years later in 1626 (= 1714 - 88). Ergo, Jacob arrived in Egypt 13 years (= 1649 - 1636) after the eruption of Mount Thera.

In order to determine whether a link with the Patriarchs is indeed possible, more information is needed about the circumstances surrounding the Hyksos rise to power.

These Amorite emigrants began banding together around 1750, after which they gradually started claiming the land they would eventually possess in the Nile Delta. To all appearances, the kings of Thebes were unperturbed by this apparently peaceful coexistence. Grimal and Shaw even emphasize the surprising continuity between the documents and monuments from the 12th Dynasty and the Second Intermediate Period. They specify: *"The most surprising aspect of the 13th and 14th Dynasties is the apparent continuation of Egyptian influence over bordering countries".*[265]

Because Egypt continued to exert influence over its neighbours, it would seem that a major event, perhaps the eruption of Mount Thera, played a role in toppling the established order by quickly shifting the balance of power to the Hyksos, who promptly seized control of all of Egypt and established the 15th Dynasty. So, what happened?

Unfortunately the history of this period is very poorly documented, since the Egyptians were prompt to wipe out all traces of their inglorious past from buildings and monuments. Only a small amount of information escaped this censorship, and what remains is fragmented, incomplete and contradictory; as such, it cannot accurately confirm the names and reigns of the Hyksos kings, or even the order in which they ruled.

While the kings of the 12th and 13th Dynasties[266], who came immediately before the Hyksos, as well as those of the 17th and

---

[265] Grimal, Nicolas. 1992. *A History of Ancient Egypt.* Oxford: Blackwell. p. 183
[266] The 12th Dynasty ruled over all of Egypt. The 13th and 14th Dynasties were

18th Dynasties, who succeeded them, are relatively well known, there is a dearth of information about the 14th, 15th and 16th Dynasties[267]. The following diagram illustrates the links between these dynasties, which ruled simultaneously.

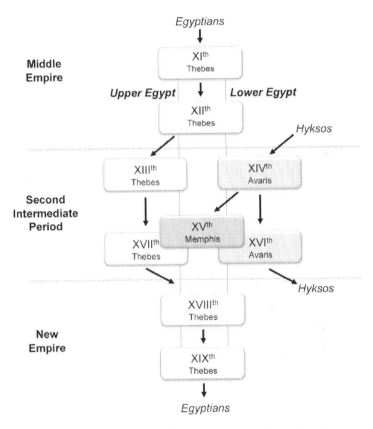

52: Dynasties of the Second Intermediate Period

Experts date the Hyksos reign based on two main sources: the king list compiled by the Egyptian historian Manetho (3rd century BCE) and the Turin Royal Canon (13th century BCE). The latter is a collection of papyrus fragments that contain important information on a number of dynasties, including the 15th Dynasty—that of the

contemporaries. The arrival of the Hyksos, who formed the 14th Dynasty, fragmented the power of the 13th Dynasty (heirs of the 12th Dynasty).
[267] The 15th, 16th and 17th Dynasties were contemporaries. The 15th Dynasty governed the country and collected taxes; the 16th Dynasty ruled Lower Egypt, whereas the 17th Dynasty (heirs of the 13th Dynasty) ruled Upper Egypt. Only the kings of the 17th Dynasty were native Egyptians; the others were of Hyksos origin.

Hyksos. Unfortunately, these fragments provide very little insight into the names and lengths of reigns of these six kings. Only the number of reigns and their total duration are known: approximately a century, maybe 108 years. The last name on this list is also legible: "Khamudi". The remaining known information comes from transcriptions, the original documents having long since been lost. These include the works of Manetho, who also reports six kings from the 15th Dynasty. On this point, the information concurs. However, Khamudi is noticeably absent from Manetho's list of six kings, and their reigns total 260 years, more than twice the length reported in the Turin Royal Canon. It would seem that the information in the Canon is more accurate—albeit too fragmented to provide a clear picture—since several artifacts dating from this turbulent period have been found. While certain facts point toward a plausible solution, they must be interpreted with caution.

The experts don't agree on the matter, since the years in which these kings reigned cannot be substantiated by any reliable data. On the other hand, based on known information about their predecessors and successors, the total length of their reign can be estimated at approximately 150 years. Incidentally, the six Hyksos kings of whom traces have been found during archaeological digs, or about whom solid clues exist, are Salatis, Sheshi, Yakub-her, Khyan, Apophis, and Khamudi.

We don't know precisely when and how the Hyksos of the 15th Dynasty seized power. However, Josephus Flavius faithfully conveys the way in which the Egyptian Manetho opens his chapter on their reign:

> *There was a king of ours whose name was Timaus.[268] Under him it came to pass, I know not how, that God was averse to us, and there came, after a surprising manner, men of ignoble birth out of the eastern parts, and had boldness enough to make an expedition into our country, and with ease subdued it by force, yet without our hazarding a battle with them. So when they had gotten those that governed us under their power, they afterwards*

[268] Timaus is known as the 13th Dynasty pharaoh who capitulated to the Hyksos.

burnt down our cities, and demolished the temples of the gods, and used all the inhabitants after a most barbarous manner; nay, some they slew, and led their children and their wives into slavery. At length they made one of themselves king, whose name was Salatis; he also lived at Memphis, and made both the upper and lower regions pay tribute, and left garrisons in places that were the most proper for them.[269]

This passage contains a few clues about the circumstances surrounding this coup. The choice of the expression "*God was averse to us*" could very well refer to the volcanic eruption and the fallout from that natural disaster. However, the ease with which the Hyksos managed to invade Egypt is in surprising contrast to the harmony and stability that appeared to reign over the country. In addition, evidence seems to indicate that the Egyptians were taken by surprise by the sudden shift in the situation.

But, why did the Hyksos benefit—more so than the Egyptians—from the chaos that followed the eruption of Mount Thera? Recall that they worshipped Seth, the Amorites' equivalent of *Baal*, god of chaos, thunder and lightning. They might have interpreted these heavenly signs as a blessing and their adversaries' weakness as a divine reward. The impending famine would have been just another motivating factor.

In fact, in the history of monotheistic religions, religious fervour has always been divinely rewarded, whereas failure to follow the rules has led to censure. The exile to Babylon is an example of this divine punishment.

But, despite everything, we would have expected the disciplined and trained army of a politically stable country to have at least attempted to fend off a hostile invader. Did the eruption of Mount Thera destabilize the country so badly that the Egyptians unwillingly became the instruments of their own defeat? If the Hyksos took the country "*without [the Egyptians] hazarding a battle with them*", this may have been because they encountered a

---

[269] Josephus, Flavius. 2006. *Against Apion.* Portland: Read How You Want

disorganized and paralyzed army... or because the Hyksos were handed the land in exchange for food!

In fact, the Bible describes how Joseph acquired land from the desperate Egyptians in exchange for food:

> Ge 47:18 When that year was ended, they came unto him the second year, and said unto him, We will not hide it from my lord, how that our money is spent; my lord also hath our herds of cattle; there is not ought left in the sight of my lord, but our bodies, and our lands:

> Ge 47:19 Wherefore shall we die before thine eyes, both we and our land? buy us and our land for bread, and we and our land will be servants unto Pharaoh: and give us seed, that we may live, and not die, that the land be not desolate.

> Ge 47:20 And Joseph bought all the land of Egypt for Pharaoh; for the Egyptians sold every man his field, because the famine prevailed over them: so the land became Pharaoh's.

The Nile Delta, where the Hyksos settled, was the most fertile part of Egypt; even today, it is still one of the most harvested areas in the world. If Joseph, aware of the imminent danger, rationed food to preserve the country's resources and then skillfully negotiated the sale of this precious commodity, this might explain the peaceful takeover.

If the eruption of Mount Thera indeed helped propel the Hyksos to power, then it is appropriate to date the start of the reign of Salatis-Sheshi, the first Hyksos king, shortly after the eruption, in around 1649. This date coincides with that proposed by most experts who date the start of his reign to around 1650. This would lead us to believe that Salatis-Sheshi was the "pharaoh" who ruled during Joseph's time. The fact he was also an Amorite would explain his great trust in Joseph and his family.

If Yabkub-her is indeed Jacob, then he probably ruled Egypt for about ten years, from 1636 to 1626 (as seen before). Consequently, the duo Salatis-Sheshi[270] could not have reigned longer than

---

[270] Some believe that these two names refer to one and the same man.

thirteen years (= 1649 - 1636), or the time elapsed between the eruption of Mount Thera and Yabkub-her's accession to the throne.

The length of Jacob's stay in Egypt corresponds to the generally accepted length of the pharaoh Yakub-her's reign. Unfortunately, since history has left us with very few details about him, we are forced to turn to the Bible for more information. This would leads us to believe that the biblical Jacob could, in fact, have been the Hyksos king of the same name.

In summary

- What little information we have about the Hyksos is often contradictory. We do not know how they rose to power in Egypt, or how long their kings reigned.

- History teaches us that the Hyksos settled in the Delta around 1750. All of Egypt was under their control by around 1650, after which they continued to rule for more than a hundred years.

- The small amount of available information seems to indicate that there were six or seven Hyksos kings: Salatis, Sheshi, Yakub-her, Khyan, Apophis I & II, and Khamudi.

- If Abraham was born in 1810, then Jacob lived in Egypt from 1636 to 1626. These years could correspond to the reign of Yakub-her.

- Manetho states that the Hyksos rose to power in Egypt *"without [the Egyptians] hazarding a battle with them"*.

- The Bible tells us that, during the famine, Joseph skillfully traded food for land in Egypt.

Yakub-her's successors

While some authors already suspected a link between Jacob and Yakub-her, it seems that none has ever theorized about his successors.

The Bible confirms that Joseph was Jacob's favorite son:

> *Ge 37:3 Now Israel loved Joseph more than all his children, because he was the son of his old age: and he made him a coat of many colors.*

The "coat of many colors" no doubt has a particular significance: it designates Joseph as the favorite son appointed to carry on the bloodline. In fact, a number of Egyptian frescoes depict the pharaoh dressed in a richly colored tunic.

> *Ge 37:10 And he told it to his father, and to his brethren: and his father rebuked him, and said unto him, What is this dream that thou hast dreamed? Shall I and thy mother and thy brethren indeed come to bow down ourselves to thee to the earth?*

> *Ge 37:11 And his brethren envied him; but his father observed the saying.*

Although Jacob was not particularly inclined to bow down before his own son, Joseph was clearly destined to rule over his brothers. The rest of the story reveals how he became a very important person.

In all likelihood, Khyan succeeded Yakub-her as king of the Hyksos. Khyan was certainly a great king, since evidence of him exists outside Egypt. Traces of his seals have been found in Knossos, Crete, Boghazkoy in Turkey (formerly Hattusas, a major Hittite capital) and in Babylon.[271] Khyan's name is generally associated with the title "Ruler of Foreign Lands". Were Joseph and Khyan the same person?

Kim Ryholt, a Danish Egyptologist specializing in the Second Intermediate Period, describes how a stele found at Avaris contains the name of Khyan, followed by a dedication that is too damaged to be deciphered.[272] Ryholt postulates that it was likely "Seth", the Hyksos counterpart of the god *Baal*, worshipped by the Amorites.

---

[271] Crew, P. Mack, I. E. S. Edwards, J.B. Bury, C. J. Gadd, Nicholas Geoffrey, N. G. L. Hammond and Edmond Sollberger. 1973. *History of the Middle East and the Aegean Region c.1800-1380 B.C.* Vol. 2 of *The Cambridge Ancient History.* Cambridge: Cambridge University Press. p. 60
[272] Ryholt, Kim. 1997. *The Political Situation in Egypt During the Second Intermediate Period c.1800-1550 B.C.* Copenhagen: Carsten Niebuhr Institute of Near Eastern Studies:

Since the Hyksos worshipped the god Seth, and Isra-El and Ishma-El worshipped the god El, we can assume that Khyan's full name was in fact "Khyan-Seth".

Ryholt states that the Amorite equivalent of "Khyan" is "*hyaan*". Supposing Khyan's full name was "*h-ya-a-n-seth*", then the contracted form "*h-ya-seth*" or "*ya-sef*". In Hebrew, the name "Joseph" is written (וסף) *yowceph*.

This link seems even more probable given the fact that Joseph's eldest son was named "Manasseh", and Khyan-Seth's eldest, "Yanassi". Two names of similar consonant.

> Ge 41:51 And Joseph called the name of the firstborn Manasseh: For Elohim, said he, hath made me forget all my toil, and all my father's house.

Based always on the assumption that Jacob was 47 years old when Joseph was born and that he died at 88 years old; and that Joseph died at the age of 66 (Ge 50:26), we can deduce that Joseph survived his father by 25 years (= 66 - (88 – 47)). Accordingly, Joseph would have inherited the throne in 1626, at the age of 41, and ruled until his death in 1601 (= 1667 - 66). This means that he would have lived in Egypt for almost 50 years (= 66 - 18) and ruled for 25 years. Once again, these dates and this length of reign make sense in reference to Khyan.

Therefore, it's no surprise that the Bible later gives a description that fits Khyan perfectly, when Moses blesses the tribes of Israel and says, in reference to Joseph:

> De 33:17 His glory is like the firstling of his bullock, and his horns are like the horns of unicorns[273]: with them he shall push the people together to the ends of the earth: and they are the ten thousands of Ephraim, and they are the thousands of Manasseh.

These traits match those attributed to Khyan, "Ruler of Foreign Lands", who worshipped the god Seth, counterpart of *Baal*, himself typically represented by a calf or horns.

Museum Tusculanum.
[273] Translated as "wild ox" in the New King James Version

Oddly, the story of the Patriarchs breaks off abruptly with Joseph's death. The trail quickly goes cold, and nothing in the Bible indicates that his descendants continued to rule over Egypt. On the Hyksos' side, Ryholt suggests that Yanassi was most likely designated as Khyan's successor.[274] However, according to history, it was Apophis, and not Yanassi, who succeeded Khyan, most likely by leading a coup upon the latter's death.

The biblical duo Joseph/Manasseh seems to correspond very well to the historical figures of Khyan-Seth/Yanassi. And, if Yanassi was indeed assassinated or overthrown, then it's only normal that the story of the Patriarchs would come to a sudden end.

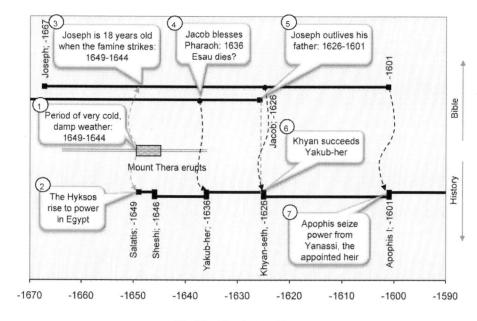

53: The famine in Egypt

Based always on the premise that Abraham was born in 1810, this chart illustrates the perfect correspondence between the Patriarchs' lineage and the Hyksos kings, two generations down. If Joseph was born when

[274] Ryholt, Kim. 1997. *The Political Situation in Egypt During the Second Intermediate Period c. 1800-1550 B.C.* Copenhagen: Carsten Niebuhr Institute of Near Eastern Studies: Museum Tusculanum.

Jacob was 47 years old, then Joseph was 18 (3) in 1649, the exact year in which the region experienced the greatest tree-section growth rate in thousands of years. The study's authors attribute these abnormally cold and damp years to the eruption of Mount Thera (1). Joseph skillfully traded land for food, a precious commodity, propelling the Hyksos to power in Egypt (2). Joseph survived Jacob by 25 years. Manasseh, who should have inherited the throne in 1601, was overthrown by Apophis, and this is how the identities of Jacob and Yakub-her, Joseph and Khyan-Seth, and Manasseh and Yanassi fuses.

The book of Genesis ends with Joseph's death. But, if this story is indeed based in historical fact, the chapter about the Patriarchs affords us only a brief glimpse at what really happened.

This leads us to question the identities of the remaining characters in this story. Are there links between the biblical Isaac, Esau and Ephraim, and the other known Hyksos kings: Salatis, Sheshi, Apophis and Khamudi? Logically, we would expect to discover new relationships as events unfold. Also, how can the Exodus be explained in light of our investigation? Unfortunately, reliable information—both biblical and historical—is in short supply and, therefore, does not permit any firm conclusions. You are nevertheless invited to pursue a more tenuous exploration of the Hyksos descendants as well as the story of Exodus and Joshua's conquest in Annex A, page 304.

In summary

- Joseph spent close to 50 years in Egypt, from the time he was almost 18 until his death at the age of 66.

- The Bible tells us that Joseph was Jacob's favorite son.

- The description of Joseph in Deuteronomy matches the description of Khyan.

- If Khyan-Seth is Joseph, then he succeeded his father, Jacob, and ruled Egypt from 1625 to 1601.

- Manasseh (Joseph's son), like Yanassi (Khyan-Seth's son), was the son appointed to succeed his father. According to the Bible, Joseph was instead succeeded by Ephraim and according to history, Khyan was succeeded by Apophis.

The Ark of the Covenant

If the story of Abraham is to be dated back to the Middle Bronze Age, how could it even have been recorded at such an early time? And how could its medium have withstood the ravages of time and its content maintained its temporal efficiency without suffering major distortions?

William Schniedewind, from the Kershaw Chair of Ancient Eastern Mediterranean Studies at UCLA, explains that during the Middle Bronze Age writing was used almost exclusively by the states for the purpose of trade, administering justice, and religion. While acknowledging that small city-states of Canaan already had their own scribe at the turn of the second millennium BCE, he underscores:

> In antiquity, writing was both complex and expensive. Writing was not a mundane activity. It required institutional support. Writing was primarily an activity of the state. [275]

Because Schniedewind believes that the Abrahamic story recounts the birth of a monotheistic religion which evolved out of a small nomadic and illiterate group living among a largely polytheistic population, his writings naturally supports the belief that this narrative has long been passed down orally, and that the formation of biblical literature does not begin until the 8th century BCE. But when ruling out the religious interpretation and considering the story from a political perspective, i.e. as a state affair, the presence of writing can be easily accepted: By recording the details surrounding the covenant, it is given a timeless and everlasting trait. Vansina's works on the reliability of oral transmission abound in the same vein. This anthropologist's historical view is that oral

---

[275] Schniedewind, William M. 2004. *How the Bible Became a Book: The Textualization of Ancient Israel.* Cambridge: Cambridge University Press. p.35

transmissions prove very reliable, but only when taken in a particular cultural context. They inevitably suffer from important limitations when reporting factual information.[276] As such, the intricate underlying story that is rediscovered and brought forward through a dissociative exegesis pledges, *a contrario*, in favor of a very efficient written transmission, and refutes the possibility of an oral transmission. In sharp contrast to the overall coherence of the rediscovered story, the few anachronisms are isolated and most often found towards the end of chapters. They can easily be explained by the deterioration of the writing medium that forced the scribes and copyists to clarify, modify or update the text, as needed, most likely in accordance with the beliefs and tradition of their times. Some critics might also raise the issue of the reliability of the translations and invoke the many possible interpretations that can be placed upon the text. But this observation is only valid in light of a theological interpretation, where one must carefully weigh punctuation and the hidden intention behind every word. In contrast, a political and literal reading reveals a rudimentary vocabulary, a clear context and meaning of words that is rarely ambiguous. That's why the dissociative exegesis can be practiced using most translations of Genesis. Only a few expressions, for which the translators visibly tried to give a theological slant, necessitate reverting to the original Hebrew texts for clarification. It is nevertheless important to recall that the dissociative exegesis suggested in this work only applies to the sections of the book of Genesis involving the story of the Patriarchs (Chapters 12-50) and not systematically to the entire Bible.

As the legal form did not exist at the time, it was by recounting the circumstances surrounding the reciprocal commitments and agreements that these people sought to formalize their covenant. Probably recorded on clay tablets, it has been carefully preserved and moved as a relic of great value to proudly display the claim of the right to land. It is hard not to think of the famous Ark of the Covenant as anything but a repository for these precious tablets.

---

[276] Vansina, Jan. 2006. *Oral Tradition: A Study in Historical Methodology*. New Brunswick: Aldine Transaction. p.172

54: The Ark of the Covenant

The tradition is clear about its existence: it already contained tablets with the "divine" laws during the time of Moses. The Ark was still around, centuries later, during the reign of King Solomon who is said to have placed it in the Holy of Holies after the construction of the first temple. In contrast, the Ark had disappeared when the Roman general Pompey arrived at the temple in the 1st century BCE. This makes perfect sense, as the "Pentateuch" assembly was completed by then. By ensuring the protection and the relocation of these precious tablets, the Ark would have effectively contributed to the preservation and the transmission of these legal documents, as well as figuratively embodying the *"spirit of Yahweh"*.

Treaties and the Ancient Near East

What do we know of ancient treaties and what parallels can be drawn with this covenant? The vast majority of research into treaties and alliances of the Ancient Near East were virtually abandoned a few decades ago. Fortunately, some authors continue to publish, including Wilhelm G. Grewe[277], Mario Liverani[278] and Noel Weeks[279].

For Noel Weeks: *"the topic of treaty and covenant was a major concern of Ancient Near Eastern scholarship in the 1950s-1960s.*

---

[277] Grewe, Wilhelm G. 1995. *Fontes Historiae Iuris Gentium: Quellen zur Geschichte des Völkerrechts. Band 1: 1380 v. Chr./B.C.-1493.* Berlin: Walter de Gruyter.
[278] Liverani, Mario. 2004. *Myth and Politics in Ancient Near Eastern Historiography.* Ithaca: Cornell University Press.
[279] Weeks, Noel. 1993. "Covenant and Treaty: A Study in Intercultural Relations." *Lucas* (16): 10-22.

After that, it virtually disappears." Among the reasons for this decline, Weeks states *"much of the interest stemmed from attempts to resolve certain issues in the biblical field. When these issues appeared to be resolved in other ways, the topic lost its immediate relevance."*

Weeks conducts a full analysis of past research and denounces circular references that do not allow to settle as easily as some would like on the question of the form of the treaties in the light of different cultures and eras. He reminds us that *form criticism* can hardly be applied after *source criticism*, since it does not allow us to rule on the consistency of the resulting text. Weeks also cautions the reader against any parallels with the biblical texts:

> *The biblical data complicates immensely the tracing of cultural interrelationships. Some scholars have emphasized the historical element of biblical covenants to relate them chronologically to second-millenium Hittites treaties. Others have emphasized the curse element to relate them to first-millenium Assyrian treaties. Others again have denied all relationship in order to preserve their particular theological version of the history of Israel. The tradition, in critical biblical scholarship, of dividing and re-dating portions of texts facilitates the arrangement of evidence to prove these quite contradictory positions.*[280]

While he considers it precarious to compare biblical texts with neighboring secular texts, it is mainly due to their specificity, because *"Treaties between humans and deities are very rare, if they exist at all in Mesopotamia."*[281]

However, if the document at the base of the Abrahamic story was issued from a secular alliance treaty with a powerful lord rather than a deity, it would be possible, according to Weeks, to compare the shape to the treaty extrinsic to Israel:

> *If a covenant in which God is a partner can be related to a covenant with only human partners in Israel, then there can*

---

[280] Ibid. p. 8
[281] Ibid. p. 32

be no insuperable objection to a relationship to human covenants (treaties) outside Israel.[282]

The land and the heir

In a collection of approximately twenty Hittite and Assyrian treaties, spanning from 1380 to 450, Wilhelm G. Grewe (1995) offers a set of texts that exhibits the great diversity of treaties, whose form tends to change over time. In the proposed samples, it can nevertheless be observed that the earlier Hittite treaties make greater use of historical background, while the later Assyrian treaties tend to incorporate more curses.

When referring to the Bible, Weeks says, *"For our purpose there is another interesting fact about such covenants of promise. They have their closest analogies outside of Israel in royal land grants."*[283] He is not the first one to make this connection. Several years before him, Moshe Weinfeld suggested while analyzing the Covenant made between *Yahweh* and Abraham in Ge 15 and that of David:

> *Although the grant to Abraham and David is close in its formulation to the neo-Assyrian grants and therefore might be late, the promises themselves are much older and reflect, the Hittite pattern of grant. "Land" and "house" (= dynasty), the objects of the Abrahamic and Davidic covenants respectively, are indeed the most prominent gifts of the suzerain in the Hittite and Syro-Palestinian political reality, and like the Hittite grants so also the grant of land to Abraham and the grant of "house" to David are unconditional.*[284]

This tends to confirm that if a link could be established between the Abrahamic story and a secular treaty it would be fair to expect that it was written as part of a royal land grant.

Thomas C. Römer says that the Abrahamic story is mainly characterized by two recurring themes that are like leitmotifs,

---

[282] Ibid. p. 151
[283] Ibid. p. 9
[284] Weinfeld, Moshe. 1970. "The Covenant of Grant in the Old Testament and in the Ancient Near East." *Journal of the American Oriental Society* 90(2): 184-203. pp. 196-200

namely the issue of the possession of the land and the issue of the son or the descendants.[285] These two fundamental themes that connect Abraham and Isaac to *Yahweh* for "eternity", also resonate in the alliance treaty made between Mursulis II and Duppi-Tessub (c. 1340), as reported by Wilhelm G. Grewe:

> *And I, the king, will be loyal toward you, Duppi-Tessub. When you take a wife, and when you beget an heir, he shall be king in the Amurru land likewise. And just as I shall be loyal toward you, even so shall I be loyal toward your son. But you, Duppi-Tessub, remain loyal toward the king of the Hatti land, the Hatti land, my sons (and) my grandsons forever!* [286]

Weeks underlines that these parallels are only useful in the context of comparisons between secular texts. If an affiliation can be demonstrated with a secular alliance treaty, then these comparisons can be considered valid.

Intimately linked to the question of its transmission is the question of the narrative's evolution. Why give a religious dimension to an historical archive? How does such a "drift" fit into the evolution of the psyche of the proto-Israelites?

By legitimizing the right to the land of Canaan, this "covenant" will gradually take on a mythical dimension for the people of Israel. *Baal* would first have been celebrated for his *berith*, magnificence and the generosity he bestowed upon a nomadic people seeking a sedentary lifestyle. His justice, laws, protection, and more importantly the land he provided, made of him a figure far more present and tangible in the collective imagination than the local gods of Canaan. To elevate him to divine status required just a small step that the cult of the ancestors would help achieve over time. Abraham's pledge, symbolized by his unwavering loyalty and enshrined in the blood[287], by the ritual of circumcision, will

[285] Römer, Thomas C. 1999. Recherches actuelles sur le cycle d'Abraham. In *Studies in the Book of Genesis : Literature, Redaction and History*, ed. Wénin, André, 179-211. Leuven; Paris; Sterling: Leuven University Press ; Uitgeverij Peeters. p. 200

[286] Grewe, Wilhelm G. 1995. *Fontes Historiae Iuris Gentium: Quellen zur Geschichte des Völkerrechts. Band 1: 1380 v. Chr./B.C.-1493*. Berlin: Walter de Gruyter. p. 12

[287] See Durand, Jean-Marie. 2005-2006. "L'idéal de vie bédouin à l'époque amorrite." *Collège de France*, Collège de France, Collège de France, http://www.college-de-france.fr/media/jean-marie-durand/UPL17281_jmdurandcours0506.pdf (retrieved May 10,

mark the birth of a new people who will make *"Yahweh"*, the *"Most High Elohim, Possessor of heaven and earth"*, their only god. *Yahweh*'s anthropomorphic nature fits perfectly into the logic of the *"God of the Father"*, with which these nomadic people were already intimate.[288] As such, *"Yahweh"*, the *"God of Abraham"* will gradually become the *"God of the people of Israel"*.

The Samaritans and the post-exilic Jews

The story of the Samaritans is another historical challenge that has been puzzling biblical scholars for generations and that is easily solved by adopting the hypothesis of a mortal Lord.

The Persian Achaemenid Empire (c. 556-330 BCE), founded by Cyrus the Great (559-529 BCE), draws our attention because it exercised power throughout the Middle East at a time that was critical for the formation of the Bible, which corresponds to the return of the Babylonian Exile in 538. The Achaemenid Empire maintained several operating structures bequeathed by the Assyrians and Babylonians and established a number of "satrapies" based on ancient territorial divisions. Rather than resorting to intimidation and brute force, the Achaemenids chose to leave some of the power in the hands of governors belonging to the ethno-dominant class. These were responsible for maintaining order and for the collection of tributes. In exchange, they would enjoy some form of autonomy in local law enforcement as well as in the practice of religious cults. This approach has enabled the Achaemenid Empire to withstand for several generations at the head of a vast territory, bringing together people with widely diverse interests and cultures.

Nehemiah, a contemporary of Ezra, was the appointed *Tirshatha* (i.e. governor) of Jerusalem under king Artaxerxes (465-424 BCE). He was mandated by the Persians to rebuild the temple of Jerusalem. When the locals wanted to join his efforts and participate in the rebuilding of their temple, they were rejected. Ezra 4:1-2 wrote that the "enemies" of the Jews wanted to

---

2008). p.614 for a reference to blood alliance.
[288] Thompson, Thomas L. 1992. *Early History of the Israelite People: From the Written and Archaeological Sources*. Leiden: E.J. Brill. p.56

participate in the rebuilding of Jerusalem and its temple. Among these "enemies" were the Samaritans, a people originating from Samaria and having Shechem as their stronghold.

From a population exceeding the million in late Roman times, there are now just a few hundred Samaritans left that are divided between Tel Aviv and mount Gerizim, in the vicinity of Nablus (biblical Shechem). To this day, the Samaritans call themselves "Bene Yisrael" (son of Israel) and pretend to be issued from the tribes of Manasseh and Ephraim.

Their history, as a distinct community, officially begins in 722 BCE with the taking of Samaria by the Assyrians. The Samaritans view themselves as the guardians of the true religion of the early Israelites, as it was practiced in the Land in the ancient times. They consider Judaism as a related, but reformed and altered religion that was brought back by those that were exiled in Babylon. The Jewish tradition, on the other hand, claim that the Samaritans are foreigners that were carried away into captivity to Assyria, and were later relocated by the king of Assyria in and around Samaria in order to intermarry with the Israelite population (2 Kings 17:24). According to the Jewish tradition, the Samaritans were taught Judaism by the priests, but retained many of their idolatrous customs.

The polemic on the exact origins of the Samaritans continues to divide the two communities as they both pretend to be more "authentic" than the other. And while historical inscriptions[289] from Sargon II (not to be confused with Sargon of Akkad) gives credence to the biblical account on their relocation, genetic analysis of mitochondrial DNA sequences also confirm that the Samaritans' Y-chromosomes have a greater affinity with their Jewish lineage than with their geographical neighbors, the Palestinians.[290] It therefore seems plausible that the relocation of some foreigners has contributed to expand their initial population.

---

[289] Chavalas, Mark W. and K. Lawson Younger. Mesopotamia and the Bible : comparative explorations. London: T & T Clark International. p. 310
[290] Shen, Peidong, Tal Lavi, Toomas Kivisild, Vivian Chou, Deniz Sengun, Dov Gefel, Issac Shpirer, Eilon Woolf, Jossi Hillel, Marcus W. Feldman and Peter J. Oefner. 2004. "Reconstruction of patrilineages and matrilineages of Samaritans and other Israeli populations from Y-Chromosome and mitochondrial DNA sequence Variation." *HUMU*

To this day, the Samaritans adhere rigidly to the Torah and have never admitted any of the later prophetical teachings. Their claims present a challenge similar to the squaring of the circle to those holding minimalistic views. Indeed, one that views Abraham and the tribes of Israel as purely fictitious characters can always pretend that Judaism developed in the aftermath of the Babylonian Exile, but then, what to do with those who refute Judaism as an altered religion and claim that the only genuine part of that religion is that of Abraham?

Could the early Israelites that were practicing the cult of *Baal Berith* be the direct ancestors to the Samaritans? One can certainly appreciate that the people of Shechem have had an ongoing history of preserving their original cult. Recall that Judges 8-9 in the Bible tells of how Abimelech killed all the Israelites that had found refuge in *Baal Berith*'s temple.

In refusing to evolve their worship by adopting some of the newer religious practices, the Samaritans eventually got marginalized by those who had been in contact with the Persians during the Babylonian Exile. It should then not come as a surprise that Nehemiah, the Jewish poster child of the Persians, wanted nothing to do with these "idolatrous" people.

The Samaritans' inability to participate in the rebuilding of what they legitimately considered their own temple, would have stirred anger and thus motivated Bishlam, Mithredath and Tabeel, to write the following letter to King Artaxerxes to denounce the reconstruction of the city by Nehemiah and "his" people:

> *Ezra 4:12 Be it known to the king that the Jews who came up from thee unto us have come to Jerusalem; they are building the rebellious and the bad city, and they complete the walls and join up the foundations.*

> *Ezra 4:13 Be it known therefore unto the king, that, if this city be built and the walls be completed, they will not pay tribute, tax, and toll, and in the end it will bring damage to the kings.*

Human Mutation 24(3): 248-60.

Ezra 4:14 Now, since we eat the salt of the palace, and it is not right for us to see the king's injury, therefore have we sent and informed the king;

Ezra 4:15 that search may be made in the book of the annals of thy fathers: so shalt thou find in the book of the annals and know that this city is a rebellious city, which has done damage to kings and provinces, and that they have raised sedition within the same of old time, for which cause this city was destroyed.

Ezra 4:16 We inform the king that if this city be built and its walls be completed, by this means thou shalt have no portion on this side the river.

Artaxerxes' response follows shortly after:

Ezra 4:18 The letter that ye sent to us has been read before me distinctly.

Ezra 4:19 And I gave orders, and search has been made, and it has been found that this city of old time has made insurrection against the kings, and that rebellion and sedition have been raised therein.

Ezra 4:20 And there have been mighty kings over Jerusalem, who have ruled over all beyond the river; and tribute, tax, and toll were paid to them.

Ezra 4:21 Now give order to make these men to cease, and that this city be not built, until the order shall be given from me;

Ezra 4:22 and take heed that ye fail not to do this: why should harm grow to the damage of the kings?

In the above letter, the expression *"the annals of thy fathers"* most likely refers to the destruction of Jerusalem and its temple in 587-586, which took place only a few generations before Artaxerxes (465- 424). However, the comment *"of old times"* could refer to a historical past much more distant. Was the region of Palestine known by the Babylonians for its historical insubordination? Although Pierre Briant, a specialist of the Persian era, expresses some reservations about the historical aspect of these letters, he considers it nevertheless plausible, especially when considering that reconstruction work of the city had been carried on before the royal decree, which only authorized the rebuilding of the temple.[291]

It was also precisely during this period that Zoroastrianism, the dominant Persian religion gained its momentum. According to the Jewish Encyclopedia:

> *The points of resemblance between Zoroastrianism and Judaism, and hence also between the former and Christianity, are many and striking. Ahuramazda, the supreme lord of Iran, omniscient, omnipresent, and eternal, endowed with creative power, which he exercises especially through the medium of his Spenta Mainyu ("Holy Spirit"), and governing the universe through the instrumentality of angels and archangels, presents the nearest parallel to Yhwh that is found in antiquity... There are striking parallels between the two faiths and Christianity in their eschatological teachings—the doctrines of a regenerate world, a perfect kingdom, the coming of a Messiah, the resurrection of the dead, and the life everlasting. Both Zoroastrianism and Judaism are revealed religions: in the one Ahuramazda imparts his revelation and pronounces his commandments to Zarathustra on "the Mountain of the Two Holy Communing Ones"; in the other Yhwh holds a similar communion with Moses on Sinai.* [292]

In his monograph *God in Translation*, Mark S. Smith shows it was common practice in Ancient Near East to translate the names of deities between peoples and languages, based on their equivalence.[293] Smith refers to a number of treaties and documents that mentions the deities of one group in one copy, and the equivalent deities of the other group in the other copy. Changing the name of a deity therefore did not imply that it would automatically lose its power or characteristics.

[291] Briant, Pierre. 2002. *From Cyrus to Alexander : A History of the Persian Empire*. Winona Lake: Eisenbraun. p. 578
[292] Kohler, Kaufmann and A. V. W. Jackson. "Zoroastrianism." Jewish Encyclopedia. http://www.jewishencyclopedia.com/articles/15283-zoroastrianism (retrieved September 10, 2015).
[293] Smith, Mark S. 2010. *God in Translation: Deities in Cross-Cultural Discourse in the Biblical World*. Grand Rapids: W.B. Eerdmans.

There is an ongoing debate among scholars as to whether it was Zoroastrianism that influenced Judaism or the other way around. As we know that the cult of *Yahweh* took over the cult of *Baal* – the temple of *Baal Berith* had already become the temple of *Yahweh* by the Persian period, it would seem far more likely that the priests in exile in Babylon refined or developed Judaism by grafting, to the ancient sacrificial worship that had been at the very core of their traditions and beliefs, some new ontological concepts acquired through syncretism with Zoroastrianism. References to the pagan deity *Baal Berith* had been evacuated, but the story of Abraham, their forefather and Patriarch, remained the umbilical cord that would unite the people of this land through their unique tradition. The lasting chasm with the Samaritans would have then developed when the later refused to change their worship.

Nehemiah clearly adhered to the original cult of the land of Israel. In a speech to his people, he recounts the story of their forefather, from the days of Abraham (Neh. 9:7-33) all the way up to the Babylonian Exile, in order to bring the clan to reaffirm their Covenant with God and to justify the establishment of the Mosaic laws. He ends his speech with these words:

> *Neh. 9:38 And because of all this we make a sure covenant, and write it; and our princes, our Levites, [and] our priests are at the sealing.*

Certainly, a theology that would leverage on the primeval emotions of the people would help Nehemiah consolidate his authority and justify the application of laws that were in support of the Persian administrative model. As Volker Glissmann concludes:

> *Overall, the Abram story provides a survival strategy for diaspora communities, through adherence to, and respect for, the community of the ancestral family line, and by winning the trust of the host nation through moral behaviour and piety, and ultimately by trusting that YHWH will come to their aid and bless their relationship with the imperial ruling class.*[294]

---

[294] Glissmann, Volker. 2009. "Genesis 14: A Diaspora Novella?" *Journal for the Study of the Old Testament* 34(1): 33-45. p. 44

It seems hard to believe that if the story of Abraham was a late and purely fictitious creation, as the scholarly community currently believes, it could have achieved such a significant unifying role among the diaspora communities. Such a position also completely denies the historical claims of the Samaritans. All evidences point to the same direction: the Abrahamic story originated from a much older tradition and was profoundly engrained in the psyche of these people.

In summary

- While writing was expensive and rare, it is very likely that such a politically motivated covenant would have been recorded in writing as far back as the Middle Bronze Age.

- There are no known examples of covenants established between men and gods, outside of the biblical one. In all known historical treaties, gods are invoked as witnesses, but never as a party.

- Parallels between the Abrahamic Covenant and attested historical treaties of the Middle Bronze Age can be established as soon as *Yahweh* is no longer seen as a God, but rather as a mortal.

- The possession of the land and the issue of the heir, which are central to the Abrahamic Covenant, are two notions common to other historical treaties.

- There is no doubt that Judaism developed significantly under the Persian administration at a time when Zoroastrianism was the state religion and that many parallels can be drawn between Judaism and Zoroastrianism.

- It appears that the Samaritans are right when they claim they were the sons of Manasseh and Ephraim, and the guardians of the original religion of the Land.

> *One fool will deny more truth*
> *in half an hour than a wise man*
> *can prove in seven years.*
> **Coventry Patmore**

Conclusion

As a plethora of scholars have pointed out before us, the history of Mesopotamia contains striking parallels with that outlined in the Bible. The *Enûma Eliš* Sumerian text tells the story of Creation, complete with the Garden of Eden and the Tower of Babel. The Epic of Gilgamesh contains a version of the Great Flood, which offers numerous parallels to the biblical story down to details such as the number of days the ark was afloat. The story of the birth of Moses as told in Exodus is almost identical to that of Sargon of Akkad a thousand years earlier. Finally, Hammurabi's code of laws bears a strong resemblance to the Ten Commandments. And, while none of these texts is found in its entirety in the Bible, there's no denying that the authors of the Torah were inspired by these sources.

But, is not the quest for God an inner one? By accepting the dogma, the prophets and the priests naturally interpreted the story of the Patriarchs from a theological perspective. Is it any surprise, then, that all research conducted to confirm the historical accuracy of the Patriarchs was destined to fail? By focusing our research on the identity of Abraham's Lord rather than on Abraham himself, this essay puts forth a systemic, logical, rational and verifiable explanation for the story of Abraham.

From the cult of the ancestors to Judaism

Each time Israel was submitted to a foreign power, its "state" religion evolved. The Abrahamic narrative offers a historical account of the *berith* ("covenant") made between Abraham and *Baal* ("lord"). As soon as one dissociates *Yahweh* from *Elohim* in the text, and considers Abraham's religion strictly from the perspective of the immaterial deity *Elohim*, it becomes obvious that his worship was perfectly in line with that of the Bronze Age. Numerous biblical references, such as the carrying of Joseph's bones, indicate that the Patriarchs were likely practicing the nomadic cult of the ancestors. The gift of the land through the covenant with *Baal* let the descendants of Abraham adopt a more sedentary lifestyle and this situation favored the emergence of the *Baal/El Berith* deity at Shechem.

The Tetragrammaton *Yhwh* could refer to *yhw*, a geographical location in Judea, but it seems more likely that the Hebrew-speaking descendants of Abraham would have understood the Akkadian expression *beliya* as "*Baal Yah*" instead of "my *Baal*". Possibly influenced by Akhenaten, the Pharaoh ruling at Amarna, the priests of Canaan would have developed a new "super deity" by compounding the attributes of *Baal, Baalah (Asherah* or *Baalah Sarah)* and *Baal Berith.* The name *Yhwh* would then be the result of the contraction of the expression *Baal Yah we* ("and") *Baalah* of which the term *Baal* was dropped, either for sake of concision or as part of the repudiation process. "*Yahweh Elohim*" would then be the perfect divine representation of the earthly couple that sits at the very head of Israel's lineage.

As the history of the Samaritans testifies, the adoption of *Yahwism* was not peaceful and unified. The priests would have sought to dissociate their new super deity from the lesser *Baals* by proscribing this name and clamping down on the rebarbative tribes. Clashes continued to occur until the exilic and post-exilic periods. Judges recounts how some of the early Israelite tribes that were still veneering *Baal Berith*, were slaughtered by king Abimelech. Book of 1 King tells of how King Jehu legitimized his coup by associating king Ahad with *Baal* – depicted as a weaker deity – while establishing the superiority of *Yahweh.* Later, and this time through contact with Zoroastrianism, the Persian state religion, the Jewish priests in exile adopted some new ontological concepts.

Historical context and influences

	Bronze Age			Iron Age	Persian period	Ancient Rome	Islamic period
1800-1700 BCE	1600-1400 BCE	1300-1100 BCE	1000-600 BCE	500-200 BCE		30-325 CE	610-632 CE

55: Evolution of the Abrahamic faith

The above diagram shows how Baal would have been first celebrated after his death for the berith ("Covenant") he made with Abraham. He would soon be elevated to the ranks of El Berith, a local deity for Shechem. Given Baal had a consort; the Tetragrammaton yhwh could represent the contracted form of Baal Yah we ("and") Baalah from which the term Baal was removed. Yahweh would soon be adopted as this new super deity's name that would further distance it from lesser Baals. It would be through contact with Zoroastrianism that new ontological concepts would be grafted to the original pagan cult that is still practiced by the Samaritans.

Deeply rooted in tradition

In their efforts to assemble the sacred texts that would eventually become the Torah, the post-exilic priests collated some older narratives relating the history of their ancestors, as evidenced by the many parallels with the ancient texts by which they were largely inspired. One of these texts tells the story of their ancestor, Abraham, and of the *berith* he once made with *Yahweh*. The case was perfect: The Hebrew of Amorite origin; the descendants of Abraham had "proof" that "*Yahweh*" had chosen the Jewish people from among all other on Earth by making an everlasting covenant with them. If their captivity was the result of a loosening of their faith; the end of their captivity should logically be the sign that He had been sensitive to their affliction and fervor.

An inalienable symbol of the pledge between their ancestor Abraham and his "God", the *sacred* text of the Covenant will likely be integrated a thousand years later, during the Babylonian Exile, as a founding narrative for the Torah. At this time, the principle of unicity (*Yahweh=Elohim*) raises no more questions among the priests. And since power has always been given and legitimized by a deity, who would dare question the divine nature of this great Lord, of whom no other tangible evidence remains? Parts of the Torah might have been assembled in order to preserve the accumulated texts and traditions in order to ensure sustainability and facilitate their transportation during the exile (the disappearance of the Ark does seem to coincide with this event). Additional texts, also related to the history of this people, would have naturally been grafted during final assembly to form a coherent body. By alternating the use of the terms *Yahweh* and *Elohim*, the editors might have simply attempted to perpetuate what they thought was a style, without fully realizing the deeper meaning of what was before their eyes, therefore contributing to the overall confusion. In fact, they will neither be the first, nor the last, in a long list of priests, scribes and copyists to perpetuate this "error"; hence the dead-end that has faced previous documentary theories.

Scholars believe that the texts relating to the story of Abraham were passed down orally, mainly because of the many inconsistencies and contradictions they contain, and which must be interpreted in order to substantiate the dogma. However, these same contradictions vanish when approached from a historico-political angle. All confusion evaporates the moment we distinguish the immaterial *Elohim* from the anthropomorphic *Yahweh*. If these texts had been passed down orally, it is certain that the smallest details would have been lost forever. In this regard, historical anthropologist Vansina's work on the reliability of oral transmissions is insightful; he believes that they are highly reliable, but only when considered in a specific cultural context.[295] However, their capacity for reporting factual information is inevitably limited. The great accuracy with which certain details reveal the hidden meaning of this earthly interpretation of the story of the Patriarchs is no coincidence. Rather, it attests to the

---

[295] Vansina, Jan. 2006. *Oral Tradition: A Study in Historical Methodology.* New Brunswick: Aldine Transaction. p. 172

accuracy of extremely well preserved sources. The mysterious Ark of the Covenant would then prove to be a simple chest used to preserve and carry the valuable treaty written on clay tablets. When considering *Yahweh* as a mortal Lord, the format and clauses related to the right of the land and the importance of an heir will be later echoed in nearby Hittite and Assyrian treaties.

Diverging interpretations from both conservatives and liberals scholars appear to find a coherent synthesis in this proposed euhemeristic hypothesis. As a result, new possibilities for the interpretations of subsequent events can be considered.

A politico-historical covenant

Archaeologists Finkelstein and Silberman, among many others, have clearly demonstrated that early-Israelites and native Canaanites were not only living together, but were also sharing a common culture.[296] The only archaeological difference is that pork bones were not found on Iron Age settlements identified as belonging to early-Israelites.

From the moment one accepts the human dimension of Abraham's "Lord", the answers flow naturally, whether from the scriptures or from history. Accordingly, an analysis of the cultural backgrounds of Abraham and Hammurabi allows us to conclude that both men were of Amorite descent. The culture of this semi-nomadic, semi-sedentary people strongly resembles that of the Patriarchs. History tells us that the Amorites took control of Ur under the rule of king Ibi-Sin and that, from that moment; they gradually began spreading their influence over all of Mesopotamia, the Levant and Egypt. The application of the 6/10 multiplier to the Babylonian sexagesimal dating system allows us to correct conversion errors likely introduced by Nabonidus' scribes in the 6th century and conclude that Sem, Abraham's ancestor, emigrated from Canaan shortly after the construction of the first ziggurats, precisely at the time the Amorites arrived in Ur. The Bible also tells us that Abraham's journey began in Ur.

---

[296] Finkelstein, Israel and Neil Asher Silberman. 2001. *The Bible Unearthed: Archaeology's New Vision of Ancient Israel and the Origin of its Sacred Texts*. New York: Free Press.

Hammurabi reinforced his power through his many conquests and alliances. His diplomatic correspondence indicates that he could have fought in the War of Kings alongside his allies prior to 1763. Again according to the "corrected" dates of the Bible, Abraham would have been 45 years old when he arrived in Canaan and 52 years old when Ishmael was born. Since several clues lead us to conclude that Abraham and Hammurabi were indeed born in the same year, namely 1810, we can date the War of Kings around 1764. Incidentally, this timeframe coincides perfectly with known information about Hammurabi's reign and indicate that the latter could have waged a military campaign with the kings of Elam and Larsa before defeating them. These victories allowed Hammurabi to expand his empire quickly. However, after hearing rumors of simmering discontent in Sodom, he would have soon felt the need to reassert his authority over the area. After witnessing the determination with which Abraham set out to rescue his nephew, Lot, Hammurabi opted to make a covenant with Abraham, promising him the land of Canaan in exchange for unwavering loyalty by him and his descendants. Strengthened by this new alliance, Hammurabi was well positioned to assert his authority through a show of force, namely by inflicting severe punishment on the rebellious city of Sodom.

However, Abraham's bloodline was problematic: how could the son of an Egyptian slave woman possibly be the rightful heir to such a vast empire? The solution: Hammurabi conceived a son with Sarah. According to the proposed chronology, Isaac would have been born in 1750, the same year that Hammurabi died. Obviously, Abraham and his descendants would then have been required to pledge allegiance to Samsu-iluna, Hammurabi's son.

By ordering the sacrifice of Ishmael, the firstborn son threatening the dynastic bloodline, Samsu-iluna severely tests Abraham's loyalty. However, the latter rises to the occasion. In the conflict between Jews and Muslims as to the identity of the son who was to be sacrificed, we must agree with the Muslims, since it was most likely Ishmael and not Isaac who was to be sacrificed.

The 1649 eruption of Mount Thera provides further evidence to this hypothesis by showing that the story of the famine in Egypt during Joseph's reign corresponds perfectly to the "dream" that he interpreted at the age of 18, and to the consequences of this major volcanic eruption on the people. This natural disaster allowed the Hyksos to take control of all of Egypt *"without hazarding a battle"*. The Bible tells us that Joseph was a highly influential man in Egypt during the years that ensued and that he skillfully traded the lands of Egypt in exchange for food. The accuracy of the dating method continues to hinge on his father, Jacob, and the Hyksos king, Yakub-her, who would have ruled Egypt between 1634 and 1626. And, although it gives no indication as to Jacob's age at the birth of his eleventh son, Joseph, this new dating system easily leads us to believe that he could have been 47 years old at the time. As such, Joseph could have succeeded him and reigned from 1625 to 1601. The Hyksos king Khyan and biblical Joseph would then be the same person; in fact, the parallels between the similar-sounding Khyan-Seth (Ya-sef) and Joseph are striking.

Moreover, neither Manasseh, Joseph's son, nor Yanassi, Khyan-Seth's son, acceded to the throne following their father's death. Biblical Manasseh and Hyksos Yanassi would have been the same man. Jacob clearly chose Ephraim—and not Manasseh—to inherit. The story of Genesis ends abruptly with Joseph's death, after which the Hyksos king Apophis rose to power. As can be seen in Annex A, the names of his children and the sequence of events lead us to believe that Apophis was Ephraim. The first years of his reign were peaceful. But his sons, including Ezer, were later killed in attacks led by the Thebans. As a result, the reins of power reverted to Shemidah, Manasseh's great-grandson, upon Ephraim's death. Biblical Shemidah and Hyksos king Khamudi were likely the same man, and, just a few years later, pursued by the Theban king Ahmose, Khamudi fled to Sharuhen, in Canaan.

The book of Genesis naturally ends with the expulsion of the Hyksos and the fall of the Babylonian empire.

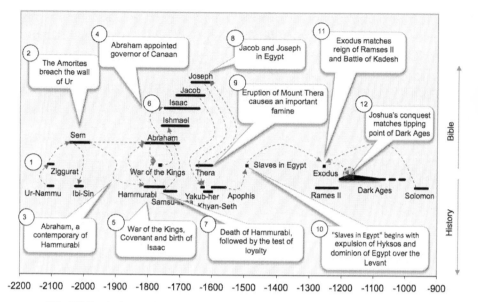

56: Biblical chronology dilemma solved using the 6/10 multiplier

Based on the premise that Abraham was merely one of Hammurabi's governors and that he did not have any special relationship with the divine, the 6/10 dating system enables us, with astonishing accuracy, to associate entire sections of Antiquity with more than forty dates in the Bible spanning fifty generations. For the first time, the biblical story of the Patriarchs lines up with historical data to provide a believable explanation of events.

Van De Mieroop expresses the impact that Hammurabi had on the Ancient Near East:

> *It is thus no surprise that later generations remembered him more than any other kings of the early second millennium. Over time, his prominence increased, and he became one of the few kings of the ancient past to whom people referred more than a thousand years after his death.[297]*

Free from dogma

In what is more than just a simple coincidence, the long chain of events in the story of the Patriarchs lines up with astonishing

---

[297] Van De Mieroop, Marc. 2005. *King Hammurabi of Babylon: a Biography*. Malden: Blackwell p.128

accuracy with the history of the region. The dates and events, the peoples' cultural practices, laws and structure of governance, and the archaeological evidence all come together to give the story a rational interpretation. Common sense finally prevails in the meeting of myth and history.

Far from being the story, or even the glorified legend, of a man who sought to revolutionize the religious culture of his time, the realization we are facing is a harsh one: Abraham was not a particularly religious man and he never sought to make a covenant with a new god. What's more, the man we consider to be the father the world's monotheistic religions was possessed of very human characteristics, including greed.

Without denying them any cultural or spiritual worth, this research invites us to acknowledge that the objectivity, credibility, and, above all, the immutability of the messages of the prophets are seriously called into question, since the evolution of their thinking and of their beliefs is based on the fact that Abraham truly became the father of a new religion upon making the Covenant with God. Once this argument is refuted, what is the basis for their logic? The real scandal lies not in the questioning of divine inspiration, but rather in the perpetuation of the illusion through complacency. As Galileo said: "*of all hatreds, none is greater than that of ignorance against knowledge*".

If we seek to find a sacred dimension to the Scriptures, it is because of their universal and symbolic nature, more than the belief in divine intervention encourages us to do so. These texts appear to have been inspired by the eternal and benevolent wisdom of man, as are philosophical, Hindus, Buddhist or Greek teachings, all of which contribute to the development of spirituality and to the enlightenment of the human being. In this respect, they possess unimaginable educational value, but, rather than seeking to sanctify them as dogma, it would be infinitely wiser to "translate" them, to modernize them and to restore them to their full measure of authenticity.

While a fair amount of work has been done, much remains to be accomplished as egos can hardly stand failures and uncertainties. Many will rather continue wearing rose-colored glasses coated with religious non-sense than admit they were wrong or that they just don't know.

President Obama was right when he said:

> *"I believe that the starting point of faith is some doubt – not being so full of yourself and so confident that you are right and that God speaks only to us, and doesn't speak to others, that God only cares about us and doesn't care about others, that somehow we alone are in possession of the truth."[298]*

If confirmed, this hypothesis should convey everyone to conduct serious introspections. I dream of the day when scholars and scientists will offer their *mea culpa* to the Jewish people and start acknowledging that their remarkable odyssey did indeed began some four thousand years ago, albeit with a twist. I also dream of the day when religious leaders of all faiths will acknowledge that their scriptures are no more sacred than the works of Plato, Descartes or Voltaire, and that it is not only ok, but essential to question them. The world should grasp this opportunity to question the role, meaning and significance of the divine in the third millennium. Times have changed and it is no longer necessary to oppose spirituality to science as the more we explore the Universe, the more we realize that matter, energy and consciousness are all interrelated. Humanity is ready to modernize itself by doing away with sectarian religions dominated by archaic-beliefs to embrace a new model of all encompassing spiritual freedom that acknowledges that all science and creatures are part of one universal living force that flourishes through love, respect and compassion.

---

[298] Office of the Press Secretary. "Remarks by the President at National Prayer Breakfast." The White House. http://www.whitehouse.gov/the-press-office/2015/02/05/remarks-president-national-prayer-breakfast (retrieved March 12, 2015).

ANNEXES

Annex A: Further study

Driven by curiosity to seek out additional clues and new unifying theories, we continue our investigation by casting the rigid scientific method aside in favor of greater intuition and speculation. It's nevertheless interesting to go on and see how well the interpretation bears out with subsequent ancestors. The results obtained are intriguing enough to merit consideration and might even offer clues for future research.

We will first revisit the story of Isaac, before expanding on the investigation carried over with Joseph and Manasseh to see what connection can be established between biblical Isaac, Jacob, Esau, Ephraim, Ezer and Shemidah and the remaining Hyksos kings. We will finally explore how Exodus and Joshua's conquest might relate to the history of the region.

The lost tablets of Isaac

Genesis provides very few details about Isaac's life, despite the fact that he was the son with whom *Yahweh* made his Covenant (Ge 17:19).

Nothing is known about his childhood. We only know that, when Sarah dies, Abraham dispatches his loyal servant to find a wife for his son:

> *Ge 24:3 And I will make thee swear by Baal*, the Elohim of heaven, and the Elohim of the earth, that thou shalt not take a wife unto my son of the daughters of the Canaanites, among whom I dwell:*
>
> *Ge 24:4 But thou shalt go unto my country, and to my kindred, and take a wife unto my son Isaac.*

Why are Canaanite girls despised in the eyes of Abraham? Why would Abraham seek a wife for Isaac among his polytheistic

---

* Yahweh in the Bible

family members? It only seems logical that Abraham is simply trying to perpetuate the practice of endogamy.

The servant returns with Rebekah, sister of Laban and daughter of Bethuel:

> *Ge 24:47 And I asked her, and said, Whose daughter art thou? And she said, the daughter of Bethuel, Nahor's son, whom Milcah bare unto him: and I put the earring upon her face, and the bracelets upon her hands.*

Chapter 25 of Genesis tells the story of the birth of the couple's children, Esau and Jacob, although without any particular emphasis on Isaac.

A feeling of déjà-vu

We finally learn more in Chapter 26, which tells the story of Isaac and Abimelech, summed up as follows:

> *A famine strikes the land. Isaac and his family leave for Guerar. The very beautiful Rebekah is introduced as Isaac's sister before being kidnapped by King Abimelech. "God" threatens the king, who then releases Rebekah. Abimelech is intimidated; he fears and respects Isaac. A discussion ensues about ownership rights to wells. In the end, Isaac makes a covenant with Abimelech and each man returns home.*

This passage from Chapter 26 is astonishingly similar to the events described in Chapters 20 and 21, which also tell of Abimelech. However, the main character in these chapters is Abraham. It is obviously the same story, starring the same actors, which repeats one generation later.

Let's examine these two stories in more detail. While the story of Isaac and Abimelech is told in its entirety in Chapter 26, that of Abraham and Abimelech begins in Chapter 20, breaks off, and then concludes at the end of Chapter 21. The similarities between the two texts become more apparent when they are analyzed side by side:

Comparison of the stories involving Abimelech		
Common event	Story of Isaac	Story of Abraham
A famine forces Abraham-Isaac to travel to Guerar.	26:1 And there was a famine in the land, beside the first famine that was in the days of Abraham. And Isaac went unto Abimelech king of the Philistines unto Gerar.	20:1 And Abraham journeyed from thence toward the south country, and dwelled between Kadesh and Shur, and sojourned in Gerar.
Abraham-Isaac introduces his wife as his sister; she is then kidnapped by Abimelech.	26:7 And the men of the place asked him of his wife; and he said, She is my sister: for he feared to say, She is my wife; lest, said he, the men of the place should kill me for Rebekah; because she was fair to look upon.	20:2 And Abraham said of Sarah his wife, She is my sister: and Abimelech king of Gerar sent, and took Sarah.
Abimelech is threatened and accuses Abraham-Isaac of having lied to him about his wife.	26:10 And Abimelech said, What is this thou hast done unto us? one of the people might lightly have lien with thy wife, and thou shouldest have brought guiltiness upon us.	20:9 Then Abimelech called Abraham, and said unto him, What hast thou done unto us? and what have I offended thee, that thou hast brought on me and on my kingdom a great sin? thou hast done deeds unto me that ought not to be done.

Abimelech knows that he risks the death sentence for "touching" a married woman.	26:11 And Abimelech charged all his people, saying, He that toucheth this man or his wife shall surely be put to death.	20:3 But *Baal* came to Abimelech in a dream by night, and said to him, Behold, thou art but a dead man, for the woman which thou hast taken; for she is a man's wife.
Abraham-Isaac negotiates access to the wells for the servants.	26:18 And Isaac digged again the wells of water, which they had digged in the days of Abraham his father; for the Philistines had stopped them after the death of Abraham: and he called their names after the names by which his father had called them.	21:25 And Abraham reproved Abimelech because of a well of water, which Abimelech's servants had violently taken away.
Abimelech knows that Abraham-Isaac has the protection of *Baal*. Phichol is the head of Abimelech's army.	26:20 And the herdmen of Gerar did strive with Isaac's herdmen, saying, The water is ours: and he called the name of the well Esek; because they strove with him. 26:28 And they said, We saw certainly that *Baal* was with thee: and we said, Let there be now an oath betwixt us, even betwixt us and thee, and let us make a covenant with thee;	21:22 And it came to pass at that time, that Abimelech and Phichol the chief captain of his host spake unto Abraham, saying, *Baal* is with thee in all that thou doest:

Abraham-Isaac promises to act like a responsible governor and to treat Abimelech and his descendants with esteem and respect.	26:29 That thou wilt do us no hurt, as we have not touched thee, and as we have done unto thee nothing but good, and have sent thee away in peace: thou art now the blessed of the *Baal*.	21:23 Now therefore swear unto me here by *Elohim* that thou wilt not deal falsely with me, nor with my son, nor with my son's son: but according to the kindness that I have done unto thee, thou shalt do unto me, and to the land wherein thou hast sojourned.
Abraham-Isaac concludes an alliance with Abimelech.	26:31 And they rose up betimes in the morning, and sware one to another: and Isaac sent them away, and they departed from him in peace.	21:32 Thus they made a covenant at Beersheba: then Abimelech rose up, and Phichol the chief captain of his host, and they returned into the land of the Philistines.

It is highly unlikely that Isaac and his father experienced the exact same events. We must not lose sight of the fact that these documents were likely inscribed on clay tablets; therefore, it seems more logical to believe that some were lost, mixed up or too damaged to be transcribed.

Without Isaac's story, the scribes could not have just pieced together a "sacred" text. A creative solution would have been to take Abraham's story and adapt it to fit his son, Isaac, a stratagem that legitimized Isaac without infringing on the sacred nature of the texts.

Unsure of the order of certain tablets, or taken aback by the obvious similarities between the two texts, the authors of the Bible may have decided to break up the story of Abraham to give it the form we know today. Nevertheless, the main objective should have been to preserve an unaltered version of the texts, even at the risk of certain events appearing out of order. In our opinion, Chapter 26 should be disregarded completely, since it doesn't fit with the original story.

This hypothesis about missing or mixed up tablets also explains why certain sections of Genesis appear disjointed and inconsistent. It seems appropriate to suggest a few corrections. By reinserting a few sections of Chapters 18, 19, 20 and 21 between Chapters 15 and 16 (see Figures 32 and 33), we not only improve continuity, but the story of the destruction of Sodom makes much more sense:

Abraham, a newly appointed governor, wishes to please Hammurabi, the new overlord visiting. He bows before him and offers him hospitality as signs of respect. Hammurabi tells him of his intention to destroy Sodom. While Abraham tries to reason with him to save the lives of the Sodomites, Hammurabi insists on setting an example by annihilating Sodom.

Abimelech's story should take place immediately after Hammurabi returns home. Sarah is still a young and presumably beautiful woman and Abraham a new governor who has not yet firmly established his authority over the region. But, the punishment leveled against Sodom is enough to convince Abimelech to submit to the new king of Babylon and to Abraham, his representative.

ANNEXES

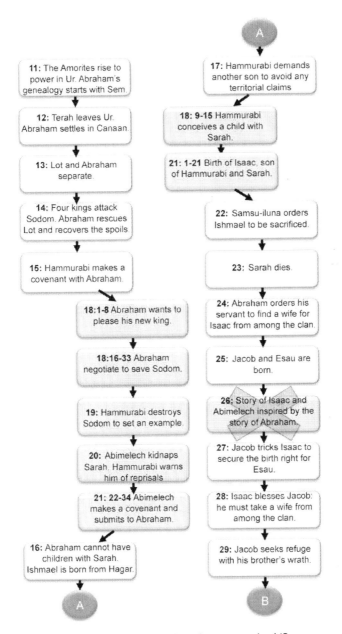

11: The Amorites rise to power in Ur. Abraham's genealogy starts with Sem.

12: Terah leaves Ur. Abraham settles in Canaan.

13: Lot and Abraham separate.

14: Four kings attack Sodom. Abraham rescues Lot and recovers the spoils.

15: Hammurabi makes a covenant with Abraham.

18:1-8 Abraham wants to please his new king.

18:16-33 Abraham negotiate to save Sodom.

19: Hammurabi destroys Sodom to set an example.

20: Abimelech kidnaps Sarah. Hammurabi warns him of reprisals.

21: 22-34 Abimelech makes a covenant and submits to Abraham.

16: Abraham cannot have children with Sarah. Ishmael is born from Hagar.

A

17: Hammurabi demands another son to avoid any territorial claims

18: 9-15 Hammurabi conceives a child with Sarah.

21: 1-21 Birth of Isaac, son of Hammurabi and Sarah.

22: Samsu-iluna orders Ishmael to be sacrificed.

23: Sarah dies.

24: Abraham orders his servant to find a wife for Isaac from among the clan.

25: Jacob and Esau are born.

26: Story of Isaac and Abimelech inspired by the story of Abraham.

27: Jacob tricks Isaac to secure the birth right for Esau.

28: Isaac blesses Jacob: he must take a wife from among the clan.

29: Jacob seeks refuge with his brother's wrath.

A

B

57: Genesis, revised and corrected - 1/2

295

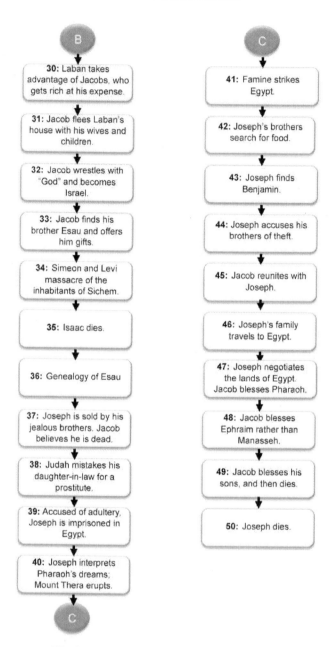

58: Genesis, revised and corrected - 2/2

Not only do these reordered verses offer better textual continuity, but they also provide more coherence and fluidity to the new sections. Thus, the pivotal passage in which Hammurabi visits Sarah to fulfill his promise of impregnating her is no longer abruptly interrupted by the passage about Abimelech.

These adjustments are completely optional, as they do not affect the substance of previous arguments, since they in no way affect the dates and relationships postulated in this analysis. However, I believe they do provide additional clarity to the story.

The original story of Abimelech

Once the tablets are reordered, a brief review of the relationship between Abraham and Abimelech is in order. We pick up Abraham's story at the beginning of Genesis, at which point this newly appointed governor is expected to exert a certain degree of authority. As a representative of the central authority, he must also advocate for the interests of the empire throughout the entire territory of Canaan. The story of Abimelech explains how this king of Guerar, initially reluctant to submit, is eventually persuaded after receiving the customary assurances.

Let's analyze this passage in more detail:

> *Ge 20:1 And Abraham journeyed from thence toward the south country, and dwelled between Kadesh and Shur, and sojourned in Gerar.*

> *Ge 20:2 And Abraham said of Sarah his wife, She is my sister: and Abimelech king of Gerar sent, and took Sarah.*

As a newly appointed governor, Abraham must have been endeavouring to fulfill his responsibilities and earn the people's respect. Was Sarah abducted or was she given to Abimelech as wife? Was this a power play by Abimelech to better negotiate with Abraham or did Abraham give his "sister" to Abimelech in hope to establish a relationship of trust?

> *Ge 20:3 But Elohim came to Abimelech in a dream[299] by night, and said to him, Behold, thou art but a dead man, for the woman which thou hast taken; for she is a man's wife.*

---

[299] Hebrew (חלום) chalowm ("dream")

Either way, Abimelech is urged to free Sarah on threat of reprisals. Incidentally, Hammurabi's code of law prohibits a man from sleeping with another man's wife, a crime one would think would be especially reprehensible if committed with the wife of his representative:

> *§ 129. If a man's wife be surprised (in flagrante delicto) with another man, both shall be tied and thrown into the water, but the husband may pardon his wife and the king his slaves.*[300]

Abimelech finds himself in a delicate situation, in which he is forced to prove that he did not have sexual relations with Sarah.

> *Ge 20:4 But Abimelech had not come near her: and he said, Baal***, wilt thou slay also a righteous nation?*
>
> *Ge 20:5 Said he not unto me, She is my sister? and she, even she herself said, He is my brother: in the integrity of my heart and innocency of my hands have I done this.*
>
> *Ge 20:6 And Elohim said unto him in a dream, Yea, I know that thou didst this in the integrity of thy heart; for I also withheld thee from sinning against me: therefore suffered I thee not to touch her.*
>
> *Ge 20:7 Now therefore restore the man his wife; for he is a prophet, and he shall pray for thee, and thou shalt live: and if thou restore her not, know thou that thou shalt surely die, thou, and all that are thine.*
>
> ...
>
> *Ge 20:14 And Abimelech took sheep, and oxen, and menservants, and women servants, and gave them unto Abraham, and restored him Sarah his wife.*
>
> *Ge 20:15 And Abimelech said, Behold, my land is before thee: dwell where it pleaseth thee.*

---

[300] Richardson, M. E. J. 2004. *Hammurabi's Laws: Text, Translation, and Glossary.* New York: Continuum International Publishing Group. p. 83
*** Adonai ("my lord") in the Bible

Ge 20:16 And unto Sarah he said, Behold, I have given thy brother a thousand pieces of silver: behold, he is to thee a covering of the eyes, unto all that are with thee[301], and with all other: thus she was reproved.

To atone for his wrongdoing, Abimelech returns Sarah to Abraham with livestock, servants, and a thousand pieces of silver.

Ge 21:22 And it came to pass at that time, that Abimelech and Phichol the chief captain of his host spake unto Abraham, saying, Baal[**] is with thee in all that thou doest:

Abimelech knows that, as Hammurabi's representative, Abraham has the latter's protection.

Ge 21:23 Now therefore swear unto me here by Elohim[***] that thou wilt not deal falsely with me, nor with my son, nor with my son's son: but according to the kindness that I have done unto thee, thou shalt do unto me, and to the land wherein thou hast sojourned.

The king of Guerar is willing to submit, although not without conditions: Abraham must swear that, if Abimelech agrees to submit to and respects the laws of Hammurabi, he and his descendants will be given due respect as merits their rank.

Ge 21:24 And Abraham said, I will swear.

Once the pact is sealed, they move on to trivial details.

Whilst the structure of this story appears logical and chronologically correct (challenge – threat – alliance – conflict resolution), the same does not hold true for the story of Isaac, since the conflict resolution (discussion about ownership of the wells) occurs *before* the alliance. This is why I believe that the story of Abraham is likely to be the original one, and that of Isaac to be a later addition.

The fact that the designation "king of the Philistines" is used only for Abimelech supports the hypothesis that Isaac's story was

---

[301] This is another application of the laws of Hammurabi where a transaction must be made in public so all can witness the fairness.

** Elohim in the Bible

*** Elohim in the Bible, but Baal would have also been appropriate

patched together during the compilation of the various sources that make up the Bible.

In this same vein, I refute the use of this argument by those who claim that the Patriarchs could not have existed during the Middle Bronze Age, based on the fact that the Philistines emerged only much later.

In summary

- Certain sources used to write the story of the Patriarchs were lost, damaged or mixed up.

- Without the story of Isaac, the scribes could not justifiably invent a "sacred" story.

- Except for the fact that it stars Isaac, Chapter 26 of Genesis is an exact reproduction of the story of Abraham's youth with King Abimelech. This stratagem legitimizes Isaac without actually infringing on the sacred nature of the texts.

- The current form of Chapter 26 post-dates the arrival of the Philistines in the Levant, hence the source of the anachronism noted by Finkelstein and many others before him.

The ruling Hyksos

We left the Hyksos at the time Apophis took over control of the ruling dynasty instead of Yanassi's (i.e. Joseph's son Manasseh). Many more questions and possible links can be further explored and might help us better understand what might have happened of the biblical characters. For instance, could a faint connection be made between the Hyksos king Salatis (Se-kha-en-Rê) and Isaac (יצחק), and between Sheshi and Esau (עשו)? Once again, the etymology of the names is similar: the contracted form "Se-kha" resembles "Isaac" and that of "Eshi" resembles "Esau".

Salatis and Sheshi were the first two Hyksos kings to rule over all of Egypt. Historians date their reigns around 1650. If Isaac really died at the age of 108 in 1642 (Ge 35:28), he could have risen to power after the eruption of Mount Thera in 1649, even at the ripe age of 101. It's thus inconceivable that he seized control by force. However, his son Jacob could have offered to symbolically share power with Isaac. And, since several experts believe that Salatis and Sheshi may have been the same king, a co-regency—which was common in Antiquity—would have been a possibility, thereby resolving the ambiguity.

But, if Sheshi and Esau were the same person, then Yakub-her was his brother. And, since all evidence points to the fact that Yakub-her was the Hyksos pharaoh who succeeded Sheshi, the question is: why did his brother Jacob become governor instead of one of Esau's many sons? (Chapter 36 of Genesis provides his complete genealogy.)

Isaac and Esau rise to power

It was pointed out earlier that the relationship between the two brothers was rife with tension. Let's summarize the facts.

While Jacob and Esau, Isaac's sons, are twin brothers, Esau is technically born first, making him the eldest. Jealous of his brother, Jacob tricks him out of his birthright, sparking conflict between the two brothers. The Bible describes how Jacob poses as Esau to steal their father's blessing. Although the Old Testament is unclear on this subject, we will see that their father, Isaac, favors Jacob because Esau chooses to marry women of "impure" blood. Isaac and Rachel reject them and appoint Jacob as heir to the dynasty. An enraged Esau forces his brother into exile. Jacob spends many years with Laban, and marries his daughters—Amorite women—in deference to his parents' wishes. During this time, Esau becomes wealthy. Upon his return from exile, Jacob finally begins to thrive, eventually becoming the ruler of Egypt.

The story of this quarrel and of Esau's choice of wives is telling. This evidence will be supported later on by facts and historical interpretations, in addition to an analysis of the biblical context.

A plate of lentils

In order to better understand the evolution of the two brothers' relationship, we need to revisit their story. The Bible describes Jacob's trickery and his determination to steal Esau's birthright. The story unfolds in Chapters 25, 27 and 28, well before the story of the famine and, as such, before the Hyksos rise to power in Egypt.

The Bible tells how a young Esau "despises" his birthright and would rather give it to Jacob; in other words, he seems indifferent to it:

> *Ge 25:34 Then Jacob gave Esau bread and pottage of lentils; and he did eat and drink, and rose up, and went his way: thus Esau despised his birthright.*

Much later, Jacob, disguised as Esau, dupes their father into giving him the blessing:

> *Ge 27:24 And he said, Art thou my very son Esau? And he said, I am.*
>
> ...
>
> *Ge 27:30 And it came to pass, as soon as Isaac had made an end of blessing Jacob, and Jacob was yet scarce gone out from the presence of Isaac his father, that Esau his brother came in from his hunting.*

But an enraged Esau would not stand for it:

> *Ge 27:41 And Esau hated Jacob because of the blessing wherewith his father blessed him: and Esau said in his heart, The days of mourning for my father are at hand; then will I slay my brother Jacob.*

Was this a simple quarrel, a case of sibling rivalry or conscious choice made in the greater interest of the Amorite dynasty? Recall that Ishmael was passed over as heir in favour of Isaac because he was not a "pure" Amorite. Terrified by his brother's death threats, Jacob flees to Laban's home to find a wife.

What was the lineage of Esau's and Jacob's wives?

> *Ge 28:6 When Esau saw that Isaac had blessed Jacob, and sent him away to Padanaram, to take him a wife from thence; and that as he blessed him he gave him a charge, saying, Thou shalt not take a wife of the daughters of Canaan;*
>
> *Ge 28:7 And that Jacob obeyed his father and his mother, and was gone to Padanaram;*
>
> *Ge 28:8 And Esau seeing that the daughters of Canaan pleased not Isaac his father;*
>
> *Ge 28:9 Then went Esau unto Ishmael, and took unto the wives which he had Mahalath the daughter of Ishmael Abraham's son, the sister of Nebajoth, to be his wife.*

Esau disregards his parents' wishes. Not only does he marry Ishmael's daughter, he also marries a Canaanite and a Hittite woman:

> *Ge 36:2 Esau took his wives of the daughters of Canaan; Adah the daughter of Elon the Hittite, and Aholibamah the daughter of Anah the daughter of Zibeon the Hivite;*
>
> *...*
>
> *Ge 26:34 And Esau was forty years old when he took to wife Judith the daughter of Beeri the Hittite, and Bashemath the daughter of Elon the Hittite:*

However, these women of Hittite, Canaanite and part-Egyptian (a descendant of Ishmael) descent do not meet Amorite standards:

> *Ge 26:35 Which were a grief of mind unto Isaac and to Rebekah.*

Esau's choices clearly displease his parents, which is why I believe Jacob is most likely appointed as heir. Jacob returns after several years of exile, during which time he becomes wealthy at Laban's expense.[302]

The Bible tells us that, in the meantime, Esau has become an influential lord, wealthier than his brother Jacob and commander of a powerful army. This takes place well before the famine and the Hyksos rise in Egypt. Esau is living in Edom when Jacob returns from Laban's house:

> Ge 32:3 And Jacob sent messengers before him to Esau his brother unto the land of Seir, the country of Edom.

> Ge 32:4 And he commanded them, saying, Thus shall ye speak unto my lord Esau; Thy servant Jacob saith thus, I have sojourned with Laban, and stayed there until now:

> Ge 32:5 And I have oxen, and asses, flocks, and menservants, and women servants: and I have sent to tell my lord, that I may find grace in thy sight.

Naturally, Jacob is worried about how Esau will react to him. However, good fortune and time seem to have cooled his brother's temper. Esau no longer appears to harbor any bitterness toward Jacob and welcomes him home with open arms.

Could the famine that strikes a few years later drive Isaac and Esau into the fertile lands of Egypt, where they could have ruled over the Delta region? The location of this geographical area supports this idea, since the region of Edom – where Esau lives – borders Egypt between the Sinai Peninsula and the Gulf of Aqaba.

If Isaac ruled over the Delta region and if Esau already controlled a portion of Edom through his marriage to Ishmael's daughter (recall that Edom was originally Ishmael's land), then it wouldn't be unusual if father and son ruled the country together.

Being twin brothers, Esau's blood is just as "pure" as Jacob's. And, as firstborn, he is the natural choice to rule. However, his lineage is an issue: by violating the rule of endogamy, Esau presents a threat to the Amorite dynasty. As a result, it seems he is allowed to reign but his descendants are barred from succeeding him. Upon his death, the throne is to revert back to his brother Jacob and his descendants. And this would explain how Yakub-her, the Hyksos, would eventually come to rule. Any

---

[302] Jacob serves Laban for "twenty years", or rather, 12 years (6/10). See Ge 31:41

archaeological evidence of Sheshi's descendants being also passed over in favor of Yakub-her, would be confirmation of the brothers' quarrel over their birthright.

Could this fratricidal quarrel be at the heart of the war still raging between the Israelis, descendants of Isaac and Jacob, and the Arabs, descendants of Ishmael and Esau?

In summary

- The Bible describes the long conflict over Esau's birthright, which eventually reverts to Jacob.

- A furious Esau threatens to kill his brother. Jacob exiles himself for many years with Laban.

- Esau rules as an influential and wealthy lord, but his descendants are considered too "impure" to carry on the dynasty.

- Several historians believe that Salatis-Sheshi rose to power around 1650. According to our calculations, Isaac and Esau took power in 1649.

- If Sheshi-Esau was the same person, then Jacob succeeded him upon his death.

- The bloody fratricidal war raging between the Israelis and the Arabs could have its foundations in this long-ago quarrel over inheritance rights.

Jacob blesses Pharaoh

The hypothesis that Esau is the Hyksos king Sheshi is in line with the biblical logic, and appears to be based on the twin brothers' choice of wives. But, this deduction is purely circumstantial; there are no concrete historical facts to confirm these links. This hypothesis would be bolstered by indications that Sheshi-Esau died at the age of 78, the same age at which his twin brother Yakub-her-Jacob rose to power in Egypt.

The Bible does not provide many details about Esau, apart from his genealogy. However, if he truly is the pharaoh who preceded

Jacob, then an analysis of Jacob's relationship with him might yield further information.

Certain details about Jacob's arrival in Egypt stand out, for example the intriguing passage in which Joseph presents his father to pharaoh. These verses could shed more light on the matter, since they occur chronologically after the famine, namely after the Hyksos rise to power in Egypt:

> *Ge 47:7 And Joseph brought in Jacob his father, and set him before Pharaoh: and Jacob blessed Pharaoh.*

> *Ge 47:8 And Pharaoh said unto Jacob, How old art thou?*

> *Ge 47:9 And Jacob said unto Pharaoh, The days of the years of my pilgrimage are an hundred and thirty years: few and evil have the days of the years of my life been, and have not attained unto the days of the years of the life of my fathers in the days of their pilgrimage.*

The traditional theological interpretation of these passages leaves the reader perplexed as to why Jacob would bless the Pharaoh of Egypt: what authority does a simple "Bedouin" presume to have over the most powerful man in the vicinity? There is no apparent explanation for this action. Moreover, Jacob's response is rather odd: he speaks of his life in the past tense and complains of having been ill and of not having lived as long as his ancestors.

If Isaac's name was inserted into the story of the test of loyalty (Ge 22) in order to make the text fit the ideology, why wasn't this also the case with the passage about Pharaoh?

A subtle manipulation of the text yields a new interpretation; the ambiguity is restored by simply replacing the subjects "Jacob" and "Pharaoh" with the pronoun "he" in Ge 47:8 and Ge 47:9:

> *Ge 47:7 And Joseph brought in Jacob his father, and set him before Pharaoh: and Jacob blessed Pharaoh.*

> *Ge 47:8 And he said, How old art thou?*

> *Ge 47:9 And he replied, The days of the years of my pilgrimage are an hundred and thirty years: few and evil have the days of the years of my life been, and have not*

*attained unto the days of the years of the life of my fathers
in the days of their pilgrimage.*

In Hebrew, the verb (ברך) *"barak" – to kneel, to bless* – is used.
Jacob shows reverence to Pharaoh, but this action takes on a very
different meaning if the latter is none other than his own brother
Esau, at death's door and on the verge of handing over the reins of
power to Jacob (as we saw previously, Jacob seems to have
survived his brother by ten years).

Since they are twins, both men can indeed be presumed to be 78
years old (= 130 x 6/10), without this affecting the chronology of
the story. However, Esau would be justified in begrudging
Abraham and Isaac, who both died at a much greater age. This
nevertheless ripe old age would also explain Esau's eagerness to
appoint the brilliant young Joseph as head of the country a few
years prior.

Naturally, from the perspective of the religion of *Yahweh*, a well-
intentioned scribe might have been tempted to "clarify" this
passage in order to eliminate any ambiguity. The following verse
clearly illustrates that the subjects are not always well defined in
this narrative style. In fact, in this discussion between Jacob and
Isaac it is unclear who "he" is:

> *Ge 27:25 And he said, Bring it near to me, and I will eat of
> my son's venison, that my soul may bless thee. And he
> brought it near to him, and he did eat: and he brought him
> wine and he drank.*

This is why I believe that the proper names "Jacob" and
"Pharaoh", used in Ge 47:8 and Ge 47:9, might have been inserted
to replace the original impersonal "he", much like the name of
Isaac would have been inserted in Chapter 22.

The anachronistic "pharaoh"

But, how could Esau be "pharaoh" if there was no pharaoh in
Egypt at this time? Many historians refute the historical
authenticity of the Patriarchs based on the anachronistic use of the
term "Pharaoh" in the story, among other things.

According to Christiane Desroches Noblecourt, a renowned Egyptologist, the first use of the term "per-aâ" to refer to the sovereign of Egypt dates back to the twelfth year of the reign of Queen Hatshepsut and her nephew, Thutmose III.[303] However, Hatshepsut was the daughter of Thutmose I, who succeeded Amenhotep I, son of Ahmose. She reigned over Egypt for some fifty years, after the expulsion of the Hyksos.

Based on this information, we must consider the possibility that this term was introduced by the Hyksos-Patriarchs themselves. The Egyptians began using this term one or two generations after the Hyksos were run out of the country. So, we shouldn't be surprised to see the term "Pharaoh" used in reference to Esau, and to the other Hyksos who ruled the Delta region to some degree before him.

The word *pharaoh* means "great house" in Egyptian. When referring to their extended family, the Patriarchs often allude to their "house". The expression "great house" is therefore a term that would apply to the ruler of Avaris and of the entire region.

In summary

- Out of tremendous respect for the scriptures, the Bible's authors obviously exercised great restraint in not altering the "sacred" texts. However, they did try to remove certain ambiguities by introducing proper names into them.

- The bizarre blessing of Pharaoh would make complete sense if Pharaoh was in fact Esau, suffering on his deathbed and ready to transfer power to Jacob.

- Since Esau and Jacob were twin brothers, both could have been 78 years old.

- The term "Pharaoh", which refers to the sovereign of Egypt, first appears in Egyptian texts at the time of Queen Hatshepsut. It seems plausible that it was already being used by the Hyksos, but that it took some

---

[303] Desroches Noblecourt, Christiane. 2002. *La reine mystérieuse*. Paris: Pygmalion. p. 134.

time to reappear after the Hyksos's expulsion from Egypt.

The expulsion of the Hyksos

Unlike the data in the story of Abraham, the information linking Esau to the Hyksos pharaoh Sheshi remains highly circumstantial. While the reported facts seem to indicate a positive identification, we would be hasty in leaping to a definite conclusion. We can only hope that future research will eventually confirm or refute this hypothesis. For the moment, let's see where curiosity takes us.

In our quest for possible ties between the last Hyksos pharaohs and the Patriarchs, let's analyze other available fragments of information. What few shreds remain offer up clues that are worth considering. The last two Hyksos pharaohs were Apophis and Khamudi. What do we know about them? Can they be linked to the Patriarchs? How did the Hyksos saga end in Egypt? Do the biblical and historical chronologies still line up? Let's turn our attention to answering these questions.

Fortunately, the rise of the 17th and 18th Egyptian dynasties, which expelled the Hyksos from the country, is much better documented than the Hyksos dynasties themselves. Chronicles and other artefacts enable us to reconstruct the sequence of events leading up to this expulsion:

- *The Papyrus Sallier I describes a conflict between the Hyksos king Apophis and the king of Thebes, Seqenenre Tao II, about noise made by hippopotamuses, which were preventing Apophis from sleeping despite the great distance between these two kings; this proves that the two were contemporaries.*[304]

---

[304] Crew, P. Mack, I. E. S. Edwards, J.B. Bury, C. J. Gadd, Nicholas Geoffrey, N. G. L. Hammond and Edmond Sollberger. 1973. *History of the Middle East and the Aegean Region c.1800-1380 B.C.* Vol. 2 of *The Cambridge Ancient History*. Cambridge: Cambridge University Press. p.72

- *The reign of Seqenenre Tao II lasted only three or four years. Seqenenre Tao II died from severe head injuries likely sustained during a battle against Apophis.*[305]

- *Seqenenre Tao II's son, Kamose, succeeded him. During a military campaign, Kamose intercepts a message that Apophis is trying to send to one of his allies. Kamose dies just five years into his reign.*[306]

- *The task of continuing and eventually concluding the battle against the Hyksos falls to Ahmose, Kamose's younger brother and successor. Apophis is still alive at this time, since the Rhind papyrus, written during the 33rd year of his reign, mentions Ahmose; this proves that Apophis lived to at least this age.*[307]

- *Upon Apophis's death, he is succeeded by Khamudi, who fends off an attack by Ahmose during the 11th year of his reign. But, Ahmose successfully conquers Avaris the following year, around the 18th year of his reign. The Hyksos are pushed back to Sharuhen in Judea and continue to fight off a siege for a further three years before fading into the obscurity of history. They never again posed a threat to Egypt.*[308]

While the above information are documented facts, there is still no unanimity on the dates of the reigns of the Theban kings Seqenenre Tao II, Kamose and Ahmose, who chased the Hyksos from Egypt.

The following table lists the generally accepted start and end dates of the reigns, as well as the proposed variations:

---

[305] Ibid. p.289

[306] Ibid. p. 291

[307] Grimal, Nicolas. 1992. *A History of Ancient Egypt.* Oxford: Blackwell. p. 186

[308] Bright, John. 2000. *A History of Israel.* Louisville: Westminster J. Knox Press. p. 60

Kings of Thebes	Dynasty	Proposed dates
Seqenenre Tao II	17th	Range: 1591/1558 to 1576/1545
Kamose	17th	Range: 1576/1545 to 1570/1539
Ahmose I	18th	Range: 1570/1530 to 1546/1504

As such, E.F. Wente suggests that Ahmose reigned from 1570 to 1546, whereas H.W. Helck believes he ruled some forty years later, from 1530 to 1504. However, most experts seem to agree on the median reign of 1550 to 1525, proposed by Reeves, Arnold, von Beckerath, Shaw and Kitchen.[309]

In summary

- The archaeological evidence points to a link between the last two Hyksos kings and the Theban kings who expelled them from Egypt.

- The expulsion of the Hyksos took place during the successive reigns of three Theban kings: Seqenenre Tao II, Kamose and Ahmose I.

- Historians date the reigns of these three kings between 1591 and 1504.

The long reign of Apophis

According to Ryholt, Apophis was the Hyksos king who succeeded Khyan—possibly the biblical Joseph—, and who reigned over all

---

[309] Shaw, Ian. 2002. *The Oxford History of Ancient Egypt*. Oxford: Oxford University Press. p. 461

of Egypt for many years.[310] To all appearances, he maintained good relations with the Theban kings during the first years of his reign. The Hebrews no doubt enjoyed a special status until the ascension of Seqenenre Tao II, who set off hostilities.

In presuming that Apophis (or two successive kings ostensibly with the same name, as N. Grimal suggests) reigned for a period of 35 to 50 years, then we will see that the chronology of the Hyksos Patriarchs previously outlined lines up perfectly with the dates generally recognized for the Theban kings of the 17th and 18th Dynasties who expelled them from Egypt.[311]

It is important to further clarify this chronological link, as it can lend further credibility to any hypothesis concerning a connection between the Hyksos and the Patriarchs. In fact, if the known dates for the Theban kings who expelled the Hyksos from Egypt do not correspond to the ends of the reigns of Apophis and Khamudi, then we fail in this demonstration.

In addition to the facts presented earlier, which suggests a possible link between the Theban kings and these last two Hyksos kings— Apophis and Khamudi—, it is also helpful to study the links that may have existed between the later and their possible predecessors, namely the Patriarchs.

To this effect, it is interesting to note that, over a century ago, Rawlinson described an ancient tradition linking Apophis to the pharaoh who lived at the same time as Joseph. He wrote:

> *There was an ancient tradition, that the king who made Joseph his prime minister, and committed into his hands the entire administration of Egypt, was Apepi. George the Syncellus says that the synchronism was accepted by all.[312]*

George the Syncellus was a Byzantine chronicler who lived in the late 8th century CE and who wrote a chronicle of world history from Genesis to the accession of Diocletian (284). According to Rawlinson, this tradition was widely accepted during Syncellus'

---

[310] Ryholt, Kim. 1997. *The Political Situation in Egypt During the Second Intermediate Period c. 1800-1550 B.C.* Copenhagen: Carsten Niebuhr Institute of Near Eastern Studies: Museum Tusculanum.
[311] Grimal, Nicolas. 1992. *A History of Ancient Egypt.* Oxford: Blackwell.
[312] Rawlinson, George. 1920. *Ancient Egypt.* Fifth ed. London: T. Fisher Unwin. p. 145

lifetime. Although it has since been influenced by theological interpretation, this tradition nevertheless supports the belief that Joseph and Apophis lived at the same time. If we maintain our hypothesis that Khyan and Joseph were the same person and that Apophis succeeded Khyan, then our research findings are perfectly consistent with this ancient tradition.

However, the fact that this tradition describes a relationship of trust between the two men seems to illustrate a contradiction. In fact, Ryholt explains that Khyan appointed his son, Yanassi, as his successor.[313] Yet, history tells us that Apophis succeeded Khyan. So, if Khyan was really Joseph, then how could the latter have been on good terms with Apophis?

In summary

- If we acknowledge that Apophis reigned for 35 to 50 years (we know he reigned for more than 33 years), then our chronology lines up perfectly with the historical timeline.

- An "ancient tradition" states that Apophis and Joseph were contemporaries. The hypothesis proposed in this essay is consistent with this notion.

- How could Joseph have been on good terms with Apophis if the latter prevented Manasseh (Joseph's son) from taking power?

Jacob blesses Apophis

The events reported in the Bible correspond to this historical account. The passages below provide significant insight. Just before his death, Jacob, also known as Israel, calls for Joseph and his two sons, Ephraim and Manasseh, to give them his blessing:

> *Ge 48:17 And when Joseph saw that his father laid his right hand upon the head of Ephraim, it displeased him:*

---

[313] Ryholt, Kim. 1997. *The Political Situation in Egypt During the Second Intermediate Period c.1800-1550 B.C.* Copenhagen: Carsten Niebuhr Institute of Near Eastern Studies: Museum Tusculanum.

and he held up his father's hand, to remove it from Ephraim's head unto Manasseh's head.

Ge 48:18 And Joseph said unto his father, Not so, my father: for this is the firstborn; put thy right hand upon his head.

Ge 48:19 And his father refused, and said, I know it, my son, I know it: he also shall become a people, and he also shall be great: but truly his younger brother shall be greater than he, and his seed shall become a multitude of nations.

Ge 48:20 And he blessed them that day, saying, In thee shall Israel bless, saying, Elohim make thee as Ephraim and as Manasseh: and he set Ephraim before Manasseh.

Given the family history, it makes sense to suspect that Manasseh married a non-Amorite, and, therefore, a woman considered by his grandfather, Jacob, to be of "impure" blood. This prompts Jacob to give his blessing to Ephraim, to the great dismay of Joseph.

This abrupt shift in the situation is not unlike the failed succession of Yanassi. If Ephraim was in the Bible chosen over Manasseh, and if history says that Apophis became pharaoh instead of Yanassi, then the question is: is Apophis actually the Ephraim of the Bible? The association seems entirely plausible.

Apophis can also be written as Apofis or Apepi. In Egyptian, this name is written as "*ipp*". We know that Apophis worshipped the god Re, since his throne name was Apepi A-Qenen-Re (*the energy of Re is great*). Therefore, the contracted form of his name could have been Apepi-Re or Ipp-Re. In Hebrew, Ephraim is written אפרים. If we ignore the Masoretic punctuations added sometimes between 700-1000 CE, we can also pronounce "*Aph-re-yim*" which means "*the anger of Re is great*".[314] We find here what appears to be a plausible match between the two names.

---

[314] The Hebrew term (אַף) aph ("nostril", "nose", "face", "anger"); letter (ר) re; and (ים) ym ("sea", also indicates plurals in Hebrew; although in this case it seems to qualify Re, rather than the anger).

59: Hyksos sphinx - king Apepi

This photograph by J. Pascal Sebah taken at the Museum of Giza in the last century, shows Hyksos sphinx; the name Apepi appears on one of them. These statues are similar in style, pose and appearance to the statue of the turquoise goddess *Baalat*. Is this simply a coincidence, or is it not evidence that the Hyksos had elevated themselves to the rank of *Baals*?

In summary

- The Bible tells us that Jacob appointed Ephraim as Joseph's successor instead of Manasseh.

- History tells us that Apophis succeeded Khyan instead of Yanassi.

- The name "Ephraim" also means "Anger of Re is great" in Hebrew.

- The statue of Apophis is the same style and shape as that of the turquoise goddess "*Baalat*".

- The word "Pharaoh" is strikingly similar to "mighty bull" in Hebrew.

Did Ezer die in combat?

Curiously, around the middle of Apophis's reign, the name Apepi A-Qenen-Re (*the energy of Re is great*) morphed into Apepi A-User-Re (*the strength of Re is great*). Given the great similarity in the meanings of the two names, most experts believe that they refer to the same person. However, this opinion is not unanimous, and some experts, including Grimal, continue to believe that they could have been two different pharaohs.

Incidentally, the Bible teaches us that one of Ephraim's sons is named Ezer (1 Chronicles 7:21) – in Hebrew (עזר) *ezer*, means "mighty is Re"[315]. This name and definition matches that of A-User-Re, who succeeded or perhaps even reigned with A-Qenen-Re. Do the timeline and the story of Ezer support this possible link?

According to the Bible, Manasseh and Ephraim were born before the famine, that is, before 1649:

> Ge 41:50 *And unto Joseph were born two sons before the years of famine came, which Asenath the daughter of Potipherah priest of On bare unto him.*

> Ge 41:51 *And Joseph called the name of the firstborn Manasseh: For Elohim, said he, hath made me forget all my toil, and all my father's house.*

Joseph was still alive when Ephraim's sons and Manasseh's grandson were born, meaning that this third generation was born before 1601, the year Joseph died:

> Ge 50:23 *And Joseph saw Ephraim's children of the third generation: the children also of Machir the son of Manasseh were brought up upon Joseph's knees.*

But, a terrible tragedy befell Ephraim:

---

[315] Hebrew (עז) `az ("strong", "mighty", "fierce")

1 Chr 7 :21 And Zabad his son, and Shuthelah his son, and Ezer, and Elead, whom the men of Gath that were born in that land slew, because they came down to take away their cattle.

1 Chr 7 :22 And Ephraim their father mourned many days, and his brethren came to comfort him.

1 Chr 7 : 23 And when he went in to his wife, she conceived, and bare a son, and he called his name Beriah, because it went evil with his house.

All of Ephraim's sons are slaughtered. Old and grief stricken, Ephraim must nevertheless father another son, Beriah, to carry on the line.

But, how and at what age did Ezer, Ephraim's son, die? The Bible says all of Ephraim's sons are killed by the men of "Gath". This city is generally thought to be Tell es-Safi in Israel, although the name could refer to several cities since in Hebrew (גת) *gath* means "wine press". Wine was also produced in Thebes, and in many other places. Frescoes depicting scenes of wine presses have been found dating precisely from the 18th Dynasty:

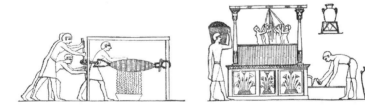

60: Wine press - Bronze Age fresco of Thebes

Is it possible that Ephraim's sons were instead killed in a battle against the rebel Thebans who were attempting to expel them? Seqenenre Tao and the other Theban kings were in fact "*born in that land*" of Upper Egypt; as such, they could very likely have "*come down*" to them in Lower Egypt. What's more, all of Ephraim's heirs were killed. It would have had to have been a crucial battle for the sons of pharaoh to have engaged in a military conflict.

Since Seqenenre Tao was the first Theban king to wage war against the Hyksos, we could date Ezer's death as early as 1591 according to high chronology. In this case, and since we know Ephraim was born before the famine, he could have been just 58 years old (= 1649 - 1591) when his sons were killed. He could have easily fathered another son at this age. However, if we use middle chronology, which dates the reign of Seqenenre Tao around 1558, then Ephraim would have been up to 91 years old (= 1649 - 1558), a little old to reproduce! But, if Seqenenre Tao was the first Theban king to openly engage the Hyksos, there might have been a few undocumented clashes in the years leading up to his ascension. In this case, Ezer could still have been killed earlier. According to the chronology applied to the kings of Thebes, Ezer could have died as early as 1591 (high chronology), but more likely died around 1558 (middle chronology).

Shemidah rises to the challenge

With all of Ephraim's sons having been slain in battle, the next in line for the throne was a member of Manasseh's family, a great-grandson named (שמידע) Shemidah. Since the Egyptian "k" is almost silent, Shemidah appears to have been Khamudi, the last Hyksos king to rule Egypt.

According to the Bible, Shemidah is the son of Gilead (1 Chr 7:19), himself the son of Machir (Nu 26:29), who is the son of Manasseh (Ge 50:23). If the sons of Machir "were brought up upon Joseph's knees", then we can deduce that one of these sons, Gilead, could have been born before 1601 (the year of Joseph's death). Based on an estimated average of 20 years between generations, Machir could have been born around 1629 (= 1649 - 20), or 20 years after the birth of Manasseh. Gilead could have been born 20 years later, around 1613 (= 1629 - 20), a few years before Joseph's death. If we extrapolate from this reasoning, Shemidah, the son of Gilead, could have been born around 1593 (= 1613 - 20), when Ephraim was 56 years old (= 1649 - 1593).

Therefore, Shemidah could have reigned alongside an aging Ephraim-Apophis.

How does this chronology correspond to that of the Theban kings who succeeded Seqenenre Tao? According to history, Ahmose was seven years old when his father, Seqenenre Tao, died after a brief reign of just three or five years, some time between 1576 and 1545. Most experts agree that he died around 1554, when his brother, Kamose, became the new king of Thebes. Apophis was still alive at this point. If Ahmose reigned jointly with his brother, Kamose, then the first year of his reign can be established as early as 1554.

History also teaches us that Apophis/Ephraim lived long enough to be the contemporary of Ahmose and that he was succeeded after his death by Khamudi. Given that the Theban king Ahmose defeated the Hyksos at Sharuhen during the 17th or 18th year of his reign, and that this event took place in the 11th year of Hyksos king Khamudi's reign, then we can conclude that Ahmose must have risen to power at least six years (= 17 - 11) before Ephraim's death.

In order for there to be a "link" between the biblical and the historical timelines, then Ephraim could only have died six years after the start of Ahmose's reign. If Ahmose rose to power in 1554, then Ephraim must have lived to the venerable age of 101 (= 1649 − 1554 + 6). Recall that Ezer died only some 10 years previously (= 1558 − 1554 + 6). This would have made Shemidah 45 years old (= 1593 − 1554 + 6) when he inherited the throne and 56 years old (= 1593 − 1554 + 17) when the Hyksos retreated to Sharuhen and the final siege played out. Beriah's young age (he was born after Ezer died), the state of war and the volatile situation that prevailed were all factors that gave Shemidah the upper hand in shaping the country's destiny.

However, since some experts, including Edward F. Wente, suggest that Seqenenre Tao, Kamose and Ahmose lived some 15 years earlier, it's also possible that Ephraim may have died at age 86.[316] If this was the case, Shemidah would have been 15 years younger,

[316] Wente, Edward F., Charles C. Van Sclen Iii and George R. Hughes. 1976. *A Chronology of the New Kingdom, in Studies in Honor of George R. Hughes.* Chicago: Oriental Institute of the University of Chicago.

or 30 years old when Ephraim died and 41 years old at the time of the siege. However, if Ezer was killed in an attack led by Sequenenre Tao, then Beriah would still have been only about 10 years old when Ephraim died, since the dates of this attack would be relative to Ephraim's death.

The proposed dates are therefore entirely consistent with either of the chronologies applied to the three Theban kings who liberated Egypt from the Hyksos.

There is still other information to support our hypothesis. The Bible says that Ephraim also had a daughter named Sherah, a name similar to Herit (Harat), the daughter of Apophis.

> *1 Chr 7:24 And his daughter was (שארה) Sherah, who built*
>
> *(בית חורון) Beth-horon the nether, and the upper, and Uzzen-sherah.*

If Sherah built Beth-horon, which in Hebrew means "house of Horon", it seems very likely that the house she built would bear her name. In this case, it seems that Sherah and Horon could be one and the same (based on phonetic similarities).

We also know the names of two of Apophis's sisters, Tany and Tcharydjet, and of one of his daughters, Harat (or Herit). A link between Horon and Harat therefore seems highly likely.

While these names and dates, and this chronology do not allow us to draw a firm conclusion, they do pave the way for new interpretations.

In summary

- If Ephraim lived to the age of 86 or older, then the proposed chronology allows us to believe that he could have been Apophis.

- If Ezer was A-User-Re, then he died as a co-regent, perhaps during an attack by the Egyptians, which explains the name change and the ambiguity about Apophis, since it is still not known whether there reigned one or two kings by this name.

- Because Ephraim no longer had any heirs, he was forced to father another son at an advanced age. However, this son would have been too young to rule upon Ephraim's death.

- If Ephraim had no heir old enough to reign, Shemidah would have been a valid choice. Shemidah, Joseph's great-great-grandson, could have been Khamudi.

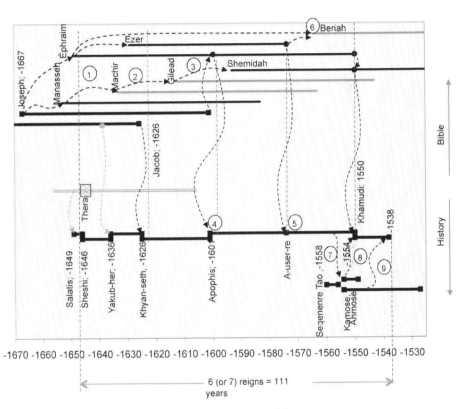

61: Ephraim and Apophis

This table illustrates the chronology linking Ephraim to Apophis. It corresponds to the traditional timelines of the expulsion of the Hyksos. Manasseh and Ephraim are born before the famine (1). Their sons, Machir and Ezer, are born before Jacob dies (2). Joseph holds his grandson, Gilead, on his knees (3). According to Jacob's wishes, Ephraim – instead of Manasseh – succeeds Joseph (4). Ephraim changes his name or rules jointly with Ezer until his death, between (5) and (7). After his sons are killed, Ephraim fathers Beriah (6), who is still too young to rule after his father dies. Seqenenre Tao dies while Apophis is still alive (7). His son, Kamose, succeeds him and perhaps rules jointly with Ahmose. After Ephraim dies, Shemidah, Joseph's great-great-grandson, takes up the charge against the Hyksos (8). Twelve years later, in the 17th year of his reign, Ahmose liberates Egypt (9).

Recap of the reigns of the 15th dynasty

According to the Turin Royal Canon	
???	??
???	??
???	??
???	??
???	??
Khamudi	??
Six reigns	108(?) years

According to Manetho (Flavius)	
Saites (Salatis)	19 years
Bnon (Sheshi)	44 years
Apacnan (Yakub-her)	37 years
Iannas (Khyan-seth)	50 years
Apofis (Apepi I&II)	61 years
Assis (Khamudi)	49 years
Total	260 years

Historical data	
Salitis (Se-kha-en-Re)	??
Sheshi (Maa-ib-Re)	??
Yakub-her (Mery-user-Re)	??
Khyan (Suser-en-Re)	??
Apophis I (A-Qenen-Re)	+33 years
Apophis II (A-User-Re)	
Khamudi	+11 years
Six (or seven) reigns	-150 max.

Proposed lengths	
Salatis (Isaac)	3 years
Sheshi (Esau)	10 years
Yakub-her (Jacob)	10 years
Khyan-seth (Joseph)	25 years
Apepi–Re (Ephraim)	51 years
A-User-Re (Ezer)	co-regency
Khamudi (Shemidah)	12 years
Six (or seven) reigns*	111 years*

* The last six reigns (excluding Salatis) total 108 years.

62: The shepherd kings

Slaves in Egypt

By recounting the enslavement of the children of Israel in the land
of Egypt and how God delivered them through the guidance of
Moses, Exodus is one of the most poignant myths of Israel. This is
why some would like to see in the expulsion of the Hyksos a
possible explanation for this myth. However, dates don't match,
and much like the story of Abraham, archaeologists have long

abandoned the idea of a historical event, primarily because they have never found any indication of a large-scale population movement leaving Egypt. Indeed, we learn in Numbers that hundreds of thousands were liberated.

> *Num 1:46 Even all they that were numbered were six hundred thousand and three thousand and five hundred and fifty.*

It is clear that if hundreds of thousands of Israelites had fled Egypt, there would be plenty of Egyptian records of this. This is why most historians now suggest that if any Exodus ever took place, it must have been limited to a community, a clan, and even perhaps to a large family.

Finkelstein summarizes the current scholarly position on Exodus:

> *Putting aside the possibility of divinely inspired miracles, one can hardly accept the idea of a flight of a large group of slaves from Egypt through the heavily guarded border fortifications into the desert and then into Canaan in the time of such a formidable Egyptian presence. Any group escaping Egypt against the will of the pharaoh would have easily been tracked down not only by an Egyptian army chasing it from the delta but also by the Egyptian soldiers in the forts in northern Sinai and in Canaan.* [317]

However, the investigation we have conducted thus far has brought us to realize that the Bible can offer very factual data, but instead of taking it at face value, we should carefully interpret it and map it to known historical events.

Keeping the Hyksos in check

After expelling the Hyksos, the Egyptians sought to consolidate and expand their territorial authority by exerting control over the Levant. By the 21st year of Thutmose III reign (1481-1425), Egypt launched a significant campaign and marched over Israel and Canaan. Although the Hyksos must have been kept in check ever

---

[317] Finkelstein, Israel and Neil Asher Silberman. 2001. *The Bible Unearthed: Archaeology's New Vision of Ancient Israel and the Origin of its Sacred Texts.* New York: Free Press. p. 61

since their expulsion, this event marked the beginning of a dominion that would last nearly 300 years.

> *We know that the solution to the problem of the Exodus is not as simple as lining up dates and kings. The expulsion of the Hyksos from Egypt in 1570 BCE ushered in a period when the Egyptians became extremely wary of incursions into their lands by outsiders. And the negative impact of the memories of the Hyksos symbolizes a state of mind that is also to be seen in the archaeological remains. Only in recent years has it become clear that from the time of the New Kingdom onward, beginning after the expulsion of the Hyksos, the Egyptians tightened their control over the flow of immigrants from Canaan into the delta.[318]*

Finkelstein hereby underlines the difficulty associated with trying to match the Exodus with the expulsion of the Hyksos (such as suggested by filmmaker Simcha Jacobvici), especially given the tight control that the Egyptians exercised onto their borders at that time.

Now, what if Exodus did not originate from a mass movement leading a large number of Israelites slaves out of Egypt, but rather an event "liberating" all Canaanites from their Egyptian yoke? Indeed, given Egypt exercised control over most of the Levant after the Hyksos were expelled, the end of this domination must have been perceived as a divine liberation. Certainly, such an interpretation would explain why no mass movement of Israelites was ever recorded leaving Egypt. In fact, the number 603,550 provided in the Bible accounts for all males *"from twenty years old and upward, all that are able to go forth to war in Israel"*. By applying the 6/10 multiplier, we get 362,130 (=603,550*6/10) males, which appears to match relatively well the most recent population estimates for entire Canaan during the Late Bronze II that was assessed by Kennedy to range anywhere between 499,000 and 650,000.[319]

---

[318] Ibid. p. 58
[319] Kennedy, Titus Michael. 2013. A Demographic Analysis of Late Bronze Age Canaan: Ancient Population Estimates and Insights through Archaeology. Doctor of Literature and Philosophy, University of South Africa.

How could we possibly validate such a hypothesis and what event should we look for? We know that there are two possible ways to calculate the date of the Exodus based on the Bible:

The first method is based on the amount of time the children of Israel have been slaves in Egypt. God tells Abram in Ge 15:13 that his descendants would be slaves in a foreign land for 240 (400*6/10) years. This number was likely taken out of Acts 7:6 *post factum*. In Ex 12:41, we learn that the Israelites were in Egypt for 258 years (430*6/10). This number also appears in Galatians 3:17. So were the Israelites in Egypt for 240 or 258 years? If the Egyptians started exercising control over the Levant immediately after – or soon after – the expulsion of the Hyksos, the "oppression" would have started somewhere between 1550 and 1515 (depending which years are retained for the reign of Ahmose) and we should therefore situate the Exodus anywhere between 1310 (1550-240) and 1257 (1515-258).

The second method is based on the construction of the Temple of Jerusalem. In this case, we are told in the Bible that Exodus should have taken place 288 (480*6/10) years before Solomon built the Temple. Given this work was undertaken in the forth year of his reign, we find that the Exodus should have taken place in 1254 (970 – 4 + 288).[320]

These two methods – which are believed by most modern scholars to be relying on bogus dates – are now converging thanks to the 6/10 multiplier and are allowing us to pinpoint the Exodus fairly accurately. What international event could have left a lasting impression on the Israelites during this time, and more importantly, how did it affect Egyptian control over the Levant?

Exodus and the Battle of Kadesh

The Battle of Kadesh is an epic and memorable battle that began in 1274. It opposed the Egyptians and the Hittites armies in the northern part of the Levant. The battle lasted over a decade and involved thousands of chariots. As there was no clear winner, a

---

p. 580
[320] The construction of Solomon's Temple began in the fourth year of his reign, in 970.

peace treaty was finally ratified in 1259. A copy of this peace treaty, the oldest recorded in history, is still on display at the headquarters of the United Nations. Ever since the Hyksos had been expelled from Egypt some 250 years prior, and up until this battle, most of the Levant was maintained under Egyptian dominion. After signing this treaty, the Egyptians started loosening up on the Levant and it is difficult not to think of this key event as an amazing opportunity for the Israelites to think of themselves as slaves being freed from Egyptian domination...

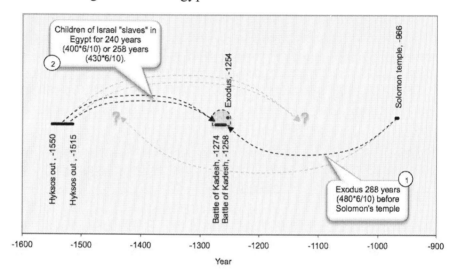

63: Dating the Exodus

The above diagram shows that date of the Exodus coincides with the end of the Battle of Kadesh. It also confirms that all the dates provided by the Bible; that is (1) 1 Ki 6:1 as well as (2) Ge 15:13/Acts 7:6 and Ex 12:41/Gal 3:17, converges to the same period, but only after being corrected using the 6/10 multiplier.

Accounts of the Battle of Kadesh were documented in the forms of a poem and bulletin. These texts can be found on many Egyptian sites. Pentaur, scribe at the Temple of Amen, wrote the epic poem that can be found on the walls of the Luxor temple in Karnak. The poem recounts the victory of Ramses II against his enemies. We know that both belligerent, Hittites and Egyptians alike, claimed victory on this battle. It is therefore not surprising to see both parties twisting reality to their advantages.

64 : The Battle of Kadesh

The above fresco is from the Great Temple of Abû-Simbel. Countless Egyptians and Israelites found death in this tragic war that lasted for well over a decade. The evocative image of Pharaoh's enemies drowning in the river finds echo in the Red Sea's story and must have had a lasting impact on the collective memories of the region.

This poem of Pentaur bears important similarities with the biblical passage of the Red Sea, where Moses tells of how the Israelites flee from Egypt. In fact, Moses' recount appears like a shortened version of the poem (and/or bulletin) that was embellished and turned to the Israelites' advantages. The original poem is rather long, but the critical passages are highlighted and can more easily be compared with the biblical account. For the most part, the main ideas and the sequence of events are the same.

Exodus 14	Poem of Pentaur
Pharaoh's heart hardens. He lifts up a large army and chariots to pursue the Israelites/Hittites.	
Ex 14:5 And it was told the king of Egypt that the people fled: and the heart of Pharaoh and of his servants was turned against the people, and they said, Why have we done this, that we have let Israel go from serving us? Ex 14:6 And he	*Beginning of the victory of king Ramses Miamun – may he live forever! – which he obtained over the people of the Khita, of Naharain, of Malunna, of Pidasa, of the Dardani, over the people of Masa, of Karkisha, of Qasuatan, of Qarkemish, of Kati, of Anaugas, over the people of Akerith and Mushanath.* *The youthful king with the bold hand has not his equal. His arms are powerful, his heart is firm, his courage is like that of the god of war, Monthu, in the midst of the fight. He leads his warriors to unknown peoples. He seizes his weapons, and is a wall, their [his warriors'] shield in the day of battle. He seizes his bow, and no man offers opposition. Mightier than a hundred*

made ready his chariot, and took his people with him:	*thousand united together goes he forwards.* *His courage is firm like that of a bull. He has smitten all peoples who had united themselves together. No man knows the thousands of men who stood against him. A hundred thousand sank before his glance. Terrible is he when his warcry resounds; bolder than the whole world; he is as the grim lion in the valley of the gazelles. His command will be performed. No one dares to speak against him. Wise is his counsel. Complete are his decisions, when he wears the royal crown Atef and declares his will, a protector of his people. His heart is like a mountain of iron. Such is king Ramses Miamun. After the king had armed his people and his chariots, and in like manner the Shardonians, which were once his prisoners, then was the order given them for the battle. The king took his way downwards, and his people and his chariots accompanied him, and followed the best road on their march. . . .*

Pharaoh positions his troops to the North. The Israelites are hiding.

Ex 14:7 And he took six hundred chosen chariots, and all the chariots of Egypt, and captains over every one of them. Ex 14:8 And the Lord hardened the heart of Pharaoh king of Egypt, and he pursued after the children of Israel: and the children of Israel went out with an high hand. Ex 14:9 But the Egyptians pursued after them, all the horses and chariots of Pharaoh, and his horsemen, and his army, and overtook	*Now had the miserable king of the hostile Khita, and the many peoples which were with him, hidden themselves in an ambush to the northwest of the city of Kadesh, while Pharaoh was alone, no other was with him. The legion of Amom advanced behind him. The legion of Phra went into the ditch on the territory which lies to the west of the town of Shabatuna, divided by a long interval from the legion of Ptah in the midst [marching] towards the town of Arnama. The legion of Sutekh marched on by their roads. And the king called together all the chief men of his warriors. Behold, they were at the lake of the land of the Amorites. At the same time the miserable king of Khita was in the midst of his warriors, which were with him. But his hand was not so bold as to venture on battle with Pharaoh. Therefore he drew away the horsemen and the chariots, which were numerous as the sand. And they stood three men on each war chariot, and there were assembled in one spot the best heroes of the army of Khita, well appointed with all weapons for the fight.* *They did not dare to advance. They stood in ambush to the northwest of the town of Kadesh. Then they went out*

ANNEXES

| them encamping by the sea, beside Pihahiroth, before Baalzephon. | *from Kadesh, on the side of the south, and threw themselves into the midst of the legion of Pra-Hormakhu, which gave way, and was not prepared for the light. Then Pharaoh's warriors and chariots gave way before them. And Pharaoh had placed himself to the north of the town of Kadesh, on the west side of the river Arunatha. Then they came to tell the king. Then the king arose, like his father Month; he grasped his weapons and put on his armor, just like Baal in his time. And the noble pair of horses, which carried Pharaoh, and whose name was "Victory in Thebes," they were from the court of King Eamses Miamun. When the king had quickened his course, he rushed into the midst of the hostile hosts of Khita, all alone, no other was with him. When Pharaoh had done this, he looked behind him and found himself surrounded by 2500 pairs of horses, and his retreat was beset by the bravest heroes of the king of the miserable Khita, and by all the numerous peoples, which were with him, of Arathu, of Masu, of Pidasa, of Keshiesh, of Malunna, of Qazauadana, of Khilibu, of Akerith, of Kadesh, and of Leka. And there were three men on each chariot, and they were all gathered together.*

[Thus spake the king:] "And not one of my princes, not one of my captains of the chariots, not one of my chief men, not one of my knights was there. My warriors and my chariots had abandoned me, not one of them was there to take part in the battle…

I hurled the dart with my right hand, I fought with my left hand. I was like Baal in his time before their sight. I had found 2500 pairs of horses; I was in the midst of them; but they were dashed in pieces before my horses. Not one of them raised his hand to fight; their courage was sunken in their breasts, their limbs gave way, they could not hurl the dart, nor had they the courage to thrust with the spear. |

The enemies fall in the water and drown. Their chariots tumble. They all died.

| Ex 14:21 And Moses stretched out his hand over the sea; and the Lord caused | *I made them fall into the waters just as the crocodiles fall in. They tumbled down on their faces one after another. I killed them at my pleasure, so that not one looked back behind him, nor did another turn round.* |

331

the sea to go back by a strong east wind all that night, and made the sea dry land, and the waters were divided.

Ex 14:22 And the children of Israel went into the midst of the sea upon the dry ground: and the waters were a wall unto them on their right hand, and on their left.

Ex 14:23 And the Egyptians pursued, and went in after them to the midst of the sea, even all Pharaoh's horses, his chariots, and his horsemen.

Ex 14:26 And the Lord said unto Moses, Stretch out thine hand over the sea, that the waters may come again upon the Egyptians, upon their chariots, and upon their horsemen.

Ex 14:27 And Moses stretched forth his hand over the sea, and the sea returned to his strength when the morning appeared; and the Egyptians fled against it; and the Lord overthrew the

Each one fell, he raised himself not up again."

There stood still the miserable king of Khita in the midst of his warriors and his chariots, to behold the fight of the king. He was all alone; not one of his warriors, not one of his chariots was with him. There he turned round for fright before the king. Thereupon he sent the princes in great numbers, each of them with his chariot, well equipped with all kinds of offensive weapons: the king of Arathu and him of Masa, the king of Malunna and him of Leka, the king of the Dardani and him of Keshkesh, the king of Qarqamash and him of Khilibi. There were altogether the brothers of the king of Khita united in one place, to the number of 2500 pairs of horses. They forthwith rushed right on, their countenance directed to the flame of fire [i.e. my face].

"I rushed down upon them. Like Monthu was I. I let them taste my hand in the space of a moment. I dashed them down, and killed them where they stood. Then cried out one of them to his neighbor, saying: 'This is no man. Ah! woe to us! He who is in our midst is Sutekh, the glorious: Baal is in all his limbs. Let us hasten and flee before him. Let us save our lives; let us try our breath.'"

As soon as any one attacked him, his hand fell down and every limb of his body. They could not aim either the bow or the spear. They only looked at him as he came on in his head- long career from afar. The king was behind them like a griffin.

[Thus spake the king:] "I struck them down; they did not escape me. I lifted up my voice to my warriors and to my charioteers, and spake to them, 'Halt! stand! take courage, my warriors, my charioteers! Look upon my victory. I am alone, but Amon is my helper, and his hand is with me.'"

Egyptians in the midst of the sea. Ex 14:28 And the waters returned, and covered the chariots, and the horsemen, and all the host of Pharaoh that came into the sea after them; there remained not so much as one of them.	
They are afraid and beg their Lord to save their lives.	
Ex 14:10 And when Pharaoh drew nigh, the children of Israel lifted up their eyes, and, behold, the Egyptians marched after them; and they were sore afraid: and the children of Israel cried out unto the Lord. Ex 14:11 And they said unto Moses, Because there were no graves in Egypt, hast thou taken us away to die in the wilderness? wherefore hast thou dealt thus with us, to carry us forth out of Egypt? Ex 14:12 Is not this the word that we did tell thee in Egypt, saying, Let us alone, that we may serve the Egyptians? For it	*"When Menna, my charioteer, beheld with his eyes how many pairs of horses surrounded me, his courage left him, and his heart was afraid. Evident terror and great fright took possession of his whole body. Immediately he spake to me: 'My gracious lord, thou brave king, thou guardian of the Egyptians in the day of battle, protect us. We stand alone in the midst of enemies. Stop, to save the breath of life for us. Give us deliverance, protect us. O King Eamses Miamun.'"*

had been better for us to serve the Egyptians, than that we should die in the wilderness.	
Halt! Stand still! The Lord will fight alone.	
Ex 14:13 And Moses said unto the people, Fear ye not, stand still, and see the salvation of the Lord, which he will shew to you to day: for the Egyptians whom ye have seen to day, ye shall see them again no more for ever. Ex 14:14 The Lord shall fight for you, and ye shall hold your peace. Ex 14:15 And the Lord said unto Moses, Wherefore criest thou unto me? speak unto the children of Israel, that they go forward:	*Then spake the king to his charioteer: "Halt! stand! take courage, my charioteer. I will dash myself down among them as the sparrow hawk dashes down. I will slay them, I will cut them in pieces, I will dash them to the ground in the dust. Why then is such a thought in thy heart? These are unclean ones for Amon, wretches who do not acknowledge the god."* *And the king hurried onwards. He charged down upon the hostile hosts of Khita. For the sixth time, when he charged upon them [says the king] : "There was I like to Baal behind them in his time, when he has strength. I killed them; none escaped me."* *[The king gives his officers a tongue lashing for leaving him in the lurch. The next morning the battle is renewed.]*
In the morning, those who had fought with him were consumed by fire.	
Ex 14:24 And it came to pass, that in the morning watch the Lord looked unto the host of the Egyptians through the pillar of fire and of the cloud, and troubled the host of	*"The diadem of the royal snake adorned my head. It spat fire and glowing flame in the face of my enemies. I appeared like the sun god at his rising in the early morning. My shining beams were a consuming fire for the limbs of the wicked. They cried out to one another, 'Take care, do not fall! For the powerful snake of royalty, which accompanies him, has placed itself on his horse. It helps him. Every one who comes in his way and falls down there comes forth fire and flame to*

the Egyptians,	*consume his body.'''*

The enemies beg for mercy.

Ex 14:25 And took off their chariot wheels, that they drave them heavily: so that the Egyptians said, Let us flee from the face of Israel; for the Lord fighteth for them against the Egyptians.	*And they remained afar off, and threw themselves down on the earth to entreat the king in the sight [of his army]. And the king had power over them and slew them without their being able to escape. As bodies tumbled before his horses, so they lay there stretched out all together in their blood.*
	Then the king of the hostile people of Khita sent a messenger to pray piteously to the great name of the king, speaking thus: " Thou art Ra-Hormakhu. Thou art Sutekh the glorious, the son of Nut, Baal in his time. Thy terror is upon the land of Khita, for thou hast broken the neck of Khita forever and ever."
	Thereupon he allowed his messenger to enter. He bore a writing in his hand with the address, "To the great double name of the king":
	"May this suffice for the satisfaction of the heart of the holiness of the royal house, the Sun-Horus, the mighty Bull, who loves justice, the great lord, the protector of his people, the brave with his arm, the rampart of his life guards in the day of battle, the king Ramses Miamun."
	The servant speaks, he makes known to Pharaoh, my gracious lord, the beautiful son of Ra-Hormakhu, as follows:
	"Since thou art the son of Amon, from whose body thou art sprung, so has he granted to thee all the peoples together.
	The people of Egypt and the people of Khita ought to be brothers together as thy servants. Let them be at thy feet. The sun god Ra has granted thee the best [people]. Do us no injury, glorious spirit, whose anger weighs upon the people of Khita.
	Would it be good if thou shouldst wish to kill thy servants, whom thou hast brought under thy power? Thy look is terrible, and thou art not mildly disposed. Calm thyself. Yesterday thou earnest and hast slain hundreds of thousands. Thou comest today, and none

will be left remaining [to serve thee].

Do not carry out thy purpose, thou mighty king. Better is peace than war. Give us freedom."

Then the king turned back in a gentle humor, like his father Monthu in his time, and Pharaoh assembled all the leaders of the army and of the chariot fighters and of the life guards. And when they were all assembled together in one place, they were permitted to hear the contents of the message, which the great king of Khita had sent to him. [When they had heard] these words, which the messenger of the king of Khita had brought as his embassy to Pharaoh, then they answered and spake thus to the king:

"Excellent, excellent is that! Let thy anger pass away, O great lord our king! He who does not accept peace must offer it. Who would content thee in the day of thy wrath?"

Then the king gave order to listen to the words of him, and he let his hands rest, in order to return to the south. Then the king went in peace to the land of Egypt with his princes, with his army, and his charioteers, in serene humor, in the sight of his [people]. All countries feared the power of the king, as of the lord of both the worlds. It had protected his own warriors. All peoples came at his name, and their kings fell down to pray before his beautiful countenance. The king reached the city of Ramses Miamun, the great worshiper of Ra-Hormakhu, and rested in his palace in the most serene humor, just like the sun on his throne. And Amou came to greet him, speaking thus to him: "Be thou blessed, thou our son, whom we love, Ramses Miamun! May they [the gods] secure to him without end many thirty-years' feasts of jubilee forever on the chair of his father Tum, and may all lands be under his feet!"

It can be observed that the events and their order of appearance are the same between the two texts; except for the drowning of the chariots that occurs at the end of the passage in the Bible. However, in the *bulletin* recounting Ramses' victory, the drowning occurs at the very end too. Given the timing of Exodus and the parallels that can be observed between the texts, I believe it is fair to suggest that the Bible has turned the "Battle of Kadesh" into a religious experience in which their "God" relieved the Israelites from the Egyptian yoke.

A breach in Sethi's dam

Lake Homs Dam, located halfway between Homs (Roman Emesa) and Tell Nebi Mend (Kadesh), was built in 1935 CE on the remains of a famous dam built for irrigation purposes by the Roman emperor Diocletian (284–305 CE). For quite some time, the dam was believed to have been built by the Egyptian ruler Sethi I (1290-1279 BCE). However, given the structure of the dam was determined to be Roman, this thought was largely abandoned.

Pierre-Louis Viollet more recently argued that the Romans could have very well established their dam on top of an older structure, much like the modern dam was constructed on top of the Roman's. For Viollet, the historical account of the Greek geographer, philosopher, and historian Strabo (64/63 BCE – c. 24 CE) who situated one of the sources of the Orontes to be *"near the Egyptian wall, toward the territory of Apamea"*[321] must have been referring to the unusual system of copious percolation that was used to let water flow downstream through the wall of the dam itself.

> *The most reasonable hypothesis, following Yves Calvet and Bernard Geyer, is that the site of the dam is a natural rocky barrier which, from very early times in Antiquity, was the site of structures built to raise the level of the natural lake.* [322]

A great builder having fought extensively in Palestine, Syria and with the Hittites to the north, Sethi is thought by many scholars to have been the greatest king of the 19th dynasty. He died just a few years before the Battle of Kadesh raged. If Sethi had indeed built a

[321] Strabo. *Geography, Book XVI, Chapter 2, 9.*
[322] Viollet, Pierre-Louis. 2007. *Water Engineering in Ancient Civilizations 5,000 Years of History.* Madrid: International Association of Hydraulic Engineering and Research.

dam in this location, it would have been situated just a few kilometers north of Kadesh, and in direct line with the path that fleeing Israelites/Hittites would have taken.

Is it therefore possible that the Israelites/Hittites would have made a breach in Sethi's dam right after having crossed the Orontes river, and while they were still being chased out? Perhaps this could explain the "wall of water" that came rushing against the Egyptians according to Exodus... If we are to give any credence to this vivid biblical passage, this might fit the bill. Perhaps the Egyptians had set up camp for the night in the middle of the valley, only to get engulfed by a huge flood in the morning. There remains the question of how practical it would have been for the Israelites/Hittites to create such a breach overnight. While a highly speculative hypothesis, it would be understandable that the Egyptians would have had no good reason to record such an inglorious event.

A Hittite connection

According to the Bible, Mount Sinai (also referred to as Mount Horeb) is the place where God gave Moses the Ten Commandments. Although no one knows for sure where this mount was located, tradition has always placed it in the Sinai Peninsula of Egypt that is bordering southern Israel. This is probably due to the fact that the *Yam Suph* (סוף ים) "sea of reeds", which is the name given to the body of water that the Israelites have crossed and where the chariots of Pharaoh have drowned, has traditionally been associated with the Red Sea. However, given the historical Battle of Kadesh took place on the Orontes river, near Kadesh, perhaps one should consider remapping the location of Mount Sinai way up to the north of Israel. We do learn from the late Burckhardt that two hundred years ago, the inhabitants of the Orontes valley were still building mud huts, of which the roofs were formed of the reeds of the river.[323] While this trait is probably

[323] Burckhardt, John Lewis. 1822. Travels in Syria and the Holy Land. In *The British Review, and London Critical Journal.* London: Baldwin, Cradock, and Joy. p.64

not unique to this river, the Orontes could nevertheless prove be the famous *Yam Suph*. By remapping the geography of the events to the north, we would still find that Exodus would have taken place on the edge of the Egyptian "borders", but the extended ones... It would then make perfect sense to match Midian, where Moses meets Jethro, his father in law and priest (Ex 3:1), with Late Bronze Mitanni, the stretch of land neighboring the Hittites, just northeast of Kadesh.[324] While the geography of this region appears to fit just as well the description made in the Bible, what else can be learned from the Hittite culture that would match the Biblical account?

Tudhaliya IV, son of Muwatali Hattusili (who fought the Battle of Kadesh against Ramses II), is known to have deified his father (it was common for Hittite kings to get deified). Deification of the dead was therefore an accepted practice. Did Tudhaliya IV take with him a small number of Israelites to Hattusa, the Hittite capital (modern day Boğazköy in Turkey) in order to serve him, and perhaps even revere him? By fighting this battle against the Egyptians, he would have indeed "liberated" them. As a liberator of the people, he could pose as either Moses or God. It is certainly interesting to note that his name ends with –*ya*, the Akkadian possessive adjective that became the theophoric diminutive name of the God of Israel at approximately the same time. Could the lasting confusion between *beliya*, which means "my Lord" in Akkadian, but "Lord *Yah*" in Hebrew not find its roots in an association made with the name of this great Hittite King that raised to power in the aftermath of the Battle of Kadesh?[325]

Tudhaliya IV, much like Akhenaten 150 years before him in Egypt, is best remembered for having undertaken major religious reforms aimed at giving some sort of system to the divine ranks of the Hittite pantheon. As Bryce puts it:

---

[324] The "D" and the "T" are two consonants are often paired together because they take the same mouth position. They were therefore often interchanged in old Near Eastern languages that were primarily spoken.

[325] While there are texts attesting that Tudhaliya IV deified his father, it is unclear whether Tudhaliya IV himself was ever deified. For a discussion on the possible confusion between the deification of Tudhaliya and Tudhaliya IV see Bryce, Trevor. 2012. *Life and Society in the Hittite World*. Oxford; New York: Oxford University Press. (Orig. pub. 2012.). p. 243

Such reforms were not just a matter of theological housekeeping. They must also have been intended to promote a greater sense of coherence and unity, both cultural and political, within the empire as a whole. Not a plethora of different gods of different regions, but the same gods for all peoples and all regions of the empire. In theory the advantages are obvious, if one takes the overlord's point of view.[326]

The King knew he had to manoeuver with tact:

On the one level, Tudhaliya obviously sought to build up as much credit as he could with the divine powers in the ever-darkening final years of the empire. But perhaps just as importantly, he was seeking to assure the peoples of his kingdom that far from threatening to destroy their cherished religions traditions, or showing indifference to them, he was in fact intent on strengthening them beyond previous measure.[327]

This balancing act would eventually lead to the construction of the rock sanctuary of Yazilikaya, a kilometer north-east of Hattusa, where one can still admire the impressive rock sculptures depicting the Hittite pantheon. Horeb (חרב) "dry, desolate, sword", is a qualifier that would fit very well to this rock sanctuary. This place was a quite unusual and a likely a very ancient site of worship (way before the Hittites) because of a water spring that used to flow from a rock alcove. It is hard not to picture Moses performing his "miracle":

Ex 17:6 Behold, I will stand before thee there upon the rock in Horeb; and thou shalt smite the rock, and there shall come water out of it, that the people may drink. And Moses did so in the sight of the elders of Israel.

While additional investigation should definitely be carried out to explore other possible ties with the Hittites, it is interesting to note that Finkelstein was able to identify early Israelites settlement in the Levant because of the absence of pork bones. And although it

---

[326] Ibid. p.138
[327] Ibid. p.138

is likely that the Hittites weren't the only people of the Near East to share this customary diet, we do know that they did not eat pork. Unfortunately, data is sparse, both inside and outside of the Bible because all civilizations of the Near East were then on the brinks of collapsing into what Eric Clines calls the "First Dark Ages".

Joshua's conquest of the Dark Ages

This was a deeply troubled period, as all major cities were savagely attacked by a seemingly unrelated and opportunistic group of warriors dubbed the "Sea People":

> *Within a period of forty to fifty years at the end of the thirteenth and the beginning of the twelfth century almost every significant city in the eastern Mediterranean world was destroyed, many of them never to be occupied again.[328]*

From the walls of the Medinet Habu, mortuary temple of Ramses III, we learn that:

> *The foreign countries made a conspiracy in their islands. All at once the lands were removed and scattered in the fray. No land could stand before their arms, from Khatte, Qode, Carchemish, Arzawa, and Alashiya on, being cut off at [one time]. A camp [was set up] in one place in Amurru. They desolated its people, and its land was like that which has never come into being. They were coming forward toward Egypt, while the flame was prepared before them. Their confederation was the Peleset, Tjekker, Shekelesh, Danuna, and Weshesh, lands united. They laid their hands upon the lands as far as the circuit of the earth, their hearts confident and trusting. [329]*

Cline explains that the Philistines are the only group of people that has been clearly identified among the looters. Others could have

---

[328] Drews, Robert. 1993. *The End of the Bronze Age : changes in warfare and the catastrophe ca. 1200 B.C.* Princeton, N.J.: Princeton University Press. p. 4
[329] Cline, Eric H. 2014. *1177 B.C. : the year civilization collapsed.* p. 3

been a mix of mercenaries and opportunists from various places, including Western Europe.

Of all the foreign groups active in this arena at this time, only one has been firmly identified. The Peleset of the Sea Peoples are generally accepted as none other than the Philistines, who are identified in the Bible as coming from Crete.[330]

It has been established that the Philistines were no different than the people surrounding them. The name "Philistia" (or "Palestine") was nothing more than a place-name, without ethnic connotations.

Since the inhabitants of Philistia worshiped Canaanite gods, and since the language of the area in the first millennium was Northwest Semitic, one must assume that the overwhelmingly majority of Iron Age Palestinians were descended from Palestinians of the Late Bronze Age.[331]

The question therefore arises as to who were these "Philistines" and what motivated them? Given what we know of the Hyksos, the Hittites, the Canaanites and the Israelites, perhaps we can conjecture a bit... Recall that Sharuhen is the Hyksos stronghold where Shemidah took refuge after being chased out of Egypt. This city is located in the southern part of Philistine. Could the *Peleset* turn out to be the descendants of the ancient Hyksos trying to take advantage of a weakened geo-political situation to regain a land they once controlled and possessed?[332] This would certainly help explain the motivation and relentlessness that these "Sea People" exhibited during their raids and it would also help explain why the Philistines sought to capture the Ark of the Covenant (1 Sam 4:3) after defeating the Israelites. Given the Philistines were still culturally indistinguishable from the Israelites at that time, we can speculate as to their exact origins and motivations. It appears, however, that resentment, power struggles and diverging religious

---

[330] Ibid. p. 4
[331] Drews, Robert. 1993. *The End of the Bronze Age : changes in warfare and the catastrophe ca. 1200 B.C.* Princeton, N.J.: Princeton University Press. p. 68
[332] The Phoenician alphabet preceded Hebrew. It was developed soon after the Hyksos were expelled from Egypt. It therefore appears as if the descendants of Khyan-Seth (biblical Joseph) leveraged their knowledge of Egyptian hieroglyphs and Akkadian cuneiform to develop their own script.

beliefs would have brought the writers of the Bible to depict the Philistines as pagan enemies, much like they would eventually disdain the Samaritans for being "half-Jews" because, although they adhere to the Torah, they reject all other books of the Old Testament.

Did Joshua, who became the leader of the Israelite tribes after Moses' death lead another one of these groups of looters? They too might have wanted to seize the opportunity. While the ruins do not match the descriptions given in the Bible, there is no doubt that multiple cities of Canaan have been destroyed between 1250-1000 BCE, with the tipping point situated around 1175. And although most biblical scholars that have tempted to solve biblical chronologies have situated Joshua's conquest of Canaan during the 15th century BCE, the revised chronology based on the 6/10 multiplier confirms that Exodus would have taken place only decades prior to the invasion of the "Sea People". If Moses, would have been 25 when he led the Israelites "out of Egypt" and died at 72 (120*6/10); we can establish that the conquest could not have started for another 47 (72-25) years after Exodus. And if Joshua, who died at the age of 66 (110*6/10), was also 25 when Moses entrusted him; the conquest could have started soon after his death and spread over 20 or even 30 years. This brings us to establish that the conquest likely took place 47 to 77 years after Exodus, but before Joshua dies (88 years after Exodus), which takes us right around the tipping point of 1177 (1254-77); precisely when Ramses III (1187-1156 BCE) reports the attacks from the "Sea People".

This said, even if one could prove that the Israelites never marched on Canaan, it is clear that, at the minimum, the redactors of the Bible rode on these historical events with the goal of enriching their own story.

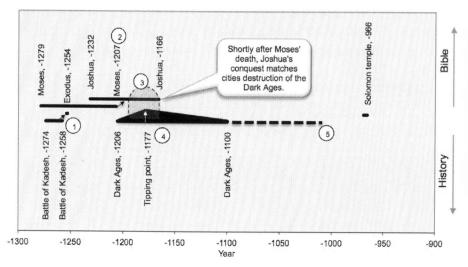

65: Joshua's conquest of the Dark Ages

With Exodus being intimately linked with the Battle of Kadesh (1), the above diagram shows how Joshua's conquest (3), taking place just a few years after Moses' death (2), likely coincided with the tipping point of the Dark Ages (4), a time when the large civilizations of the Near East collapsed and numerous Canaanite cities were destroyed. The entire region remained in turmoil until the turn of the millennium (5).

As attested by the early biblical scholars, several details of the Bible reveal a historical reality that is compatible with that of the Middle and Late Bronze Age. When the minimalists, such as Finkelstein, criticize this view, it is mostly the conclusions and the claims that these early authors drew from the limited historical data that they reject. They accuse the maximalists of building theories that only seek to confirm a conservative view professing the historical reliability of the biblical narratives.[333] Without actually being able to refute the idea that the story itself could be dated as far back as the Middle Bronze Age, the minimalists rationalize its improbability because dates do not fit; because no trace of monotheism has been found prior to the Iron Age; and because they believe the story can be better explained as a post-exilic fictitious saga.

---

[333] Bright, John. 2000. *A History of Israel.* Louisville: Westminster J. Knox Press. p. 469

As soon as it is acknowledged that that there have always only been a single, homogeneous and polytheistic people in Canaan, the notions of amphictyony, inter-tribal unions living on the fringe of society, as well as religious revolutions are no longer needed to explain the origin of an early and separate monotheistic Israel. And while in total disagreement with the analysis of the available data that brought Finkelstein to conclude that Exodus could not possibly have taken place during the 13th century, I could not agree more with his final observations:

> *The process that we describe here is, in fact, the opposite of what we have in the Bible: the emergence of early Israel was an outcome of the collapse of the Canaanite culture, not its cause. And most of the Israelites did not come from outside Canaan – they emerged from within it. There was no mass Exodus from Egypt. There was no violent conquest of Canaan. Most of the people who formed early Israel were local people – the same people whom we see the in highlands throughout the Bronze and Iron Ages. The early Israelites were – irony of ironies – themselves originally Canaanites!* [334]

Minimalists and maximalists should therefore find a synthesis of this complex and often paradoxical dialectic through the hypothesis of a mortal lord as, on the one hand, it allows us to set the Patriarchs as far back as the Middle Bronze Age through a politically motivated covenant, and on the other, it confirms a late birth of monotheism by acknowledging that the Patriarchs and their descendants were pagan and that Israel, as a separate and monotheistic identity, only existed at a much later date.

Such a rereading of the Bible obviously raises the problem of the *writing* and the *transmission* of the Abrahamic narrative. Is it realistic to believe that such a document was drafted in the Middle Bronze Age?

---

[334] Finkelstein, Israel and Neil Asher Silberman. 2001. *The Bible Unearthed: Archaeology's New Vision of Ancient Israel and the Origin of its Sacred Texts.* New York: Free Press. p. 118

Annex B: The "anchor point"

A substantial part of the above demonstration rests on the postulate that Abraham and Hammurabi were born c. 1810. This said, it is important to keep in mind that all dates are relative to the reign of Hammurabi, and could therefore be moved along with it. But, how is it possible to arrive at such a precise date when no traces of this man exist? Does this process not leave room for error or uncertainty? Could Abraham have been born a few years earlier or later, and how would this affect this new hypothesis? We must first look at the evidence suggesting that Abraham was indeed born in 1810. Let's examine the repercussions of shifting this date either forward or back. The most reliable event for situating Abraham in time is the War of Kings, since it permits us to establish a connection with Hammurabi.

Recall that the reasoning outlined earlier states that Abraham and Hammurabi were very likely contemporaries and members of the same group of Amorite conquerors who immigrated to Mesopotamia at the turn of the second millennium. According to this logic, Abraham must have lived sometimes during the 18th century BCE.

On Hammurabi's reign

Hammurabi's diplomatic correspondence indicates that he began expanding his empire after the 25th year of his reign. He defeated the kingdoms of Elam and Larsa, respectively, in the 28th and 29th years of his reign, and later died around the 42nd year of his kingship.

Since, according to the proposed hypothesis, the War of Kings preceded Hammurabi's rise to power, we can logically date this event somewhere between the 25th and 29th years of his reign. We can rule out the possibility that it took place after the 29th year of his reign, since Elam and Larsa, had already been defeated by then. However, there is nothing to rule out the possibility that this war took place before the 25th year of Hammurabi's monarchy.

The window of opportunity for Hammurabi's involvement in this war appears to be at least four years, since the war could have started before the 25th year of his reign, but it could not have continued beyond the 29th year.

On the story of Abraham
The dates set out in the Scriptures and subjected to the 6/10 multiplier reveal that Abraham arrived in Canaan at the age of 45. His arrival in Canaan and the War of Kings were interspersed by the famine, which drove him to flee to Egypt for a time. He could only have participated in the War of Kings after the drought and his return to Canaan. Incidentally, the story's timeline suggests that Abraham made his Covenant with Hammurabi after this war, but before the birth of Ishmael. Therefore, the Covenant must have been made before Abraham was 52, his age at the time of Ishmael's birth.

The window of opportunity for Abraham's involvement in this war is therefore seven years: it started when he was 45 and it ended when he was 52.

On the relationship between the two men

Isaac was born when Abraham was 60 years old, fifteen years after his arrival in Canaan. In order for Hammurabi to be Isaac's genitor, he obviously must have fathered him before dying, that is, no later than the 42nd year of his reign. As such, Abraham could not have arrived in Canaan after the 28th year of Hammurabi's reign (= 42 - 15), which narrows the window of opportunity for Hammurabi by one year. Instead of Hammurabi's windows being 25th-29th as indicated earlier, it should now be reduced to 25th-28th year.

The Scriptures also confirm that the city of Sodom was still ruled by the king of Elam during the War of Kings. This is likely because Hammurabi had not yet defeated the king of Elam. However, Hammurabi had to become the new ruler of Sodom before he could make the Covenant with Abraham. Therefore, the defeat of Elam could only have occurred after Abraham's arrival in Canaan, but before Ishmael's birth. This leads us to conclude that Abraham could not have arrived in Canaan more than seven years prior to the defeat of the kingdom of Elam. And, knowing that Elam was overthrown during the 28th year of Hammurabi's reign, then Abraham could not have arrived in Canaan before the 21st year of Hammurabi's rule (= 28 - 7).

Abraham's arrival into Canaan would therefore have taken place somewhere between the 21st and 28th year of Hammurabi's reign.

On the "correct" chronology

The above dates used regarding Hammurabi's reign correspond to what is commonly called "middle chronology". According to this chronology, Hammurabi was born in 1810 and rose to power in 1792.

Since the War of Kings had to have occurred between the 21st and the 28th years of Hammurabi's reign and because Abraham was 45 when he arrived in Canaan, the War of Kings had to have taken place between 1771 (= 1792 - 21) and 1764 (= 1792 - 28). Given Abraham was born 45 year earlier; he would have been born between 1816 (= 1771 + 45) and 1809 (= 1764 + 45).

On the birth of Abraham

If Abraham could have been born anywhere between 1816 and 1809, why focus on 1810?

The Bible confirms that Isaac's genitor was 60 when Sarah became pregnant. It also states that Abraham was 60 when Isaac was born. This double confirmation allows us to conclude that Hammurabi and Abraham differed in age by only a few months. Since this information is open to interpretation, let's confirm it in another way.

If Abraham was born during the same year as Hammurabi, then he was necessarily born in 1810. In this case, he would have arrived in Canaan in 1765 (= 1810 - 45), one year before the defeat of

Elam. If a famine took place in Egypt, then he no doubt would have travelled to Canaan after this famine.

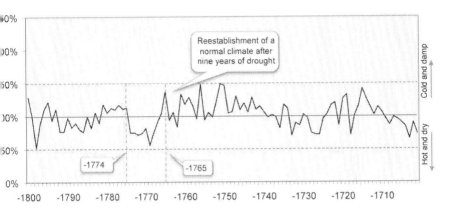

66: Dendrochronological data of the XVIIIth century BCE

Data from the 18th century BCE show a return to normal in the year 1765, after the longest period of drought during that century. Could this period match the famine that forced Abraham to flee to Egypt? If so, this dendrochronological data would confirm that Abraham is likely to have returned to Canaan in 1765 or early 1764, after the perils of the famine had dissipated. As such, he would have stayed in Egypt for only a few months. Since it is unlikely that Abraham left Egypt before the end of this long drought, the War of Kings could not have taken place before this date.

Presuming that Abraham returned to Canaan in 1765, this in fact allows him enough time to have participated in the War of Kings, prior to Hammurabi's defeat of Elam in 1764.

The War of Kings must therefore have taken place between the years 1765-1764, and this date would not allow Abraham to be born any other year than 1810. This pinpoints to a remarkably small window that relies on the convergence of multiple data sets. Can such a small window truly be coincidental?

On the margin of error

Most of the above calculations are not absolute, but relative to Hammurabi's reign. Once it is established that the two men are contemporaries, one only need to align the known ages of the Patriarchs with the known reigned years of Hammurabi to end up with a very high level of accuracy. An absolute date is only obtained by aligning the resulting data with the start of Hammurabi's reign (i.e. any change to this absolute date would not affect the validity of these calculations which are based on the relative relationship between the two men). A certain margin must nevertheless be allowed due to the fact that, while an event may be associated with a specific year, we do not know whether it occurred at the start or the end of the year. Moreover, while the vast majority of years can be converted to the 6/10 system without a remainder, a simple method of rounding (e.g. 1.4 = 1 but 1.6 = 2) was occasionally used, which provides for up to a six-month margin of error. The dendrochronological data set, on the other hand, is absolute and has a margin of error of +4/-7 years (standard deviation information not available). Any change to Hammurabi's absolute reign or the dendrochronological data set would therefore have an impact on the use of the dendrochronological data to correlate any events.

Annex C: Reference material

Genesis 12-25

Authorized King James Version

In order to practice a Dissociate Exegesis, do a first pass by paying special attention to the first-degree relationship between "Lord/God" and Abraham. When encountering an earthly relationship, insert the term *"Yahweh"*. In contrast, insert *"Elohim"* when Abraham addresses an immaterial deity. When done, re-read the story and envision *Yahweh* as being in league with the Four Eastern Kings. Expect some remaining editing noise, but pay close attention to the relationships, the actions and the motivations of the various characters.

Ge 12 *Now the Lord had said unto Abram, Get thee out of thy country, and from thy kindred, and from thy father's house, unto a land that I will shew thee: 2 and I will make of thee a great nation, and I will bless thee, and make thy name great; and thou shalt be a blessing: 3 and I will bless them that bless thee, and curse him that curseth thee: and in thee shall all families of the earth be blessed. 4 So Abram departed, as the Lord had spoken unto him; and Lot went with him: and Abram was seventy and five years old when he departed out of Haran. 5 And Abram took Sarai his wife, and Lot his brother's son, and all their substance that they had gathered, and the souls that they had gotten in Haran; and they went forth to go into the land of Canaan; and into the land of Canaan they came.*

6 And Abram passed through the land unto the place of Sichem, unto the plain of Moreh. And the Canaanite was then in the land. 7 And the Lord appeared unto Abram, and said, Unto thy seed will I give this land: and there builded he an altar unto the Lord, who appeared unto him. 8 And he removed from thence unto a mountain on the east of Beth-el, and pitched his tent, having Beth-el on the west, and Hai on the east: and there he builded an altar *unto the Lord, and called upon the name of the Lord. **9** And Abram journeyed, going on still toward the south.*

***10** And there was a famine in the land: and Abram went down into Egypt to sojourn there; for the famine was grievous in the land. **11** And it came to pass, when he was come near to enter into Egypt, that he said unto Sarai his wife, Behold now, I know that thou art a fair woman to look upon: **12** therefore it shall come to pass, when the Egyptians shall see thee, that they shall say, This is his wife: and they will kill me, but they will save thee alive. **13** Say, I pray thee, thou art my sister: that it may be well with me for thy sake; and my soul shall live because of thee. **14** And it came to pass, that, when Abram was come into Egypt, the Egyptians beheld the woman that she was very fair. **15** The princes also of Pharaoh saw her, and commended her before Pharaoh: and the woman was taken into Pharaoh's house. **16** And he entreated Abram well for her sake: and he had sheep, and oxen, and he asses, and menservants, and maidservants, and she asses, and camels. **17** And the Lord plagued Pharaoh and his house with great plagues because of Sarai Abram's wife. **18** And Pharaoh called Abram, and said, What is this that thou hast done unto me? why didst thou not tell me that she was thy wife? **19** Why saidst thou, She is my sister? so I might have taken her to me to wife: now therefore behold thy wife, take her, and go thy way. **20** And Pharaoh commanded his men concerning him: and they sent him away, and his wife, and all that he had.*

***Ge 13** And Abram went up out of Egypt, he, and his wife, and all that he had, and Lot with him, into the south. **2** And Abram was very rich in cattle, in silver, and in gold. **3** And he went on his journeys from the south even to Beth-el, unto the place where his tent had been at the beginning, between Beth-el and Hai; **4** unto the place of the altar, which he had made there at the first: and there Abram called on the name of the Lord.*

***5** And Lot also, which went with Abram, had flocks, and herds, and tents. **6** And the land was not able to bear them, that they might dwell together: for their substance was great, so that they could not dwell together. **7** And there was a strife between the herdmen of Abram's cattle and the herdmen of Lot's cattle: and the*

Canaanite and the Perizzite dwelled then in the land. 8 And Abram said unto Lot, Let there be no strife, I pray thee, between me and thee, and between my herdmen and thy herdmen; for we be brethren. 9 Is not the whole land before thee? separate thyself, I pray thee, from me: if thou wilt take the left hand, then I will go to the right; or if thou depart to the right hand, then I will go to the left. 10 And Lot lifted up his eyes, and beheld all the plain of Jordan, that it was well watered every where, before the Lord destroyed Sodom and Gomorrah, even as the garden of the Lord, like the land of Egypt, as thou comest unto Zoar. 11 Then Lot chose him all the plain of Jordan; and Lot journeyed east: and they separated themselves the one from the other. 12 Abram dwelled in the land of Canaan, and Lot dwelled in the cities of the plain, and pitched his tent toward Sodom. 13 But the men of Sodom were wicked and sinners before the Lord exceedingly.

14 And the Lord said unto Abram, after that Lot was separated from him, Lift up now thine eyes, and look from the place where thou art northward, and southward, and eastward, and westward: 15 for all the land which thou seest, to thee will I give it, and to thy seed for ever. 16 And I will make thy seed as the dust of the earth: so that if a man can number the dust of the earth, then shall thy seed also be numbered. 17 Arise, walk through the land in the length of it and in the breadth of it; for I will give it unto thee. 18 Then Abram removed his tent, and came and dwelt in the plain of Mamre, which is in Hebron, and built there an altar unto the Lord.

Ge 14 And it came to pass in the days of Amraphel king of Shinar, Arioch king of Ellasar, Chedorlaomer king of Elam, and Tidal king of nations; 2 that these made war with Bera king of Sodom, and with Birsha king of Gomorrah, Shinab king of Admah, and Shemeber king of Zeboiim, and the king of Bela, which is Zoar. 3 All these were joined together in the vale of Siddim, which is the salt sea. 4 Twelve years they served Chedorlaomer, and in the thirteenth year they rebelled. 5 And in the fourteenth year came Chedorlaomer, and the kings that were with him, and smote the Rephaims in Ashteroth Karnaim, and the Zuzims in Ham, and the Emims in Shaveh Kiriathaim, 6 and the Horites in their mount

Seir, unto El-paran, which is by the wilderness. 7 And they returned, and came to En-mishpat, which is Kadesh, and smote all the country of the Amalekites, and also the Amorites, that dwelt in Hazezon-tamar. 8 And there went out the king of Sodom, and the king of Gomorrah, and the king of Admah, and the king of Zeboiim, and the king of Bela (the same is Zoar;) and they joined battle with them in the vale of Siddim; 9 with Chedorlaomer the king of Elam, and with Tidal king of nations, and Amraphel king of Shinar, and Arioch king of Ellasar; four kings with five. 10 And the vale of Siddim was full of slimepits; and the kings of Sodom and Gomorrah fled, and fell there; and they that remained fled to the mountain. 11 And they took all the goods of Sodom and Gomorrah, and all their victuals, and went their way. 12 And they took Lot, Abram's brother's son, who dwelt in Sodom, and his goods, and departed.

13 And there came one that had escaped, and told Abram the Hebrew; for he dwelt in the plain of Mamre the Amorite, brother of Eshcol, and brother of Aner: and these were confederate with Abram. 14 And when Abram heard that his brother was taken captive, he armed his trained servants, born in his own house, three hundred and eighteen, and pursued them unto Dan. 15 And he divided himself against them, he and his servants, by night, and smote them, and pursued them unto Hobah, which is on the left hand of Damascus. 16 And he brought back all the goods, and also brought again his brother Lot, and his goods, and the women also, and the people.

17 And the king of Sodom went out to meet him after his return from the slaughter of Chedorlaomer, and of the kings that were with him, at the valley of Shaveh, which is the king's dale. 18 And Melchizedek king of Salem brought forth bread and wine: and he was the priest of the most high God. 19 And he blessed him, and said, Blessed be Abram of the most high God, possessor of heaven and earth: 20 and blessed be the most high God, which hath delivered thine enemies into thy hand. And he gave him tithes of all. 21 And the king of Sodom said unto Abram, Give me the persons, and take the goods to thyself. 22 And Abram said to the king of Sodom, I have lift up mine hand unto the Lord, the most high God, the possessor of heaven and earth, 23 that I will not take from a thread even to a shoelatchet, and that I will not take any thing that is thine, lest thou shouldest say, I have made Abram rich: 24 save only that which the young men have eaten, and the portion of the men which went with me, Aner, Eshcol, and Mamre; let them take their portion.

Ge 15 *After these things the word of the Lord came unto Abram in a vision, saying, Fear not, Abram: I am thy shield, and thy exceeding great reward. 2 And Abram said, Lord God, what wilt thou give me, seeing I go childless, and the steward of my house is this Eliezer of Damascus? 3 And Abram said, Behold, to me thou hast given no seed: and, lo, one born in my house is mine heir. 4 And, behold, the word of the Lord came unto him, saying, This shall not be thine heir; but he that shall come forth out of thine own bowels shall be thine heir. 5 And he brought him forth abroad, and said, Look now toward heaven, and tell the stars, if thou be able to number them: and he said unto him, So shall thy seed be. 6 And he believed in the Lord; and he counted it to him for righteousness. 7 And he said unto him, I am the Lord that brought thee out of Ur of the Chaldees, to give thee this land to inherit it. 8 And he said, Lord God, whereby shall I know that I shall inherit it? 9 And he said unto him, Take me an heifer of three years old, and a she goat of three years old, and a ram of three years old, and a turtledove, and a young pigeon. 10 And he took unto him all these, and divided them in the midst, and laid each piece one against another: but the birds divided he not. 11 And when the fowls came down upon the carcases, Abram drove them away. 12 And when the sun was going down, a deep sleep fell upon Abram; and, lo, an horror of great darkness fell upon him. 13 And he said unto Abram, Know of a surety that thy seed shall be a stranger in a land that is not theirs, and shall serve them; and they shall afflict them four hundred years; 14 and also that nation, whom they shall serve, will I judge: and afterward shall they come out with great substance. 15 And thou shalt go to thy fathers in peace; thou shalt be buried in a good old age. 16 But in the fourth generation they shall come hither again: for the iniquity of the Amorites is not yet full. 17 And it came to pass, that, when the sun* *went down, and it was dark, behold a smoking furnace, and a burning lamp that passed between those pieces.* **18** *In the same day the Lord made a covenant with Abram, saying, Unto thy seed have I given this land, from the river of Egypt unto the great river, the river Euphrates:* **19** *the Kenites, and the Kenizzites, and the Kadmonites,* **20** *and the Hittites, and the Perizzites, and the Rephaims,* **21** *and the Amorites, and the Canaanites, and the Girgashites, and the Jebusites.*

Ge 16 *Now Sarai Abram's wife bare him no children: and she had an handmaid, an Egyptian, whose name was Hagar.* **2** *And Sarai said unto Abram, Behold now, the Lord hath restrained me from bearing: I pray thee, go in unto my maid; it may be that I may obtain children by her. And Abram hearkened to the voice of Sarai.* **3** *And Sarai Abram's wife took Hagar her maid the Egyptian, after Abram had dwelt ten years in the land of Canaan, and gave her to her husband Abram to be his wife.* **4** *And he went in unto Hagar, and she conceived: and when she saw that she had conceived, her mistress was despised in her eyes.* **5** *And Sarai said unto Abram, My wrong be upon thee: I have given my maid into thy bosom; and when she saw that she had conceived, I was despised in her eyes: the Lord judge between me and thee.* **6** *But Abram said unto Sarai, Behold, thy maid is in thy hand; do to her as it pleaseth thee. And when Sarai dealt hardly with her, she fled from her face.*

7 *And the angel of the Lord found her by a fountain of water in the wilderness, by the fountain in the way to Shur.* **8** *And he said, Hagar, Sarai's maid, whence camest thou? and whither wilt thou go? And she said, I flee from the face of my mistress Sarai.* **9** *And the angel of the Lord said unto her, Return to thy mistress, and submit thyself under her hands.* **10** *And the angel of the Lord said unto her, I will multiply thy seed exceedingly, that it shall not be numbered for multitude.* **11** *And the angel of the Lord said unto her, Behold, thou art with child, and shalt bear a son, and shalt call his name Ishmael; because the Lord hath heard thy affliction.* **12** *And he will be a wild man; his hand will be against every man, and every man's hand against him; and he shall dwell in the presence of all his brethren.* **13** *And she called the name of the*

Lord that spake unto her, Thou God seest me: for she said, Have I also here looked after him that seeth me? 14 Wherefore the well was called Beer-lahai-roi; behold, it is between Kadesh and Bered. 15 And Hagar bare Abram a son: and Abram called his son's name, which Hagar bare, Ishmael. 16 And Abram was fourscore and six years old, when Hagar bare Ishmael to Abram.

Ge 17 *And when Abram was ninety years old and nine, the Lord appeared to Abram, and said unto him, I am the Almighty God; walk before me, and be thou perfect. 2 And I will make my covenant between me and thee, and will multiply thee exceedingly. 3 And Abram fell on his face: and God talked with him, saying, 4 As for me, behold, my covenant is with thee, and thou shalt be a father of many nations. 5 Neither shall thy name any more be called Abram, but thy name shall be Abraham; for a father of many nations have I made thee. 6 And I will make thee exceeding fruitful, and I will make nations of thee, and kings shall come out of thee. 7 And I will establish my covenant between me and thee and thy seed after thee in their generations for an everlasting covenant, to be a God unto thee, and to thy seed after thee. 8 And I will give unto thee, and to thy seed after thee, the land wherein thou art a stranger, all the land of Canaan, for an everlasting possession; and I will be their God.*

9 And God said unto Abraham, Thou shalt keep my covenant therefore, thou, and thy seed after thee in their generations. 10 This is my covenant, which ye shall keep, between me and you and thy seed after thee; Every man child among you shall be circumcised. 11 And ye shall circumcise the flesh of your foreskin; and it shall be a token of the covenant betwixt me and you. 12 And he that is eight days old shall be circumcised among you, every man child in your generations, he that is born in the house, or bought with money of any stranger, which is not of thy seed. 13 He that is born in thy house, and he that is bought with thy money, must needs be circumcised: and my covenant shall be in your flesh for an everlasting covenant. 14 And the uncircumcised man child whose flesh of his foreskin is not circumcised, that soul shall be cut off from his people; he hath broken my covenant.

15 And God said unto Abraham, As for Sarai thy wife, thou shalt not call her name Sarai, but Sarah shall her name be. 16 And I will bless her, and give thee a son also of her: yea, I will bless her, and she shall be a mother of nations; kings of people shall be of her. 17 Then Abraham fell upon his face, and laughed, and said in his heart, Shall a child be born unto him that is an hundred years old? and shall Sarah, that is ninety years old, bear? 18 And Abraham said unto God, O that Ishmael might live before thee! 19 And God said, Sarah thy wife shall bear thee a son indeed; and thou shalt call his name Isaac: and I will establish my covenant with him for an everlasting covenant, and with his seed after him. 20 And as for Ishmael, I have heard thee: Behold, I have blessed him, and will make him fruitful, and will multiply him exceedingly; twelve princes shall he beget, and I will make him a great nation. 21 But my covenant will I establish with Isaac, which Sarah shall bear unto thee at this set time in the next year. 22 And he left off talking with him, and God went up from Abraham.

23 And Abraham took Ishmael his son, and all that were born in his house, and all that were bought with his money, every male among the men of Abraham's house; and circumcised the flesh of their foreskin in the selfsame day, as God had said unto him. 24 And Abraham was ninety years old and nine, when he was circumcised in the flesh of his foreskin. 25 And Ishmael his son was thirteen years old, when he was circumcised in the flesh of his foreskin. 26 In the selfsame day was Abraham circumcised, and Ishmael his son. 27 And all the men of his house, born in the house, and bought with money of the stranger, were circumcised with him.

Ge 18 And the Lord appeared unto him in the plains of Mamre: and he sat in the tent door in the heat of the day; 2 and he lift up his eyes and looked, and, lo, three men stood by him: and when he saw them, he ran to meet them from the tent door, and bowed himself toward the ground, 3 and said, My Lord, if now I have found favour in thy sight, pass not away, I pray thee, from thy servant: 4 let a little water, I pray you, be fetched, and wash your feet, and rest yourselves under the tree: 5 and I will fetch a morsel of bread, and comfort ye your hearts; after that ye shall pass on: for therefore are ye come to your servant. And they said, So do, as thou hast said. 6 And Abraham hastened into the tent unto Sarah, and said, Make ready quickly three measures of fine meal, knead it, and make cakes upon the hearth. 7 And Abraham ran unto the herd, and fetcht a calf tender and good, and gave it unto a young man; and he hasted to dress it. 8 And he took butter, and milk, and the calf which he had dressed, and set it before them; and he stood by them under the tree, and they did eat.

9 And they said unto him, Where is Sarah thy wife? And he said, Behold, in the tent. 10 And he said, I will certainly return unto thee according to the time of life; and, lo, Sarah thy wife shall have a son. And Sarah heard it in the tent door, which was behind him. 11 Now Abraham and Sarah were old and well stricken in age; and it ceased to be with Sarah after the manner of women. 12 Therefore Sarah laughed within herself, saying, After I am waxed old shall I have pleasure, my lord being old also? 13 And the Lord said unto Abraham, Wherefore did Sarah laugh, saying, Shall I of a surety bear a child, which am old? 14 Is any thing too hard for the Lord? At the time appointed I will return unto thee, according to the time of life, and Sarah shall have a son. 15 Then Sarah denied, saying, I laughed not; for she was afraid. And he said, Nay; but thou didst laugh.

16 And the men rose up from thence, and looked toward Sodom: and Abraham went with them to bring them on the way. 17 And the Lord said, Shall I hide from Abraham that thing which I do; 18 seeing that Abraham shall surely become a great and mighty nation, and all the nations of the earth shall be blessed in him? 19 For I know him, that he will command his children and his household after him, and they shall keep the way of the Lord, to do justice and judgment; that the Lord may bring upon Abraham that which he hath spoken of him. 20 And the Lord said, Because the cry of Sodom and Gomorrah is great, and because their sin is very grievous; 21 I will go down now, and see whether they have done altogether according to the cry of it, which is come unto me; and if not, I will know. 22 And the men turned their faces from thence, and went toward Sodom: but Abraham stood yet before the Lord.

23 And Abraham drew near, and said, Wilt thou also destroy the righteous with the wicked? 24 Peradventure there be fifty righteous within the city: wilt thou also destroy and not spare the place for the fifty righteous that are therein? 25 That be far from thee to do after this manner, to slay the righteous with the wicked: and that the righteous should be as the wicked, that be far from thee: Shall not the Judge of all the earth do right? 26 And the Lord said, If I find in Sodom fifty righteous within the city, then I will spare all the place for their sakes. 27 And Abraham answered and said, Behold now, I have taken upon me to speak unto the Lord, which am but dust and ashes: 28 Peradventure there shall lack five of the fifty righteous: wilt thou destroy all the city for lack of five? And he said, If I find there forty and five, I will not destroy it. 29 And he spake unto him yet again, and said, Peradventure there shall be forty found there. And he said, I will not do it for forty's sake. 30 And he said unto him, Oh let not the Lord be angry, and I will speak: Peradventure there shall thirty be found there. And he said, I will not do it, if I find thirty there. 31 And he said, Behold now, I have taken upon me to speak unto the Lord: Peradventure there shall be twenty found there. And he said, I will not destroy it for twenty's sake. 32 And he said, Oh let not the Lord be angry, and I will speak yet but this once: Peradventure ten shall be found there. And he said, I will not destroy it for ten's sake. 33 And the Lord went his way, as soon as he had left communing with Abraham: and Abraham returned unto his place.

Ge 19 And there came two angels to Sodom at even; and Lot sat in the gate of Sodom: and Lot seeing them rose up to meet them; and he bowed himself with his face toward the ground; 2 and he said, Behold now, my lords, turn in, I pray you, into your servant's house, and tarry all night, and wash your feet, and ye shall rise up early, and go on your ways. And they said, Nay; but we will abide in the street all night. 3 And he pressed upon them greatly; and they turned in unto him, and entered into his house; and he made them a feast, and did bake unleavened bread, and they did eat.

4 But before they lay down, the men of the city, even the men of Sodom, compassed the house round, both old and young, all the people from every quarter: 5 and they called unto Lot, and said unto him, Where are the men which came in to thee this night? bring them out unto us, that we may know them. 6 And Lot went out at the door unto them, and shut the door after him, 7 and said, I pray you, brethren, do not so wickedly. 8 Behold now, I have two daughters which have not known man; let me, I pray you, bring them out unto you, and do ye to them as is good in your eyes: only unto these men do nothing; for therefore came they under the shadow of my roof. 9 And they said, Stand back. And they said again, This one fellow came in to sojourn, and he will needs be a judge: now will we deal worse with thee, than with them. And they pressed sore upon the man, even Lot, and came near to break the door. 10 But the men put forth their hand, and pulled Lot into the house to them, and shut to the door. 11 And they smote the men that were at the door of the house with blindness, both small and great: so that they wearied themselves to find the door.

12 And the men said unto Lot, Hast thou here any besides? son in law, and thy sons, and thy daughters, and whatsoever thou hast in the city, bring them out of this place: 13 for we will destroy this place, because the cry of them is waxen great before the face of the Lord; and the Lord hath sent us to destroy it. 14 And Lot went out, and spake unto his sons in law, which married his daughters, and said, Up, get you out of this place; for the Lord will destroy this city. But he seemed as one that mocked unto his sons in law.

15 And when the morning arose, then the angels hastened Lot, saying, Arise, take thy wife, and thy two daughters, which are here; lest thou be consumed in the iniquity of the city. 16 And while he lingered, the men laid hold upon his hand, and upon the hand of his wife, and upon the hand of his two daughters; the Lord being merciful unto him: and they brought him forth, and set him without the city.

17 And it came to pass, when they had brought them forth abroad, that he said, Escape for thy life; look not behind thee, neither stay thou in all the plain; escape to the mountain, lest thou be consumed. 18 And Lot said unto them, Oh, not so, my Lord:

19 behold now, thy servant hath found grace in thy sight, and thou hast magnified thy mercy, which thou hast shewed unto me in saving my life; and I cannot escape to the mountain, lest some evil take me, and I die: 20 behold now, this city is near to flee unto, and it is a little one: Oh, let me escape thither, (is it not a little one?) and my soul shall live. 21 And he said unto him, See, I have accepted thee concerning this thing also, that I will not overthrow this city, for the which thou hast spoken. 22 Haste thee, escape thither; for I cannot do any thing till thou be come thither. Therefore the name of the city was called Zoar.

23 The sun was risen upon the earth when Lot entered into Zoar. 24 Then the Lord rained upon Sodom and upon Gomorrah brimstone and fire from the Lord out of heaven; 25 and he overthrew those cities, and all the plain, and all the inhabitants of the cities, and that which grew upon the ground.

26 But his wife looked back from behind him, and she became a pillar of salt. 27 And Abraham gat up early in the morning to the place where he stood before the Lord: 28 and he looked toward Sodom and Gomorrah, and toward all the land of the plain, and beheld, and, lo, the smoke of the country went up as the smoke of a furnace.

29 And it came to pass, when God destroyed the cities of the plain, that God remembered Abraham, and sent Lot out of the midst of the overthrow, when he overthrew the cities in the which Lot dwelt.

30 And Lot went up out of Zoar, and dwelt in the mountain, and his two daughters with him; for he feared to dwell in Zoar: and he dwelt in a cave, he and his two daughters. 31 And the firstborn said unto the younger, Our father is old, and there is not a man in the earth to come in unto us after the manner of all the earth: 32 come, let us make our father drink wine, and we will lie with him, that we may preserve seed of our father. 33 And they made their father drink wine that night: and the firstborn went in, and lay with her father; and he perceived not when she lay down, nor when she arose. 34 And it came to pass on the morrow, that the firstborn said unto the younger, Behold, I lay yesternight with my father: let us make him drink wine this night also; and go thou in, and lie with him, that we may preserve seed of our father. 35 And they made their father drink wine that night also: and the younger arose, and lay with him; and he perceived not when she lay down, nor when she arose. 36 Thus were both the daughters of Lot with child by their father. 37 And the firstborn bare a son, and called his name Moab: the same is the father of the Moabites unto this day. 38 And the younger, she also bare a son, and called his name Ben-ammi: the same is the father of the children of Ammon unto this day.

Ge 20 And Abraham journeyed from thence toward the south country, and dwelled between Kadesh and Shur, and sojourned in Gerar. 2 And Abraham said of Sarah his wife, She is my sister: and Abimelech king of Gerar sent, and took Sarah. 3 But God came to Abimelech in a dream by night, and said to him, Behold, thou art but a dead man, for the woman which thou hast taken; for she is a man's wife. 4 But Abimelech had not come near her: and he said, Lord, wilt thou slay also a righteous nation? 5 Said he not unto me, She is my sister? and she, even she herself said, He is my brother: in the integrity of my heart and innocency of my hands have I done this. 6 And God said unto him in a dream, Yea, I know that thou didst this in the integrity of thy heart; for I also withheld thee from sinning against me: therefore suffered I thee not to touch her. 7 Now therefore restore the man his wife; for he is a prophet, and he shall pray for thee, and thou shalt live: and if thou restore her not, know thou that thou shalt surely die, thou, and all that are thine. 8 Therefore Abimelech rose early in the morning, and called all his servants, and told all these things in their ears: and the men were sore afraid. 9 Then Abimelech called Abraham, and said unto him, What hast thou done unto us? and what have I offended thee, that thou hast brought on me and on my kingdom a great sin? thou hast done deeds unto me that ought not to be done. 10 And Abimelech said unto Abraham, What sawest thou, that thou hast done this thing? 11 And Abraham said, Because I thought, Surely the fear of God is not in this place; and they will slay me for my wife's sake. 12 And yet indeed she is my sister; she is the daughter of my father, but not the daughter of my mother; and she became my wife. 13 And it came to pass, when God caused me to wander from my father's house, that I said unto her, This is thy kindness which thou shalt shew unto me; at every place whither we shall come, say of me, He is my brother. 14 And Abimelech took sheep, and oxen, and menservants, and womenservants, and gave them unto Abraham, and restored him Sarah his wife. 15 And Abimelech said, Behold, my land is before thee: dwell where it pleaseth thee. 16 And unto Sarah he said, Behold, I have given thy brother a thousand pieces of silver: behold, he is to thee a covering of the eyes, unto all that are with thee, and with all other: thus she was reproved.

17 So Abraham prayed unto God: and God healed Abimelech, and his wife, and his maidservants; and they bare children. 18 For the Lord had fast closed up all the wombs of the house of Abimelech, because of Sarah Abraham's wife.

Ge 21 And the Lord visited Sarah as he had said, and the Lord did unto Sarah as he had spoken. 2 For Sarah conceived, and bare Abraham a son in his old age, at the set time of which God had spoken to him. 3 And Abraham called the name of his son that was born unto him, whom Sarah bare to him, Isaac. 4 And Abraham circumcised his son Isaac being eight days old, as God had commanded him. 5 And Abraham was an hundred years old, when his son Isaac was born unto him.

6 And Sarah said, God hath made me to laugh, so that all that hear will laugh with me. 7 And she said, Who would have said unto Abraham, that Sarah should have given children suck? for I have born him a son in his old age. 8 And the child grew, and was weaned: and Abraham made a great feast the same day that Isaac was weaned.

9 And Sarah saw the son of Hagar the Egyptian, which she had born unto Abraham, mocking. 10 Wherefore she said unto Abraham, Cast out this bondwoman and her son: for the son of this bondwoman shall not be heir with my son, even with Isaac. 11 And the thing was very grievous in Abraham's sight because of his son. 12 And God said unto Abraham, Let it not be grievous in thy sight because of the lad, and because of thy bondwoman; in all that

Sarah hath said unto thee, hearken unto her voice; for in Isaac shall thy seed be called. 13 And also of the son of the bondwoman will I make a nation, because he is thy seed.

14 And Abraham rose up early in the morning, and took bread, and a bottle of water, and gave it unto Hagar, putting it on her shoulder, and the child, and sent her away: and she departed, and wandered in the wilderness of Beer-sheba. 15 And the water was spent in the bottle, and she cast the child under one of the shrubs. 16 And she went, and sat her down over against him a good way off, as it were a bowshot: for she said, Let me not see the death of the child. And she sat over against him, and lift up her voice, and wept. 17 And God heard the voice of the lad; and the angel of God called to Hagar out of heaven, and said unto her, What aileth thee, Hagar? fear not; for God hath heard the voice of the lad where he is. 18 Arise, lift up the lad, and hold him in thine hand; for I will make him a great nation. 19 And God opened her eyes, and she saw a well of water; and she went, and filled the bottle with water, and gave the lad drink. 20 And God was with the lad; and he grew, and dwelt in the wilderness, and became an archer. 21 And he dwelt in the wilderness of Paran: and his mother took him a wife out of the land of Egypt.

22 And it came to pass at that time, that Abimelech and Phichol the chief captain of his host spake unto Abraham, saying, God is with thee in all that thou doest: 23 now therefore swear unto me here by God that thou wilt not deal falsely with me, nor with my son, nor with my son's son: but according to the kindness that I have done unto thee, thou shalt do unto me, and to the land wherein thou hast sojourned. 24 And Abraham said, I will swear. 25 And Abraham reproved Abimelech because of a well of water, which Abimelech's servants had violently taken away. 26 And Abimelech said, I wot not who hath done this thing: neither didst thou tell me, neither yet heard I of it, but to day. 27 And Abraham took sheep and oxen, and gave them unto Abimelech; and both of them made a covenant. 28 And Abraham set seven ewe lambs of the flock by themselves. 29 And Abimelech said unto Abraham, What mean these seven ewe lambs which thou hast set by themselves? 30 And he said, For these seven ewe lambs shalt thou take of my hand, that they may be a witness unto me, that I have digged this well. 31 Wherefore he called that place Beer-sheba; because there they sware both of them. 32 Thus they made a covenant at Beer-sheba: then Abimelech rose up, and Phichol the chief captain of his host, and they returned into the land of the Philistines.

33 And Abraham planted a grove in Beer-sheba, and called there on the name of the Lord, the everlasting God. 34 And Abraham sojourned in the Philistines' land many days.

Ge 22 *And it came to pass after these things, that God did tempt Abraham, and said unto him, Abraham: and he said, Behold, here I am. 2 And he said, Take now thy son, thine only son Isaac, whom thou lovest, and get thee into the land of Moriah; and offer him there for a burnt offering upon one of the mountains which I will tell thee of.*

3 And Abraham rose up early in the morning, and saddled his ass, and took two of his young men with him, and Isaac his son, and clave the wood for the burnt offering, and rose up, and went unto the place of which God had told him. 4 Then on the third day Abraham lifted up his eyes, and saw the place afar off. 5 And Abraham said unto his young men, Abide ye here with the ass; and I and the lad will go yonder and worship, and come again to you. 6 And Abraham took the wood of the burnt offering, and laid it upon Isaac his son; and he took the fire in his hand, and a knife; and they went both of them together. 7 And Isaac spake unto Abraham his father, and said, My father: and he said, Here am I, my son. And he said, Behold the fire and the wood: but where is the lamb for a burnt offering? 8 And Abraham said, My son, God will provide himself a lamb for a burnt offering: so they went both of them together. 9 And they came to the place which God had told him of; and Abraham built an altar there, and laid the wood in order, and bound Isaac his son, and laid him on the altar upon the wood. 10 And Abraham stretched forth his hand, and took the knife to slay his son. 11 And the angel of the Lord called unto him out of heaven, and said, Abraham, Abraham: and he said, Here am I. 12 And he said, Lay not thine hand upon the lad, neither do thou any thing unto him: for now I know that thou fearest God, seeing thou hast not withheld thy son, thine only son from me. 13 And Abraham lifted up his eyes, and looked, and behold behind him a ram caught in a thicket by his horns: and Abraham went and took the ram, and offered him up for a burnt offering in the stead of his son. 14 And Abraham called the name of that place Jehovah-jireh: as it is said to this day, In the mount of the Lord it shall be seen.

15 And the angel of the Lord called unto Abraham out of heaven the second time, 16 and said, By myself have I sworn, saith the Lord, for because thou hast done this thing, and hast not withheld thy son, thine only son: 17 that in blessing I will bless thee, and in multiplying I will multiply thy seed as the stars of the heaven, and as the sand which is upon the sea shore; and thy seed shall possess the gate of his enemies; 18 and in thy seed shall all the nations of the earth be blessed; because thou hast obeyed my voice. 19 So Abraham returned unto his young men, and they rose up and went together to Beer-sheba; and Abraham dwelt at Beer-sheba.

20 And it came to pass after these things, that it was told Abraham, saying, Behold, Milcah, she hath also born children unto thy brother Nahor; 21 Huz his firstborn, and Buz his brother, and Kemuel the father of Aram, 22 and Chesed, and Hazo, and Pildash, and Jidlaph, and Bethuel. 23 And Bethuel begat Rebekah: these eight Milcah did bear to Nahor, Abraham's brother. 24 And his concubine, whose name was Reumah, she bare also Tebah, and Gaham, and Thahash, and Maachah.

Ge 23 And Sarah was an hundred and seven and twenty years old: these were the years of the life of Sarah. 2 And Sarah died in Kirjath-arba; the same is Hebron in the land of Canaan: and Abraham came to mourn for Sarah, and to weep for her.

3 And Abraham stood up from before his dead, and spake unto the sons of Heth, saying, 4 I am a stranger and a sojourner with you: give me a possession of a buryingplace with you, that I may bury my dead out of my sight. 5 And the children of Heth answered Abraham, saying unto him, 6 Hear us, my lord: thou art a mighty prince among us: in the choice of our sepulchres bury thy dead; none of us shall withhold from thee his sepulchre, but that thou mayest bury thy dead. 7 And Abraham stood up, and bowed himself to the people of the land, even to the children of Heth. 8 And he communed with them, saying, If it be your mind that I should bury my dead out of my sight; hear me, and intreat for me to Ephron the son of Zohar, 9 that he may give me the cave of Machpelah, which he hath, which is in the end of his field; for as much money as it is worth he shall give it me for a possession of a buryingplace amongst you. 10 And Ephron dwelt among the children of Heth: and Ephron the Hittite answered Abraham in the audience of the children of Heth, even of all that went in at the gate of his city, saying, 11 Nay, my lord, hear me: the field give I thee, and the cave that is therein, I give it thee; in the presence of the sons of my people give I it thee: bury thy dead. 12 And Abraham bowed down himself before the people of the land. 13 And he spake unto Ephron in the audience of the people of the land, saying, But if thou wilt give it, I pray thee, hear me: I will give thee money for the field; take it of me, and I will bury my dead there. 14 And Ephron answered Abraham, saying unto him, 15 My lord, hearken unto me: the land is worth four hundred shekels of silver; what is that betwixt me and thee? bury therefore thy dead. 16 And Abraham hearkened unto Ephron; and Abraham weighed to Ephron the silver, which he had named in the audience of the sons of Heth, four hundred shekels of silver, current money with the merchant.

17 And the field of Ephron, which was in Machpelah, which was before Mamre, the field, and the cave which was therein, and all the trees that were in the field, that were in all the borders round about, were made sure 18 unto Abraham for a possession in the presence of the children of Heth, before all that went in at the gate of his city. 19 And after this, Abraham buried Sarah his wife in the cave of the field of Machpelah before Mamre: the same is Hebron in the land of Canaan. 20 And the field, and the cave that is therein, were made sure unto Abraham for a possession of a buryingplace by the sons of Heth.

Ge 24 And Abraham was old, and well stricken in age: and the Lord had blessed Abraham in all things. 2 And Abraham said unto his eldest servant of his house, that ruled over all that he had, Put, I pray thee, thy hand under my thigh: 3 and I will make thee swear by the Lord, the God of heaven, and the God of the earth, that thou shalt not take a wife unto my son of the daughters of the Canaanites, among whom I dwell: 4 but thou shalt go unto my country, and to my kindred, and take a wife unto my son Isaac. 5 And the servant said unto him, Peradventure the woman will not be willing to follow me unto this land: must I needs bring thy son again unto the land from whence thou camest? 6 And Abraham said unto him, Beware thou that thou bring not my son thither again. 7 The Lord God of heaven, which took me from my father's house, and from the land of my kindred, and which spake unto me, and that sware unto me, saying, Unto thy seed will I give this land; he shall send his angel before thee, and thou shalt take a wife unto my son from thence. 8 And if the woman will not be willing to follow thee, then thou shalt be clear from this my oath: only bring not my son thither again. 9 And the servant put his hand under the thigh of Abraham his master, and sware to him concerning that matter.

10 And the servant took ten camels of the camels of his master, and departed; for all the goods of his master were in his hand: and he arose, and went to Mesopotamia, unto the city of Nahor. 11 And he made his camels to kneel down without the city by a well of water at the time of the evening, even the time that women go out to draw water. 12 And he said, O Lord God of my master Abraham, I pray thee, send me good speed this day, and shew kindness unto my master Abraham. 13 Behold, I stand here by the well of water; and the daughters of the men of the city come out to draw water: 14 and let it come to pass, that the damsel to whom I shall say, Let down thy pitcher, I pray thee, that I may drink; and she shall say, Drink, and I will give thy camels drink also: let the same be she that thou hast appointed for thy servant Isaac; and thereby shall I know that thou hast shewed kindness unto my master. 15 And it came to pass, before he had done speaking, that, behold, Rebekah came out, who was born to Bethuel, son of Milcah, the wife of Nahor, Abraham's brother, with her pitcher upon her shoulder. 16 And the damsel was very fair to look upon, a virgin, neither had any man known her: and she went down to the well, and filled her pitcher, and came up. 17 And the servant ran to meet her, and said, Let me, I pray thee, drink a little water of thy pitcher. 18 And she said, Drink, my lord: and she hasted, and let down her pitcher upon her hand, and gave him drink. 19 And when she had done giving him drink, she said, I will draw water for thy camels also, until they have done drinking. 20 And she hasted, and emptied her pitcher into the trough, and ran again unto the well to draw water, and drew for all his camels. 21 And the man wondering at her held his peace, to wit whether the Lord had made his journey prosperous or not.

22 And it came to pass, as the camels had done drinking, that the man took a golden earring of half a shekel weight, and two bracelets for her hands of ten shekels weight of gold; 23 and said, Whose daughter art thou? tell me, I pray thee: is there room in thy father's house for us to lodge in? 24 And she said unto him, I am the daughter of Bethuel the son of Milcah, which she bare unto Nahor. 25 She said moreover unto him, We have both straw and provender enough, and room to lodge in. 26 And the man bowed down his head, and worshipped the Lord. 27 And he said, Blessed be the Lord God of my master Abraham, who hath not left destitute my master of his mercy and his truth: I being in the way, the Lord led me to the house of my master's brethren.

28 And the damsel ran, and told them of her mother's house these things. 29 And Rebekah had a brother, and his name was Laban: and Laban ran out unto the man, unto the well. 30 And it came to pass, when he saw the earring and bracelets upon his sister's hands, and when he heard the words of Rebekah his sister, saying, Thus spake the man unto me; that he came unto the man; and, behold, he stood by the camels at the well. 31 And he said, Come in, thou blessed of the Lord; wherefore standest thou without? for I have prepared the house, and room for the camels.

32 And the man came into the house: and he ungirded his camels, and gave straw and provender for the camels, and water to wash his feet, and the men's feet that were with him. 33 And there was set meat before him to eat: but he said, I will not eat, until I have told mine errand. And he said, Speak on. 34 And he said, I am Abraham's servant. 35 And the Lord hath blessed my master greatly; and he is become great: and he hath given him flocks, and herds, and silver, and gold, and menservants, and maidservants, and camels, and asses. 36 And Sarah my master's wife bare a son to my master when she was old: and unto him hath he given all that he hath. 37 And my master made me swear, saying, Thou shalt not take a wife to my son of the daughters of the Canaanites, in whose land I dwell: 38 but thou shalt go unto my father's house, and to my kindred, and take a wife unto my son. 39 And I said unto my master, Peradventure the woman will not follow me. 40 And he said unto me, The Lord, before whom I walk, will send his angel with thee, and prosper thy way; and thou shalt take a wife for my son of my kindred, and of my father's house: 41 then shalt thou be clear from this my oath, when thou comest to my kindred; and if they give not thee one, thou shalt be clear from my oath. 42 And I came this day unto the well, and said, O Lord God of my master Abraham, if now thou do prosper my way which I go: 43 behold, I stand by the well of water; and it shall come to pass, that when the virgin cometh forth to draw water, and I say to her, Give me, I pray thee, a little water of thy pitcher to drink; 44 and she say to me, Both drink thou, and I will also draw for thy camels: let the same be the woman whom the Lord hath appointed out for my master's son. 45 And before I had done speaking in mine heart, behold, Rebekah came forth with her pitcher on her shoulder; and she went down unto the well, and drew water: and I said unto her, Let me drink, I pray thee. 46 And she made haste, and let down her pitcher from her shoulder, and said, Drink, and I will give thy camels drink also: so I drank, and she made the camels drink also. 47 And I asked her, and said, Whose daughter art thou? And she said, The daughter of Bethuel, Nahor's son, whom Milcah bare unto him: and I put the earring upon her face, and the bracelets upon her hands. 48 And I bowed down my head, and worshipped the Lord, and blessed the Lord God of my master Abraham, which had led me in the right way to take my master's brother's daughter unto his son. 49 And now if ye will deal kindly and truly with my master, tell me: and if not, tell me; that I may turn to the right hand, or to the left.

50 Then Laban and Bethuel answered and said, The thing proceedeth from the Lord: we cannot speak unto thee bad or good.

51 Behold, Rebekah is before thee, take her, and go, and let her be thy master's son's wife, as the Lord hath spoken. 52 And it came to pass, that, when Abraham's servant heard their words, he worshipped the Lord, bowing himself to the earth. 53 And the servant brought forth jewels of silver, and jewels of gold, and raiment, and gave them to Rebekah: he gave also to her brother and to her mother precious things. 54 And they did eat and drink, he and the men that were with him, and tarried all night; and they rose up in the morning, and he said, Send me away unto my master. 55 And her brother and her mother said, Let the damsel abide with us a few days, at the least ten; after that she shall go. 56 And he said unto them, Hinder me not, seeing the Lord hath prospered my way; send me away that I may go to my master. 57 And they said, We will call the damsel, and enquire at her mouth. 58 And they called Rebekah, and said unto her, Wilt thou go with this man? And she said, I will go. 59 And they sent away Rebekah their sister, and her nurse, and Abraham's servant, and his men. 60 And they blessed Rebekah, and said unto her, Thou art our sister, be thou the mother of thousands of millions, and let thy seed possess the gate of those which hate them.

61 And Rebekah arose, and her damsels, and they rode upon the camels, and followed the man: and the servant took Rebekah, and went his way.

62 And Isaac came from the way of the well Lahai-roi; for he dwelt in the south country. 63 And Isaac went out to meditate in the field at the eventide: and he lifted up his eyes, and saw, and, behold, the camels were coming. 64 And Rebekah lifted up her eyes, and when she saw Isaac, she lighted off the camel. 65 For she had said unto the servant, What man is this that walketh in the field to meet us? And the servant had said, It is my master: therefore she took a vail, and covered herself. 66 And the servant told Isaac all things that he had done. 67 And Isaac brought her into his mother Sarah's tent, and took Rebekah, and she became his wife; and he loved her: and Isaac was comforted after his mother's death.

Ge 25 *Then again Abraham took a wife, and her name was Keturah. 2 And she bare him Zimran, and Jokshan, and Medan, and Midian, and Ishbak, and Shuah. 3 And Jokshan begat Sheba, and Dedan. And the sons of Dedan were Asshurim, and Letushim, and Leummim. 4 And the sons of Midian; Ephah, and Epher, and Hanoch, and Abida, and Eldaah. All these were the children of Keturah. 5 And Abraham gave all that he had unto Isaac. 6 But unto the sons of the concubines, which Abraham had, Abraham gave gifts, and sent them away from Isaac his son, while he yet lived, eastward, unto the east country.*

7 And these are the days of the years of Abraham's life which he lived, an hundred threescore and fifteen years. 8 Then Abraham gave up the ghost, and died in a good old age, an old man, and full of years; and was gathered to his people. 9 And his sons Isaac and Ishmael buried him in the cave of Machpelah, in the field of Ephron the son of Zohar the Hittite, which is before Mamre; 10 the field which Abraham purchased of the sons of Heth: there was Abraham buried, and Sarah his wife.

11 And it came to pass after the death of Abraham, that God blessed his son Isaac; and Isaac dwelt by the well Lahai-roi.

12 Now these are the generations of Ishmael, Abraham's son, whom Hagar the Egyptian, Sarah's handmaid, bare unto Abraham: 13 and these are the names of the sons of Ishmael, by their names, according to their generations: the firstborn of Ishmael, Nebajoth; and Kedar, and Adbeel, and Mibsam, 14 and Mishma, and Dumah, and Massa, 15 Hadar, and Tema, Jetur, Naphish, and Kedemah: 16 these are the sons of Ishmael, and these are their names, by their towns, and by their castles; twelve princes according to their nations. 17 And these are the years of the life of Ishmael, an hundred and thirty and seven years: and he gave up the ghost and died; and was gathered unto his people. 18 And they dwelt from Havilah unto Shur, that is before Egypt, as thou goest toward Assyria: and he died in the presence of all his brethren.

19 And these are the generations of Isaac, Abraham's son: Abraham begat Isaac: 20 and Isaac was forty years old when he took Rebekah to wife, the daughter of Bethuel the Syrian of Padanaram, the sister to Laban the Syrian. 21 And Isaac intreated the Lord for his wife, because she was barren: and the Lord was intreated of him, and Rebekah his wife conceived. 22 And the children struggled together within her; and she said, If it be so, why am I thus? And she went to enquire of the Lord. 23 And the Lord said unto her, Two nations are in thy womb, and two manner of people shall be separated from thy bowels; and the one people shall be stronger than the other people; and the elder shall serve the younger.

24 And when her days to be delivered were fulfilled, behold, there were twins in her womb. 25 And the first came out red, all over like an hairy garment; and they called his name Esau. 26 And after that came his brother out, and his hand took hold on Esau's heel; and his name was called Jacob: and Isaac was threescore years old when she bare them. 27 And the boys grew: and Esau was a cunning hunter, a man of the field; and Jacob was a plain man, dwelling in tents. 28 And Isaac loved Esau, because he did eat of his venison: but Rebekah loved Jacob.

29 And Jacob sod pottage: and Esau came from the field, and he was faint: 30 and Esau said to Jacob, Feed me, I pray thee, with that same red pottage; for I am faint: therefore was his name called Edom. 31 And Jacob said, Sell me this day thy birthright. 32 And Esau said, Behold, I am at the point to die: and what profit shall this birthright do to me? 33 And Jacob said, Swear to me this day; and he sware unto him: and he sold his birthright unto Jacob. 34 Then Jacob gave Esau bread and pottage of lentiles; and he did eat and drink, and rose up, and went his way: thus Esau despised his birthright.

Description of roles

Italics = assumptions!

Character	Source	Description
A-User-Re	Hyksos	Name taken by the Hyksos king Apophis around the middle of his reign. *Biblical Ezer?*
Aaron	Bible	Brother of Moses called to the priesthood. Builds a golden calf during the Exodus.
Abimelech	Bible	King of Guerar who kidnaps Sarah. Threatened by *Baal*, he allies with Abraham and submits to his authority
Abram, Abraham	Bible	Son of Terah. First Patriarch. Governor of Canaan. He makes a covenant with *Baal* in exchange for the "promised land".
Ahmose	Egypt	Theban king of the 18th dynasty who oversees the expulsion of the Hyksos in the mid-16th century BCE.
Amraphel	Bible	Fights in the War of Kings against Sodom. *Hammurabi, king of Babylon?*
Apophis, Apepi	Hyksos	Last Hyksos king, enjoys a very long reign. *Biblical Ephraim?*
Arioch	Bible	Fights in the War of Kings against Sodom. *Eriaku, king of Larsa?*
Asherah	Levant	Mother goddess of Israel. Often associated with Astarte and Ishtar. *Biblical Sarah deified?*
Baal, Bel	Levant	Important deity of the Levant. Represented by a calf, a bull or its horns. Also an honorific title meaning "master" or "lord". Equivalent of Marduk.

Baal Berith	Levant	Litterally "Lord of Covenant". Important Shechemite deity of the Middle Bronze Age. Shares many characteristics with Yahweh/Elohim. *Deified Hammurabi?*
Bethuel	Bible	Son of Nahor and nephew of Abraham. Father of Rebekah, Isaac's wife.
Beriah	Bible	Son whom Ephraim conceives after his other sons are killed.
Ephraim	Bible	Son of Joseph to whom Jacob gives his blessing instead of Manasseh. *Apophis, Hyksos king?*
Eriaku	Mesopotamia	Generally associated with Rim-Sin, king of Larsa, who was captured by Hammurabi. *Biblical Arioch?*
Esau	Bible	Jacob's twin brother who loses his birthright. *Sheshi, Hyksos king?*
Ezer	Bible	Son of Ephraim. *Apophis A-User-Re, Hyksos king?*
Gilead	Bible	Son of Machir and great-grandson of Joseph. Father of Shemidah.
Gilgamesh	Mesopotamia	Mythical king of the Great Flood whose story is very similar to that of Noah.
Hammurabi	Mesopotamia	Famous king of the Babylonian empire. Known for his Code of Laws. *Abraham's "lord"? Baal Berith after death?*
Haran	Bible	Son of Terah and brother of Abraham. Father of Lot.
Ibi-Sin	Mesopotamia	King of Ur. During his reign, Abraham's ancestors, the Amorites, rise to power.
Ishmael	Bible	Abraham's son with his servant, Hagar. The Muslims believe that he was the son whom God ordered Abraham to sacrifice.
Isaac	Bible	Son given to Sarah by "God". Heir to the dynasty. *Son of Hammurabi?*

Jacob	Bible	Son of Isaac and grandson of Abraham. *Yakub-her, Hyksos king?*
Joseph	Bible	Son of Jacob and great-grandson of Abraham. Father of Manasseh and Ephraim. *Khyan, Hyksos king?*
Joshua	Bible	Succeeds Moses in leading the Exodus of the Hebrew people.
Kamose	Egypt	Theban king of the 17th dynasty. Son of Sequenenre Tao. Involved in the expulsion of the Hyksos from Egypt.
Kedor-Laomer	Bible	King of Elam. Fights in the war against Sodom. *Siwe Palar Khuppak, king of Elam?*
Khamudi	Hyksos	Last Hyksos king. Flees to Sharuhen and finally capitulates after a three-year siege. *Biblical Shemidah?*
Khyan	Hyksos	Hyksos king. *Biblical Joseph?*
Laban	Bible	Son of Bethuel. Jacob takes refuge with him for several years and marries his daughters, Leah and Rachel.
Leah	Bible	Daughter of Laban. Jacob's first wife.
Lot	Bible	Son of Haran and nephew of Abraham. Lives in Sodom. Kidnapped during the War of Kings.
Manasseh	Bible	Son of Joseph. *Yanassi, son of Khyan?*
Machir	Bible	Son of Manasseh and grandson of Joseph. Father of Gilead.
Marduk	Mesopotamia	Important god of Babylon. Equivalent to the god (and not the title) *Baal*.
Melchizedek	Bible	Usually called "King of Salem". Pagan priest and peace advisor. Celebrates Abraham's victory against the four Eastern kings. *Officiates a local covenant between Abraham and the righteous King of*

		Sodom?
Moses	Bible	High priest and legislator of the Hebrew people, whom he leads out of Egypt during the Exodus.
Nahor	Bible	Son of Terah and brother of Abraham. Father of Bethuel.
Naram-Sin	Mesopotamia	Akkadian king. Expands the borders of the Empire. First to proclaim himself a "living king".
Rachel	Bible	Daughter of Laban and wife of Jacob.
Rebekah	Bible	Daughter of Bethuel and wife of Isaac.
Rim-Sin	Mesopotamia	King of Larsa, captured by Hammurabi. Generally associated with Eriaku. *Biblical Arioch?*
Salatis	Hyksos	First Hyksos king. *Biblical Isaac?*
Samsu-iluna	Mesopotamia	Hammurabi's heir. Tests Abraham's loyalty after his father's death?
Sarai, Sarah	Bible	Daughter of Terah. Half-sister and wife of Abraham. *Goddess Asherah (i.e. Baalah Sarah)?*
Sargon of Akkad	Mesopotamia	Akkadian king. First to unify Mesopotamia, creating a vast empire.
Sequenenre Tao	Egypt	Theban king of the 17th dynasty. Wages war against the Hyksos. Dies a violent death.
Siwe Palar Khuppak	Mesopotamia	King of Elam, contemporary of Hammurabi. Plots to defeat Hammurabi, who emerges victorious. *Biblical Kedor-Laomer?*
Shemidah	Bible	Great-grandson of Manasseh. *Khamudi, last Hyksos king?*
Sheshi	Hyksos	Second Hyksos king. *Biblical Esau?*

Solomon	Bible	King of Jerusalem at the turn of the millennium. Builds the Temple of Jerusalem.
Terah	Bible	Father of Abraham, Nahor, Haran and Sarah. He leaves Ur for Canaan.
Tidal	Bible	Fights in the War of Kings against Sodom. *Tudhaliya, Hittite king?*
Tudhaliya	Mesopotamia	Hittite king who was likely a contemporary of Hammurabi. *Biblical Tidal?*
Ur-Nammu	Mesopotamia	King of Ur. First to build ziggurats.
Yakub-her	Hyksos	Third Hyksos king. *Biblical Jacob?*
Yanassi	Hyksos	Son of Khyan. *Biblical Manasseh?*

Patriarchs' Genealogy – corrected

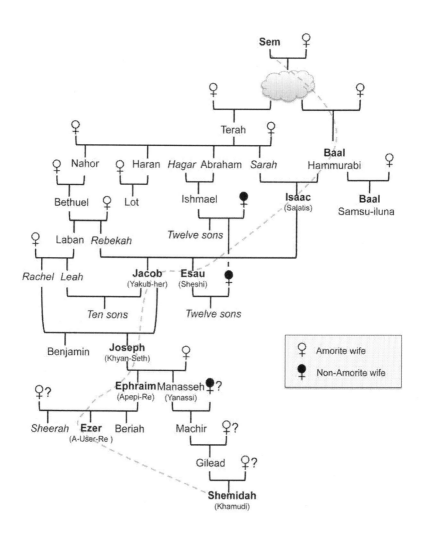

The Near East during the Bronze Age

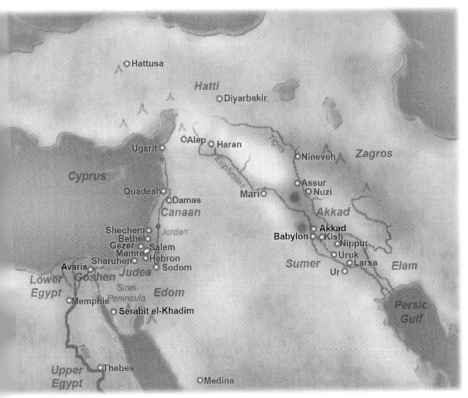

Friends of the Earthly Covenant

While the bulk of the work is done, much remains to be accomplished! Please help raise the awareness of this work by calling for an unbiased scientific investigation into it. You can show support by joining the community of the Friends of the Earthly Covenant on Facebook:

www.facebook.com/FriendsoftheEarthlyCovenant

Our objective is to raise awareness and bring the world to realize that there is a different and more efficient way to interpret the Abrahamic Covenant than that offered by tradition. Through dissemination and education, there is hope that a rational interpretation will one day oppose the faith-based and emotionally charged discourses that fundamentalists use to highjack the souls of our youth.

Acknowledgements

I will be forever grateful to Christine, love of my life and my first critic, for her *inémesurable* patience and constant encouragements. I also want to extend sincere thanks to my mother Myrèse, whose genuine faith brought me to seek authenticity in the scriptures, as well as to my father Raymond, for his invaluable support and tireless ear.

I would also like to express my love and thanks to my family and friends, especially my daughters, Émilie and Chloé, as well as my colleague and business partner, David, for putting up with me. They are a constant source of inspiration and motivation.

I also want to express my gratitude to professor Robert David for being such a great source of motivation and a wonderful Hebrew teacher, despite the fact that we could never see eye to eye on the subject of the historicity of Abraham.

The original title *Quiproquo sur Dieu* was initially translated to English by Ann Marie Boulanger before some significant additions were made. Timothy Gorman and Sandra Lange revised them most of them. I therefore want extend my earnest appreciation to all of them for their invaluable help and the countless hours they put into this project. This said, and as I cannot resist making ongoing changes, I must take full responsibility for any remaining typos and grammatical errors that could only be mine.

This book would remain incomplete without a very special thanks to Alex Zieba for the great feedback, suggestions and compelling

Foreword; to Claude Émilie Marec and André Serra, who were first to believe and commit to this project by publishing *Quiproquo sur Dieu*, as well as to the following readers for their support and encouragements: Daniel Anderson, Brian Austin, Daniel Baril, Michel Boutin, François Brochu, Marcel Bruneau, Robert David, Dominic Desroches, Michel Feeney, Gary Gruber, Scott Hansen, Maurice Lafleur, Gérard Laurençon, Stella Mathon, Valéda Melanson, Julie Mercier, Jean-Paul Michon, Jean-Pierre Mouvaux, Michel Pion, Thierry Pouliart, André Reny, Andréa Richard, Normand Rousseau, Howard Solomon, Paul-André Turcotte and Michel Virard.

List of illustrations

Iconography

I would like to thank the following people and institutions for allowing me to use the copyrighted images and photos in this book.[335]

1, 2, 3, 4, 5, 6, 7, 8, 9, 10, 11,	
12, 13, 14, 15, 16, 17, 18, 19,	
21, 22, 24, 25, 26, 28, 27, 31,	
33, 34, 37, 38, 39, 40, 41, 42,	
43, 44, 45, 46, 47, 48, 49, 50,	
52, 53, 54, 55, 56, 60, 62, 63,	
64, 65	© Bernard Lamborelle
16:	© iStockphoto.com/Fabio Bianchini
14:	© iStockphoto.com/Mark Goddard
31:	© iStockphoto.com/John Said

Public domain images reproduced with permission:

17:	Israel Antiquities Authority/Israel Museum
20:	Oriental Institute Museum, 1896 (scarab)
23:	Iraqi Directorate General of Antiquities
27:	Lasse Jensen, 2004
29, 30, 32:	Fritz-Milkau-Dia-Sammlung
35:	NASA/JPL-Caltech
36:	University of British Columbia (2)
51:	James Jacques Joseph Tissot, 1836-1902
57:	A.H. Gardiner, 1916
59:	OldBookArt/W. Struse Collection (1)
58, 61:	Boston Public Library's photostream (2)

(1) Images taken from:

Mathematical Astronomy by C.W.C. Barlow & G.H. Bryan (1893); Dawn of Astronomy by Sir Norman Lockyer (late

---

[335]Although every effort was made to obtain the necessary authorizations, I apologize for any omissions that may have occurred and I commit to making the appropriate corrections in all future editions.

1800s); Baedeker's Palestine and Syria (1912); An Illustrated History of the Holy Bible, published by Henry Bill (1871); and The Holy Bible, published by John E. Potter and Company (late 1800s).

(2) GNU Free Documentation License:

Verbatim copying and distribution of this entire article are permitted worldwide, without royalty, in any medium, provided this notice is preserved.

(3) Project Gutenberg License:

This eBook is for the use of anyone anywhere at no cost and with almost no restrictions whatsoever. You may copy it, give it away or re-use it under the terms of the Project Gutenberg License included with this eBook or online at www.gutenberg.org

Bibliography

(cited in this work)

2008. *La Civiltà Cattolica* 3795-3796(2-16 August).

Arendzen, John. 1907. *The Catholic Encyclopoedia*. New York: Robert Appleton Company.

Becking, Bernhard, Engelbert, Jan and Hendrik. 2001. *Only One God? : Monotheism in ancient Israel and the veneration of the goddess Asherah*. London; New York: Sheffield Academic Press.

Best, Robert M. 1999. *Noah's ark and the Ziusudra Epic: Sumerian Origins of the Flood Myth*. Fort Myers: Enlil Press.

Biggs, Robert D., John A. Brinkman, Miguel Civil, Walter Farber, Ignace J. Gelb, A. Leo Oppenheim, Erica Reiner, Martha T. Roth and Matthew W. Stolper. 1999. *The Assyrian dictionary of the Oriental Institute of the University of Chicago*. Vol. 14 of. Chicago: The Oriental Institute, University of Chicago.

Bottéro, Jean. 1992. *L'épopée de Gilgames: le grand homme qui ne voulait pas mourir*. Paris: Gallimard.

Bottéro, Jean and Samuel Noah Kramer. 1989. *Lorsque les dieux faisaient l'homme: mythologie mésopotamienne*. Paris: Gallimard.

Boucher, Claude. 2009. *Une brève histoire du Proche et du Moyen-Orient*. [Montréal]: Fides.

Briant, Pierre. 2002. *From Cyrus to Alexander : A History of the Persian Empire*. Winona Lake: Eisenbraun.

Bright, John. 2000. *A History of Israel*. Louisville: Westminster J. Knox Press.

Bromiley, Geoffrey William. 1979. *The International Standard Bible Encyclopedia*. Grand Rapids: W.B. Eerdmans.

Brown, F., S. Driver and C. Briggs. 2007. *The Brown-Driver-Briggs Hebrew and English Lexicon: Coded with Strong's Concordance Numbers*. Peabody, Mass.: Hendrickson Pub. Inc. (Orig. pub. 1907.).

Bryce, Trevor. 2012. *Life and Society in the Hittite World*. Oxford; New York: Oxford University Press. (Orig. pub. 2012.).

Bucaille, Maurice. 2008. *Moses and Pharaoh in the Bible, Qur'an and History*. Selangor: Islamic Book Trust.

Burckhardt, John Lewis. 1822. Travels in Syria and the Holy Land. In *The British Review, and London Critical Journal*. London: Baldwin, Cradock, and Joy.

Burnett, Joel S. 2001. *A Reassessment of Biblical Elohim*. Atlanta: Society of Biblical Literature.

Butler, Edward P. 2012. *Essays on a polytheistic philosophy of religion*. New York: Phaidra Editions.

Cassuto, Umberto, Joshua Berman and Israel Abrahams. 2006. *The Documentary Hypothesis and the Composition of the Pentateuch: Eight Lectures*. Jerusalem [Israel]; New York [N.Y.]: Shalem Press.

Chapman, Arthur Thomas. 1911. *An Introduction to the Pentateuch*. Cambridge: University Press.

Charpin, Dominique and Nele Ziegler. 2003. "Mari et le Proche-Orient à l'époque amorrite: essai d'histoire politique." *Mémoires de NABU 6* Florilegium marianum 5

Chavalas, Mark W. and K. Lawson Younger. Mesopotamia and the Bible : comparative explorations. London: T & T Clark International.

Cline, Eric H. 2007. *From Eden to Exile: Unraveling Mysteries of the Bible*. Washington, D.C.: National Geographic.

Cline, Eric H. 2014. *1177 B.C. : the year civilization collapsed.*

Clines, David J. A. 2006. "What Happened to the Yahwist? Reflections after Thirty Years." *SBL Forum,* SBL Forum, SBL Forum, http://sbl-site.org/Article.aspx?ArticleID=551 (retrieved June 4, 2006).

Cluzan, Sophie. 2005. *De Sumer à Canaan: l'Orient ancien et la bible.* Paris: Éditions du Seuil.

Cohen, Ronald and Judith D. Toland. 1988. *State Formation and Political Legitimacy.* New Brunswick: Transaction Books.

Crew, P. Mack, I. E. S. Edwards, J.B. Bury, C. J. Gadd, Nicholas Geoffrey, N. G. L. Hammond and Edmond Sollberger. 1973. *History of the Middle East and the Aegean Region c.1800-1380 B.C.* Vol. 2 of*The Cambridge Ancient History.* Cambridge: Cambridge University Press.

Damrosh, David. 2007. *The Buried Book: The Loss and Rediscovery of the Great Epic of Gilgamesh.* New York: Macmillan.

Davaine, Casimir-Joseph. 1857. *Recherches sur l'anguillule du blé niellé considérée au point de vue de l'histoire naturelle et de l'agriculture, mémoire couronné par l'Institut.* Paris: J.-B. Baillière.

De Angelis, Franco De Angelis and Benjamin Garstad. 2006. "Euhemerus in Context." *Classical Antiquity* 25(2): 211-42.

De Pury, Albert and Thomas Römer. 2002. *Le Pentateuque en question: les origines et la composition des cinq premiers livres de la Bible à la lumière des recherches récentes.* 3e ed. Genève: Labor et Fides.

De Pury, Albert, Thomas Römer, Jean-Daniel Macchi, Christophe Nihan and Philippe Abadie. 2004. Ge 12-36. In *Introduction à l'Ancien Testament.* Genève: Labor et Fides.

De Vaux, Roland. 1971. *Histoire ancienne d'Israël, des origines à l'installation en Canaan.* Paris: Lecoffre.

Desroches Noblecourt, Christiane. 2002. *La reine mystérieuse.* Paris: Pygmalion.

Desroches Noblecourt, Christiane. 2006. *Le fabuleux héritage de l'Egypte*. Paris: Pocket.

Dever, William G. 2005. *Did God Have a Wife?: Archaeology and Folk Religion in Ancient Israel*. Grand Rapids: Eerdmans.

Drews, Robert. 1993. *The End of the Bronze Age : changes in warfare and the catastrophe ca. 1200 B.C.* Princeton, N.J.: Princeton University Press.

Driver, Godfrey Rolles and John C. L. Gibson. 1978. *Canaanite Myths and Legends.* Edinburgh: T. & T. Clark. (Orig. pub. 1956.).

Driver, Samuel Rolles. 2005. *An Introduction to the Literature of the Old Testament*. Tenth ed. Whitefish: Kessinger Publishing.

Durand, Jean-Marie. 2005-2006. "L'idéal de vie bédouin à l'époque amorrite." *Collège de France,* Collège de France, Collège de France, http://www.college-de-france.fr/media/jean-marie-durand/UPL17281_jmdurandcours0506.pdf (retrieved May 10, 2008).

Elgavish, David. 1999. The Encounter of Abram and Melchizedek King of Salem: A Covenant Establishing Ceremony. In *Studies in the Book of Genesis : Literature, Redaction and History*, ed. Wénin, André, 495-508. Leuven; Paris; Sterling: Leuven University Press ; Uitgeverij Peeters.

Eliade, Mircea and Willard R. Trask. 1979. *A History of Religious Ideas: From the Stone Age to the Eleusinian Mysteries.* Vol. 1 of 3. London: Collins.

Escudier, Alexandre. *De Chladenius à Droysen. Théorie et méthodologie de l'histoire de langue allemande (1750-1860)Annales. Histoire, Sciences Sociales 2003/4 - 58e année.* Paris: Editions de l'EHESS.

Evans, Elaine A. "The Sacred Scarab." McClung Museum. http://mcclungmuseum.utk.edu/sacred-scarab (retrieved August 17, 2015).

Falk, Avner. 1996. *A Psychoanalytic History of the Jews*. Madison: Fairleigh Dickinson University Press.

Fatoohi, Louay and Shetha Al-Dargazelli. 1999. *History Testifies to the Infallibility of the Qur'an: Early History of the Children of Israel*. Kuala Lumpur: A.S. Noordeen.

Finkelstein, Israel and Neil Asher Silberman. 2001. *The Bible Unearthed: Archaeology's New Vision of Ancient Israel and the Origin of its Sacred Texts*. New York: Free Press.

Finkelstein, J. J. 1966. "The Genealogy of the Hammurapi Dynasty." *Journal of Cuneiform Studies* 20(4): 95-118.

Foltz, Richard. 2007. *L'Iran, creuset de religions: de la préhistoire à la République islamique*. Québec: Presses de l'Université Laval.

Forbes, Robert James. 1936. *Bitumen and Petroleum in Antiquity*. Leiden: E.J. Brill.

Forsyth, Phyllis Young. 1997. *Thera in the Bronze Age*. New York: P. Lang.

Foucart, Stéphane. "Gilgamesh l'immortel." *Le Monde* (July 13, 2007).

Frank, Philipp and Shuichi Kusaka. 2002. *Einstein: His Life and Times*. Cambridge: Da Capo Press.

Frankfort, Henri. 1978. *Kingship and the gods : a study of ancient Near Eastern religion as the integration of society & nature*. Chicago: University of Chicago Press.

Freedman, David Noel , Allen C. Myers and Astrid B. Beck. 2000. *Eerdmans Dictionary of the Bible*. Grand Rapids: W.B. Eerdmans.

Freud, Sigmund and Katherine Jones. 2013. *Moses and monotheism*. Milton Keynes: Lightning Source UK Limited. (Orig. pub. 1939.).

Gardiner, Alan H. 1964. *Egypt of the Pharaohs: An Introduction*. London: Oxford University Press.

Gardiner, Alan H. 1990. *The Admonitions of An Egyptian Sage: From a Hieratic Papyrus In Leiden (Pap. Leiden 344 recto)*. Hildesheim: Georg Olms. (Orig. pub. 1909.).

Gardner, Chris and Başak Güner Gardner. 2014. *Flora of the Silk Road : an illustrated guide.*

Garfinkel, Yosef. 2011. "The Birth & Death of Biblical Minimalism." *Biblical Archaeology Review*, 30(03), http://www.basarchive.org (retrieved October 12, 2007).

Glissmann, Volker. 2009. "Genesis 14: A Diaspora Novella?" *Journal for the Study of the Old Testament* 34(1): 33-45.

Gottheil, Richard , Victor Ryssel, Marcus Jastrow and Caspar Levias. "Captivity." Jewish Encyclopedia. http://www.jewishencyclopedia.com/articles/4012-captivity (retrieved September 10, 2015).

Grabbe, Lester L. 2009. *Ancient Israel: What do we Know and How do we Know It?* New York: Continuum. (Orig. pub. 2007.).

Green, Alberto Ravinell Whitney. 2003. *The Storm-God In the Ancient Near East*. Winona Lake: Eisenbrauns.

Green, Margaret Whitney. 1975. Eridu in Sumerian Literature. University of Chicago.

Greenberg, David F. 1988. *The Construction of Homosexuality*. Chicago: University of Chicago Press.

Grewe, Wilhelm G. 1995. *Fontes Historiae Iuris Gentium: Quellen zur Geschichte des Völkerrechts. Band 1: 1380 v. Chr./B.C.-1493*. Berlin: Walter de Gruyter.

Grimal, Nicolas. 1992. *A History of Ancient Egypt*. Oxford: Blackwell.

Hadley, Judith M. 2000. *The Cult of Asherah in Ancient Israel and Judah: Evidence for a Hebrew GoddessUniversity of Cambridge Oriental Publications*. Cambridge: Cambridge University Press.

Hamilton, Victor P. The Book of Genesis: Chapters 18-50. Grand Rapids: W.B. Eerdmans.

Hattem, Willem C. Van. 1981. "Once Again: Sodom and Gomorrah." *The Biblical Archaeologist* 44(2): 87-92.

Heidel, Alexander. 1963. *The Babylonian Genesis: The Story of Creation*: University of Chicago Press.

Hirsch, Emil G. and W. Max Muller. "Goshen." Jewish Encyclopedia. http://www.jewishencyclopedia.com/articles/6819-goshen (retrieved September 10, 2015).

Hoffner, Harry A., Gary M. Beckman, Richard Henry Beal and John Gregory Mcmahon. 2003. *Hittite Studies In Honor of Harry A. Hoffner Jr.* Winona Lake: Eisenbrauns.

Hooper, Franklin Henry. 1909. *The Encyclopaedia britannica: Eleventh Edition.* London: Cambridge University Press.

Jacobs, Joseph "Ancestor worship." Jewish Encyclopedia. http://www.jewishencyclopedia.com/articles/1488-ancestor-worship (retrieved September 10, 2015).

Jacq, Christian. 1976. *Akhenaton et Néfertiti : le couple solaire.* Paris: R. Laffont.

Jastrow, Morris. 1894a. "The Element בשת in Hebrew Proper Names." *Journal of Biblical Literature* 13(1): 19-30.

Jastrow, Morris. 1894b. "Hebrew Proper Names Compounded with יה and יהו". *Journal of Biblical Literature* 13(1): 101-27.

Jeanrond, Werner. 1995. *Introduction à l'herméneutique théologique: développement et signification.* Paris: Éditions du Cerf.

Jobes, Gertrude. 1962. *Dictionary of Mythology, Folklore and Symbols.* New York: Scarecrow Press.

Joffe, L. "The Elohistic Psalter : What, How and Why?" *Scandinavian Journal of the Old Testament* 15(1): 142-69.

Johnson, Luke Timothy. 1998. *Religious Experience in Earliest Christianity: A Missing Dimension in New Testament Studies.* Minneapolis: Fortress Press.

Jones, Gareth. 2004. *The Blackwell Companion to Modern Theology.* Malden: Blackwell Publishing.

Josephus, Flavius. 2006. *Against Apion.* Portland: Read How You Want

Kaiser, Walter C. 2001. *The Old Testament Documents: Are They Reliable & Relevant?* Downers Grove: InterVarsity Press.

Katz, Victor J. and Annette Imhausen. 2007. *The Mathematics of Egypt, Mesopotamia, China, India, and Islam: A Sourcebook.* Princeton: Princeton University Press.

Kennedy, Titus Michael. 2013. A Demographic Analysis of Late Bronze Age Canaan: Ancient Population

Estimates and Insights through Archaeology. Doctor of Literature and Philosophy, University of South Africa.

King, Leonard William. 1996. *The Code of Hammurabi.* Edition Richard hooker ed. Washington: Washington University. (Orig. pub. 1910.).

King, Leonard William. 2004. *Babylonian Religion and Mythology.* Kila: Kessinger Publishing. (Orig. pub. 1903.).

King, Philip J. and Lawrence E. Stager. 2001. *Life in Biblical Israel.* Louisville: Westminster John Knox.

Kitchen, Kenneth Anderson. 2003. *On the Reliability of the Old Testament.* Cambridge: Eerdmans.

Kittel, Rudolf. 1925. *The Religion of the People of Israel.* New York: Macmillan.

Knight, Christopher and Robert Lomas. 2001. *The Hiram key : pharaohs, Freemasons and the discovery of the secret scrolls of Jesus.* Gloucester, MA: Fair Winds Press.

Kohler, Kaufmann and A. V. W. Jackson. "Zoroastrianism." Jewish Encyclopedia.

http://www.jewishencyclopedia.com/articles/15283-zoroastrianism (retrieved September 10, 2015).

Kuniholm, Peter I., Maryanne W. Newton, Carol B. Griggs and Pamela J. Sullivan. 2005. Dendrochronological Dating in Anatolia: The Second Millennium BC. Ithaca: Cornell University.

Lamborelle, Bernard. 2009. *Quiproquo sur Dieu: 3,500 ans pour élucider la véritable identité du seigneur d'Abraham*. Montréal: Éditas.

Lamm, Norman. 1999. *The Religious Thought of Hasidism: Text and Commentary*. Hoboken: KTAV Publishing House.

Lemche, Niels Peter. . 1991. *The Canaanites and Their Land: The Tradition of the Canaanites*. New York: Continuum International Publishing Group

Lewis, Theodore J. 1996. "The Identity and Function of El/Baal Berith." *Journal of Biblical Literature* 115(3): 401-23.

Lewis, Theodore J. 1999. "Israel's Beneficent Dead: Ancestor Cult and Necromancy in Ancient Israelite Religion and Tradition by Brian B. Schmidt." *Journal of the American Oriental Society* 119(3): 512-14.

Liverani, Mario. 2004. *Myth and Politics in Ancient Near Eastern Historiography*. Ithaca: Cornell University Press.

Lurton Burke, Madeleine and Paule Jarre-Chardin. 1963. *Dictionnaire archéologique des techniques: (1-2. A- Z)*. Paris: Éditions de l'Accueil.

Lutkehaus, Nancy. 2008. *Margaret Mead : the making of an American icon*. Princeton: Princeton University Press.

Magill, Frank Northen. 1992. *Great Events from History II: Human Rights*. Pasadena: Salem Press.

Manning, S. W., C. B. Ramsey, W. Kutschera, T. Higham, B. Kromer, P. Steier and E. M. Wild. 2006. "Chronology for the Aegean Late Bronze Age 1700-1400 B.C." *Science (New York, N.Y.)* 312(5773): 565-9.

Manning, Sturt W., Felix HöFlmayer, Nadine Moeller, Michael Dee, Christopher Bronk Ramsey, Dominik Fleitmann, Thomas Higham, Walter Kutschera and Eva Maria Wild. 2014. "Dating the Thera (Santorini) Eruption : Archaeological and Scientific Evidence Supporting a High Chronology." *Antiquity.* 88(342): 1164-79.

Menninger, Karl Augustus and Paul Broneer. 1992. *Number Words and Number Symbols: A Cultural History of Numbers.* New York: Dover.

New World Encyclopedia Contributors. "Baal." *New World Encyclopedia,* http://www.newworldencyclopedia.org/p/index.php?title=Baal (retrieved August 30, 2015).

Nocquet, Dany. 2004. *Le livret noir de Baal: la polémique contre le dieu Baal dans la Bible hébraïque et l'ancien Israël.* Genève: Labor et Fides.

Office of the Press Secretary. "Remarks by the President at National Prayer Breakfast." The White House. http://www.whitehouse.gov/the-press-office/2015/02/05/remarks-president-national-prayer-breakfast (retrieved March 12, 2015).

Oppenheim, A. Leo and Erica Reiner. 1999. *The Assyrian Dictionary of the Oriental Institute of the University of Chicago* 27. Chicago: Oriental Institute.

Pinches, Theophilus G. 2002. *The Old Testament in the Light of the Historical Records and Legends of Assyria and Babylonia.* New York: Elibron Classics. (Orig. pub. 1902.).

Purvis, James D. 1966. "Shechem: The Biography of a Biblical City by G. Ernest Wright." *Journal of Near Eastern Studies* 25(2): 140-42.

Rallis, Irene Kerasote. 1986. Nuptial Imagery in the Book of Hosea: Israel as the bride of Yahweh.

Rawlinson, George. 1920. *Ancient Egypt.* Fifth ed. London: T. Fisher Unwin.

Rendtorff, Rolf. 1989. L'histoire biblique des origines (Gen 1-11) dans le contexte de la " rédaction sacerdotale " du Pentateuque. In *Le Pentateuque en question*, eds De Pury, Albert and Römer, Thomas. Paris: Labor et Fides.

Richardson, M. E. J. 2004. *Hammurabi's Laws: Text, Translation, and Glossary*. New York: Continuum International Publishing Group.

Rodkinson, Michael Levl, Godfrey Taubenhaua and Isaac Mayer Wise. 1918. *Tract Sabbath*. Vol. 1 of 9 *New edition of the Babylonian Talmud*. Second ed. Boston: The Talmud Society.

Römer, Thomas. 1996. La formation du Pentateuque selon l'exégèse historico-critique. In *Les premières traditions de la Bible*, eds Amphoux, C.-B. and Margain, J., 17-55. Paris: Éditions du Zèbre.

Römer, Thomas C. 1999. Recherches actuelles sur le cycle d'Abraham. In *Studies in the Book of Genesis : Literature, Redaction and History*, ed. Wénin, André, 179-211. Leuven; Paris; Sterling: Leuven University Press ; Uitgeverij Peeters.

Ross, Robert B. 1988. *Handbook of Metal Treatments and Testing*. London; New York: Chapman and Hall.

Rudgley, Richard. 2000. *The Lost Civilizations of the Stone Age*. New York: Simon & Schuster.

Ryholt, Kim. 1997. *The Political Situation in Egypt During the Second Intermediate Period c.1800-1550 B.C.* Copenhagen: Carsten Niebuhr Institute of Near Eastern Studies: Museum Tusculanum.

Sabbah, Messod and Roger Sabbah. 2004. *Secrets of the Exodus : the Egyptian origins of the Hebrew people*. New York: Helios Press.

Sarton, George. 1993. *Ancient Science Through the Golden Age of Greece*. Harvard: Harvard University Press. (Orig. pub. 1952-59.).

Schniedewind, William M. 2004. *How the Bible Became a Book: The Textualization of Ancient Israel*. Cambridge: Cambridge University Press.

Segal, Robert Alan. 1996. *Psychology and Myth*. New York: Taylor & Francis.

Shahrukh, Husain. 2003. *The Goddess: Power, Sexuality, and the Feminine Divine*. Ann Arbor: University of Michigan Press.

Shanks, Hershel. "Losing Faith: Who Did and Who Didn't." http://www.basarchive.org (retrieved October 12, 2007).

Shaw, Ian. 2002. *The Oxford History of Ancient Egypt*. Oxford: Oxford University Press.

Shen, Peidong, Tal Lavi, Toomas Kivisild, Vivian Chou, Deniz Sengun, Dov Gefel, Issac Shpirer, Eilon Woolf, Jossi Hillel, Marcus W. Feldman and Peter J. Oefner. 2004. "Reconstruction of patrilineages and matrilineages of Samaritans and other Israeli populations from Y-Chromosome and mitochondrial DNA sequence Variation." *HUMU Human Mutation* 24(3): 248-60.

Simonnet, Dominique and Pascal Vernus. "Graver le nom du roi, c'était le rendre immortel." *L'Express* (July 13, 2006).

Smith, Mark S. 2001. *The Origins of Biblical Monotheism : Israel's polytheistic background and the Ugaritic texts*. New York: Oxford University Press.

Smith, Mark S. 2002. *The Early History of God: Yahweh and the Other Deities in Ancient Israel*. Grand Rapids: Mich. : Eerdmans. (Orig. pub. 1990.).

Smith, Mark S. 2010. *God in Translation: Deities in Cross-Cultural Discourse in the Biblical World*. Grand Rapids: W.B. Eerdmans.

Spencer, Herbert. 1893. *The principles of sociology Vol. 1*. New York: Appleton and Company.

Stoneman, Richard. 1994. *Palmyra and its Empire : Zenobia's revolt against Rome*. Ann Arbor: University of Michigan Press.

Strabo. *Geography, Book XVI, Chapter 2, 9.*

Talbott, Strobe. 2008. *The Great Experiment : The story of Ancient Empires, Modern States, and the Quest for a Global Nation*. New York: Simon & Schuster.

Taylor, J. Glen 1994. "Was Yahweh Worshiped as the Sun? Israel's God was abstract, but he may also have had a consort." *Biblical Archaeology Review* 20(03): 53-61, 90-91.

Thompson, Thomas L. 1992. *Early History of the Israelite People: From the Written and Archaeological Sources*. Leiden: E.J. Brill.

Torres-Heredia Julca, Jaime Vladimir. 2005-2006. "Un lien géométrique entre le cercle et le système sexagésimal." *Université de Genève,* Université de Genève, Université de Genève, http://halshs.archives-ouvertes.fr/docs/00/03/44/42/PDF/Un_lien_geometrique_entr e_le_cercle_et_le_systeme_sexagesimal.pdf (retrieved January 23, 2009).

Trigger, Bruce G. 2003. *Understanding Early Civilizations: A Comparative Study*. Cambridge: Cambridge University Press.

Valbelle, Dominique. 1998. *Histoire de l'État pharaonique*. Paris: Presses universitaires de France.

Van De Mieroop, Marc. 2004. *A History of the Ancient Near East: ca. 3000-323 B.C.* Oxford: Blackwell Publishing.

Van De Mieroop, Marc. 2005. *King Hammurabi of Babylon: a Biography*. Malden: Blackwell

Van Der Waerden, B. L. 1961. *Science Awakening*. New York: Oxford University Press.

Van Selms, A. 1954. *Marriage and Family Life in Ugaritic Literature*. London: Luzac.

Vansina, Jan. 2006. *Oral Tradition: A Study in Historical Methodology*. New Brunswick: Aldine Transaction.

Vincent, Hugues. 1907. *Canaan d'après l'exploration récente*. Paris: J. Gabalda.

Viollet, Pierre-Louis. 2007. *Water Engineering in Ancient Civilizations 5,000 Years of History*. Madrid: International Association of Hydraulic Engineering and Research.

Weeks, Noel. 1993. "Covenant and Treaty: A Study in Intercultural Relations." *Lucas* (16): 10-22.

Weinfeld, Moshe. 1970. "The Covenant of Grant in the Old Testament and in the Ancient Near East." *Journal of the American Oriental Society* 90(2): 184-203.

Wente, Edward F., Charles C. Van Sclen Iii and George R. Hughes. 1976. *A Chronology of the New Kingdom, in Studies in Honor of George R. Hughes*. Chicago: Oriental Institute of the University of Chicago.

Westermann, Claus. 1995. *Genesis 12-36*. Minneapolis: Fortress Press. (Orig. pub. 1985.).

Young, Dwight W. 1988. "A Mathematical Approach to Certain Dynastic Spans in the Sumerian King List." *Journal of Near Eastern Studies* 47(2): 123-29.

Zandee, J. 1956. "Le Roi-Dieu et le Dieu-Roi dans l'Egypte ancienne." *Numen Numen* 3(3).

ABOUT THE AUTHOR

BERNARD LAMBORELLE is a secular humanist with an engineering degree from École de Technologie Supérieure. In 2003, a simple question triggered a lengthy and passionate investigation into the origin of the Abrahamic faith. He first published *Quiproquo sur Dieu* (ed. Editas) in2009, which received praises from a few, left many dubitative, and raised excellent questions that called for answers. This led him to sign up for a Master in Theology at Université de Montréal in 2011, where he studied biblical Hebrew, historico-critical methods and narrative analysis. Armed with this new academic background, he widened the scope of his analysis to develop a comprehensive evolutionary model on the origin of monotheism.